PRISONER
OF DREAMS

Confessions of a Harlem Drug Dealer

RICK TALLEY

13-digit ISBN 978-19395210-2-6

10-digit ISBN 193-95210-2-5

Ms. Lady

*I have known you only for a moment in time…yet
your presence has lived in my heart for an eternity.*

*I loved you before I knew of your existence or the cool
summer breeze whispered your name softly in my ear.*

*The touch of your hand now comforts my being, and your
smile soothes me like the warmth of the summer sun.*

*From the moment we met I instinctively knew that
you were the dream I had hoped would come true.*

*I have loved you for a lifetime…and now I know your
name and all that you truly mean to me.*

NICOLETTA CHESARU
Beautiful Dreamer

Celebrating the Life Of

Leonard McNeil

1959 to 2011

The Gentle Giant
A Giant of a Man

In Memory of a Man
George Fulellen, passed in June of 2011

George, Larry, Moe and I walked the big yard at Auburn Correctional Facility for more than 5 years, each of us with more time to do than most people could imagine possible. We talked about old times, this book, and the freedom we knew one day would come. Rest in peace, my Good Brother.

CONTENTS

INTRODUCTION

In writing this book there were a number of things I had to consider. The story had to be told in a way that would keep you, the reader, interested. At the same time, I had to be careful in its wording because of the content. I could never betray the trust placed in me by those whom I choose to walk with. My lifestyle was and is mine by my own choosing.

In the late sixties no one had any idea how enormous the drug trade would become. For some black people it was simply a way to improve one's lifestyle. It gave him a stature in life that was unreachable any other way. The tomb-like buildings that made up Harlem became his own private kingdom. He ruled as the Lord over his chosen blocks. He defended his turf with deadly force.

History has shown that the streets of the black community have always belonged to the youth. In a world of instant gratification it was never a question of morals. The drug trade was and is just a way for the youth in the community to improve himself and his family's way of life.

A legitimate job in one of the fast food places, for 40 hours, does not pay much. The cost of living in New York City is high, and a third of their pay goes out for taxes. Everywhere they look they are confronted with the lifestyle of "The Rich and Famous" and "The American Dream."

It is not a realistic concept to believe that these youth should turn away from thousands of dollar to be made in the drug trade. The standards of living that have been set by those who sell the idea of the great American dream have closed their doors on the youth of the black community. There are those black people who have slipped through the cracks that were open by the guilt of white American. These black people have gone on to become the Bill Cosbys, Eddy Murphys, Julius (Doctor J) Ervings and Michael Jordans. Those of us who remained behind, endured as best we could. For some it was a matter of choice. It was either the road to a drug-induced dream or to become the merchant of those dreams.

The attitude of prosecutors, judges and the police, as well as the white communities was that it is the black problem, and indeed it was. The rundown rat and roach-infested buildings that once held black families together were now abandoned as more drugs came into the community.

Today, the Americans are outraged at the drug problem. Yet there was no drug problem in America as long as it remained in the black community.

Now that drugs' have touched the lives of those living in the white communities, the war has been declared and billions of dollars are being spent on the drugs fight. Nowadays, the courts are overloaded. The legal system is on the verge of collapse and the prisons are overcrowded.

Black and Latinos make up 90 percent of the prison population while whites consume 70 percent of all drugs sold in this county. [1]

In one of his news conferences on the subject of the drug situation in America, America's first appointed Drug Czar, when asked by a black reporter to comment on the drug arrest phenomenon in the black community, showed little regard as to what the contents of his statement really meant to Black Americans. The reporter stated, "The population of black people in this country is 12 percent of the total, why then do blacks account for 90 percent of the prison population? It appears that black people are being targeted for arrest." To which the president of the United States' Drug Czar replied, *"So, what is wrong with that?"*

The billions of dollars that are spent on education and rehabilitation

---

[1]   When I speak of the Black Community, it is representative of the **Latin Community** as well.

programs have little or no effect for those living in the black community. Politicians juggle statistics to meet their own political needs. Rehabilitation programs work only when dealing with kids who return to the sanctuary of their white community. Most Blacks and Latinos receive their rehabilitation in prison, (which is different from the outside society?) where conditions are unrealistically set. It is beyond anything that one can imagine to believe that these (inmates/offenders) will find success once they are returned to the society, where the same temptations had once led them to their initial downfall.

The glitter of success includes new cars, jewelry, fine clothes and a nice home. The rewards of being in the drug trade are extremely tantalizing that little thought is given to the risk of life or imprisonment. With the passage of new drug law such as the Federal statute 848, a conviction can lead to a life sentence without parole including the forfeiture of all properties and cash. However, this law is perhaps the best scenario that has occurred in the so-called drug war against the black youth. It is a sword that cuts both ways. Nowadays, the youth have to master the techniques of legitimate business as they are involved in the drug trade; by doing so the communities that have paid them so well can be rebuilt. Today's youth can easily earn a million dollars in one weeks' time, a sum of money that is far greater than anything Alphonse Gabriel "Al" Capone earned in the best of his times. The drug trade to blacks is what bootlegging was to Joseph Kennedy (and history has shown that he placed his son in the White House).

The black youth must learn the true power of the dollar, as did those white powerbrokers who came before them. The American dream is a commodity that is brought and paid for. The black youth of today's drug trade is the largest earning business group in the world. Who does it better than these youth to buy a new beginning in the so-called American dream?

It has never been a question of anything other than money and a chance to remove oneself and his family from the *ghetto*. As for those who took the other road saw no hope in any form of lifestyle. They were lost and doomed to self-destruction from the moment they first heard about the American Dream. They woke up only to find it was not their dream to dream.

Politicians preach the woes of drugs. The fear of drugs and what we have become because of drugs is at an all-time high. Black Americans have always known the hardships of drugs in our community. Drugs have taken Billy Holiday and the Len Bias from us, not to mention the many other names who are forgotten or were never known.

We murder and are murdered. There are more weapons in our neighborhoods than ever before. However, we do not manufacture the drugs or weapons..We only bury our children.

RICK TALLEY
IN THE ERA OF SUPERFLY AND
THE FRENCH CONNECTION

When reading the previous introduction, some of you may have come to the conclusion that I am pro-drugs. The contents hereafter are of a lifestyle that did have merit. Nevertheless, the introduction is a statement of facts in regards to today's drug situation. The problematic combinations of circumstances, which I spoke of, are in such way that few who can will think in terms of giving back to the suffering communities. For the majority, drugs are and always will be a hardship of destruction, long prison sentences and death. Drugs are a sickness that has entrapped the dealer as well as the user. The dealer is addicted to the money, power and fame. The user is addicted because he knows none of the luxuries of the dealer's lifestyle. He knows only the illusion of good times brought on from the drug high. Therefore, my position is clearly in the belief that until society gives the youth community something other than no hope, drugs will remain their number one choice for escape.

We Are Family

If a man is fortunate he will know the love of many. Yet, he will never find a love as pure as his mother's. A mother gives life and guards it with her own. A mother stands by when others turn away. In Mama's eyes her child can do no wrong. I will always love my mother. She brought me into this world and showed me love. My mother gave me a sister and three brothers, and showed us all love so we would love one another.

I gave Mama a grandson so her love would carry on.

Pamela

Claude

William

Jeffrey

Grandchildren,

Sean

Lisa, Shevon and Tiffany

Shannon and William

Kristal

A Father's Love

I chose a life that few dared to live. So great is the price I have paid that I must wonder? To lose even one moment that you can't see the glow in your child's eyes as he grows. To know he must look to another when he should be looking to you. To lose these things is the cause for the pain in my heart. To waste away in prison and not know them is a matter for my dying soul.

If there were a way, I would say to you, my child, look at my life and do not do as I have done. I would say, be there for your child so he will grow up to love others and forgive me, because in my search for the pot of gold at the end of the rainbow… I did not realize the pot of gold is the sparkle in your eyes.

We Live with Love
True Friendship Never Dies

In Memory Of
Sonny (Boy) Thomas
Arthur (Moon) Cromer
William Taylor
Ronald (Crime) Brown
Nathaniel (Nanny) White
Joseph (Young Blood) Cobham
Earl (The Goat) Manigault
Walt (Cha Cha) Peterson

The Spring Of 1984

H E SAT QUIETLY watching his reflection on the window of the train. The buildings flashed by quicker than his eyes could fix on any one in particular. The steel wheels beat their own rhythm against the rails as the Amtrak train raced towards New York City. At each stop, his thoughts would return to the reality of the train car as he watched the empty seats fill. He hoped no one would take the seat next him; it would be an invasion of his privacy. He was not ready to share this small piece of the world that he had chosen for his own. He watched the women as they made there way on and off of the train, and he felt the other five ex-cons were doing the same.

It had been four long years and he had seen each of these cons on numerous occasions. However, they had never spoken. It was strange how they had all chosen seats in the same train car. There was an unmentioned closeness they felt for each other at this most peculiar of times. Each of them knew when the train reached its destination at Grand Central Station, they would go on their own separate ways. They were most likely never to see one another again in life.

It was far too late in the evening for these cons to be making this trip. If they had been in any prison other than Sing Sing, they would have been released early that morning. As it is, they would now have to face the rush hour crowd at Grand Central Station.

The double knit, tan pants and dark brown jacket did not fit his lean muscular body, and in his subconscious mind he was sure all eyes were upon him. At 35, he was in better shape than any men ten years below him. His boyish good looks led you to believe he was much younger than his actual age.

The uneasy nervousness felt by the first hours of freedom held each of these men in one another's eyesight. They stayed close for protection as though they had just landed on Mars.

He had waited so very long for this moment to have the freedom to walk and not be bound by a wall. To shop, look in store windows and have your own choice of food. Just to be able to watch the people as they went about the business of being people. And, tonight there would be no bell to signal the end of the day. His pleasure would not come from the ads he had seen in magazine or on television, the pretty bikini clad women in the Bud Light commercials on television, the women of *Vogue*, *Vanity Fair*, *Ebony* and *Essence* magazine, not to mention the beauty of the week in Jet magazine.

The beauty of the women who danced on Soul Train were enough to make a grown man cry. A beauty larger than life as seen by his minds' eye made him weak in the knees. The women stared back at him from the pages of these magazines and came to life on television. So close in his imagination, yet so far away in the reality of his days. These women set a burning desire loose in his groin, turning his manhood rock hard, hot to the touch. He was consumed by a heat that engulfed his whole body, driving him to the edge of madness.

Tonight his satisfaction would not have to come from a search into the inner sanctum of his mind. His sex-starved mind sometimes knew no limit. It would reach into the unknown to find fulfillment because his body knew no such pleasure. Masturbation held no real promise of satisfaction for him. His mind played a game; his fantasies took on their own reality. Forbidden worlds of unknown sex and desire held a moment in his thoughts. Then a faked orgasm by way of hand drove them back, only for them to reappear again when the pain became so great he needed release once more. Yet, at this moment he did not feel the familiar burning in his groin. The excitement of freedom far exceeded any other feeling that he could possibly imagine.

His thoughts drifted with the steady motion of the train. One question played back in his mind, over and over again. He asked himself, '*Are you truly the person you believe yourself to be?*' His eyes stared back at him through the reflection on the train window; they reached deep into his soul to find the man that made him who he is, and he answered to himself. *I have always known just what I would do and how I would accomplish it. There is no doubt, my lifestyle, the awareness of myself as a man speaks for itself. I am a dedicated man who works hard to enjoy the many wonders of life. Though the odds have been and are against me, I have never, nor will I ever bend or break. My needs in life have always been met by my demands for the best life has to offer. My presence in this city will insure that the road I have chosen for myself is one of success. The limitations known by man are based on how far his mind's eye can see. In some men it can be guided by blind emotion. I know now which is the greater. I will never allow myself to be guided by such emotions. I am not a child who is trying to play in a man's world. I will know no limitations; in time my actions will speak. They will say to others just who I am. Others will see me as I see myself. I am a man whose time has come. I have known the hardships of life, just as I have known its pleasures. Success in all I do is my destiny. Yes, I am the man I believe myself to be. I am no longer a "Prisoner of my dream".*

Book One

CHAPTER ONE

Street Life
Fourth of July Weekend 1970

THE LAZY MORNING sunlight shinning through the window along with the rhythmic tapping of the lawn sprinkler's head gently eased Rick out of his sleep. He laid there for a few moments watching the spotlight effect of the sunlight coming through the window shinning on Jeff, his youngest brother. The silence of the street below brought a peaceful calm to the three bedroom apartment.

Rick walked over to the dresser that sat by the bedroom door. He looked over the things he had placed there early that morning before going to bed. He picked up the fist-sized roll of money, studying it briefly before placing it back on the dresser in disappointment.

The warm shower felt good to Rick. It cleared his head and seemed to bring an ease to his thinking. On this day he was not sure of what his future would be. He did know, however, that he would never in life go through the same shit he did this past Friday with that whitey in the employment office. The whitey made him realize that he was closed out of the job market, completely.

Rick had very little understanding for what was going on in the society at this time, nor did he really care. He still felt the edginess of spending a year in the jungles of Vietnam. He moved in deadly silence, said little to anyone and never seemed to smile or laugh. In fact, the 4th of July was a bad time for his nerves. It was just last night that he had rolled 15 feet on the ground before he realized the firecrackers were not machine gun fire much to the delight of his man, Moon, and startling his woman, Jenny.

Rick stood quietly in front of his building in the Fredrick Douglas Housing Projects. It was 11 o'clock in the morning. The hot July sun had kept most everyone indoors. Rick looked around. Seeing no one, he decided to walk across 102nd street to Amsterdam Avenue. He thought there might be someone in the park shooting baskets on the court named Lucky Star.

Rick stopped for a moment in the dead-end horseshoe in front of his old elementary school. The shade from the old castle-like building had kept the pavement cool. Looking at the empty school building brought back memories, not good or bad, just memories.

Rick stepped out from the shade of the school building and the heat of the sun assured him that no one would be playing ball at this time of day. Rick looked over to the park once more and it was just as he thought it would be.

Rick stood on the east corner of Amsterdam Avenue, undecided as to if he should just turn around and go back home. He also thought about crossing the avenue and hanging out in front of the Spanish store for a while. The one cool spot of shade on the side of the Spanish store won out.

Rick stood in the shade for a few minutes before he saw anyone. Then he saw her. How could he miss those long thick shapely legs in short shorts? She knew how to strut and move her behind.

Rick recognized the man walking beside her. He was a friend of his and his family. Rick called him and his call startled Donny because he had not seen Rick standing in the shadow of the building.

"Yo, Donny," Rick called again, "let me see you for a moment."

Donny left the female on the corner and crossed over to where Rick was standing.

"Donny who's that girl, she with you or what?" Rick asked.

"No, she's just a friend," Donny replied.

"Is that what you called me for?" Donny asked.

Before Rick could respond, Donny had already begun to ask the next question. "When are we going to take care of that business we talked about?" Donny asked.

"We can do that now," Rick replied as he reached in his pocket, pulling out a fistfull of money. Donny's eyes lit up, he was ready to go.

"Come on Rick," Donny said.

Rick only laughed. "Yo, Donny, we can't do anything with this money. It's not enough," Rick informed him.

"How much is it?" Donny asked.

"It's not enough for us to go into business with," Rick insisted. "It's only ninety dollars, and what can we do with ninety dollars?"

"That's enough," Donny vigorously insisted.

"Get the fuck out of here," Rick said. "We can't do shit with this little bit of money."

"With that ninety dollars we can get rich," Donny stated.

Rick thought about the scenario in the employment office and the attitude of the white man when he told him about the dishwashing job. Rick knew the money in his pocket would not last more than a day or so. "Fuck it," Rick said, "We'll give it a try."

Donny and Rick walked over to Broadway from Amsterdam Avenue. Rick asked Donny about the young lady he had left standing on the corner.

"She'll be alright; that's her building, 868."

Donny intensely told Rick about the plan he thought would make them rich as they walked downtown on Broadway.

Rick handed the store clerk 14 dollars in exchange for the box of glassine bags, roll of scotch tape and rubber bands. Once outside Rick asked how much dope would be enough to fill all the glassine bags in the box.

Donny chuckled, "It takes about a thousand dollars or so to use all 900 bags in the box. One day," Donny said smiling.

Rick handed Donny 65 dollars and stepped up on the stoop of the corner building on 111th street, on 8th Avenue. There was no need for both of them to walk over to 7th Avenue to cop one quarter of dope. Besides, Donny was the one who knew who had the best product.

Rick could see Donny coming back up the block and at the same time he spotted Michelle crossing the street. Michelle was a pretty deep dark chocolate woman. Rick had known Michelle for years than they both could remember. Rick had always been impressed by her style. She was a woman of many men's fantasies. Her beauty had not began to fade, but the dull look in her eyes let him know that she fucked around.

"Well Rick," Michelle asked, "What brings you uptown?"

Rick did not bother to answer her question knowing that she was only looking to get high. Michelle looked in Donny's directions just as he called to Rick. Rick could see the sparkles in Michelle's eyes, the kind a dope fiend gets when they are about to get high.

"Hello, Donny," Michelle said in her sexiest voice.

"Everything alright Rick?," asked Donny.

"Everything is cool," Donny replied. Neither man paid attention to Michelle as she went into her best performance, thinking it would entice Donny or Rick to take her with them.

"I can show you a real good time, I feel like getting real freakish," Michelle said

"It ain't like that Michelle," Donny said. "Rick and I are scrambling. We just came up here to check on our business. If you want to cop you can find us in front of 868 in the projects."

Michelle was impressed by what Donny had just told her. She knew now that it was not about getting high but about getting money.

Rick and Donny did the ten blocks it took to get to the projects in no time at all. They talked about what the future held in store for them.

Rick and Donny sat at the table in the dining area of the 9th floor apartment. Ronda handed Donny an album cover and the package they had dropped off before going uptown, Isaacs Hayes, "Hot Butter Soul". They all laughed, each at their own private joke, as Rick read the title of the album cover.

Donny took two stacks of 50 each of the glassine bags out of the box. Donny placed the bags next to the album cover.

"Look Rick, this is how we will do this," Donny said. "I'll put the dope in the bags, you fold and tape them."

Donny carefully opened the quarter of dope pouring the contents into the small sifter. There seemed to be more dope after it had been sifted, yet the pile was so small it led Rick to wonder.

"That doesn't look like shit," Rick told Donny. "How the fuck are we going to make money with that little bit of shit?" Rick protested.

"You'll see," Donny replied.

Donny filled the bags, measuring to make sure each bag had a nice amount but not too much. Rick counted 81 bags and there was still some dope left on the album cover.

'What are you going to do with that?" Rick asked.

"I'm going to take care of my sickness and give some to Ronda for letting us use her apartment."

Donny took the album cover with the remaining dope and he and Ronda disappeared into one of the back rooms. Rick placed the bags in neat stacks of 15 each bound with a rubber band. Five stacks plus six extra bags, $162.00. *It's a start*, Rick thought to himself.

Rick shot a few hoops on the Lucky Star while Donny stood in front of 868 to let everyone know he was straight. In less than 10 minutes Donny handed Rick 55 dollars and took the other 3 half loads from Rick's shirt on the ground.

Rick was a little surprised at how quickly Donny sold the first two halves. After shooting a few more baskets, Rick walked over to where Donny was. As usual, Donny sat talking with a cutie pie. Donny introduced Rick to her as his partner and both men felt the sensation of pride. They both knew they were making a step up in life.

Another kid from the neighborhood approached Donny to cop the last few bags. He nodded his head to acknowledge Rick and the young lady. It was nearly 3 in the afternoon. Rick and Donny made their way to Rick's house. They sat at the dining room table with the money in a neat pile in front of them.

"Look Rick," Donny said, "if we are going to get money I'm going to kick. It should only take me a few days."

Rick listened and could feel the sincerity in what his young friend said.

Rick counted out $130.00, "this is for us to cop two quarters and 16 dollars each for pocket money."

"What do you want to do now, Rick?" Donny asked. "We can cop now and knock them off tonight. Or we can do it in the morning."

"Let's do it now," Rick enthusiastically responded.

"I'm glad you said that," Donny replied.

The two men once again set at Ronda's table counting halves. They had packaged 12 halves in all with just enough left to pay Ronda and to get Donny straight in the morning.

"Check this out, if I were going to keep getting high I would be back there with Ronda right now," Donny said. "What I'll do is get off in the morning. That should hold me all day. Two days like that and I will be able to go the third day with nothing. The first day we bagged up I was so damn sick and the smell of the dope made me want to throw up. I was glad when we finished so I could get off. Man was I glad; I had never felt that bad before."

Rick, Donny, and Moon sat in the little playground area next to Rick's building. It had taken Rick and Donny two hours to flip the last package. Word had spread like wildfire through dry grass; Rick and Donny have got something nice.

Rick listened as his friends talked, the way only old and good fiends do. The projects were alive in the hot summer nights. The older people sat talking on the benches in front of most buildings. The younger children played in groups of girls and groups of boys.

The projects always seemed festive on summer nights. Everyone enjoyed the peace and familiarity of having done everything there is to do together for so many years. In another hour or so all of the younger children would be upstairs along with the older people who had to get ready for work the next day. The quiet dark corners of the projects would become lovers' lane.

The invisible boundary line drawn by the first group of teenage kids there brought a uniquely different lifestyle on each side of the border in the housing project simply known as the Douglas.

There was up the hill, it ran from 102nd street to 104th street. Then there was down the hill, it ran from 102nd street to 100 streets. The projects themselves set between Manhattan and Amsterdam Avenues with Columbus Avenue running down its center.

The boundary line really had no meaning until it came to the argument of who was better at what. Down the hill believed they had better basketball players and dressers, as did up the hill. Sometimes the challenge of the game would be played in back of the community center between 103rd and 104th street. At other times the games would be played next to the 24th precinct, between 101st and one hundred streets. At no time did anyone know a limitation as to where they could go in the projects.

CHAPTER TWO

Donny's Busted
A Few Days Later

THE HOT AFTERNOON made for a lazy time watching the summer programming on television. The living room of Rick's mothers' apartment was always nice and cool at this time of day. Rick enjoyed the solitude of the afternoon peace. This afternoon, however, his instincts told him something was not right. Rick had the same feelings now that he always got before an ambush in Vietnam. The sound of the metal doorknocker intensified his awareness of trouble. Rick gazed through the peephole of the apartment door. He could see Mia, Donny's woman, standing there crying.

Rick opened the door to a shaken Mia and a lady he did not know. Donny's busted, Mia managed to say while frantically crying. Mia's words stunned him. He looked at Mia then to the lady beside her. Mia must have sensed his thoughts; she stopped crying just long enough to introduce the lady as Donny's aunt.

Rick had the two women stepped into the apartment, closing the door behind them. Mia had stopped shaking, yet Rick perceived the despair of the two women. The river of tears still flowed down Mia's face as she asked Rick what he was going to do. *What the fuck am I going to do?* Rick thought but said nothing. The plea in Mia's eyes led him to lie.

"I will bail him out when the time comes," Rick said.

Rick knew his words had not reassured them. In fact his words had not sounded convincing to him either.

"Look," he told them, "once I find out what his bail is I will get the money from the people uptown." Rick could see that the mention of someone other than himself eased the tension felt between the three of them.

Rick sat silently in the living room; he paid very little attention to the news bulletin that flashed across the TV screen. The scene was of the tombs, and there appeared to be some kind of troubles going on.

"Rick, Rick." The call of his name brought him out of the tranquil escape from the scenario that had taken place earlier. Rick got up from where he was seated to look out of the window to see whom it was calling him. The female voice sounded familiar, but he could not place it at the moment. Rick got to the window just as she called again. It was Carmen, a girl he had known since they were in the same class in the second grade and throughout most of their schooling. She wanted Rick to come downstairs. Rick wondered what she could possibly want.

Carmen explained to Rick how Donny had gotten arrested during the short walk from Rick's building to hers, which was just across and in front of his. Carmen told Rick that Donny could not have had more than 5 or 6 bags on him. She explained that the police had grabbed him because he pulled out a lot of money to give her a change for twenty. Rick asked if she knew whether the police had taken the money from Donny. Carmen said she did not think so but could not say for sure. Rick was pleased with the little information Carmen had provided.

They could see the police barricades as they came closer to the court building. Rick knew it was much too early for Donny's case to be called. However or whatever, Mia and Donny's aunt had showed up at his apartment door at 9 o'clock this morning. To them it appeared as if Rick were dressed and ready for court. When in truth, Rick had been out all night.

Newspaper reporters, television crews and other kinds of camera people were all over the place. The fire department stood by and watched the smoke coming from the top floor of the Tombs. Broken glass fell to the sidewalk breaking into millions of tiny pieces. Prisoners waved white bed sheets and held signs out of the broken windows asking for help in changing the conditions in the old prison.

The police were turning away anyone who did not have immediate business in the Tombs. Rick stood reading the court docket, found Donny's name, and read the charges. Rick was relieved to see that he was only charged with possession.

Rick sat with the two women in the back of the arraignment courtroom. They had been there for what seemed like years. Rick could see the long wait was getting to the women. He wished that they were not. He could have handled it better by himself. Rick excused himself and went to stand in the corridor of the ancient court building. The halls were crowed with people. Pimps and hoes, players and dealers, and the families of those down on their luck.

The news people moved freely about. The police and anyone who had anything to do with law enforcement were noticeable and moved about in an uncertain manner because of the situation in the building.

Rick approached a well-dressed black man who was talking with a pretty white girl. When the young pimp turned to see what his hoe was looking at, he recognized Rick at once. The two men threw their arms around one another. Their greeting was warm and sincere. The hoe stood dumbfounded, she had never seen two pimps show so much affection for one another.

"Damn," Rick said, "I have not seen you since Vietnam but you sure look like you are doing it."

"Yeah, Rick," Brown the young pimp replied, "I'm kicking it with these hoes'. You look like you're stepping to".

"I'm doing alright," Rick replied. "Right now I'm just here to bail my partner out. He's got a possession case."

"Fuckin' with these hoes, this place has become my office," Brown stated. "It seems like I spend more time bailing these bitches out than they put on the job."

"I know what you mean," Rick said, "But that's the life."

The two men smiled at one another in agreement. Brown's other hoe exited the court after paying her fine. She stood with her wife-in-law while her man and Rick exchanged telephone numbers.

Rick leaned against the wall across the hall from where Donny was to be arraigned. He watched the hoes and drag queens exit the courtroom and make a B-line to the front door. Ozzie Davis, the actor, stood just across from Rick. Rick wondered what would bring him there on a day like today or why he would be there at all. It was just the night before that Rick had seen his new movie. Rick cursed himself for not being able to remember the name of the movie. He knew Ozzie had played some kind of cop in a white Southern town. The movie also starred his real wife. *What the fuck is the name of the movie?* Rick asked himself again.

Mia signaled to Rick that they had brought Donny out and all of his thoughts about the name of the movie disappeared. Rick stomach muscles tightened, his nerves felt raw. Rick was ready to spring into battle, but there was no battle to be fought.

Donny sat on the small crowded bench that held prisoners. The bench was in the corner near the exit that led to the holding cells, placed so the prisoners could step in front of the judge when their names were called.

After hearing your named called there was only one of two things that could happen. One could walk through the gate that separated the judges' bench and lawyers table from the rest of the courtroom. Or, one could be returned through the same exit back to the holding cells.

Donny tried to signal a message to Rick and the two women. The court correction officer told Donny that if he did not be cool he would put him back in the holding pen until sometimes tomorrow.

The court clerk called Donny's docket number and name. The Legal Aid lawyer was just about to speak on Donny's behalf when a captain from the Department of Correctional Services approached the side of the judge's podium and whispered in the judge's ear.

The judge made an announcement to the people in his courtroom. "As you know," he began, "We are having a problem upstairs. We had a belief that the situation was under control. However, it appears that it has flared up once again. I am informing you so you will know that no one in this courtroom waiting for family or friends to be arraigned has anyone in the part of the jail that has the problem. Okay, let's get on with the next case."

The district attorney and the legal aid lawyer argued the merits of the case as they each saw them. The judge asked the legal aid lawyer if the defendant could make a bail. The Legal Aid lawyer read the report on Donny's bail status. Rick and the two women moved closer, sitting on the edge of the bench trying to hear all that was being said.

The judge informed the district attorney and Legal Aid lawyer that he did not want to send anyone else upstairs under the conditions of the present circumstances if possible.

"Especially in a case like this one; How much money does the defendant have on him?" the judge asked.

"Two hundred and twenty-five dollars," the district attorney read from the arrest report.

"Bail is set at one hundred dollars," the judge ordered.

Donny walked over to the bailiff to post his bail and the two women breathed a sigh of relief. Rick could see the color return in the two women's complexions. Rick listened as the judge politely explained to the district attorney, "The reason I did not set bail at two hundred dollars is because you never want to send a man home broke. Being broke could cause a man to commit a crime." Rick found the judge's comments rather strange, and he knew he would never forget the name of the only black judge he had ever seen, Judge Bruce Wright.

CHAPTER THREE

Stayin' in The Game

RICK SAT SILENTLY in the front seat of the taxicab. He listened but Donny's conversation with Mia did not register. Rick wondered what it was he felt about Donny's aunt. They had said less than two words to each other. She was quiet the whole time; her eyes told a sad story. Rick wondered if it was important to him or not. The only thing he really knew was that he wanted to get away from both women. Being there forced him to be other than what he wanted at the moment.

Rick's nerves were on the edge. He really wanted to stop the cab and get out. Every so often Donny would say something to Rick, yet he did not reply.

The cab pulled into the horseshoe in front of the school on 102nd street. By the time Rick had paid the cab fare everyone else had already gotten out.

"What are you going to do Donny?" asked Rick

"I'm going to my mother's house," Donny replied. I am going to take Mia home. I will come by later so we can talk," Donny said.

Before Rick could get settled in, he heard a knock on the door. When he answered it he found Donny standing there.

"I thought you would be with your woman for a while," Rick said.

"Hell no, I will see her later," Donny replied. "She knows I'm alright so everything's cool."

The two men eased back to enjoy the comfort of the large sofa. They both were worn out from the excitement of the past two days.

"So what's it going to be my brother Rick?" asked Donny " I'm going home to take a shower and get cleaned up. Then I'll come back and pick you up so we can go cop," Donny informed Rick.

"You know, Donny the cops will be looking to bust you from now on."

"I know we will just have to get a worker. We won't make as much or grow as fast as we want, but it's safer," Donny said.

Rick and Donny had been everywhere they could think of to cop but it seemed everyone had sold out.

"Yo Donny, I'm going home. Fuck this shit I'm tired, we can cop tomorrow."

"That's cool Rick, I'm going to stay up here for a while longer. I will be by your house later on," Donny said.

Claude's deep voice had awakened Rick before he could complete what he was saying. "Yo, man, Donny's in the living," Claude stated.

"Tell him to come back here," Rick replied.

"Damn Rick," Donny said, "How long you going to sleep?

"Shit, it only seems like I've been asleep for ten minutes."

"Hey Claude," Rick called to his brother, "Where's Ma?"

"She didn't come from church yet," Claude replied.

"What time is it?" Rick asked.

"Ten thirty, time for you to get your lazy ass the fuck up," Claude said, fucking with his brother.

"Yo Claude, what the fuck are you doing here anyway?" Rick asked.

"I just came over to hang out," Claude replied. "Bruce and I are going to the "Devil's Inn".

"What's up Rick?" asked Donny. "After you cut out I went back to Nat's Bar and I ran into Rafael. He told me not to fuck with quarters. He said Jesse had hundred dollar things of scramble that are smoking."

"So when can we cop?" Rick asked.

"We have to be at the Shalimar at 12 o'clock tomorrow night."

"That's a long wait, what are we going to do for tomorrow morning?" Rick asked. "People are going to think you're getting busted has put us out of business."

"I've thought about that, but fuck what people think. Anyway, maybe we can cop a few quarters in the morning to make back the money we put up for bail."

Standing in front of the Shalimar, Rick felt every nerve in his body dancing. Rick checked out the Cadillac Broughams', Coupe deVilles', Buick Electra 225's, Rivera's', Oldsmobile 98's and Toronados', and the young men who dressed in outfits to match the color of the cars' they drove.

Rick knew most of these young men from playing basketball or having gone to school with them or from just hanging out. It had been three years or more since Rick had seen some of them. They had all come light years since he had last saw them.

The changing red, green and yellow of the traffic light, the headlights of passing autos' hitting the shiny new cars double parked in front of the Shalimar, along with the loud music coming from inside the bar held Rick captive in a surreal spell.

Rick could hear The Chit-Lites singing "For God sake you've got to give more power to the people". The parade of beautiful women in all shades, sizes and different styles of dress, going in and out of the Shalimar made for a carnival like atmosphere on the corner of 123rd street 7th Avenue.

Rick and Donny stood watching the show that they had now become apart of. They could also see the same show going on across the avenue at the Gold Lounge. For a brief moment Rick recalled a story he had heard. Watusi, Pat Smith, one hell of a basketball player who had allegedly turned down a pro contract. He and Rick had played in several tournaments together. Some times on the same team, other times against each other. Rick pictured Watusi walking out of the Gold Lounge, a gunman steps from the shadow firing a shot knocking Watusi to the ground. Only to stand over him pumping 4 more slugs into his body. Rumor had it he owed money. However, they supposedly had found three hundred thousand dollars in the truck of his car. *So how much could Watusi have owed for them to kill him*? Rick thought to himself. But then again, it was just a rumor.

It was nearly an hour past midnight when Jesse and Willie pulled up in the black Coupe deVille. Rick had known Jesse from high school. At the time they were just students and would never have dreamed they could meet again like this.

Jesse had a good reputation for taking care of business. Rick had heard the many rumors on how he got started in the drug game. The one rumor that made the rounds more than the others was that he and two others stuck up a liquor store or something. Jesse and one kid became partners in the drug game, never to look back. The other kid had fucked his share of the money, up getting high. Jesse being the man he is, to this day still looked out for him.

Donny spoke with Willie and gave him the hundred dollars.

"Come on Rick, lets get out of here," Donny said.

"You got it already?" Rick asked

"No," Donny replied. "We have to meet them on 110th street Lenox Avenue at 4 o'clock in the morning."

Rick and Donny walked over to and then down 8th Avenue. The image of the night still danced in their fantasies. They stopped on 118th street to kick it with Skull who they knew would be shooting crap on the corner.

"What brings you two Douglas niggers uptown?" Skull asked, greeting them.

"Nothing really, we just had a little business to take care of with Jesse," Rick said.

"He's a good man," Skull stated.

"I'm doing something with him too," Skull informed them. "Jesse and Willie came through here about half an hour ago. Anyway, it's about time somebody out of the Douglas decided to get some of that money. It's alot of money to be made in the Douglas," Skull informed both Donny and Rick.

"That's' how we see it too," Donny replied.

Rick and Donny walked across 110th street on the park side; it was 3:45 *a.m.* They both were excited and as nervous as schoolboys about to get their first shot of pussy. Their conversation was full with anticipation and what was to become of the move they were making.

Lenox Avenue was deserted except for the small group of men who stood on the corner of 111th street. As Rick and Donny came closer to the group they recognized the men as the ones' from the Shalimar. The group of men greeted them with silent recognition. Several others arrived after Rick and Donny.

Willie appeared at 4 o'clock on the nose approaching the group walking from the 110th street Lenox Avenue exit of Central Park. Rick and Donny were unsure of what was to happen next and waited like the others for Willie's instructions.

Willie checked the group to make sure everyone was there. He told Rick and Donny that both of them did not need to come with him.

"I'll go with you," Rick responded.

"I will wait for you on 110th and 7th Avenue," Donny told Rick.

Willie took the group of men just inside of the Lenox Avenue exit on 110th street and down in a ravine. From this vantage point everyone could see oncoming car traffic in the park or anyone walking on the streets without being seen.

Willie pulled a shopping bag from behind one of the trees. He called each man by name, handing them small brown bags or freezer size plastic bags filled with white power. Willie told one kid that they had run out of cut and to see them later that day. The

kid told Willie that he had enough cut to put something out but that he would need the cut to finish the package. As each man received their package they walked out of the park.

Rick could not believe the size of some of the packages given out. Willie handed Rick a small brown paper bag with John written on it.

"I wrote John on the bag because I didn't know your name."

"Rick's my name," Rick said as he turns to walk out of the park.

"Okay Rick," Willie replied.

Donny sat on the bench in the shadow of the wall that held Central Park back from the concrete sidewalk and buildings of Manhattan. Rick had seen Donny from half a block away, just like he heard the rats moving under the cover of darkness along the wall in search of food.

Rick's perception of his persona was that of moving through the jungles of Vietnam. He could hear the still wind move the leaves of the trees ever so gently. Rick knew that his heightened sense of alert was because of the small bag of drugs in his pocket.

Donny had not seen Rick until he called to him. Rick showed Donny the golf ball size bag of dope and Donny was ecstatic. Rick was reluctant in expressing his enthusiasm because of the large bags of drugs he had just seen the other receive. Rick told Donny about the drop and the size of the bags he had just seen given out. Rick expressed in no uncertain terms his intentions that they would be buying the large size bags soon, real soon.

Ronda peered through the peephole, then opened the door for Rick and Donny. Her bathrobe hung open and they viewed the nakedness of her body.

'*Damn*' Rick thought to himself, *she sure looks good*. Rick knew that it was the excitement and the danger of the business that had increased his sexual appetite.

Ronda sat at the table watching Rick and Donny worked. Rick flirted boldly with Ronda building his passion almost to the point of exploding. Even though he knew she would not be the one to satisfy his burning desire.

The golf ball size bag was much more dope than Rick had realized once it had been sifted.

"Yo Donny, you know one of those large bags of dope must fill up two or three album covers like this. I mean look at what we have here. I know one of those bags was at least 150 to 200 times more dope than we've got here. I wonder what one of those bags cost and how much you can make from one of them," Rick thought out loud.

"I don't know," Donny replied, "But we are sure going to find out."

Rick and Donny counted 21 half loads and both men were happy with the count. They gave Ronda enough to keep her straight for the next few days and 50 dollars cash to take care of the baby and household needs.

The 21 halves would bring in 420 dollars using a worker. Both men thought about the 630 dollars it would bring if they sold it themselves, knowing that was out of the question.

"So Donny what time you going to meet Junie? I'm going to take 5 halves by his house at 8 o'clock."

They both looked over at the clock.

"That's just a little while from now," Rick said.

"Yeah, I know," Donny replied. "What I will do is give him the 5 and go get some sleep until 12 noon. By then he should be ready to re-up. Then sometime around 6, I will give him more and around 9, I will give him the last of it."

"Yeah, that's cool," Rick said. "What are you going to do, Donny?"

"I was thinking about going somewhere to get some pussy."

"Stop the bullshit Donny, said you know you are going to stay here and fuck Ronda. That's what she thinks," Rick replied.

"I know when she comes out of the back she is going to be all doped up looking for me to hit her. But she can't have me," Rick stated. They both laughed at Rick's statement.

Rick threw 16 halves in the metal box and locked it, then placed it on the top shelve of the hall closet. Donny walked down the hallway to the elevator and Rick stood in the doorway of Ronda's apartment talking to her. She wanted him to stay there while Donny took the dope to June. Rick played, teasing her with his mind game. He stuck his hand in her panties and tickled the hair on her mound. Her legs open slightly so his finger could find home.

"I see it's all wet," Rick teased. She held his hand in place by closing her legs. "I've got to go baby, business before pleasure, but I'll come back later," Rick told her.

Donny and Rick sat in Phil's restaurant on the corner of 102nd street Broadway, laughing over a scramble egg and toast breakfast. The early morning light of day had given both men renewed energy. Neither Rick nor Donny felt like sleeping at this point. They both wanted to see how things would go for Junie on his first morning.

"You know Rick, I could get a year for this bullshit case," Donny said. Their attitudes changed to a serious mode. They spoke on the many possibilities.

"The first thing we have to do is get you a real lawyer," Rick said.

"That will cost us about 15 hundred for a case like this," Donny stated.

"No problem, we should have that money in three or four days," Rick calculated.

"If you should get any time you will be on when you come back. I know we are going to come off so I will just run things until you get back," Rick proclaimed.

Donny paid the check and they walked back to Amsterdam Avenue. They stood on the corner of 102nd street; they did not see Junie in front of 868. A few people asked Donny if he was straight.

"Junie has our thing; you can see him from now on," Donny told them.

Junie came from the back of 868 and walked over to where Donny and Rick stood.

"You looking for me," Junie asked.

"No, we're just checking things out," Rick replied.

"Anyway, I'm almost finished," Junie said.

"If that's the case you can give that money to Donny," Rick said.

Donny and Junie walked off towards Broadway. Junie took a seat on a stoop when they where in the middle of the block. Donny stood guard while Junie counted the money. Junie handed Donny the money then walked across the street and headed back towards 868. Donny went back to stand on the corner with Rick.

"How much did he give you?" Rick asked.

"Eighty-four dollars, he still owes 16," Donny replied. "In an hour we'll give him something else. An hour should be enough time for him to sell everything including his profit," Donny stated.

Rick and Donny enjoyed the atmosphere that was unique to the Shalimar. Tonight they were greeted differently, sharing in the spotlight. At the same time they knew they were accepted as members in a secret society, royalty of Harlem's underworld.

Rick spoke with Skull, kicking it about a 5 foot 11 inch tall chocolate beauty that was new to the set.

"If I did not have business to take care of, I would have her tonight,"

Skull thought out loud. Rick's mind was more on the business at hand than the lovely ladies. It was the third time they were going to cop. Things had gone well for them since Donny's arrest. Junie still had to turn in another hundred dollars, which they would pick up in the morning when they gave him his new package. Yes, all in all things were looking real good, money in the stash to get Donny a lawyer and enough to cop again.

Donny was standing with Joe Frog and the two brothers, George and Reggie Fluellen. They listen to a young kid named William Underwood talk about his plans for the record business. *If Berry Gordy could do it, so can I,* he told them.

Willie parked the Caddy in the block just around the corner from the Shalimar, and walked over to a group of men standing in front of the bar. He asked the group of men if Jesse had shown yet.

"No," Joe Frog told him.

"Okay, let me get a drink first, and then we can take care of business," Willie stated.

Willie opened the trunk of the Caddy just so he could easily get in and out of it, then leaned against the fender of the car. Skull handed Willie a large grocery bag of money.

"Is it all there Willie?" asked Skull.

"Yeah, every dime," Willie replied.

Willie wrote Skull's name on the bag and threw it in the trunk of the car. One after another they handed Willie large and small bags and huge rolls of money held by rubber bands. Willie marked each order on a sheet of paper and told everyone what time and where the drop would be made. Rick felt out of place when Donny handed Willie the small fold of a hundred dollars, which he placed in his pocket.

By the time Jesse had shown up, Willie had taken all of the orders. Most of the young hustlers had told the lady of their choice for that night what after-hour-spot to meet them at and gone off to set up for the night's business.

It was a clear sunny evening, Rick leaned against the park fence talking with Jenny. This was the first time he had seen her since they had broken up. She had no idea Rick was scrambling.

"Yo Rick, Mel a kid who was going nowhere in life called, I tried your thing today. At first I was a little skeptical about it, but you have a good bag." Rick could not believe this fool was telling him this shit and in front of a woman he had know idea of who she may or may not be.

"Yeah okay Mel, thanks you, later," Rick replied.

Jenny was still mad about their break up sarcastically stated, "You think you are big time now?"

"No, not really, not yet anyway," Rick replied. '*But I am the biggest thing to come out of these projects,*' Rick thought to himself.

Rick called to a kid sitting on the steps of the elementary school, motioning for him to come over.

"Yeah Rick, what's up?"

"Do me a favor, get me two bags of smoke and get one for you," Rick told him.

"Where do you want me to get it from?" the kid asked.

"It doesn't matter as long as it's good."

"Rick, are you going to the party with Denise and me?" Jenny asked.

"I don't think so, I've got something to do tonight," Rick replied.

"What about your son, when are you going to come see him?" Jenny wanted to know. "I'll come get him in the morning; he can stay with me for a couple of days. You can pick him up at Nanny's house, that's were he is spending the night," Jenny informed Rick.

"Yo Rick, here's the smoke. I got two bags; I'm just going to keep the five dollars."

"Yeah, that cool, it was yours anyway," Rick said. Rick told the kid to give the smoke to Jenny. After the kid had walked off, Jenny asked Rick, "Why did you tell the kid to give me the smoke?"

"It's yours' isn't it?" Rick replied.

"I don't want people all up in my business," Jenny scolded Rick.

"Look girl, he doesn't know if it's for you or if you are holding it for me," Rick informed her. "You ready to go or what?" Rick asked Jenny..

"Are you trying to get rid of me?" Jenny asked Rick. "I came all the way up here just to see you,"

"Stop the bullshit; you came so I could get you some smoke." Rick was not in the mood to go through any changes with her. Rick called a taxi for Jenny. When the cab pulled over and Jenny had gotten in, Rick told the cabdriver to take Jenny to 93rd and Columbus Avenue.

"Come on Rick, at least you can ride with me home."

"No, no, here's the money to pay for the cab. You can tell nanny I will pick Sean up around 8:30 or 9 in the morning."

The old lady peered through the glass window of the back door. She could not speak English but she could call Rick's and Sean's name clearly with her broken accent. Mairmare had to be at least 80 years old, she was Sean's great grandmother. For someone her age she sure moved around good. Nanny, the lady who looked after her and Sean was also up in age. Nanny had been brought over from Haiti to care for Mairmare. After the birth of Sean, Nanny cared for him sometimes during the day.

Nanny who also could not speak English much better than Mairmare, had gone to the store. Rick could see Sean sitting on the bed from where he stood in the kitchen. The expression on Sean's face as he watched Mairmare trying to speak English was as if he were trying to seriously make out what was being said. When Sean saw his father his eyes lit up.

Rick rolled Sean over and over on the bed. Rick blew air bubbles on Sean's stomach making him laugh and kick his legs in the air with joy. Mairmare asked if Sean will go out, waving her hands back and fourth as though it brought understanding to what she was trying to say.

"I'm taking Sean," Rick replied shaking his head yes.

Mairmare pulled Sean's clothes from the closet and watched Rick dress him. She stood guard to help out if she thought Rick was doing it wrong. Nanny came back from the store just when Rick was about to place Sean in his stroller.

"No eat, no eat," she told Rick. She had a worried look on her face, like if she did not feed Sean, he would not get to eat. Rick told her that he would feed Sean and had to reassure her several times. Rick found the two women humorous, for them to think he could not care for his child make him wonder about the men in their county.

Rick pushed Sean around in circles making him laugh. The other kids in the park watched Rick playing like a madman laughed also, so Rick played with them. Rick chased them, and then fell on the ground rolling over making strange noises. The kids screamed and laughed. Sean seemed to be having a good time with the other kids. The little girls played with Sean like he was their doll. When the Good Humor ice cream man came along pushing his cart, Rick brought all of his ice cream and handed it out to the kids and their mothers.

Rick was having a good time with his son. The innocence of the children's play eased the harshness of the horror from the year that he spent in the jungles of Vietnam. Rick could see no wrong in the sloppy wet smile of his son's face. The giggles and laughter of the other children was the hope of the world to him. Playing with the children was the only time he felt no danger and could relax. Even when he had a chance to be around the children of war torned in Vietnam, he sensed the purity of their young souls. Rick had always took the time to play with them regardless of the danger.

Rick had been up all night but had not felt tired until him and Sean had left the park. Rick put Sean in his crib after cleaning him up and feeding him. The hot shower had relaxed Rick, he felt good as he laid on the sofa. The television played and Rick drifted off to sleep. Rick slowly opened his eyes because he realized that Sean was lying on his chest with his head resting on his shoulder. Rick moved carefully so as not to wake Sean. Rick was puzzled, how did Sean get out of the crib? Rick wondered if Jeff had come in and took Sean out of the crib and laid him on his chest. No, that couldn't happen. Rick knew he would have woken up at the slightest movement of that kind. Rick tried but could not figure it out.

When Jeff came in later that evening, Rick asked him if he had taken Sean out of the crib and laid him on his chest. Jeff responded with a no, maybe Fred came in from work or something and did it, Jeff stated.

It was close to 10:30, a comfortable summer night. Rick and Donny sat on the stoop of a building just off 114th street, 7th Avenue. They had been there for 15 minutes when Skull showed up. They sat kicking it while waiting for Jesse.

"How much dope you copping now?" Skull asked. Donny's reply of a hundred dollars scramble sent Skull into a rage.

"What?" Skull jumped up, "A hundred in scramble?"

Donny meekly responded in defense, "We took a fall. In the last two weeks we have been scrambling to pay off the 25 hundred to the lawyer on my case."

"Fuck that!" Skull shouted back.

Skull saw Jesse approaching just as he was about to cut into Donny and Rick's business habits.

"Yo Jesse, what the fuck's wrong with you?" Skull asked.

Jesse was startled, "What the fuck are you talking about?" Jesse asked.

Rick and Donny were also taken by surprise, they had no idea Skull would go off like this.

"Give them some dope," Skull stated.

"What, I don't even know these niggers like that," Jesse shouted back.

"Fuck that," Skull said, "You see them every night, you see they are trying to get money."

Jesse pulled Skull off to the side and they spoke for several minutes, then Skull walked off.

"Look," Jesse told Rick and Donny, "You meet Willie at Wells at 2 o'clock and he will give you that thing. Then tomorrow night at the regular time meet me at the Shalimar. Bring me some money, like two, three hundred. What I'm going to do is start you out with half piece for 450 dollars. After that, whatever you buy I will give you the same amount on consignment. Can you handle it?" Jesse asked them.

"Yeah we can handle it," they both replied.

"I'm giving you a shot at getting paid so don't fuck me," Jesse stated making a point they both understood.

Rick and Donny sat in the bedroom of Rick's mother's apartment going over the events that had just taken place. Donny played with Sean on his lap as they talked.

"Ricky," his mother called from the living room, "Put that baby to bed"

"Yeah, okay Ma, in a few minutes."

"No, put him to bed now!" she said. "He's already just like you sleeping all day and staying up all night."

"Come on little man, grandma said daddy has to put you back to bed."

"Yo Donny," Rick said, "As soon as he's asleep we can cut out."

It had been a long night and Rick was beat. At this hour of the morning the projects were always nice and cool. Rick listened to his mother sing along with the gospel group on the radio as she got ready for work.

"Don't fall asleep Ricky, and let your baby run around this house."

"I'm not going to sleep; we are going to the park in an hour or so."

She kissed Rick and Sean who were sitting on the sofa watching cartoons before she walked out the door.

Rick stared at Sean as he watched cartoons. Sean seemed fascinated by the cartoons. Sean could barely say 'mama', 'daddy' or 'yes' and 'no' but his eyes lit up and he laughed at the images on the television screen. Rick wondered what he was really seeing at 11 months of age. What did the cartoons say to him that the other programs failed to say?

Rick played vigorously with Sean and the other children in the park. Rick did not feel the weariness from staying up all night. The children's laughter made him feel alive. Rick watched Sean's reaction as the female Doberman pinscher that had been playing with the other children walked up to Sean's stroller. Sean showed no fear and played with the animal as it ran in circles around him.

Rick found delight in the little girl who had run over to Sean and the dog. She was 3 years old, trying to teach Sean to say dog, barking and all. Sean found the barking easy and laughed as he threw the ball for the dog to chase.

When the Good Humor man saw Rick playing with the children he smiled, and again Rick brought all of his ice cream. On the way home, Sean barked at a pigeons and then at a cat that sat in the window of a store on Broadway.

Rick bathed Sean and the two of them sat in the tub throwing water on one another. Sean put his face in the water and blew bubbles, then laughed with delight. Sean laughed even harder when his father blew bubbles in the water.

Sean barked and laughed as his father got him ready for bed. Rick picked Sean up.

"Let me hear daddy's little man say "dog".

"Dog".

"That's it," Rick replied. "Dog, daddy, dog, dog. That's my man, but it's time for you to get some sleep. Besides little man, daddy is tired."

Rick turned the volume down on the television and drifted off to sleep. When Rick awoke some two hours later he found Sean asleep on his chest once again. "How did you get here?" Rick asked. But Sean had no answer, he just went on sleeping.

The pile of dope seemed enormous lying on the black album cover. Donny had sifted it 4 or 5 times to make sure it was mixed to perfection. Rick and Donny filled the glassine bags as Ronda folded and taped them. It took what seemed like forever to finish the bags. Donny and Rick put the bags in half loads while Ronda went in the back room to get high. They counted 88 half loads at 1,760 dollars. Both men were ecstatic.

"Junie is not going to be able to handle all of this dope," Rick said.

"Maybe we should put something down 102nd street," Rick went on to say.

"I was just going to mention that," Donny replied "I've already got a worker in mind."

"Who?" Rick asked

"Buckie. You know the one that lives in the building next to yours. He's married to that real pretty Spanish girl, Millie. We can talk to him in the morning," Donny said.

"Check this Donny; first off, I don't want to leave all this dope in this apartment. So what we can do is buy another strong box and keep half the dope at Cheryl's apartment on West End Avenue."

"That's cool," Donny replied.

"I also think we should give Junie 20 half's and start Buckie out with 10. That way we will bring in six hundred a day. We can pay the 450 we owe and every third day we can re-up," Rick stated.

"Sounds good," Donny responded, "Sounds real good to me."

Rick felt real good, like he owed the world. He stood against the wall in the Shalimar. Rick was fly. He was dressed in a pair of black tailor-made silk slacks, with matching silk shirt. The shoes, handmade in a natural color snake skin, trimmed along the bottom half by black lizard skin accenting his outfit. Rick took pride in knowing that his shoes were one of a kind. No matter how much money any of the other hustlers made or how fly they dressed, they could not get a pair like these. Rick had many, many pairs of hand made shoes done during the time he spent in Vietnam.

Rick and Donny took a seat at a table by the window. The view from where they sat allowed them to see only the legs of the women standing on the sidewalk in front of the Shalimar. Her legs, a golden brown color, short, shapely, almost bow. The sandal-style high heels brought out the muscle contour of their shape beautifully. Rick was in love and didn't care what the rest of her attributes were. Donny found Rick's sexually detailed description of her legs humorous and both of them laughed.

"Me," Donny said, "I like women with nice firm tits."

"I don't give a fuck if she has no tits just as long as she has nice legs," Rick proclaimed.

Rick invited Donny to go outside with him so they could check out the rest of the lady with the lovely legs. Jesse had arrived and stood just to the side of the bar talking with a few of the crew. When Jesse saw Rick and Donny he excused himself and came over to speak with them.

"Everything alright?" Jesse asked

"Everything's cool, we just came up to give you this money," Donny said.

"You finished?" Jesse asked

"No," Rick replied, "We've got your money but we need another day before we will be ready to re-up.

"Okay that's cool," Jesse responded. "I see you are taking care of business," Jesse stated. "What you want to do, double up next time?"

"No, we are not ready yet." Rick told him. Jesse was impressed, they did not jump on his offer to get more dope than they were ready to handle.

"Yo Ricky, where did you get those shoes? They are some bad mother-fuckers," Jesse asked.

"I got them when I was in Hong Kong," Rick replied.

"I didn't know you were overseas. We got to talk about that one day. What they run you over there?" Jesse questioned.

"Fifty four-dollar and they are handmade in a style that I designed," Rick stated.

"If I were to buy them downtown they would run about 3 to 5 hundred," Rick proclaimed. "Now let me ask you something Jesse. See that girl over there, the one wearing the glasses. Do you know who she's with,"

"That's Shemika, she is a bad lady and if your game is tight she could be with you," Jesse joked.

"Pardon me Ms. Lady; May I speak with you for a moment?" Rick asked as he stopped just in font of the lady with the pretty legs.

"Who are you?" she politely answered.

"I am just a man who is interested in getting to know you," Rick answered. "If you will excuse yourself from your friends for a moment, I am sure we have things we can talk about."

Rick liked the chase and he was about to lay down his best game. The chase gave Rick the opportunity to showcase all that he believed himself to be. Rick knew his game was sharp. But the chase allowed him to enjoy the pleasure of being in the company of beautiful women such as this young lady.

Rick drank orange juice and Shemika had a rum and coke. The music was loud and talking inside the Shalimar was all but impossible. Rick excused himself and went over to the jukebox. He inserted several dollar bills, selecting the slow records as he came to them. Smokey sang 'Oooh Baby Baby' and Rick asked the bartender to turn the volume down just a bit. Rick took Shemika by the hand and led her to the center of the floor. Rick slowly eased his arm around Shemika's slim waist holding her just close enough to whisper the words he felt for her. Shemika smiled, their eyes embraced and all else was lost to them.

"I look at you and I feel all kind of wonderful things," Rick whispered to Shemika. They stopped dancing; standing in the middle of the floor as she listens intently to all Rick had to say. "You are a rare and truly beautiful lady," his voice soft and easy. "You have a style that sets you apart from others," she moved closer to him dawned by what he made her feel.

"Shemika, I have this feeling that tells me we can be good to and for each other. If you give me the chance, time will show you that all I have said is true."

Shemika stood on her tiptoes and their lips met for the very first time. Rick felt the tenderness of her lips as he tasted the sweetness of her kiss. Shemika was soft and warm. Rick knew she was a delicate but strong woman.

Rick took Shemika by the hand and they walked out of the bar together. Rick saw Donny and Jesse talking and excused himself, Shemika went back to talk with her friends.

"Yo Donny, what are you going to do," Rick asked.

"I'm going to take Belinda to the hotel. What are you going to do?" Donny asked Rick.

"I guess I am going to do the same," Rick replied.

"You know Ricky," Jesse said, "Niggers shoot at her all the time and she don't give them no play. I'm talking niggers with a lot of money. You just hit on her once and she's ready to go off with you. A lot of motherfuckers are going to be mad at you," Jesse stated.

"I'm not talking trouble, but they are going want to know who the fuck you are. She is one of the baddest ladies in this town, plus her father is a bad man too," Jesse informed Rick.

"I figure the reason they never got no play was because they tried to let their money do the talking," Rick said. "It's all in what you have to say about yourself and how you say it..What you say has to be who you are and it's got to be real. Woman want a man that knows he is a man," Rick went on to say. Rick made it clear it could never be about having money when he chose a woman.

Rick sat lazily in the back seat of the cab. Shemika leaned against him rubbing his chest; it seemed so natural, as if they had done it many times before. Shemika surprised Rick. He had told the cab driver to take them to the Hilton Hotel. She instructed the cab drive to do otherwise by giving him her home address.

Shemika had a nice body to go along with those beautiful legs. Her face was pretty and the large frame glasses she wore added to her charm. Shemika had a sweet innocence about her. She was not like most of the women that ran with hustlers. Shemika was not like most women, period.

Shemika's apartment was spacious and nicely done, reflecting her personality. Rick made himself to home and the comfort of her apartment brought on the weariness of too many late nights. Rick picked up her phone and dialed a number.

"Hello Ma, sorry to wake you."

"Is everything alright Ricky?" she asked.

"Yeah, tell Jeff to watch Sean for me in the morning. I will be there before he gets ready to go out."

"I will tell him," she replied, "But make sure you get here to take care of your baby."

"Okay Ma, I will be there."

"Who is Sean?" Shemika asked. "That is if you don't mind telling me."

"He's my son, I take care of him sometimes."

The way Rick spoke of his son drew Shemika closer to him, but he knew her next question.

"His mother and I are not together. We're just alright," Rick stated.

"I did not ask about her," Shemika said.

"I just didn't want any unanswered questions to come between what we can become to one another," Rick replied.

Shemika took Rick by the hand and led him to her bedroom. There was no mistaking it. It was a woman's bedroom. The room had a relaxing effect, from the canopy bed to the silk-laced pillows. Rick thought a moment about Shemika, the person he met in the bar and now about Shemika the woman he was coming to know something about. Her taste was excellent, a lady with a lot of class. Shemika was a year or so younger than him, yet her breeding was that of a woman much older than her years.

"You look like you are tired," Shemika said, "Come on, let's take a shower and afterwards I will give you a nice message."

Rick felt her nakedness as she sat on his behind and messaged the muscles of his neck and shoulder. Rick could feel her hard nipples on his back when she leaned forward, and he had begin to waver in and out of sleep.

"See," she said "You are more tired than you thought. What time do you want me to wake you?" she asked.

"Something around 8, 8:30," Rick replied. Shemika set the alarm on the clock radio and eased in bed beside Rick.

Rick could feel the warmth of her body and her silky nakedness when she laid her leg across the back of his legs. Rick wrapped her in his arms, he kissed her forehead, and Shemika kissed his neck and cheek.

When their eyes met, their tongues played and they kissed passionately.

"Rick," Shemika whispered, "I just want you to hold me. Can you hold me please?" she whispered again. Shemika turned around so her backside fit into his chest and stomach. Her body fitted him like a hand in a glove. Rick held her firm but tenderly. Rick knew she could feel his hardness and the heat from it against the softness of her behind. Shemika took his hardness and placed in between her thighs so she could feel its hardness resting against her womanhood. Shemika slept peacefully and Rick felt her soft breathing throughout the night.

Rick was able to relax his consciousness though his instincts kept him totally aware of his surroundings. When the alarm sounded Shemika jumped slightly.

"Easy," Rick said, "It's alright."

Shemika found herself just about in the same position she had fell asleep in. She slid back bringing herself as close to Rick as she could. He laid there quietly, enjoying the tranquility of the early morning.

Shemika found it hard to break the pleasure of Rick's embrace, but she did. Rick watched her naked beauty as she walked to the bathroom. When Shemika called for him to join her in the bathroom, Rick found everything he needed to freshen up.

"I will fix breakfast while you get cleaned up," Shemika said.

Rick noticed that Shemika had nicely ironed and laid his clothes on the bed when he came out of the bathroom. *I could get use to this*, Rick thought to himself. Rick put on his pant and shoes then made his way to the kitchen. Rick stood in the doorway watching Shemika preparing breakfast. Shemika did not realize that Rick was standing there watching her. Rick walked over and put his arms around her and he knew that he had frightened her. It was a good thing he had waited until her hands were empty.

"Do you always move so quietly, sneaking up on people?" she asked.

"It's a habit I picked up. Most of the time I don't realize it until I see that I have frightened someone," Rick replied. "I did not mean to frighten you."

Rick was enjoying the breakfast Shemika made, pancakes, eggs, beef and turkey bacon, served with ice cold milk.

"I like to watch a man eats," Shemika informed him. "Some of my best memories are from home watching my father eat while we talked."

"So I remind you of your father," Rick said playfully.

"Yes, yes you do," Shemika replied. "Only your manner is much quieter than his ever was or is. You don't say much and what you do say, to me anyway. It is enough for me to know you have your own private world that you do not invite many people into. I knew last night, from the moment I asked you to hold me and you did not try to have me, that you are a special kind of man. You are definitely the kind of man that I want to get to know better."

"I understand your lifestyle and the business you are in," Shemika said. "Most men in your business pass women around like they are toys. That is the number one reason I never went off with anyone," Shemika stated.

"You seem to know a lot about men in what you think is my business," Rick responded.

"It's all the talks I had with my father at meal times," Shemika playfully shot back. "My father's in the life, who do you think paid for all of this?" Shemika asked.

"You are a lady who is full of surprise," Rick said.

They sat on the floor in the living room watching cartoons. Jeff and Sean had a box of Frosted Flakes and a large bowl between them. Jeff would take a spoon full of cereal than he would give Sean one. When

Sean saw his father standing in the doorway he tried to stand up. In his excitement, Sean was trying to do too much at once and fell back on the seat of his diaper. Jeff helped him up and Sean used the furniture for balance to walk to his father. Rick picked him up and threw Sean in the air. Sean laughed and slobbered all over his father.

"What's up?" Rick asked Jeff.

"Jenny called this morning; she wants you to call her."

"Where did she say she was?" Rick asked Jeff again.

"She said she would be home around 3 o'clock, but she still might be home now. It was only about 10 minutes ago when she called," Jeff informed Rick.

Fuck it. I know what she wants," Rick thought out loud. "She wants to know when I am going to bring Sean home. Hey little man, your mother wants to know when I am going to bring you home? But we are going to hang out in the park and chase the ladies," Rick told Sean, as if he really knew what his father was saying.

Rick heard someone calling to him from outside. Jeff being closer to the window knew it was Donny calling his brother. "Rick that's Donny calling you," Jeff said.

"Tell him to come up," Rick told his brother.

Rick and Donny talked as Rick set out a pair of burgundy alligator shoes with matching slacks and shirt for himself. Rick selected two nice cool summer outfits for Sean.

"I just hit Junie and Buckie," Donny informed Rick. "We will be able to re-up tonight instead of tomorrow," Donny stated.

"Sounds good," Rick replied.

Donny handed Rick a large roll of bills and he threw it in the dresser draw.

"So what are you going to do today?" Donny asked.

"I'm going to take my man to the park, then shopping," Rick replied.

"What about you?" Rick asked Donny.

"I'm just going to hang loose and keep an eye on things," Donny replied. "Where did you go last night Rick? I was looking for you at the Motor Inn. I had some crazy good blow."

"I went to Shemika's house," Rick answered. "She has got a bad apartment. Besides, if we would have gone to a hotel, it would not have been the Motor Inn. Check this, I went to her house and went to sleep."

"Get the fuck out of here!" Donny responded to what he thought had to be the dumbest shit he ever heard.

"No bullshit, I went to sleep!" Rick said. "Joe Frog said that she wouldn't give you any pussy. I could have fucked her, we slept naked and the whole shit."

"So what you are telling me is that you and she were in bed butt ass naked and you did not fuck her?" Donny said in disbelief.

"That's right," Rick stated.

"That Vietnam War fucked you up more than you realized," Donny said jokingly.

"For you not to fuck a woman as fine as she is you have to be all the way out of your mind."

"Rick gave me a few balls," Jeff asked.

"What for?" Rick questioned.

"I don't have any money," Jeff stated.

"Oh, I thought you wanted money to buy something. Look in the top dresser draw and take 10 dollars," Rick told him.

"Thanks man," Jeff answered.

"So what's up with you and Belinda?" Rick asked Donny.

"She's cool," Donny replied, "and she may be my next piece since Mia and I are coming to the end of the road."

"When did this thing with you and Mia come about?" Rick asked

"I don't know," Donny stated. "But she's starting to act real funny."

"Yeah, I wonder why? It's only been like what, 3, 4 weeks since the last time you spent any time with her," Rick said. "The only time you see her is by accident when she is coming from work or the store. The rest of the time you are with me or in the hotel with a freak. So tell me my brother, how is she supposed to act?"

Rick sat the carrying case on the bench and laid a blanket out for Sean to play on the grass with the other children. The children were happy to see Sean and Rick. They asked Rick if he was going to play with them today. *I don't think so, not today kids.* Ah, the children sighed, and Rick could feel their disappointment deep in the pit of his stomach. "Maybe in a little while," he told them. They jumped up and down with joy. "But for right now Sean can play with you in my place," Rick told the children. "Come on," they told Sean and grabbed him by the hands to help him walk.

This was the first time Rick had not brought Sean's stroller, so he watched Sean carefully as he played on the grass with the other children. This was also the first time that Rick really took the time to talk with the mothers of the other children. They flirted with him, some boldly and others with a little reserve. Once they had found out that he and Sean's mother were not together, they made their intentions clear. Any other time the invitations they offered would have been welcome. Right now, however, he had someone else on his mind. Rick excused himself from the ladies and went to play with the children.

Rick did not jump around as usual and play run and catch games but he still made the children laugh. The children and some of the mothers sat in front of him and listen to his funny stories. They all went crazy with laughter when Rick acted out the different parts of the story. Rick had not seen her (Shemika?) standing in the distance watching him at play. When she started to approach him, he felt her movement but did not turn to look at her. When she came to stand just off to his side, he made her a character in his story. Rick turn to kiss her, just a quick peck on the lips. The children oooed and ah-ed.

It was 12:30; the Good Humor man could see Rick entertaining the children so he stood off to the side and watched the show. Rick knew now was the time to end the show without the kids asking him to do more.

"Ice cream!" Rick yelled, "Ice cream! Is everybody ready for ice cream?"

"Yeah!" the children screamed at the top of their little lungs.

"Well you can't have any," Rick teased.

"Ah!" they sang in harmony.

"Okay, okay, if you really want some ice cream you can buy me some," Rick continued to tease.

"We don't have money," the children yelled back.

"Okay, then I will buy you some," Rick told them.

"Yeah!" they screamed.

Shemika watched Rick feeding Sean with ice cream while he played with him. Rick would rub the ice cream on the tip of Sean's nose then lick it off. The little boy laughed and tried to do the same to his father.

"Did you have any problems finding us?" Rick asked Shemika.

"No, your instructions were right on the money."

Shemika had a pretty smile and a warm personality. She was wearing a summer print dress with her hair in a ponytail. Her look was as fresh as the summer morning. Rick could not keep his eyes off of her legs, and she knew it as she teased him by displaying them for his pleasure.

"You know Rick," Shemika said, "If anyone from uptown saw you now they would not believe you are the same person."

"Why, because I take care of my son and play with the other kids.?"

"No, that's not really the reason," Shemika said. "It's like you are two people who live in two different worlds. Meeting you the way I did," Shemika said, "I would never have guessed about this part of your life. In the other world you are just too cool for words, a man who understands the world he lives in and what his place in it is. Today, I see a softer size of you. You are just as cool, I don't know how to put it," Shemika told him. "It's like these children and me have been invited to see who you really are."

Out of nowhere and all of a sudden a little girl ran up behind Rick to ask if Sean was going to be able to play with them some more. The little girl had startled Shemika, but Rick had not moved. Yet when the Good Humor man came within 20 or 30 feet of Rick, he turned fully and Shemika notice the way Rick's demeanor stiffened, and how alerted he now was.

"Rick," Shemika said softly, "I noticed how guarded you seemed when the ice cream man walked up behind you, but when the little girl ran up behind us scaring me, you did not move. How do you know when some-one is behind you like that and how did you know the difference between the man and a chil?", Shemika asked

"I just came back from Vietnam, well, not just back, I've been home almost a year. My nerves are still razor sharp so when I sense danger I become guarded. People give off a scent, fear, danger and so on. From the little girl I did not sense anything; from the ice cream man I just sensed his presence behind me. I could also hear his footsteps, he walks heavy. I don't know Shemika, it took a lot for me to stay alive in Vietnam and I brought some of it home with me," Rick said, feeling a bit uneasy. "It's just a part of me now."

"That explains a lot," Shemika said, "The quiet sneaky way you move and your reaction to other people's movement."

"I really don't notice any difference in myself before or after Vietnam," Rick stated. "I guess Vietnam is just so much a part of me that it is me now. My mother and sister have asked me the same questions you just did. My mother asked why I always keep myself on alert. I think my mother is afraid, not of me, but of what I might do to someone one day. I guess I will be this way for the rest of my life."

"You must have gone through hell for it to become a part of you like that," Shemika said.

"I would not call it hell; it was just something I went through, as for effect. Others have told me about it but I can't see it, I feel the same as I always have."

Shemika handed Rick the keys to the Mercedes 450. "Is it yours?" he asked.

"No, it's one of my fathers' but I can use it or any others any time I choose. I drive this one the most," she added. Shemika held Sean on her lap and bounced him up and down. Sean laughed with her like he had known her all of his young life. Sean had always been a friendly child. Rick slowed down to pay the toll on the George Washington Bridge before entering New Jersey. Sean waved at the other cars in the line.

"Can you say car?" Shemika asked Sean. "Let me hear you say car," she repeated. "Say car for me."

"Car!" Sean yelled.

"Car daddy car. That's right my man, cars. Daddy is stuck behind all of these cars."

Rick held Sean in his arm as they strolled around the stores in the Paramis shopping mall. Shemika held Rick by his other arm. The trio drew a lot of stares. Rick did not like being in the crowded stores and it was only when Shemika mention it did he ease his guard. Besides clothes, Rick brought Sean several ABC book with pictures of animals and clowns. Shemika had excused herself and when she returned she had a large bag. They had lunch in one of the mall cafes'. The conversation was good and they both played with Sean.

Shemika pulled the Mercedes over on 102nd street Columbus Avenue and turned the engine off.

"I want you to know Rick, that I had a really good time with you and Sean today. I enjoyed the pleasure of your company also and I know my man here likes you. Will I be able to see you later Rick?"

"I don't know, I've got to see what is going on since I've been gone all day. I may have some business to take care of. I will be at the Shalimar around 11:30 tonight," Rick told her. "After that I don't know what it's going to be."

"Do you see that kid standing by the mailboxk?" Rick asked Shemika.

"Yes, I see him; he looks a lot like you. He must be your brother," Shemika stated.

"He is my brother," Rick replied. "It's kind of early for him to be over here," Rick thought to himself out loud. "He must have the day off from work. He lives in Queens," Rick informed Shemika.

"The only time he comes over is when he wants to hang out. Yo, Claude!" Rick called his brother, "Come here for a minute."

"What's up," Claude said to his brother and greeted Shemika before being introduced. "Claude this is Shemika, a very close friend. Shemika this is my brother, Claude."

"Nice to meet you," they both said.

Claude took Sean through the car window.

"Claude will you take Sean upstairs?" Rick asked. "I will be up in a few minutes Rick told his brother.

"It was nice meeting you," Claude said.

"Same here," Shemika replied.

Rick leaned to kiss Shemika and she met him half way.

"Look, I am not sure what I have to do tonight," Rick said. I have to talk to my partner and see what's what. Are you going to be at the Shalimar?" Rick asked.

"I had not plan on it," she replied. "I don't go there every night.

"If you don't come to the bar I will call you as soon as I know something," Rick said. "I really want to see you tonight," Rick added.

Rick took the package from the back seat of the car.

"Take that one too," Shemika told him, "It has something for Sean in it." Rick thanked her and kissed her before he got out of the car.

Rick checked the things he bought earlier and then checked the bag that Shemika had given him. He found that she had brought Sean a stuffed dog. Rick took the dog out of the bag and found a silk shirt underneath it. It was the same shirt he had looked at but decided not to buy. The sales ticket had a message written on it. "Only because it will look so good on you, Shemika". Rick smiled.

"Come on little man, it's time for you to take a nap, you have been up all day." Rick said to Sean.

"That's a pretty girl," Claude said, "But then again, you always have pretty girls. Was that her car?" Claude asked his brother.

"No, it's her father's."

"Shhhh—Claude, don't say anything."

"What, what's the matter?" Claude asked.

"Nothing, just be quiet for one minute." Rick eased down the hall and stopped in the bedroom doorway. Rick was surprised to see Sean climbing out of his crib. Rick stepped back so Sean could not see him and watched as Sean went through the maneuvers of climbing to the floor. Rick walked backwards to the living room and told Claude to sit down and act like he was asleep.

"Why?" Claude asked, "Are you loosing your fuckin' mind?"

"No I have not lost my mind; I will tell you after Sean comes up here." Rick laid on the sofa like he was asleep and Sean crawled straight to him and climbed up on his chest. Rick waited for a minute so he would not startled Sean.

"Okay my little man; daddy knows how you do it. So you can get out of your crib, now I know I have to watch you better. You know Claude, for the last two days I have tried to figure out how it was that every time I woke up, Sean was asleep on my chest. Now I know he knows how to climb out of his crib."

Rick had just finished changing, he had on the dress slacks, silk shirt, new white Pro-Keds, and the outfit was accented with a diamond pinky ring along with a Cuban gold bracelet on his wrist. When Rick was assured that the outfit he had on matched his personality, he was ready to go.

"Come on little man, it's time for you to say so long to grandma."

Claude called Rick to the window,"There's your man Donny."

"Yo, Donny!" Rick yelled out of the window, "Wait, I'll be right down!"

Rick kissed his mother and picked his baby up.

"You coming back tonight?" she asked Rick.

"I'm not sure Ma, I don't think so."

"Hold up Rick," Claude said, "I'll go down with you."

Claude kissed his mother and told her he did not know if he would be back before he went home.

"What's up?" the two brothers greeted Donny.

"Ain't nothing," Donny replied. "Rick I need to talk to you."

"Okay, let me take Sean home and I will be right back."

"Get out of here," Donny said. "You hear your brother?" Donny told Claude.

"Everybody knows when you go down there that you never come right back."

" That's right Rick," his brother said. "I don't know why you are lying to yourself, Claude added.

"Look," Rick said. "I will be right back," with a little attitude.

"What time is it?" Rick asked.

"It's 10 after 8." Donny told him.

"Okay, I'll be back at 15 to 9, not later than 9."

"I'll wait for you in front of 840," Donny told him. "I've got this money on me."

"Give it to Claude. Claude take that money upstairs for me and put it in the drawer."

Sean was happy to see his mother, he laughed and hugged her. Jenny kissed Sean then Rick. Rick sat on the sofa watching the two of them played. Rick's thoughts went back to the time when he had first seen her. She was 15 and he was only 17. It was not love at first sight, though it was something that drew them to be together. Rick remembered clearly when fascination turned into love for both of them. They enjoyed the pleasure of their teen years dancing in the clubs and late nights walking hand in hand along Riverside Drive Park. Rick thought about the many times they had played at making love on the steps of one building or another. The pure serenity of love that had never known another and the promise to love forever was all they cared to know. Rick had known the sexual pleasure of a woman's body and he teased Jenny's sexual desires, desires that she had not known existed, yet he did not push her to go all the way.

One afternoon as they talked on the stoop of her building, Jenny told him that her mother and her new husband had just gotten an apartment. Jenny told him also that they would be moving in sometimes next week. Jenny informed him that they had left the keys at the apartment where she stayed with her cousin. Rick knew what she had in mind and when she told him that she could get the keys tomorrow night after her cousin went to bed, Rick knew as she did. This coming Friday would be a night they both would always remember.

The power was on, but they did not use the lights. They sat a candle at each end of the mattress, the only thing besides them in the apartment. They played at being lovers on the mattress and she was more than ready to receive him. But Rick found it difficult to enter her and gave up on the third or fourth try. They talked for a long time. They studied one another's naked beauty. This time when they embraced, Jenny found relaxation alone with sexual arousal and Rick entered her easily. They made passionate love into the early hours of the morning.

Rick came back to the reality of where he was when Sean called him. Rick also knew that he had to get out of there because the memories had brought on the desire to have Jenny again, and he knew she would let him.

"Jenny, I've got to go."

"You just got here," Jenny replied softly.

"Yeah, I know but I've got some people waiting for me, business. Here, take this money, what time are you going to be home tomorrow?" Rick asked Jenny.

"All day." she responded.

"Okay, I'll call you some time in the afternoon." Rick told her.

Rick kissed Sean and started to leave. Jenny told Sean to say 'bye daddy.'

"Bye daddy," Sean said.

Rick waved back to Sean and Jenny walked him to the door.

"You can come by later on tonight, I will be here." Jenny informed Rick.

The offer was tempting and it took a lot for Rick to say he could not make it tonight anyway.

"I can't believe it," Donny said.

"Yeah," Rick replied, "I told you I would be back before 9 o'clock. So what's up Donny, what's so important?"

"Nothing, I just wanted to let you know that I would meet you at the Shalimar tonight. I'm taking Mia to the show and after the show I will drop her off and shoot uptown."

"What's the rush?" Rick asked. "I can take care of everything. You can meet me at Ronda's house after I make the drop. That way you can spend some time with your woman. You know, you don't have to give her a quickie and cut out," Rick teased.

"Get the fuck out of here," Donny said, "I wasn't going to do that shit anyway.

"Whatever." Rick replied. "I'm just saying this so you have some time to do something to please her."

"Look," Rick said, "Buckie and Junie are rocking the half pieces pretty fast, so I think we should get a piece tonight."

"I was thinking about that," Donny replied, "But I was going to wait until we finished the next half before I mentioned it."

"Fuck it," Donny said, "if you think we are ready, let's do it."

Willie and Rick kicked it in the doorway of the building next to the Shalimar. Rick told him that they wanted a piece and gave Willie 450 dollars to cover half the cost.

"I see you are ready to move up," Willie commented.

"Yeah, things are coming along," Rick replied.

The crowd was a little larger than on most nights. There were noticeably fewer women as well. The Shalimar was jumping though. The socialites of Harlem had gathered. George Fluellen and Frank Matthews stood talking with Nicky Barnes. George's brother Reggie leaned against the fender of his brown Electra 225 rapping to a very pretty young lady in a mini skirt. The triple yellow Cadillac Brougham came to a stop next to Reggie's Electra. When the driver opened the door to the Caddy, the car sang the theme from the movie Goldfinger. Goldfinger greeted Reggie and walked over to Guy Fisher who was standing just off of the doorway to the Shalimar with a drink in his hand. The boss of the Council was expected tonight and the bosses of all the crews were there to greet him.

There was a special kind of excitement in the air. The crowd was sprinkled with men that Rick had never seen before. They seemed a little out of place, not really out of place, but he easily noticed them as he checked over the crowd. They all had that same glitter of success.

Jesse had not shown on the set as of yet. However, Rick recognized a lot of the men who did business with him. They all waited for Jesse to show, the same as he was. Rick knew just as everyone else there did, who was with what crew and how important each man was, with the exception of those few faces he did not know.

Willie introduced Rick to a couple of kids out of Buffalo New York as part of the crew and now Rick knew every face in the crowd. Rick and the kids from Buffalo kicked it while Willie mixed it up with the other lieutenants and bosses.

The kids from Buffalo told Rick that Jesse flew them down once every two weeks to re-up. Their conversation was one that could not be shared with anyone outside of their very own crew.

Shemika double-parked the blue Caddy Brougham with the white interior right in front of the Shalimar. Shemika had three of the most beautiful black women you could imagine with her. All eyes were watching as they got off the car, their beauty silenced the crowd. Shemika saw Rick standing off to the side as he talked with two men. She waited until Rick finished talking before approaching him. Rick excused himself to talk with Shemika. As though a switch had been turn on, the crowd came back to life. Shemika's girlfriends went inside the Shalimar.

"I did not think you were going to show," Rick said to Shemika.

"I knew that I would not be home to receive your call. So, I decided to stop by for a little bit. I wanted to see you. Besides, you may not have had the time to call," Shemika added, searching for reassurance and teasing at the same time.

"My friends and I are going to the Dome," Shemika informed Rick.

"I still don't know what I'm going to do, not yet anyway." Rick responded. "I don't know if I will have work or not."

"If you get the chance, come by the Dome please."

"If it's possible I will do just that," Rick replied. "If I don't make it by the Dome I will call you sometime during the day."

"I will be looking forward to you coming for me at the Dome," Shemika said. "Let me get my girlfriends so we can go."

Rick went back to talk with the kids out of Buffalo and Shemika honked the car horn and waved to Rick as she pulled off.

"That's your woman?" one of the kids from Buffalo asked Rick. "She sure is fine." Rick did not answer his question, nor was the kid really looking for one.

Jesse pulled up and the boss of the Council was right behind him in a pearl white Rolls Royce. Both men double-parked. Jesse and the man spoke briefly while standing on the street before they joined others on the sidewalk.

The boss was about to enter the Shalimar when he saw Rick standing off to the side. He excused himself from the crowd walked over to where Rick stood.

"What's up?" He asked Rick.

"Ain't nothing, I haven't seen you in a long, long time. Let me think, when was it? It was at the airport in Houston Texas," Rick added, re-membering. "You had Country and some girls with you. We did not get to talk because I was in a rush to catch my plane." Rick said.

"Yeah, that's right." The boss said, "And the time before that it was at the airport in Hong Kong. Seems like we always run into each other at the airports. Tell me Rick, everything alright? Are you getting money or what?" The boss asked.

"I'm with Jesse," Rick replied.

"Jesse is a good man," The boss stated. "If you stick with him and do the right thing I know you will come off. If you need anything let me know."

"You still ballin'?" The boss asked Rick.

"You know it." Rick replied.

"We're going to run this Saturday at Teachers College. Come over, you can get some run with my squad," The boss informed him.

"I'll be there." Rick responded.

"Okay, excuse me. I've got some business inside. I'll kick it with you later."

It seemed now that everyone noticed Rick because of the attention that The boss gave to him. What did it mean? Rick didn't really know, not yet anyway.

"What's up Rick?"

"How you doing Pete, Jervis," Rick replied. *This seems to be the night for reunions*, Rick thought.

"It's been a long time." Pete said.

"Yeah. I've been hearing a lot of good things about you and Jervis."

"Things are okay," Pete replied.

"I didn't know you were doing something," Jervis commented.

"A little something," Rick replied. "Me and my man got something in the projects."

"You still in the Douglas?" Pete asked.

"Yeah."

"How's Gloria and her brother Sonny?"

"They're both okay, I see them every now and then."

"You and Sonny don't hang out, what happen?" Pete asked.

"Nothing, he's still my man. But business, you know how it goes. You still in Convent?" Rick asked Pete.

"I can still be found there, but I live out on the island. I've got me a nice big house with five acres of land. If you want to find me or Jervis," Pete told Rick, "Just look in the same old places." They both laughed.

Willie approached Rick, Pete and Jervis, excusing himself he asked to speak with Rick in private. Later Rick told Pete and Jervis, "I'll catch up with both of you at another time."

"Okay Rick," they both replied, We'll get with you later."

"What's up?" Rick asked Willie.

"I'm going to have to give your package at 7 in the morning. Meet me on 7th Avenue at the restaurant on the corner of 112th street. Sorry it's going to be so late, but we ran out of cut."

"No problem." Rick said.

"If you want pure, you can get your package at 4 o'clock." Willie added.

"No, we don't have any cut either," Rick replied.

"Okay Rick, then I will see you at 7."

Rick listened to the music and moved his head to the beat. Shemika was on the dance floor with her back to him, she had not seen him come in. Rick got a thrill watching her moved to the beats of the music. Rick also could see that the young kid who danced with her had more than just dancing on his mind by the way he tried to get up on her.

Rick saw Fat Stevie standing at the end of the bar, just across the dance floor. There were lesser crowd at this early morning hour, making it easy for Rick to get across the dance floor.

"What's up?" Rick greeted Stevie, and they gave each other **five**.

"Ain't nothing." Stevie replied.

"I just left Pete," Rick told Stevie.

"I didn't know you knew my brother."

"Yeah, we've known each other way back in Junior High. I remember you, Stevie, when you used to play in front of your building. We used to all hang out in the basement and I would rap to that girl, Alvis."

"No shit! I thought we just knew each other from getting money. I don't remember anywhere else." Both men laughed and their talk had given new understanding to the friendship.

"I'm getting ready to cut out," Stevie told Rick. "These funny time bitches that hang out here, they look at a fat nigger with sneakers on like something's wrong. They don't know I can buy this place a thousand times over. So you want to hang?"

"I don't know, I just came here to see someone. Let me speak to her than I'll let you know."

"Who?" Stevie asked. "If she's got a friend we all can hang."

Rick pointed to Shemika, whom still dancing with her back to them. It seemed home boy did not want to let her off of the dance floor.

"That's my home girl," Stevie said. "Treat her right Rick, she is good people. Her father's a monster, he's got it good."

"She's here with three of her friends, but I don't know what the deal is with them." Rick told Stevie.

"I know them, they're like my sisters. Okay, let me speak to Shemika to see what's up."

When Shemika spinned, turning her back on her dance partner she found Rick standing in front of her. She kissed him and waved goodbye to her dance partner. Shemika wanted Rick to come to the table where her friends were. Rick took her to where he had left Stevie standing.

"Hi Stevie," Shemika said.

"How are you Shemika."

"I've got to be at work." Rick told Shemika. Rick could see the disappointment written on her face.

"My friends are ready to leave," she told Rick. "The only reason we're still here is because I did not want to miss seeing you. We're going to get something to eat and I am going to drop Jacqueline and Cheri off, while Ann is staying at my house. We should be at my apartment no later than 7."

"I will be working until at least 12 in the afternoon then I am going to get some sleep." Rick informed Shemika.

"You can come by my house and rest," Shemika offered.

"How much sleep do you think I will get with you and your girl friend hanging out?"

"We are going shopping, so you will have the whole place to yourself."

"It sounds good, if I finish what I'm doing before you are ready to go shopping, I will be there. Don't wait for me, when you are ready, go. If I don't make it, when you come back from shopping you can call me at home and wake me up, okay?"

Stevie and Rick sat in Stevie's car, parked between 7th and St. Nichols Avenue on 112th street. The steel gray dawn was a familiar sight, known mostly by the people who broke night, a spiritual renaissance with the birth of a new day. Rick felt good, real good. Stevie passed Rick the hundred-dollar bill with blow in it. Rick leaned back in the comfort of the car seat and took a hit. The music filled the car and overflowed out into the street.

The block was deserted; every now and then they would see a car pass on 7th Avenue.

"Yo Rick, I'm going to the Fast Track and get me a freak, you down or what?"

"No my brother, I can't hang. I've got to meet Willie in less than 20 minutes."

"Alright. Besides, it ain't going to be many freaks still there at this late hour. I only need one." Stevie said and they both laughed.

Stevie stopped at the green light on the corner of 112th street 7th Avenue. Later Rick and Stevie both said and gave each other five. Rick got out and crossed the avenue while Stevie waited for the light to turn back to green before he pulled off.

Rick eyed the small crowd of men and women in front of the restaurant, most were hoes and street hustlers who had been out working the night and wanted to cop before heading in. It was a no frills restaurant that served good food. Rick took a seat on the stool next to Willie in the rear of the restaurant.

"Want something to eat?" Willie asked.

"No, I'm skied the fuck up," Rick replied. The Chinese waitress asked in her squeaky accent, "You want order.?"

"No." Rick answered.

"You no hang here, go outside, no eat, outside." Willie put up his hand to quiet her.

"He your friend, he should say so," she chattered and walked away.

"Yo Willie, I'll wait outside for you," Rick finally said.

Rick leaned against one of the cars parked in front of the restaurant. To a stranger, the busy-bee-like movement of the crowd would have never been interpreted. However, Rick knew the cause behind the whispers and the frantic pacing back and forth very well. The anticipation of the crowd was so great, he could feel it. Rick knew once they cracked the doors to the dope spot on 111th street, the crowd in front of the restaurant would disappear, only to have another take its place when word spread that they were now open.

Jesse pulled the black Tornado to a stop in front of the restaurant.

"Yo Ricky, you got that yet?"

"No, not yet." Rick replied.

"What? Did you see Willie?"

"Yeah, he's inside, he should be out in a minute."

"What time is it?" Jesse asked.

"It's about 7:30," Rick answered.

"You should have gotten that thing. I don't know what the fuck's up with Willie; he knows he's got other business to take care of. Get in my car and wait for me," Jesse told Rick, "I'll be right out."

Willie and Jesse came out of the restaurant together; Willie got in his car and drove off. Jesse got in the car and pulled into the early morning traffic. Jesse weaved in between the other cars at a very high speed. This was the way he liked to drive and he did it well.

"Yo Ricky man, I'm sorry about the delay. I'll take you to get that thing now. We ran out of cut again. Goldfinger let me borrow enough to take care of my workers. Willie just went to meet Nicky; he's going to let me cop six hundred pounds of cut. It's getting harder to get good quinine. I don't have any problems with beneta but quinine is a motherfucker. The government started putting that shit in quinine so it won't cook up. Now you've got motherfuckers making just as much money selling quinine as niggers selling dope. Ricky if you come across anyone selling quinine let me know. If it's good, I'll buy all he's got. I don't care how much he's got, I'll buy it all," Explained Jesse.

Jesse parked the car on 168th street where Broadway crosses St. Nicholas.

"I'll be right back." Jesse said. Rick listened to the sweet sound of music coming from the cassette player in the car. Rick turned the music down low and relaxed in the comfort of the leather car seat. Rick looked at the reflection of the Audubon Ball Room in the side view mirror. It was a ghost of a building now. The Audubon had long passed the good times when he and his friends would danced the night away to the music of local groups and singers, Frankie Lyman and the Teenagers, The Four Seasons, and Jackie and the Starlights. The Audubon had become known throughout the world when Malcolm X was gunned down on its stage years earlier. *Look at it now*, Rick thought. *Run down and forgotten.*

Rick watched the sparrows and pigeons sticking their beaks between the cobblestones on the island that split Broadway and St. Nicholas. Rick studied the Black, White, Spanish and Oriental nurses that crossed the street to pass in front of the car and walked the long stretch of sidewalk in front of the Presbyterian Medical Center. He eyed their legs and felt the rise in his 'lion' and wondered what made the white uniforms so sexy.

Rick saw Jesse when he came out of the block and crossed St. Nicholas. The dip in Jesse's walk and the way he moved his head back and forth alerted Rick to the fact that he was dirty, or was it that Rick already knew Jesse would be dirty that made him pick up on the signals.

Jesse opened the driver's door and got in. "Yo Ricky, I added a little more pure to your package. When you bag it up, sift it real good. Good looking. I wanted you to have a bomb. This is the largest package you ever got and I don't want you to have any problems getting it off. The more money you get," Jesse said, "The more I make." They gave each other five in agreement.

Jesse pulled the car into traffic and made a U-turn and headed downtown on Broadway.

"Look here Ricky, I'm going to take you pass this hot ass neighborhood and drop you off so you can catch a cab the rest of the way. Is that alright? Do you have money with you?"

"Yeah, that's cool." Rick replied. "I've got money with me."

By the time they had reached 125th street, Jesse decided to drive Rick all the way to the projects. Jesse's driving was not as reckless or carefree because of the contents of the package Rick held. They continuously spoke during the drive, mostly about business. "How many half loads have you been getting out of the half pieces?" Jesse asked.

"We get 85 to 90," Rick responded.

"You should easily get a hundred ten to a hundred twenty-five."

"We make our deuces as big as nickels, that way we don't get any complaints. They always look for our thing first. Nobody can work when we put our thing out," Rick stated.

"You have the right idea," Jesse said. "You make your money on volume instead of maximum profit per half piece. That's how I sell this thing too. I give it to you good, real good. When I get it, it takes as little as a 9 or as much as a 14. If it's a 9, I put it on 5 or 6. Everybody else puts it on 7 or 8. I know when you get my thing it's going to be the best thing out. That way you can move it with no problem and re-up faster," Jesse explained. "You re-up fast and I can do the same and because I can buy more at such a steady pace, I can get it cheaper."

The black machine kept a steady speed and took the ruff streets with little disturbance to its passengers.

"Yo Ricky, I'll drop you off on the corner of 104th and Columbus so I can make the turn and head back uptown. That block over there is cool?" Jesse asked.

"Yeah, it's cool."

When they came to 105th street Jesse took a real good look around.

"Damn Ricky, you should be able to get plenty of money down here. Where do your workers scramble?"

"We've got them on both ends of the projects and in 102nd street between Manhattan and Central Park."

"That's a good layout. You can catch everyone that way."

Rick stepped briskly as he made his way to Ronda's building. The projects were teeming with people who had come out to enjoy the cool of the early morning, knowing when the sun rose high in the sky it would be to hot to stay outside. Donny called to Rick from where he stood with a small group of people in front of 840. Rick raised his hand in the air to acknowledge that he saw him and kept on stepping.

Donny caught up with Rick just as he was about to enter the elevator.

"Everything's alright." Rick stated.

"You know I've got to go to court today," Donny reminded Rick.

"I forgot all about that!"

Donny pulled the key ring from his pocket and opened the door. Ronda was sitting on the sofa watching television with her baby asleep on her lap. Donny relocked and chained the door. Rick took the shopping bag from the closet while Ronda took her baby to the room.

Ronda watched as Donny and Rick set up to begin packaging what was the largest bag of dope she had ever seen.

"I collected 750 dollars," Donny said, "And both workers are ready for something else.

"Give me 225 dollars." Rick said. "And keep the rest with you in case the judge locks you up."

"I don't think they will."

"I don't think so either, at least I hope not. But it's better to be safe than sorry."

Rick sifted the dope 5 times then measured out 16 and a half table spoons. Rick scooped up the remaining 16 and a half spoons putting them back in the plastic bag.

"Since you've got to go to court, I'm only going to bag up half," Rick said to inform Donny and Ronda.

"Rick, let's knock out a quick 20 half's, that way I can hit Junie and Buckie on the way to court," Donny suggested. They had become so proficient at bagging that it took the trio less than 15 minutes to package the 20 half's.

Rick and Ronda packaged the 70 half's so quickly that he decided to knock out the other half piece. Once they had finished, 165 halves laid on the table. Rick wondered if they should get another worker to handle the extra product.

Rick picked up the phone on the kitchen wall and dialed. The phone rang several times before it was picked on the other end.

"Hello?" She came with her husky but female sounding soft voice.

"Yeah, this is Rick, come over to Ronda's house."

"Now?" She asked.

"Yeah, right now." Rick told her and hung up.

Rick took a hundred dollars from his pocket and gave it to Ronda.

"What's this for?" She asked.

"Just a little something extra. It will hold you until payday."

"Thank you," she replied and kissed him on the cheek.

"You haven't even noticed, by the way," Ronda protested. "I haven't gotten high since the day you got on my case about it. You talked so bad about me getting high and so good about me as a person that I had to take a look at myself. I asked Donny to show me how he did it and it wasn't so bad. The things you said made me realize I want to be better for my daughter and myself."

"If you feel that way about it, what does it matter whether I noticed or not?" Rick asked her.

"I want you to care, to notice me as a woman. You are the first man I wanted who I couldn't just give some pussy to get with."

"If I didn't care about you do you think I would have told you the things I did? Or do you believe I need you because of your apartment? Let me set you straight, I can pay anybody to let me use their apartment." There was a knock at the door just as Rick was about to really get deep with Ronda.

"That must be Cheryl," Rick said.

Rick looked through the peephole to make sure it was Cheryl before

STAYIN' IN THE GAME   87

he opened the door. Cheryl kissed Rick as soon as she stepped through the door and before Rick could re-locked the door.

"Hi Cheryl." Ronda greeted her.

"Hello Ronda, what do you say about us teaming up to rape Rick?"

"I'm all for it!" Ronda excitingly replied.

"When you two silly bitches finished dreaming, we have business to take care of." Rick jokingly said.

"It's always business with him," Ronda told Cheryl, "But we both know he's giving it to somebody."

Rick sat at the table and counted out 80 half's and dropped them in a small brown paper bag.

"Come here Cheryl, take these."

Cheryl stood very close to Rick; he felt a temptation, to rub her ass as he placed the bags in her pocketbook.

"I know about you white girls," Rick teased. "Everybody knows that white girls always are trying to play a black man for some. And you Cheryl, you have Ronda trying to help you trick me into bed."

"Listen to him Ronda; trick him like he wouldn't enjoy the both of us at the same time. And, what is this white girl shit?" Cheryl asked. "Mine's is just as pink as hers."

"I would give both of you a shot but I'm afraid I will ruin you for the next man. Once you have had me you will never settle for another."

"Ooooh!", the girls both cooed.

Rick put the other 85 half's in the strong box and asked Cheryl if she were ready to cut out. "Yes," she replied.

"Okay, you know the deal. Once we get outside I will follow you," Rick said just as a reminder. "What time it is anyway? You've got this big ass clock on the wall and the shit doesn't work."

"The only reason I keep that clock is that it is so beautifully crafted, and it 1:15!" Cheryl yelled from the back bedroom of her apartment.

"Yo Cheryl, I'm leaving, come lock the door behind me."

"Use your key," she replied.

"If I wanted to use my key I wouldn't have called you."

Cheryl sashayed up to Rick who was standing by the door.

"Look at you!" Rick said, "Why didn't you put on a robe? If I *wanted to see your naked ass,* I would have told you."

"What's the big deal; you've seen me like this before. Besides, when I let you out and that nosey bitch across the hall sees me like this she will think that you come here all hours of the day and night just to fuck me."

Rick walked through the projects like he was on point again in the jungles of Vietnam. It was nearly two o'clock in the afternoon. The sun set high in the sky. The pavement was hot and the hot tar burnt through the sole of his sneakers. The projects were deserted except for the few people who used the thoroughfares to reach their destinations. From the horseshoe, Rick could see Junie, Buckie and his wife Millie sat on one of the benches in front of his building.

"What's up?" Rick greeted them, "Everything alright?"

"Yeah, everything's alright with us," Buckie said.

"We've been waiting for you for more than an hour!" Junie said, almost yelling.

"You finished or what?" Rick asked all of them.

"It took about 20 minutes to bump everything," Junie said, "Yours and my profit."

"That dope is a monster, everybody likes it!" Buckie boasted.

"Rick," Millie cut in, "You've got to give me and my husband double what we have been getting. We have the cliental to handle it. Look at all the business we lost sitting here," she added.

"Yeah, I know." Rick replied. "The reason you only got 10 was because we took the first 20 off the table so you would have something to work with this morning. I'm going to give you something else right now. I've got to go upstairs for a minute. Who's got the money?"

"I've got mine," Junie said. "Millie got ours in her bra." Buckie informed Rick.

"Junie give that money to Millie, and then you and Buckie wait for Millie in the playground by the full court. Millie, after you get the rest of the money wait for me in the lobby of my building. I'll be right back down." Rick instructed them all. "I'm going to give you 25 half's each. Each of you has got to turn in 500 dollars. I don't want a problem with this money from any of you. Do we understand each other?" Rick asked, to re-assured.

"Yeah, we got you." Both Junie and Buckie responded.

Rick opened the door to smell his brother's cooking. Rick could hear the noise of the shower coming from the open door of the bathroom. Rick checked the food cooking on the stove and he knew it was his brother Fred in the shower. Rick put the money he got from Donny in the dresser drawer. His brother was just stepping out of the shower.

"What's up, you see those people waiting outside for you?" Fred asked.

"Yeah, I just got finished talking with them. Millie is waiting downstairs for me," Rick said.

"She is a fine motherfucker." Fred commented. "I just don't know what she sees in Buckie," Fred added.

"Right, Rick replied, "And she sure loves him. Yo Fred, you going to be around tonight?"

"Yeah, why? What's up?" Fred asked.

"I don't know yet. I'll let you know when I see you tonight. I've got to go take care of this business now." Rick told his brother.

"I'll see you later," Fred said. Rick stood and watched Millie as she looked out of the lobby window. Millie did not realize Rick was standing there watching her. She was tall and the short shorts and high heel shoes accented her legs nicely. Rick's eyes followed the raw texture of her bare legs to the pear shape of her ass. Her long black hair fell down her back, almost to her waist.

"Millie," Rick called to her as she leaned over, her arms resting on the windowsill.

"Damn man, you scared me!"

"Sorry, come over here," he said and they walked around the corner of the lobby. They took the elevator to his floor because the building porter had come into the lobby. Millie reached into her bra for the money. Rick studied the un-tanned skin color of her breast. *Damn* he thought, *small and firm, just the way I like them.* Rick counted the money out loud and then told Millie that she would have to meet him in the lobby of 826 to get the package. They left the building together, she asked him how long it would be before walking down the steps to 826. Rick did not reply and took the long route before going to Ronda's building to get the 50 half's.

The two brothers stood in front of Nat's bar on the corner of 114th street, 8th Avenue. The music blared from the giant speaker in front of the record shop next to the bar. Fat Al nodded his head to acknowledge Rick before he went in the record shop that he and his brother Ned owned. The record shop also doubled as a number spot. A few young girls danced in front of the candy store that set on the other side of the bar.

Willie pulled up and doubled-parked the rush gold colored Toronda next to the car Rick sat on. Willie got out and the trio stood on the corner talking. Rick introduced his brother to Willie, and Willie extended a friendly welcome.

"What's it going to be?" Willie asked. "Did you get the rocks from your man?"

"No," Rick replied, "He wasn't home when I went by his house."

"Damn," Willie sighed, "He's got that crazy good shit. You see Fish out here?"

"No, but Fat Al just went in the record shop." Rick informed him. "Get it from him because I don't feel like running all over the place trying to cop."

"What do you want to get, a quarter or half a half?"

"Get the quarter, that way we can take some to the show."

"Go ahead to my house," Willie told them. "Tell my sister I will be there in a few minutes."

The three of them sniffed, laughed and checked out Willie's jewelry collection. By the time they were supposed to break out for the movie, the only thing they had on their minds was women and more blow.

The three of them rode to different spots and could not find any blow or women.

"You know Willie," Rick said, "Every time we get skied up we never make it to the show. Tonight is really fucked up. This is the first time my brother hangs out and we can't find shit."

The green Toreno pulled up at the red light. Neither Willie nor Rick paid attention to its driver.

"Yo, you fellows too fly to speak?" The driver yelled. Willie and Rick did not respond, possibly because their thoughts were focused elsewhere. Fred tapped his brother on the shoulder, "Rick I think that guy in the car next to us is calling one of you."

Willie and Rick both turn to look at the same time.

"Oh shit, Flat Top! What the fuck are you doing in that car?" Rick asked.

"What's up Flat Top?" Willie greeted him As well.

"You two fellows too fly to speak because of the car a guy drives?" Flat Top joked. The light changed from red to green several times and the occupants of both cars just set there continued talking without knowing what was going on around them.

"I just drive this when I want to get around without being noticed," Flat Top told them.

"Yo Flat Top who got some good blow" Willie asked.

"I've got some, pull in the block." Willie backed up and pulled in back of Flat Top to make the right turn into the block. Flat Top stopped midway down the block and got out of his car. Willie stopped right in back of his car and Flat Top got in the back seat with Fred.

"Yo Flat Top, this is my brother Fred, Fred that's Flat Top."

"Glad to know you," Flat Top said.

"Same here." Fred replied.

"Your brothers' good people so I know you're alright too. What's up with you fellows tonight, where are you headed?" Flat Top asked.

"Don't really know, we were going to the show but now it's too late for that." Willie said.

"And it's too early for the Fast Track or the Piggy Back," Rick added.

Flat Top opened the half-full sandwich size baggie and took a hit, then passed it to Fred. The baggie made the rounds back to Flat Top.

"Give me a bill, somebody." Flat Top ordered.

Rick pulled a roll of bills from his pocket and gave Flat Top a 50.

"What the fucks with you, you poor or something?" Flat Top joked. "No self-respecting, man sniffs out of a 50. Give yourself a bad name. Give me a hundred."

"All I've got are fifties and twenties, so I guess I am a poor nigger." Rick replied. They all laughed. Flat Top took another hit and passed the baggie. Flat Top took a roll of bills from his pocket. It must have been 5 or 6 hundred one hundred-dollar bills.

"Since you fellows are so poor, I'm going to give you one of these to sniff out of. When you are done you can frame it for the memory," Flat Top joked. "When I've got anything smaller than a hundred I give it to the kids on the street, twenties and tens I throw away for the bums and winos to find." They all broke in to laughter at Flat Top's comedy skit. Flat Top filled the hundred-dollar bill to over flowing.

"What do we owe you?" Willie asked.

"Are you trying to insult me? I don't sell blow, but I like your style for asking. Look, I'm out of here." Flat Top told them.

"Okay Top," Rick said, "You be cool and thanks."

"Anytime for good people like you. Good to know you my brother," Flat Top told Fred. "Willie, tell Jesse I will see him later, and you be cool."

The Toronda weaved in and out of traffic as the trio watched the hoes offering their services along Lexington Avenue. Dressed to kill they strolled back and forth in the latest fashions.

"Damn, they are some fine motherfuckers, I feel like giving one of them bitches some of this money." Willie commented to no one in particular. Rick's voice cut in sharply, not at Willie, in general. "I wouldn't give one of them hoes a dime, even if I had a room full of thousand dollar bills."

"Shit as fine as these bitches, they can get some of mine." Willie stated.

"Before I let one of those hoes touch me, she would have to pay me." Rick argued.

"What, you on some pimping shit now?"

"No, but let me tell you this. I'm a hoes' pleasure and for her to enjoy the rewards of my company and the pleasure of my touch she's got to pay cash money. And when she pays there isn't a guarantee she is going to get some. She'd have to wait until I decide she deserves some."

"You are crazier than shit Rick, but I know you are serious." Willie said.

"Damn right I'm serious. Let's get the fuck out. I'm tired of watching another motherfucker get money. Let's go back uptown where I can watch my money working," Rick suggested.

"Uptowns are where the real money is," Willie commented.

"Don't get it wrong now," Rick said. "A man who plays hoes is coming off."

"Check this out," Rick quickly began to calculate. "Each one of these hoes' makes at least 3 to 4 hundred a night. That's 21 to 28 hundred a week. A hoe brings in 84 hundred to 11 hundred and change in a month's time. A player takes down somewhere between 100 thousand and 125 thousand dollars off each hoe every year. You and I both know a pimp has to sit two or three deep or they ain't pimpin.' So you figure if the pimpin' is right they clock about 400 thousand or better in a year."

"Yeah, they're coming off but not as good as us." Willie responded, agreeing.

"I know," Rick replied, "Nobody clocks money the way we do. We have the best paying job in the world."

"Yo Rick, you can drop me off on 102nd street and Amsterdam?" Fred asked. "I'm going to my girl's house."

"What is her mother going to say? It's damn near three in the morning." Rick asked.

"Her mother ain't going to say shit; she loves me just like her daughter does. You know how it goes, when you've got it like me, everything's always cool."

"Yo Rick," Willie cut in, "Your brother talks shit just like you."

"What he's saying is the truth. When it comes to women, the Talley men have got it." Rick defended. Fred reached over the seat and gave his brother five in agreement.

Willie pulled over on the corner of 102nd street; Fred gave him five and said later.

"Hey Fred, take some of this blow with you." Willie said.

"Nah, I'm cool." Fred replied.

"You need some money?" Rick asked.

"No, everything's cool, you going to be at the house later?" Fred asked his brother.

"Yeah. Okay, be cool, I'll see you at the house then." They gave each other five.

When Fred got of the car, he saw Junie sitting in front of 868 and mentioned it to his brother.

"Tell him I said to come here." Fred crossed the Avenue and spoke with Junie. They crossed back together and Fred gave his brother and Willie the high sign and kept stepping. Junie came around to the passenger side of the car to speak with Rick.

"Rick, I was hoping you would show. I'm finished." Junie said.

"You got that money with you?" Rick asked.

"Yeah, I got it." Junie pulled a 6 inch ball of money from his pocket and handed it through the open car window to Rick.

"Can I get something else right now?" Junie asked.

"I'll give you something later. I'll come by your house," Rick responded.

"Shit, if I can get something now I'll be finished by nine in the morning."

"It sounds good, but I'm high and I don't feel like going to the stash. Besides that, my man and I have got something to take care of. Get yourself one of them young freaks and hang out," Rick told Junie. "You need a few dollars or what?"

"No, I'm cool." Junie replied. "Rick, Buckie told me to tell you if I saw you that he was finished and that he would be home."

"Okay Junie, I'll see you later."

Willie pulled off and they cruised up Amsterdam Avenue.

"Yo Willie, take this money because if I keep it I'll fuck it up."

"What do you think I will do if you give it to me?" Willie replied.

"Yeah, if you fuck it up at least some of my bill is paid. Besides, Jesse will just take it out of your pay. That's what always happens because I fuck up so much money. I get paid 10 thousand a week plus a bonus. I have not got a full payday in I don't know how long," Willie informed Rick.

"You know Rick; your brother is just like you. Really quiet and the whole shit. The only time you talk is when you are skied up. Then it's hard to get you to shut up. Your brother doesn't really say much at all. Are you going to put him down or what? He sounds like he is ready."

"He's too young," Rick answered.

"Bullshit, I started scrambling when I was 15!" Willie boldly stated.

"He's not really too young, but I could never explain it to my mother if something happens to him. If she knew I was doing this shit, I would have all hell to pay."

"I know what you mean," Willie cut in. "I didn't tell my people. They knew something was up because I got real fly real fast. When I would come in from shopping I'd have crazy bags and I tried to hide them. Then my mother started to find money I left in the house. Not a lot of money, two, three thousand here and there. Sometimes it wouldn't even be my money. It would be money I picked up for Jesse. I'd be too lazy or tired to take it to the stash after collecting it."

"The way things are going for us," Rick said, "It won't be long before I have to tell her something. It won't be anyways for me to hide all this money, not that I would even try."

"I understand." Willie said as he pulled over in front of the Oasis Bar on the corner of 148th street Broadway.

Jesse was standing with a crowd in front of the Oasis.

"Looks like you've got to work," Rick said to Willie.

"Nah," Willie replied.

"How do you know?" Rick asked.

"Jesse is just as high as we are. I can always tell when he is high." Willie continued, "And we never work when he is high."

CHAPTER FOUR

Life in The Fast Lane
Months Later

RICK AND DONNY walked across 102nd street, they stood on the project side of Manhattan Avenue and watched what was going on in the block. They did not see their elusive worker Les, but watched Prince and his girlfriend doing a nice amount of business.

It was an unusually warm night for October, many had thought the chill weather that had been in the air few weeks prior would have made it much colder by now. Rick and Donny saw Les when he came out of his sister's first floor apartment, just across from where they stood. Before they could call him, he turend around and went back into the apartment. They found his actions strange and the first thought to both of them was that he had fucked the package up. It was as if Les were trying to duck them.

"Wait here, I'm going to see what that was all about," Rick told Donny. Rick knocked at the oversized metal door. He studied the bars on the windows and thought about the many reasons why he would never live in an apartment like this. The bars kept the danger out, however, fire was an even greater danger for the people on the inside not being able to get out. Paulette broke his momentary thoughts when she opened the door.

"Hello Rick," Paulette greeted him.

"How are you doing Paulette?" Rick replied to her warm hello. "Is your brother here?"

"No, you just missed him. As he walked out the door, he realized that he should've stayed on the block."

"Okay, when he comes back tell him I came by." As Rick walked away, he wondered if Les had forced his sister into lying for him. But Rick knew she was not that kind of woman. When Rick was just about to cross the avenue, Paulette called him. She had come out onto the sidewalk. Rick went back to see what she wanted, and she was very apologetic.

"My brother is inside." Paulette said. "I did not realize he had come back into the house." She led the way as they entered the apartment.

It was a very large apartment and it seemed you could almost get lost in it.

"My brother is in the kitchen," informed Paulette, pointing in one direction and walking off in another.

"Yo Les, what's up?" Rick asked.

"Ain't nothing Rick."

"You finished with that or what?"

"No, not yet, it's too damn hot out. I like to work when it gets late," Les foolishly told Rick. "That way I don't really have to worry about the police."

"Shit, I gave you the package early this morning. Everyone else has already done theirs and re-up. If 25 halves are too much for you to handle, then you should cut this business loose especially in a block like this!" Rick was somewhat furious. "You should be pumpin' at least a hundred halves a day. You're the only worker we give 25 halves to. Everyone else is getting a hundred to two hundred and loose dope every day. I don't know about you Les, I really don't. Look, I'll see you in the morning. I know that you will be finished and have our money by then, right?" Rick demanded.

"He did not see us standing here when he came out, but everything's cool." Rick informed Donny. "He had only come out to see how things looked in the block. He will have our money in the morning."

"Alright. You ready to go downtown or what?" Donny asked Rick.

"Yeah, I guess so. We might as well; it's our money that paying for this shit anyway," Rick replied. "Once the rent runs out on these fuckin' suites that is. We will only rent a suite when we have something special we want to celebrate." Rick continued. "We can't just keep fuckin' our money off this way," Rick said to Donny, but his statement was for him to recognize as well as Donny.

They made the ride through Central Park and down 7th Avenue in silence. They listened to the tape "Sexy Mama" by The Moments, smoked a joint and took several hits. By the time they reached the suite on the upper floor of the Americana Hotel, Rick's mood had turned into stone-cold ice.

Rick watched the rhythmic movements of the women behind and the smiles on their faces as they danced to the beats of the music. Rick saw no one he liked. Even though many of the women there were more than willing to be his plaything and had come for that reason along. He knew he could have as many of them as he liked, one, two, three or more at the same time. He took a seat on a stool behind the bar and listen to the sexually stimulating conversation of the two women who stood near. Laughter danced in his mind, his facial expression never changed to reveal his thoughts. The crowd played each person in his or her own private fantasy. Rick did not like crowd, for in a crowd he knew how to distance himself from everyone.

Donny came over to the bar with a pretty Spanish girl on his arm. They both took a seat near Rick. Donny introduced the lovely lady as Joyce. Joyce was most attentive to Donny's every need, just as all women who wanted a man who scrambled.

"I see you have found your fantasy for the night." Rick sarcastically teased Donny.

"As good as I am" Joyce said, "It will be for more than one night."

Rick paid no attention to her remark and spoke directly to Donny.

"I'm going over to the other spot and see what's what. I may come back, if not I'll see you in the morning."

Rick stood across from the Howard Johnson Hotel on 8th Avenue and 50th street and watched the traffic as it made its way up the avenue. Rick liked the bright neon lights and was always transfixed by the show they displayed. Rick spotted the casually dressed young white girl who had exited the hotel and was now crossing the street headed in his direction.

Her blonde hair fell down her back, almost reaching her backside. She had beautiful legs and her stride had him loss in a world of fantasy. Her blue eyes fixed on Rick as she entered the delicatessen. Rick knew she was a high-priced working girl. He also knew as well that the look of hunger in her deep blue eyes was because she had played for pay without any satisfaction other than the money.

"What's up Rick?"

"Ain't nothin Chris, Lefty, where you coming from?" Rick responded.

"We were at the Cheetah but ain't nothing happening there." Chris said.

"Where you headed?" Lefty asked Rick.

"There is a private party in the Howard Johnson."

"How is it?" Chris asked.

"I haven't been up yet but you can check it out for yourself." Rick shrugged.

"Who's giving it?" Chris asked.

"I guess I am." Rick stated.

Lefty watched through the delicatessen window as the blonde paid the cashier.

"Fine ain't she?" Rick said.

"Yeah, she is." Lefty replied. "I thought she was with you the way she crossed the street walking in your direction."

"We will see who she's with when she comes out." Rick boasted.

"She is on her way out now," Lefty challenged him, "Let's see what you can do."

"Excuse me. Are you looking for me?" Rick asked the blonde lady.

"What makes you think I would be looking for you?" She replied.

"If you were not, then you would have just kept going instead of saying anything."

"You are very sure of yourself, I like that in a man." She responded, giving Rick her warmest smile.

"Yes, I am sure of myself. That makes me all that I am. But there is much more to me than just my confidence. I can feel that you and I have a lot in common."

"Oh really? And just what might that be?"

Lefty watched Rick work his magic. It was a game they played since junior high school when they had hung out at different clubs partying. Back then, they had always tried to catch two females to party with. Being older and wiser now they played for the conquest of a single night's pleasure in the arms and bed of some lovely lady. Rick played with his prey until he was ready for the kill. Rick told his friends later and to enjoy the party.

They sat conversing in the Howard Johnson bar. She drank a vodka martini and Rick had a large orange juice. The quiet attention paid the young lady by the doorman and bartender only confirmed Rick's belief that she was a working girl. He knew she must have worked in this hotel on a regular basis. He sensed her uneasiness, as though a secret were about to be told… yet he made no mention of it. Once his mannerisms had eased her guard she paid no attention to anyone or thing other than him… she hung on his every word.

"You mentioned a party, would you care to take me?" She asked. Rick call for the check, she paid it.

During the elevator ride up to the party she commented on her paying the check.

"You know, most men would have made a big thing out of me paying the check.

"It ain't nothing; your money spends just as well as mine does. Besides, you now know that you are with a man who is not about the image of posing as a man… but a real man."

Rick was speaking her language and she knew he was aware of her lifestyle. She felt good and appreciated the fact that she could be herself and enjoy the pleasure of his company. For her to know she was accepted by him made all the difference in the world. She knew the games so-called men played all too well. The way things have changed between a man and a woman when a woman was in her line of work.

They danced, rocking to the beats of the music. Her hips followed every beat of the music. The music lifted them higher and higher. This party was a lot smaller than the one at the Americana Hotel. The atmosphere was so much more intimate. Rick took her hand and led her from the dance floor and they sat in the corner watching the others do their thing. They shared a joint and brief kiss which let her know everything was truly alright between them. It was nearly 5:30 in the morning, just about everyone had cut out. Rick spoke with Lefty while the lady Lefty caught talked with Rick's lady friend. Rick picked up the phone and spoke with the front desk.

"The party is over, don't let anyone else up." He informed them.

"Okay Lefty, the place is yours, I'm going across the hall."

"Come on Ms. Lady, it's time for us to go."

She was a little surprised when Rick took her just across the hall. He put on a nice mellow tape by Nancy Wilson. Rick liked the cut "Now I'm A Woman". She removed the wrapping from the bowl of fresh cut canta-loupe, honeydew melon and strawberries, commenting on how sweet the fruit was. They did a ritual like movement in the center of the room to the soulful rhythm of the music. She fed Rick fruit as they slow danced, their bodies never really touching, only playing in their closeness.

"You are full of surprises," she whispered. "Are you trying to turn my head so you can get some of this body?"

"Now would I do a thing like that?" Rick teased back.

"If you are not," she said as she stepped away, "I am going to be an aw-ful disappointed lady."

"Well, well Ms Lady, if you feel that way about it."

"I do. And if you will give me a moment to freshen up, I will show you a real good time."

"Everything you need." Rick responded as she made her way to the bathroom.

Rick turned out the lights in the sitting room of the suite and went into the bedroom. He set the mood for comfort by adjusting the bed-room lights, removed his shirt and sat on the edge of the bed. He rolled another joint, took a hit and lit the joint. He listened to Harold Melvin and the Bluenoses sing "I Miss You".

Rick leaned back against the headboard of the bed, waiting for her grand entrance. And grand it was. She entered the room on cue to the beat of the music, naked except for high heel shoes. Her long blonde hair fell over her shoulders, partially covering her firm breasts. She moved her hips in, then out. She bumped and grinded slowly and threw her hair back over her shoulders all in time to the music. She worked at her pleasure, all for his entertainment.

She did a slow stroll over to the bed, Rick handed her the joint. She took a long pull on the joint then kissed Rick, blowing the smoke into his mouth. Rick excused himself to use the bathroom and when he returned, he was naked as well.

CHAPTER FIVE

Gettin' High, The Name of The Game

THE SHABBY FIGURES of Bosco and Billy swiftly made their way up the narrow stairway in building number 9. Both men were now shades of what they once were. Bosco, the tallest of the two, in his mid thirties, frame only showed traces of what it was when he was an All-City basketball star. Bosco had played all across the country and showed signs of what might have led to a pro career. Billy at one time was a boxing hopeful and could have won a championship of the world in his weight class. Billy's fame came only as a street fighter now. In his late twenties or early thirties, his body was frail to the point of breaking. Billy at one time had made a great deal of money in the drug trade. However, on this day neither man had any thoughts of yesterdays that have gone by.

They stopped to knock on the second floor apartment door just off to the right of the stairway. The door was opened by Sharon, a brown skin woman in her bathrobe. It was a three bedroom apartment that had seen better days. The walls were scorched with smoke, the windows were dirty with broken shades and torn curtains. The furnishing consisted of a broken down sofa, mix and match chairs and two or what could be three mattresses on the floor of each bedroom. A man sat in the corner trying to get a hit, and from the look of things, anyone in the know realized he had been at it for awhile. Two other men and three females nodded in a zombie like state on the old sofa and chairs.

The three females in the living room came to life knowing that Bosco and Billy only came to the apartment when they wanted to get high. Joanne quickly spoke up not wanting to miss out on a chance to get high. Joanne knew that her body, most of all her big round ass, still held an attraction and could be exchanged for the price of getting her high. Her reputation for being a stone cold freak kept her high 24/7. Bosco told Joanne to be cool that she could hang with him. Billy did not really want to deal with Sharon knowing that she would have to be paid for the use of her apartment. *So what the hell,* he thought, *she might as well do the freaky deaky too.* Sharon, sensing Billy's apprehension, let her robe fall open. Where there had once been a young tender body with nice firm breast to entice any man, he signs of shooting too much dope and coke with little or no food had taken it total. Her breast had all but disappeared; her ribs and tracks were there for the counting.

Gloria, who was quick to act before she was left out of the getting high session, rushed over to where Sharon was and took her flat breast in her mouth. Sharon understood fully what Gloria's move was all about. The two of them had done this act many times before they get high, and they had become real good at it. Gloria told Billy and Bosco that she and Sharon did the real freaky deaky, something both men already knew.

"Be cool all of you bitches." Bosco commanded, "Let me and Billy take care of this business, then we will party."

Bosco and Billy had taken off a nice sting, 34 hundred dollars. They had 17 hundred a piece and felt like they were on top of the world. Bosco asked who had the best thing and all three females sang in harmony, "Donny and Rick."

"Hey Billy, you and Sharon go cop the coke. I'm going to try and find Rick or Donny, you come with me Joanne."

"I will go with you," Joanne said, "But I don't think you will find Rick or Donny this early in the day. That kid Les on the corner has their thing."

Les told Bosco that Rick and Donny both had come through the block earlier and that he would have to see them because he could not give him the kind of play he wanted. Les told Bosco to look in the projects for them. They might be in front of Donny's woman's building or Rick's mother's building.

"Fuck it!" Bosco said to know one in particular, "I want to get high now. If I get lucky I will catch them later, but for right now Les, you can let me get two halfs.

"Get the money ready." Les told him then walked across the street and ran up the steps of building 15. Les knocked on the wall several times and spoke into a hole in the lobby wall.

Bosco and Billy fixed quickly.

"Damn, this is some good dope." Billy said nodding off. However, the cocaine he had mixed with the dope would not allow him to fall into a full nod.

The three women knew that the cocaine would make Bosco and Billy want to get freakish with them. Joanne told Bosco, "As soon as I get off daddy, I'm going to take real good care of you." Joanne as well as the other women knew all so well that as soon as they did the wild thing with and for Billy and Bosco that they would want to fix again, and then freak off once more. The women knew as long as they could be freakish enough to satisfy Bosco and Billy's cocaine induced nature, they would keep turning them on. For getting high, these women were willing to perform just about any act.

Maribel Caraballa and Tiffany Clark
Are Truly Very Special Ladies

A man who had fallen to the depths of despair looked around and saw no hope. Yet in his despair never once did his mind wander into self pity. When he heard her voice so faintly calling out for help, he looked around but could see no one. Then he looked down and there she was. At that moment he realized he had not reached the bottom of the endless pit, someone else's life had taken them deeper into despair. With a helping hand he reached down in the hope that she would no longer have to face her despair along...

CHAPTER SIX

Trudy, Bad, Bad Mis-as

THE CHILL OF this fall night was a harsh reminder of the cold winter that lays ahead. Rick enjoyed the mood that this kind of weather brought about in New York City. New York was alive with a feeling that only the fall weather could induce. The living room in his mother's apartment had that familiar warm coziness. Rick sat watching television and listen to his mother sing spirituals in the kitchen as she put the dishes away. Rick likes to hear his mother sing, it reminded him of his grandmother's church in Brooke, Virginia. The ring of the telephone interrupted his mother's singing.

"Ricky, it's for you, it's Donny!" She called him.

Rick took the receiver and walked the length of the long cord so he would not be in his mother's way as she worked in the kitchen. Rick's conversation did not take long and his mother did not pay attention to what her son was saying or the change in his disposition. She did, however, heard him utter the word 'shit' in disgust before he hung up.

"I'm going out." Rick told his mother.

"Is everything alright?" She asked him.

"Yeah Ma, everything is alright." His words did not reassure her.

"Are you sure Ricky?" She asked again.

"Yeah Ma, it's just that damn car, brand new Cadillac. The one we got from that pimp kid who owed us money. The damn car is costing more than it is worth to me." Rick could sense that his mother felt better with the explanation he provided. He saw the sparkles returned in her eyes, it made him feel the warmth of her love. He kissed her and walked out the door.

Rick saw the car sitting between 102nd and 103rd streets as he crossed the horseshoe making his way to Amsterdam Avenue. He did not see Donny, but Frank and Trudy sat in the front seat of the Caddy. Rick asked them where Donny had gone and they told him that Donny had gone to use the phone in the bar. Rick made a dash across the avenue, the long butter soft leather coat he wore flapped in the fall breeze.

Rick greeted the regulars in the bar then took a seat in the corner to wait for Donny to get off the phone.

"Look Donny, by the time Greg brings us the 10 thousand he owes, we will have to buy him a brand new car. We have already spent 15 hundred fixing it. I don't understand how a man can fuck up a brand new car so fuckin' fast."

"So what you want to do?" Donny asked Rick. "We can put it in a garage and leave it."

"I don't know yet." Rick replied. "Let's see what the problem is this time and how much it's going to cost."

Trudy came in the bar to let them know the tow truck was there.

Rick handed the tow truck driver 50 dollars then pulled the Cadillac into traffic.

"What are we going to do?" Rick asked Donny.

"I told them I would buy them something to eat after we got the car fixed."

"Where to?"

"Go to Erving's donut shop, that way I can get some blow at the same time."

Rick pulled the Cadillac in front of the donut shop on 103rd street Broadway, and parked it at the bus stop.

They took the seats in the rear of the counter. Frank sat on the stool next to Donny with his back towards Rick. Frank once again was trying to talk Donny into giving him a package. Rick and Trudy sat facing each other on the last two stools at the counter. Erving came over to take their order after he had finished waiting on another customer.

Frank ordered a cheeseburger and fries while Donny, Rick and Trudy ordered vanilla egg creams and assorted doughnuts. Donny spoke briefly to Erving then they both went into the kitchen.

Rick had known Trudy since junior high school, when one of his close friends had gone with her sister. Now her sister was his partner Donny's woman. For the first time Rick really looked at Trudy. He studied her features. They were soft and refined. Trudy and her sister shared a similar beauty. Only Trudy was smaller in statue with larger breasts. Rick looked into her large brown eyes and got lost. Her eyes were warm and drew him in. Yet they seem to be crying out though he did not know for what.

Rick and Trudy became lost in one another's conversation forgetting all else. Trudy's voice had a pure innocence's that stirred a sensation deep within him and now he knew the story her eyes told. Rick wanted to reach out to her, to hold her in his arms so she would know he held the peace of heart her eyes searched so desperately for.

When Donny returned from the kitchen, he tapped Rick on the leg as he passed him to let him know he had scored. Donny handed Frank a few bills as thanks for watching the car and asked Rick if he was ready to cut out. Frank realized he would not get another chance to talk business with Donny so he asked again about a package. Rick let Donny know he would be ready to leave in a minute.

The momentary spell that had held Trudy and Rick captivated was now broken. They came back into the moment to face the harsh reality of the bright lights in the doughnut shop. Rick leaned closer to Trudy and asked her if he could make love to her. He could see his words freezed her body stiff. She turned her head away and began to tremble. Her reaction took Rick by total surprise and he wondered if the others had also seen Trudy's change in behavior. Still trembling she faced Rick and asked him if he was trying to hurt her. Her question gave Rick an even deeper understanding of what he had seen in her eyes earlier. Rick reached over and massaged her arm as her head laid resting on them. Trudy raised her head when she felt Rick's touch. Their eyes spoke for them and her trembling stopped. As Rick spoke, his voice was soft and reassuring. "I would never do anything to hurt you." He told her. Trudy smiled to let him know they had reached an understanding between them.

Rick let Donny know he was ready to leave. Rick placed his arm around Trudy's shoulder. She slid her arms under the long leather coat and around Rick's waist. They followed Donny and Frank out of the doughnut shop. Standing in the cool breeze in front of the doughnut shop, Trudy looked up at Rick and told him that she wanted him to make love to him. Her words brought his manhood to life and he held the leather coat open for her to see. Trudy smiled and held Rick tighter.

Donny informed Frank that he would see him later before he got any idea in his head that he was going to ride with them. Donny asked Trudy about her plans but Rick answered for her. Rick got behind the wheel of the car, while Donny sat in the front passenger seat and Trudy climbed in the back. The three of them sat in the Caddy at the bus stop while Donny took some of the coke out of the aluminum foil and put it in two one hundred dollar bills. Donny folded both bills, passing one to Rick and he put the other in his shirt pocket. Donny took a one on one from the blow still in the aluminum foil then passed it to Rick. Rick started the car before he took a hit and passed the blow to Trudy. Trudy took a small rock and seductively spread it over her lips as Rick watched her in the rear view mirror.

"Yo Rick, let's get some smoke." Donny said.

"Sounds good to me," Rick replied.

"After we get the smoke you can drop me off. I am going to my woman's house. What are you going to do?"

"I'm going to keep Trudy with me, and just ride."

Rick took another drag off the joint and listened while Trudy told him why she did not want to go to the Castle Hotel on 106 street.

"If we go there, everyone will know our business and I'll be just another freak you can cut a notch on your belt for. Besides, I won't feel comfortable."

Rick handed Trudy the bill with the blow in it. She took a hit and fed him as he drove.

Rick liked the feel of the bright lights on Broadway as the Caddy cruised downtown. The Caddy was warm and felt secure. The music was set to easy listening. The combined effect made the Caddy as Rick and Trudy's private world. Rick pulled the Caddy into the drive-in-garage of the Manhattan Hotel on 44th street and 8th Avenue. The garage attendant informed Rick that he would have to go through the lobby to register due to the fact the registration window was closed.

Rick told Trudy to have a seat on the sofa in the lobby of the hotel while he registered. The old and gray-haired white man at the clerk's desk stared hard at Rick. He checked out the diamond pinky ring, and then he eyed the yellow gold chain and diamond medallion. He looked Rick up and down and noticed the long black leather coat, and the tailored look of the black outfit Rick wore. The clerk shook his head and did not bother to hide his disgust. Rick knew that the whitey did not want Rick to stay in his so-called respectable hotel. Rick thought that the clerk believed him to be an out of town pimps, one of the many who found their way to Time Square.

Rick asked the clerk for a room for himself and wife. The clerk asked Rick where his wife was and Rick pointed to Trudy on the sofa.

"How many nights do you want the room for?" The clerk asked.

"Just for tonight." Rick replied.

The clerk smiled and informed Rick that the only rooms they had were the more expensive suites. The clerk quoted a price of 350 dollars hoping it would drive Rick away.

"A suite will be fine.' Rick informed the clerk, and then smiled wickedly.

The clerk called the bellhop and handed him the key to the suite. The bellhop asked Rick if he had any luggage. Rick shook his head no and signaled Trudy to come over and follow him. Rick watched the old black man as he led them to the elevators. Rick's mind wandered to a time long since passed and the history of his people. Rick realized that a hotel such as this would not have rented rooms to blacks. Rick thought about the

old black bellhop as a young man carrying white folk's bags and it sad-
dened him. However, he felt a sense of pride in knowing the old man had
endured through the hardest of times and was still going strong.

Rick gave the others waiting for the elevator the once over. Rick felt
them all watching him as Trudy stood close to his side. He read the
questions in the white businessman's eyes as he lusted for Trudy's golden
brown body. Rick could feel the burning interest of the three black attractive females and the older black gentlemen. He felt the lust in the
eyes of the two females who stared at him. Everyone looked at him on
the sneak, then to Trudy and back to him again. Rick knew the questions
they wanted to ask.

Riding up in the elevator, one of the black females whom Rick assumed to be about 35, stood close to him gazing into his eyes. Her brown
eyes smiled at him and the question was written all over her face. *How old
is that girl with you and why are you with her when you can have me?* All of
their eyes seemed to be asking how old Trudy is. Rick politely said good
night to everyone when the elevator came to a stop at his floor. Trudy
held onto Rick's arm as they exited the elevator following the bellhop.
Rick turned and took one last look at the puzzled faces in the elevator.
His polite mannerisms made them wonder even more about the handsome couple, and for them there was no answer to be found.

Rick handed the bellhop a twenty dollar bill. The old man looked at
the bill then thanked him. "You be careful young-blood." The old black
man warned. "That desk clerk ain't no good. He'll send the house cops
around looking."

It was now Rick's turn to thank the old man. Rick was well aware of the
hatred the old white man felt for him. Rick had felt it from the moment
he spoke to the clerk. Right now though, he could care less about what the
clerk or anyone else thought of him. He was here to enjoy the pleasure of
this pretty young thing, and that is just what he was going to do.

Trudy stepped into the bathroom closing the door behind her. Rick
did a security check of the room to make sure there was nothing there he
could be arrested for if the desk clerk sent the house detective looking.

Rick turned the television to an off channel so it would pick up the black public radio station that played a lot of music and had very little talking if any. He turned the covers back on the bed and rolled another joint. By the time Trudy reappeared, Rick was laying back on the bed smoking the joint and listening to the sweet soulful music coming from the T.V.

Trudy did a slow flirtatious walk across the floor. Her sexuality filled the room. Rick laid there transfixed by her beauty. Her statue was tiny but strong. She stood boldly at the side of the bed. Rick's approving eye told Trudy he liked what he saw. Rick felt something; he had not quite figured it out as he studied her beauty from the floor up. Her small feet with painted toenails and open-toe high heel shoes would drive any foot fetish crazy. Her slim, beautifully shaped legs seemed longer than her 5 foot 2 inch frame. Rick's eyes followed her shapely legs to her full round ass. The black bikini panties highlighted the shape of her hips. The black bra she wore held her breast at attention. He had never seen such large breast on so small a framed woman or any woman for that matter. In reality the only time he had ever seen such large and perfectly shaped breast was when they had been drawn for one of those cartoon sex magazines. He wondered if they would stand as tall without the bra. Trudy's creamy brown skin color highlighted by the black bra and bikini panties aroused Rick, she was raw sex.

Trudy had sensuous full lips that quivered as though she wanted to speak but could not find the words. Her starving eyes begged for fulfillment. Rick looked deep into Trudy's eyes, her body trembled and her eyes continued to ask the question. Rick knew her eyes had asked the same question many times before. And as sure as she stood before him she had yet to find the answer to satisfy the plea in her eyes. It was the same look he had first seen in the rich white woman's eyes when he was 15 years old. It was she whom at 45 years old taught Rick how to make women worship him. He learned the fine art of making a woman fall to her knees and then begged for his touch and to be punished so that she enjoyed the pleasure of pain. Rick had come to know many such women like her in his life. These women's eyes always told the same story. They cried out to him, *please, please be the man who knows my true sexual desires*. Most times their pleas went unanswered. This was the same look that Rick now saw in Trudy's eyes, and he knew what it was he had felt earlier.

Rick motioned for Trudy to sit on the bed beside him. His fingertips did a slow run down than up her spine to find the hook of her bra. His skilled fingers easily opened Trudy's bra and her full large breast fell free. Rick could see that she did not need the bra, her breast were firm. In a stern voice Rick commanded Trudy to remove the bra the rest of the way. She was obedient, never taking her eyes from his. At that moment Rick leaned forward as if he was about to kiss the nipple of her breasts. Instead of Trudy feeling the warmth of his kiss on her breast, Rick ran his hand up her back. He locked his fingers in her hair at the base of her neck and with one swift move; he savagely pulled her head back. Rick bit her nipple at the same time. Rick forced Trudy to lay back by pulling her head by her hair to the pillow. Rick looked into her eyes and spoke.

"I know you, and I know your needs. You belong to me and will do as I say." Trudy's eyes became glassy. Rick felt her body shake in an orgasmic pleasure.

"Did I give you permission to cum?" Rick scolded. Trudy just laid there with that far off look of pleasure in her eyes. Rick pulled her face to within an inch of his. He tightens his grip in her hair.

"When I speak, what are you supposed to do bitch?" Still Trudy did not respond. Rick knew she was testing him. They always tested him. He was so young. They wanted to see if he really had it in him. They wondered did he really have what it took to become their master. Rick pulled her hair even tighter. He gazed deeper into her eyes, making himself apart of her soul. Rick understood that his will had to dominate above all else. Trudy had to be made to understand that Rick's commands must be obeyed.

"Look. You little tramp ass bitch. When I speak, you jump. When I give a command, you do as I order. Do you understand me hoe?" Trudy was barely able to utter a response because of how tight Rick was pulling her hair. "Yes Daddy", I understand." Rick released his grip and Trudy wrapped her arms around him as if she were trying to get inside his body. She held him so tight that Rick could not believe that a small-framed woman could be so strong. Rick could feel the wetness of her tears on his chest. Game over. Rick knew as did Trudy, he was now her Lord and Master.

Rick pushed Trudy away.

"What's wrong Daddy?"

"You don't deserve to touch me, or be in the same room with me." Rick scolded. Trudy meekly crawled to the foot of the bed. She began to kiss Rick's feet and beg.

"Please Daddy, please don't send me away. I will do anything you want me to do. Punish me but please don't send me away." Her child like pleas was enough to melt a heart of stone. Rick knew however if he showed any weakness, Trudy would use him and throws him away like an old pair of shoes.

Rick sat with his back against the headboard of the bed. Trudy sat on his lap facing him. She had inserted him in her. Rick did not allow Trudy to move as they talked.

"Where did you get turn out?" Rick asked.

"In Jamaica when I lived there." She replied. "I got turned out by a 72 year old man when I was 13. For two years we played, it was great. The only thing he did that I didn't care for was anal."

"Why?" Rick asked in curiousity.

"Because it hurts!"

Rick thought it is strange that she did not like to be fucked from in the ass. His experience had taught him that woman who enjoyed this fetish always like the pleasure of pain by being fucked from her behind.

Rick and Trudy smoked, sniffed and talked for what seemed like a life time. Trudy bared her soul and sexuality. She told Rick how none of her other so-called boyfriends knew her true sexual desires.

"How many 18 year olds do you think have the experience to handle a woman with your taste in sex?" Rick asked. It was more of a statement than a question for Trudy to answer.

"I became so frustrated at one time when I showed J.J. how to please me," Trudy sighed.

"What did he say about your passion for the unusual?"

"He said it was different."

"Did he please you?"

"It was okay, but it's really not much fun when you have to teach a man how to be your master. It is great with you because you already know how to handle me. And I am yours for as long as you will have me Rick. Ah-hhhh Master!"

Rick did not respond to Trudy's statement or little slip of the tongue, he just gave her a stinging slap on her behind.

Rick slapped Trudy's behind several more times and dared her to move. On command, Trudy began to move back and forth riding Rick's manhood. Each time Trudy slid back, Rick would slap her behind a little harder. Trudy's voice grew deeper with her pleasure.

"That's it Daddy! That's it, whip your slave girl's ass. Beat me good because I am cumming all over your dick!"

CHAPTER SEVEN

Workin' The Streets

I T WAS SNOWING hard. The snow was piled high on the streets and sidewalks. The city streetlights reflecting off of the snowflakes created an exotic atmosphere. The exhaust from the tailpipe of the Mark IV seemed to be the only sign of life on this lonely stretch of St. Nicholas Avenue between 142nd and 145th street. Darkness came to the city early on winter days, the winter and all of the snow flurries made it difficult to move about bringing the city and its people to a halt. At the same time, there was a peaceful air about the city and its people.

It was so difficult to get around on the streets that Rick had taken the subway uptown. The knee high snow made it a painstaking walk to get from the subway to the garage, just off the corner of 145th and St. Nicholas Avenue. Rick found the garage empty but he could see Jesse's black Mark IV parked just down the block. The interior light of the car was on but Rick could not see anyone sitting in the car. As Rick got closer to the car, he could see the exhaust coming from the tailpipe. Rick walked around to the passenger side and opened the door. The bone chilling cold of the winter night made the warmth and comfort of the car seem like paradise.

It was several minutes before Rick saw Jesse and Jerome tracking through the snow making their way to the car.

"What's up Rick?" Jesse and Jerome greeted him as they got into the car.

"Ain't nothing." Rick replied.

"It's cold as a motherfucker out!" Jerome commented. "How did you get here Rick? I didn't see your car?"

"I took the subway."

"No shit! I might just leave this car here and take the subway back myself."

"Yo Ricky, you see anyone else come by since you been here?"

"No."

"I didn't think anyone would show on a night like this. This snow will all be gone by tomorrow, though." Jesse stated.

"I hope so," Rick continued, "I remember when I was a kid, I use to love playing in the snow. Now I hate it, but it's good for business. At least you know the police are not on the roof listening or taking pictures in a weather like this."

"Look Jesse, I need four keys." Rick asked Jesse.

"That's a lot of dope Rick! Do you think you can handle it?" Jesse responded.

"It's not for me, not all of it anyway. I want three for my man."

"I don't want to meet your man."

"Ain't no worry. I'm going to handle it." Rick responded, trying to assure Jesse.

"How well do you know these people?"

"I know them well. I was in the army with them."

"You been out to where they scramble?" Jesse replied.

"Yeah, I checked out their whole operations. They do a good business in DC."

"They've got to pay up front, Rick. I can't let them get it on consignment just

because he is your man. Unless you want to be responsible for the money." Jesse added.

"I could never be responsible for another man business."

"When can I get that from you Jesse?"

"I've got something now but I want to take care of the crew first and my regular customers. I will have the new thing tomorrow or Friday." Jesse said. "It's going to be a smoker, takes an 18, but to make it a real monster put it on a 14."

"Okay. I'll give them a call and have them bring the money up on Friday. I'm charging them 30 G's for a key so I can come off with something for my efforts. I will bring the 25 G's I owe you from our last package along with the 75 G's for the three keys for them."

"That sounds alright with me." Jesse nodded. "It don't look like no one else is going to show, let's get out of here."

Jesse locked the car up and they made their way to the subway struggling with the snow. They talked about business as they stood on the platform waiting for the subway train.

"You know," Jesse commented, "This looks like a safe place to make a drop one day. Have everyone wait at different stations and hit them one at a time as we get to that station."

"Shit, at three or four in the morning there won't be anyone in the station to get in our business. That might work." Both men agreed once a time table was worked out.

Rick laid in bed watching Johnny Carson on TV, Jenny rolled another joint for them to smoke. As Rick lay in the warmth of the bed, he wanted to shake the chill from the long walk he made from his mother's building to his building. He had stopped at his mother's house just to say goodnight before he went home. The ten block walk from his mother's house in the deep snow seemed like 10 miles.

In his off and on relationship with Jenny, it appeared now that it was going to work out. What Rick liked most was the time he got to spend with his son, Sean, while Jenny was at work. Rick's schedule did not allow him to see Jenny a lot. When she came home at 6 or so in the evening, it was time for him to check on his workers. Then he would return around 9 and stay home until 11 or 11:30 when he had to meet Donny. They would get the money together, do the books and be at the Shalimar no later than 12:15 or 12:30. Rick's work schedule did not make a good home life. Maybe it was for the better, who knows. Most times when he came in the mornings, Jenny was on her way out the door for work. On the rare occasions when he stayed home or came in early, all they did was get high and fuck.

The ringing of the telephone interrupted Rick's thoughts and Johnny Carson's monologue. Rick grabbed the receiver, "Hello."

"Yeah Rick it's me."

"No shit!" Rick replied, "Like I would not recognize your voice. So what's up Donny?"

"Ain't nothing, I'm at Under the Stairs; I was going to drop by."

"Who've you got with you?" Rick asked

"Joyce".

"Okay, come on over."

Joyce and Jenny sat in the living room listening to music as they smoked a joint, joking and taking hits. Rick and Donny stayed in the bedroom talking business and watching television. Sean had woken up and came in the room to sit on his father's lap. Sean knew how to play his father so he could stay up.

"Look Donny, we are in the hole. We are not hurting or broke but the overhead is killing us. I spoke with Jesse about the three keys for my man in DC. He said it's going to be a real smoker. I figure like this, if we get three keys for ourselves on consignment we can come off."

"Did you asked Jesse for the three keys already?" Donny was really curious to know.

"No, but he shouldn't have a problem with it. It's like this, if we bag one key up we should make 140 to 150 thousand. We also have 15 thousand coming in from the three keys for my man. So we will end up with somewhere around 400 to 500 thousand after we pay the 75 thousand we owed Jesse. Our overhead now is the money for the cut, paying the girls for working the mill. The rent on the stashes is also due and we have to give those crook-it cops their weekly take. I think the best way to go is bag the dope all up. You know Donny, the biggest mistake we make was to start giving our workers loose dope. When we started that we only cleared 15 to 20 thousand per key."

"Yeah, the best way is to go back to bagging it ourselves. Now we sell more dope and make less money. We started out getting 20 dollars a half. Now our crew is getting crazy money while we get shit. We get 112 pieces out of a key and rock them for 900 or 950. It's less work doing it this way but sometimes I just don't know. Crazy ain't it?" Donny responded.

"Your plan sounds good Rick, I can live with it."

"Let's make it happen then." Rick stated.

"By the way Rick, Moose and Sledge keep asking me for a package. They think because I used to shot dope with them and they turned me on once in awhile that I am supposed to give them work."

"So what do you want me to do about it?" Rick asked.

"I told them they had to see you."

"What do you want me to give them?"

"I don't want you to give them shit. They ain't going to do nothing but fuck it up."

"So what you are saying is you want me to be the bad guy?"

"No, not really." Donny replied. "You tell them no, Rick. It's business. When I say no, it becomes personal."

"Excuse me," Jenny cut in, interrupting Rick's discussion with Donny. "Joyce wants to use the bathroom, would you please take the dog out."

"If I wasn't here, who would you get to take him out for you?" Rick asked.

"Sean," Jenny replied. "I don't believe you're afraid of your own dog!"

"I don't know Rick," Donny commented, "That is the biggest and craziest dog I have ever seen in my life."

"And he is vicious," Jenny added. "Sean, go get the dog out of the bathroom, don't let him go in the living room. Your mother is afraid to get him."

"Okay, daddy." Sean took off running towards the bathroom.

"Wait a minute Sean," Jenny said, "Let me go by first." Once Jenny passed the bathroom Sean opened the bathroom door and the large animal broke for freedom. He leaped pass Sean and headed for the living room. Sean's quick reflexes enabled him to catch the dog by his collar.

"No, no!" Sean yelled at the dog. "You have to go in the back!" When the dog did not respond Sean hit him in the head with his little fist and called him a bad dog. Rick waited until Sean had full control of the dog before he gave Sean a helping hand by calling to the dog. Sean followed the dog into the bedroom hitting him on his hindquarters telling him what a bad dog he was. Sean was excited and tried to explain in his excitement, to his father, just what the dog had done. Each time he felt he had explained a point to his father he would hit the dog calling him bad. Rick just looked at Sean in disbelief. Sean barely came up to the animal head, yet he showed no fear. The dog looked at Rick with sad eyes as if to say, *will you please get this crazy kid away from me?*

Rick knew once the dog was tired of Sean, he would grabbed him in the seat of his pamper and swing him around. It was a way for the animal to know that this was the signal for Sean to play harder. Rick would let Sean have a few minutes more of fun before him calling off of the dog. Looking at the way Sean handled the dog, you would never believe he had to wear a choke collar and muzzle to be walked.

Sean had stretched out on the rug next to the dog, where both of them had fallen asleep. Rick and the others sat in the living room enjoying each other's company. The music and the get high added to the pleasant surroundings. Rick said very little, he mostly listened. Joyce commented on Rick's quiet callousness and thought it may because he did not like or approve of her.

"No girl," Jenny said, "It's not you. Rick has been that way since he came back from Vietnam. Sometimes he scares the shit out of me the way he acts."

Rick got a bit tired of Jenny talking about him like he was not there. "It's nothing wrong with the way I act so we can talk about something else." Rick responded in defense.

It was near four in the morning when Donny and Joyce were about to walk out the door. Rick pulled Donny off to the side to speak with him so Jenny and Joyce could not hear their conversation.

"Look, I'm going to call DC. sometimes tomorrow afternoon." Rick informed Donny. When they get to New York, I'm going to put them up at the Howard Johnson on 53rd street. I've been promising Jenny I'd take her out, so I will take her to the Cheetah. That way I can step off for a minute and go upstairs to their suite and get the money. Once I leave the Cheetah, I'll drop Jenny off at home and meet you uptown. We can make any other arrangements once they get in town."

"Okay it sounds cool to me; I'll kick it with you later on today." Donny replied.

"Yeah my brother," Rick said as Donny and Joyce walked out the door.

The black Cadillac Eldorado flowed over the pot holes as it worked its way downtown on 7th Avenue. Crossing 116th street the Caddy made its way between the tomb-like buildings that lined both sides of the street. Inside of the black machine, Rick listened to the smooth sounds of the Chi-Lites. Rick was dressed in an Italian cut doubled breasted one-button suit, black shirt and alligator shoes with an off-setting charcoal gray colored tie. Jenny was dressed in a black short dressed and heels, both of which showed off her pretty legs. Jenny's head swayed to the music. They had a good time tonight. Dinner, then off partying at the Cheetah. Rick had driven to the Shalimar instead of taking Jenny straight home. Rick had informed Donny of the plans he made to drop off the three keys. Rick had also given Donny the hundred thousand dollars before he and Jenny headed home.

The headlights of the long black machine cut through the darkness of Central Park. The red light brought them to a stop at the west 106th street exit. Driving two blocks west to reach Columbus Avenue, the machine roared out on the green light. Rick turned left once he reached Columbus Avenue, again heading the machine downtown. Rick slowed the machine to a crawl at 105th street, checking the Avenue for signs of the business his crew was doing tonight. Rick picked up speed again at 100th street.

The neatly kept streets lined with high rise condominiums seemed light years away from the dead end streets of Harlem, where he spent most of his time. Rick pulled the machine into the building garage, the attendant rushed to open the passenger door. Jenny stepped out gracefully from the car, the split in her gown allowed the attendant to see more than he should have. The attendant quickly looked away. Rick laughed to himself thinking this is what the rich white society ladies have been doing to attendants and doormen for years.

In his on and off relationship with Jenny, Rick had selected to get another apartment. Rick's apartment was elegantly done, a bachelor's palace. One look was enough to let you know that whoever lived in these quarters was truly successful. Nevertheless, to him it was just another place to rest his head. As Rick leaned back on the rich feel of the silk sofa, Jenny removed his shoes. Rick laid back reflecting on the events of the past six months. Since he and Donny had gone into business together this would be the largest buy they would make.

Meanwhile, somewhere on the streets of Harlem, Donny riding in the gray Chevron pulled in front of the dimly lit corner grocery store. Moving with confidence Donny walked down the dark street. At 3 o'clock in the morning the block was empty of all life except those who came to take care of tonight's business.

When Donny reached the stoop where five other men stood, he was greeted warmly by them on this cold winter night.

"What's up Donny?" One of the men greeted.

"Ain't nothing Boo." Donny replied.

"Yo Donny! When was the last time you saw Jesse?" One of them asked.

Before Donny could reply, they all spotted Willie approaching. They each greeted Willie as the excitement of the moment grew.

Another man that none of them had seen up until now, stepped out from the shadows just a few buildings from where they all stood. He was recognized at once by all of them as he walked over to where they stood. The man from the shadows walked over to the pile of garbage at the curve. He removed one of the large black plastic bags from under the pile. Willie took the bag moving into the shadows of the stoop for cover.

"Yo Turk," Willie softly called out to hand him a large brown grocery size bag from inside the black plastic one. Turk took the bag from Willie and quickly began walking towards the nearest corner. Willie called the names of each man and handed them a bag and without a word each man made their way in different directions.

Donny drove carefully through the streets of the city knowing if he were stopped the four kilos of heroin in the back seat of the car would land him in prison for the next 25 years. Donny parked the car on a quiet neighborhood street and walked to a nearby payphone.

The telephone in the luxurious apartment rang only once before the receiver was picked up.

"Yo Rick," Donny said into the receiver.

"Yeah, this is me." Donny replied.

"The car is parked just off Broadway on the downtown side of 88th street."

"Okay, I'm on my way." Rick stated. "I'll call you when I'm finished."

Rick carefully checked the surrounding area before he approached the gray car. Once he was sure of the moment he got in and drove off. Rick drove around to make sure no one was following him before driving to the building where they had just gotten another stash apartment.

Rick sat there quietly for several minutes. For some reason, he did not trust the superintendent of the building or his son. Once Rick was sure of his safety, he reached over the front seat and removed the brown bag from under the front seat where Donny had placed it before leaving. Rick moved quietly and swiftly towards the building. Once safely inside the apartment Rick took three keys of the heroin and placed them in a suitcase. Rick placed the suitcase with the drugs in the front hallway closet. Rick took the other key and placed it in the waist band of his pants fixing his coat so that the key could not be seen. Rick placed his ear to the door and listened for movement before he turned the latch to let himself out of the apartment.

Rick made his way to the other stash apartment across town. Once he had settled in he made a call. "Hello," the reply on the other end came very soft and sweetly.

"Yeah Charlotte, it's me Rick. Are you ready?"

"Yes we are," she answered, "We have been waiting for your call."

"Okay. I'll pick you up in ten minutes at Mr. Wells," and then he hung up.

When Rick walked into Mr. Welles, Charlotte greeted him with a smile.

"Hello Rick."

"Hey girl," Rick replied as he looked around the restaurant. At this hour Mr. Welles was packed with freaks looking to go off with any one of the scrambling men who came here looking for them. In fact, if he did not have business he would grab the pretty little thing in the corner booth that had caught his eye. The women always looked better to him when he could not hang out. Then to there was the sexual excitement caused by the danger of business that always engulfed him.

Rick took the seat right next to Charlotte in the booth.

"You ready girl? He asked. Before she could answer he had asked her another question. "Who've you got to work with you tonight?"

Charlotte pointed to two females sitting at the bar. Rick knew both of them. They had worked for him with Charlotte many times before.

"Okay," Rick said, "Charlotte you ride with me. Tell the girls where to go and to take a cab. Tell them we will follow them in the cab."

Charlotte and the two other females made themselves at home in the kitchen. They worked quickly and quietly making sandwiches. Rick took a six foot mirror from the bedroom wall and laid it across the dining room table. Rick got the two large pots from under the kitchen sink and the large sifter that hung on the kitchen cabinet wall.

Rick took the key of dope and sifted it into a large mountain that sat at the end of the mirror. Rick then opened the large drum of Bonita and quinine mix while the females watched television. Rick sifted enough mix to fill both pots to the rim. Rick was now ready to begin the job of cutting the dope. Each of the pots held seven key of cut. Rick carefully sifted a blanket of mix across the mirror using the contents of one full pot. Then he filled the sifter from the mountain of dope. Rick sifted the dope evenly over the blanket of mix. He took the other pot of mix and sifted it over the blanket of mix and dope. Then he sifted the remaining dope over the white mountain of power that had grown on the mirror. Rick sifted the contents on the mirror several more times to insure an even blend. He had become good at cutting dope, and good dope cutters were hard to find. One mistake and a package could be ruined.

Rick refilled each pot and made a mountain of white power at the center of the mirror. He now had 15 keys of some of the best dope ready to hit the streets of New York City. Rick placed two shopping bags each by the side of the three chairs that sat on one side of the table. He sat a stack of boxes with glassine bags in front of each seat along with the trademark of red tape that would identify the brand of the dope.

Charlotte and the other two females who had been watching television were ready and itching to go. As if as remote control, Charlotte and the other two females removed their clothes and sat in the three chairs at the dope that filled the table.

Rick took a seat across the table from them. He built a fare size mountain of dope in front of each female. The machine like movement of the female's hands always fascinated him as they worked. Each time they placed just the right amount in the glassine bag, folding and taping it before dropping into the shopping bag at the side of the chair they each sat on.

They worked through the rest of the early morning, stopping only to use the bathroom or grab a bite to eat or to get something to drink. This procedure went on until mid-afternoon. It had taken them just over eleven hours to package the entire 15 keys of cut dope. It came to one hundred and seventy-five thousand two dollar bags. After counting each of the 78 hundred half loads, Rick handed Charlotte an envelope and told her to pay the girls.

Rick sat watching the girls get dressed as he dialed a number on the telephone. The receiver on the other end was picked up before the first ring was completed. Donny's familiar voice needed no introduction.

"Yo Donny, I'm finished." Rick informed Donny.

"Okay, what time do you want me to meet you?" Donny replied.

"Meet me at my mother's house at five this evening."

"Alright, later." And Donny hung up the phone.

The danger, the excitement of working in the mill always increased Rick's sexual desires. As he looked at the curvaceous shape of Charlotte's behind, he knew where his desires would find satisfaction on this day.[2]

Rick and Charlotte rode in silence to his hide-away apartment in Westchester County. Once there, Rick laid restlessly on the bed and took another hit of blow. He always like to relax in this apartment after working in the mill. It was a large bedroom that could have been the living room of any one family's home. However, it was the bedroom of his playpen. It was the kind of room that spelled success. It also tells you that the man who played in the large 20 x 20 foot bed was secure in who and what he was.

The thick dark blue carpet flowed across the room. The bed sat on a two foot high walnut round platform. The head of the platform was covered in black leather. The sheets were made of black silk and had the letter "R" monogrammed in the center. The bedspread was made from the finest mink pelts laid out in rows of black with thin blue strips in the folds to match the carpet. Several large throw pillows made of blue silk and black mink laid at the foot of the bed. The head of the bed rest against a blue smoke glass mirror. The mirror covered the wall from the floor to the ceiling, from wall to wall. The mirror also opened at its base to reveal a control console. Running across the length of the ceiling at the foot of the bed are the track lamps, six in all, each bearing its own color. The track lamps could be set to change with the beat of the music just by hitting a switch on the console. The lamps could be used in a number of different combinations. The lamps also worked as spotlights, leaving the room in darkness lighting only the bed. The lamps had the effect he dreamt about as he worked at becoming the man he knew himself to be. The drapes hung over the widows shielding out any evidence of what time of day or night it may be.

The music was soft and easy. Rick's lean frame rested against a pillow on the bed. His broad shoulders were reflecting in the mirror. Rick was naked, covered up to his waist by the mink bedspread. Rick enjoyed the

---

2   Females working in dope mills must remove their clothes to hold down thievery. Only females are used in professional mills, thus holding down the possibility of being set up for a robbery.

cool feeling of the silk on his back and the warmth of mink on his bare manhood.

As Rick laid down motionless, his eyes fixed on the sliding door of the master bathroom. Rick reached for the special made tray that sat on the stand next to the bed. . Rick picked up one of the 14 karat gold boxes that had his name craved on it. He opened the box and pulling a sheet of paper from its lid. Rick took some of the finely ground brown leaves and rolled a nice size joint. Rick turned off the blue florescent lamp on the side of the tray, and then lit the joint.

Taking a deep pull from the joint Rick then hit a switch on the console that sent the large wheels rolling on the tape deck. The numbers jumped in the small box as the big wheels moved silently in the dime light. Hitting the stop switch, then the play, Smokey Robinson belted out the rich tones of 'Ooooh Baby, Baby.' The music came from four of the finest speakers made, one in each corner of the room.

As Rick puffed on the joint he began to grow just a little impatient and his anticipation fueled the fire burning deep within him.

The door to the master bathroom slid open. Charlotte stepped into the arch way of the door. The light from the bathroom cast a halo like glow around her figure as she stood there. She wore black stockings, G-string panties and high heel shoes. As she paused, legs spread slightly, arms raised as if she wanted to touch the sky. The light encased her every curve giving her long slender form the aura of a Goddess. She was nasty and when she spoke her voice was low and sexy.

"Rick, am I worth the wait?" She teased. She knew what he liked and she was more than willing to give it to him. Charlotte closed the bathroom door behind her, closing out any trace of life outside of the room.

Rick hit the switch that controlled the red track lamp and it covered Charlotte from head to toe. The dim red light changed her creamy brown skin color to that of a bronzed gold. Her cat like walk was followed by the timer on the red spotlight right up to the foot of the bed. Her long, shapely legs and with a slight curve tantalized Rick's deepest fantasies.

Charlotte gracefully placed one knee on the bed, bending at the waist and coming to rest on both hands. Her smile was sexy and sweet. Her eyes showed the passion that burned within her.

"Take me, I'm yours." She whispered, her words burning in Rick's ears. "Use me for your pleasure," She purred. I love the way you make me feel, Rick."

Rick sat up on the bed, at the same time he motioned for Charlotte to sit in front of him. Of all the women he had known, she was one of the few that really brought out the raw sexual rage in him. He poured her a glass of cool white wine. He ran his finger down the shape of her nose as she placed the glass of wine to her lips.

"This wine tastes good, it has a nice sensation going down," She commented. Charlotte removed the glass from her lips and traced the outline of her mouth with her finger. Rick reached over, placing his hand on top of her hand, he stuck the tip if his finger in her mouth. She bit Rick's finger lightly then took another sip of wine. There was no rush. They were free to enjoy each other and the pleasantries they offered each other for the rest of the day.

Rick re-lit the joint and took a long slow drag. He blew out a cloud of smoke as her mouth came to meet his. The wine had cooled the touch of her lips and Rick could feel the heat of Charlotte's body.

Rick placed what was left of the joint in the ashtray next to the bed. Rick reached for Charlotte, she moved into his embrace. Rick gently laid her down and his lips met her lips once again. Rick's hand moved up then down the shape of Charlotte's body. Her skin was smooth and silky. Rick's fingers slid across Charlotte's skin as though they were skating on ice. The touch of Rick's hand brought a moan from Charlotte. Rick's manhood became hard as steel once again by her naked beauty.

Rick kissed and sucked at her every emotion until Charlotte was mad with desire.

"Damn Rick, only you who could get me worked up like this," Charlotte whispered. Rick bit her neck softly. Rick played with her breasts as if he was a master surgeon performing a difficult operation. Rick ran his hands down her stomach and between her legs. Charlotte opened her legs to receive Rick's touch. Rick could feel the wetness of her passion as he stroked the inside of Charlotte's thighs. The mastery of Rick's tongue on Charlotte's breast seemed to make them grow larger.

Charlotte ran her fingers through Rick's hair, moving her hand down and around the muscles of his shoulders and back. Rick sucked and played with every part of her body.

"Rick, oh Rick, your mouth has me dripping wet," Charlotte cried out in pleasure.

Charlotte legs were spread wide, her feet rested firmly on Rick's back. Rick's hands were wrapped around the outside of Charlotte's thighs. Rick's mouth toyed with Charlotte's body. His tongue played her like a virtuoso playing a concert piano.

"That's it Rick, that's it! I'm cumming" Charlotte moaned.

It took Charlotte a few moments to catch her breath, yet she knew the best was about to come. Rick slowly wrapped himself around her body like a snake. Charlotte's arms made their way around his back and shoulders. Charlotte's touch was hot and exciting. Rick's tongue danced in Charlotte's mouth and she sucked it for dear life. Rick's manhood was hot and hard and seemed easily finding the opening of Charlotte's womanhood by itself. The head of Rick's manhood cut through Charlotte's opening like a hot knife through soft butter. As Rick's manhood parted her she let out a loud growling moan. Charlotte's pelvis rose to meet Rick's thrush, driving him deep and all the way in her. Rick could feel Charlotte's hot juices on his manhood. The deep wet cavern of Charlotte's womanhood held Rick's manhood tight and deep inside her. They rocked back and forth in a slow hard rhythm. When Rick exploded in her she felt his manhood swelled stretching her with joy. She knew then that she had satisfied him just as he had her. But Rick was not ready when she said, "I'll never forget how you fucked me tonight, never, ever."

Donny sat at the bar in the dimly lit Tiger Lounge. As Rick entered he looked around and could see that Donny was the only customer. The warmth of the bar felt good coming out of the bitter cold. This was the first time in more than two years that Rick had set foot in the Tiger Lounge. As he looked the place over he wondered how it made any money. Then too, he had heard the rumors about Senior Hawkins turning the bar and his other business over to the Junior Hawkins and brother. Whatever the story was with Sam Hawkins Jr., it was their business. Rick took a seat on the bar stool next to Donny, the two men greeted each other.

"So how did the drop go?" Rick asked.

"Everything went as planned. His girl came uptown and I gave her the three keys and she jumped in a cab and went back downtown or where ever the fuck she had to meet him. They should be half way back to DC by now if not all the way there." Donny explained.

"When you spoke to Jesse, did he tell you why he wanted to meet us at this spot so early?"

"Nah, he didn't say shit. I was at Nat's bar when he came in looking for Willie."

Rick was looking out the window of the bar when he saw Jesse's custom made black Mark IV pulled up. Rick could not tell who the driver was but he knew it wasn't Willie. Jesse got out on the passenger side and came in the bar.

"Yo my brothers, what's up?" Jesse greeted them.

"Ain't nothing."

"Look, wait in the car for me. I need to make a call and I'll be right out."

Donny went to pay the bill, Jesse told the barmaid to put the bill on his tab.

Donny opened the car door, climbed in and greeted the driver at the same time. Rick and the driver's eyes locked and they greeted each other warmly.

"Oh shit!" Rick said. "I haven't seen you in a long time. So what's up?"

"Ain't nothing, I just came home from up north last week and I've been chillin.' I did five years." Crime informed him. When Jesse got in the car, Crime and Rick were still kickin' it.

"I see you know my man." Jesse commented.

"Yeah, we go back a long way." Rick replied.

"We were in the 600 school together." Crime added. "So, where to?

"Let's see who else we can find," Jesse said, "Just hit a couple of spots. Ricky, Donny, you don't mind riding do you?"

"Nah, so what's up?"

"I've got a big crew and with everybody else's crew meeting at the Shalimar I decided to move my operation for the time being. So until I give the word our meets will be at the Oasis. Right now I'm riding around trying to find everyone to let them know the deal."

CHAPTER EIGHT

America's Black History

RICK STUDIED THE view of the projects from the window of his mother's apartment. The fresh blanket of snow was untouched awaiting the kids who would play in it later on that morning. Rick was surprised that there were no children already out on this bright sunny winter Saturday morning. Rick's mother sat at the dining room table drinking her tea with lemon. She was checking her shopping list before getting ready to do her weekly shopping.

The tiny figure plowed through the snow in front of the building. Rick watched as the frail old woman beat out a path in the deep snow.

"Hey Ma," Rick called to his mother. "I see Mrs. Chaney. I didn't know she was still around."

"Yes, she is still around Ricky," His mother responded.

"This is the first time I have seen her since they made the movie about her son. I wonder how much money they paid her for the rights?" It was a story that shocked the world." Rick thought out loud. "The racist Klansmen killed her son and the others in Mississippi. I am sure glad it was not one of my brothers that they killed. With everything I know about weapons and explosives from being in Vietnam, I would have tried to take them all out."

"If I am not mistaken," Rick's mother responded, "That just what her youngest son Ben did. Do you remember him? He was that small dark skinned kid who used to play in front of the building when Mrs. Chaney and the rest of us sat on the benches. He was always so nice and polite, real quiet."

"Not that I can recall."

"He was younger than James. I don't know what he did after he got older, but Ben sure went down there. It was kept kind of quiet, but they put Ben away for it if I am not mistaken. If someone does your family wrong then family is supposed to take care of it no matter what the cost."

"That's what's wrong now; nobody takes care of their own," Rick stated more to himself than his mother. "Everyone runs to the police and asks for justice. Like there is justice in this country for a black man. If the Klan knew that for every black man, woman and child they hung that we would hang two of them, you can believe they would think twice about doing it. But no, what do we do, we run to the police and we know damn well his hood is in the closet."

"Slow down Ricky, you get so emotional when you talk about these things. That's right, look at the condition of the blacks in this country. Our communities use to be called just that or neighborhoods. Now they're called ghettos. Tell me, how can you raise a child with pride when all the time they are being told they live in the ghetto? The ghetto is a place of broken dream and a place where families live life with no hope. The ghetto is the worse place in the United States to live and die. Then we have the government with their bullshit civil rights bills. Our so-called leaders praise the busing act. Mark my words; this is the worst thing that could ever happen to our schools. If I were white, I would not let my child be taken out of a good school and placed in some run down school in a black ghetto. Not only will he not get the education he deserves, he's going to have to fight everyday. Who wants to worry about their child's safety while in school?"

"No, if I was white I would place my child in private school. See Ma, it's a game. The good black students will take the bus ride across town and all the heartship that goes with it to get a good education. The border line kids will drop out of school. No students, no money. If the government was serious they would rebuild the black schools and make them a place where you can get the best education in the land. Then if white kids wanted to go to one of our schools it would be by their choice. To me, it seems like all the blacks with a few dollars in their pockets are rushing to show how white they can be. We forgive you for stealing our grandparents from their homeland. We can fit in perfectly, we can act just as white as you are."

"I believe we can live together, Ricky."

"Sure we can Ma, but we've got to make them understand. No more hangings, no more second hand lifestyles. We have to build our own system within a system. Every other group of people who has ever come to these shores has built their own. They have their own banks and built their communities into places they are proud of. Sure, we started out as slaves in this country. But how long are we going to use that as a crutch for not having our own? You know what I really believe Ma? I believe that if you control the cash flow from graft, you control a power that will allow you to become anything within the framework of this system that you want. I have studied the powerful men for the last two hundred years in this country. The men who dictated policy all had their hand in some kind of graft. Sure they preach the garbage everyday to the man and woman in the streets about virtue and righteousness. They prosecute those amongst themselves that are stupid enough to have the public find out about their goings on. The Rothschild's, the Vanderbilt Clan, Kennedys and Rockefellers made enough money so there is no question about them being respectable. But if you look deep you will find they were nothing but cold blooded gangsters. Al Capone is known for being one of the biggest gangsters in history, but those American families wrote the book on crime."

The true crime families in America dictated policy to the President of this country and that office has been exposed several times. Land and oil scandals with the last one being Spiro Agnew the Vice President. I don't know why I am telling you this Ma, I guess it is just something that is on my mind. I do know this; blacks are taking control of the streets. No longer do we pay the larger amount of money made from graft to the white bosses. They don't sit in their penthouses or out on their country estates and tell black folks how and what to do on the streets of our neighborhood. The time is coming when we must buy our own politicians and judges. And, if there are none for sale because they are owned by the powers that be we must then raise own," Rick continued.

"I don't know Ricky, all that stuff is beyond me," his mother smiled.

"Yeah Ma, I know, it's beyond our so-called leader too. If they understood the true power of the dollar instead of being loss in the American dream they could see how to build a nation in our own communities. They would be searching for the men with the cash to invest in the black American dream. The men I worked with are the ones in this country who can buy the American dream for a race of people who once were slaves. They have the dollars to build factories and buildings. Where are the thinkers amongst our leaders? The government is not going to do it for us. No white bank is going to work at helping us become a power in this country. The standard of living for us as a people is one that says we will never have as long as we rely on government programs. Sure one or two of us will become the shining star for all to see. There is more money on the street than the white man ever dreamed, that's why they have new law like the Rockefeller Law. They want to put us away before we wake up and realize what can be done with all that money instead of buying cars, clothes and other bullshit. No, what do the white masters have our leaders singing, put them in jail because they are hurting your people. Never once have they thought to ask the master how many of our people did he hurt to get where he is today."

"Well, I'm going out now Ricky, are you going to be here when I get back?"

"I don't know Ma, why?"

'I need someone to meet me at the store to bring these groceries home."

"I'll stay here until you call. I will probably fall asleep on the sofa."

'If you want to go home, go ahead, your little brother is here."

"No, I'll stay," Rick insisted.

She kissed her son on the forehead as he lay down on the sofa, and then walked out the door.

In a matter of just a few moments there was a knock at the door.

"Who the fuck could that be this early in the morning?" When Rick peeked through the peephole, he could not believe this fool was knocking on the door this early in the morning. Rick opened the door and knew at once James could see the disgust written on his face.

"What's up James?"

"Ain't nothing, I saw Ma on her way to store. She told me that you were here."

"Yeah, come in. I'm kind of tired," Rick said as he lay back down on the sofa. James sat in the chair to watch TV. Rick fell into a semi-sleep.

It was several minutes before James decided to disturb Rick.

"Yo Rick, I spoke to Donny about getting a package. He told me that I had to see you about it."

"If, and I said if. If I give you something where are you going to do it?"

"I've got this spot in Queens. Robert and I are going to work it."

"Let me tell you something James. Donny told me not to give you shit because you wouldn't do nothing but fuck it up."

"Nah man, I wouldn't fuck you around. We go way back to elementary school and we have been hanging out ever since. You're coming off now and I want to get money too. The only way for me to get money is if you put me down. You don't have to worry Rick. I'm going to do the right thing."

Rick knew by the speech James had just made that it would be a bad move to give him a package. Yet he wanted to believe that his old and good friend would do the right thing.

"Look James, I don't have anything right now. I should have something in a week. If and I said if. If I decide to give you something, it's between me and you. Not Donny or anyone else. I may give you a half piece. I sell them for 450 or 500 dollars. I will let you have it for 350 dollars. That way it won't be a strain for you to get your business set up right."

Rick could see the happiness and excitement written all over James' face.

"So when and where do want to see me?" James asked.

"You see me damn near every day so just leave things the way they are.

When I'm ready to give it to you I will let you know. Okay, I'm going to cut out so you can get some sleep." James then took off and they both said 'later' at the door.

Rick sat in a booth with Shemika at Mr. Welles. They spoke quietly and truly enjoyed the pleasure of one another's company.

"I hardly see you anymore since you got back with your son's mother," Shemika said.

"Do I detect a note of jealousy?" Rick asked.

"No, yes, I don't know," Shemika said that she was really sure of what she felt. "I am just so unsure of how you feel about me and what is going on with you Rick. You make me feel like I never have before and when you are not with me I feel like a part of me is missing."

"I feel all those things about you too, Shemika. When I am with you, don't ever get it wrong, you have all of me."

"If I had never told you about Jenny, you would not be having those feelings. But every time we met I would have to lie to you. Tell me Shemika, what would we have and what would we be to each other if the foundation of our relationship was built on a lie? We share a relationship that is built on trust and understanding. As long as we have an understanding about what we mean to one another we will continue to grow together."

"So what you are saying Rick? If I had another man it would be alright with you?"

"If you are saying you have another man."

"No," Shemika cut in before Rick could finish his thought and statement. "That is not what I am saying, I don't have another man."

"Listen Shemika, you know that Jenny and I have a love-hate relationship and that we always try to make it work. Sean, my son bonds us together and there is this fantasy in my head about family. It's difficult for me to explain my emotions, this is complex matter of family responsibility. But let me tell you this, if you had another man there would be a number of things I would first ask myself. Is it infatuation and who is this man who has infatuated you so? If your feelings for him go deeper than infatuation I would look within myself to find those needs you have, that I couldn't meet."

"I don't meet all of your needs and desires, is that why you went back to Jenny?"

"Me going back to Jenny has nothing to do with the way I feel about you, Shemika. You fulfill a passion that burns deep inside of me. You bring to my life a kind of fulfillment I have never known with anyone else. With Jenny there is a responsibility to family and emotions we felt long ago that made up our relationship. Don't ever doubt it; what I feel for you is real. When I am near you and I see the look that is in your eyes. I know it is you and you alone and that means the world to me."

Rick continued, "But to answer your question Ms. Lady, if you had another man and felt you had to lie to me about it. It would mean that I could not trust you because you lied and that everything we supposedly had together was based on a lie. Then you would not have to worry about sneaking behind my back because I would be gone. You could have him and he could have all of your time and whatever else it is you want him to have out of your life."

Shemika reached across the table and placed her hands on Rick's. "I don't have another man. I'm not looking for another man. Rick, you satisfy all of my needs in life. Before I met you I would never have accepted these terms for a relationship. Now because of them, my life has taken on new meaning. I am a stronger woman than I ever believed, and I know that you are my man."

All heads turned to see Pee Wee Kirkland and New York Freddy Myers as they entered Mr. Welles. Both men were impeccably dressed. Pee Wee in a black shadow strip suit and black alligator shoes. Freddy's suit was a burgundy shadow strip with matching alligator shoes. Pee Wee's black full length mink hung from his shoulders. Freddy's 3/4 length brown mink hung from his shoulder's also.

Rick waited and watched as Jerome Harris, Pete and Jervis, as well as the many others spoke with the two debonair men. Rick excused himself from Shemika and went over to speak with the two men whom now stood at the bar. Freddy's greeting was ice cold but friendly. Pee Wee greeted Rick warmly and Freddy walked over to a statuesque beauty at the other end of the bar. Pee Wee and Rick rapped about their favorite passion basketball, clothes and women.

"I hear you are coming off," Pee said.

"Yeah, I'm trying to make a living."

"If you stay down for it, it will all come together for you, Rick." Pee Wee glanced at the diamond watch on his wrist then signaled to Freddy that it was time for them to leave. Rick said 'later' and stepped off to give the others time to speak with Pee Wee before he left.

When Rick returned to the booth, Shemika was talking with one of her friends. Shemika's friend was about to get up and leave, Rick told her it would be alright to sit and talk with them. Rick took the seat beside Shemika; he put his hand under the table placing it on her thigh pushing her dress back. She knew no one could see what he had done so she did not mind.

Shemika and Rick were both ready to leave but Rick knew it would be another twenty minutes or so before Donny returned from doing the books and counting the money. It was nearly 4 o'clock in the morning when Donny and Joyce entered Mr. Welles. They took a seat in the booth with Rick and Shemika who were now talking with Cisco and his conquest for the night. The three men excused themselves and went outside. Once outside the three men climb into Cisco's Thunderbird. Cisco turned the car on to heat it up. They all knew they would be out of the car before that happened. Rick broke open a sealed plastic bag. He took out two golf ball size rocks of cocaine. He gave one to Donny and the other one to Cisco. He passed the bag after taking a hit so Donny and Cisco could take a hit.

"This blow is crazy good," Cisco stated. "You always have good blow Rick."

"I get it from my man Lefty."

"You're going to have to take me down there one night."

"If I don't take you, Donny can. Donny knows him as well as I do."

Nicky Barns and one of his Lieutenants pulled alongside of Cisco's car in his green Mercedes. They all exchanged greetings before Nicky's Lieutenant got out. He stepped quickly in the cold making his way to the entrance of Mr. Welles. In just a few minutes he came out with two bad freaks. Rick had noticed the two freaks when he first came in. He knew they had been waiting for awhile, which was not unusual for women attracted to men with this lifestyle. When the two women and Nicky's Lieutenant got in the Benz, he said later and pulled off. The three men sat in the car laughing and relished the splendor of the cold winter morning. Cisco cracked a few jokes when Jesse's black Torondo pulled alongside his car.

"This motherfucker goes to sleep at night, has a dream about hooking up a car, gets up in the morning and goes to the car dealer to have it made. Jesse is living the American dream." All three men's attention was focused on the stagecoach lights placed near the rear window that now flashed with the emergency lights Jesse had turned on. They added a nice dimension to the machine. Jesse had Crime and Willie with him. They all greeted one another.

"Yo Ricky, you got something for me?" Jesse asked.

"Yeah, I've got a little something for you," Donny replied.

"You can give that to Willie," Jesse told him as he went into Mr. Welles with Crime.

"I'll be right with you," Donny informed Willie, and then he pulled Rick off to the side. This was the first time the two had had time to talk business since Donny had counted the money in the stash and done the books.

"I've got 22 thousand on me," Donny informed Rick. The books are fucked up and we aren't going to make a dime off this package. Besides that we are going to be three thousand short."

"The books are alright, I've got three thousand plus on me," Rick told Donny. "I sold an 8th early this morning."

"You should have told me that before I went to do the books. That's what took me so long. I was trying to figure out where the rest of the dope had gone and who didn't turn in all of the money."

"I put a marker in the book," Rick replied.

"Yeah, I saw that bullshit. That made it worse. I didn't know what the fuck it meant!" They both laughed.

Donny and Rick got in to Jesse's car with Willie. They started counting the money and Willie stopped them.

"I don't know what makes you think I want to count that money now."

Rick responded, "I have to count three thousand out of this for you. Donny has the other 22 thousand of what we owed."

Willie took the money from Donny and placed a couple of rubber bands around it. When Rick had finished counting out three thousand, Willie took it and placed a rubber around it also, marking their names on both bundles of money. Willie threw the money under the front seat of the car.

"Are you ready for something else?" Willie asked them.

"Yeah, but we don't want it tonight. Gives us two keys this time," Rick said.

"You have to talk to Jesse. I don't know if he wants to give you that much dope."

Donny, Rick and Jesse stood near the music machine at the rear of Mr. Welles as they spoke.

"You think you're ready for two joints?" Jesse asked. "How long is it going to take you to finish those two?"

"We will rock the two in the same amount of time it took us to do one," Rick told him.

"Okay, you can get that," Jesse replied. "But you have to wait a few days. I don't have enough dope to give you that much now."

"That's cool with us," Donny said.

"Look, I'm out of here," Rick told them. "I'm tired as a fuck. I know Shemika is going to be upset when I take her home and just go to sleep."

"You better take care of your homework before you blow her," Jesse commented.

"Check this out, Jesse. If a man is not going to do his best work then he should not take on the job. I've been sniffing blow all night and I'm so tired, I'm so ready to fall asleep. Besides, I know I am not going to blow her."

"I don't know, niggers be shooting at her all the time. She's a fine motherfucker."

"Yeah, I know about all of them. They pop shit all the time about *Rick ain't never going to get as much money as me. Baby I can give you the world.* She tells me all about those sorry rapping motherfuckers. They better be glad I don't want their girls. The shit they kick, my son's got more game than them."

"Rick talks plenty of shit doesn't he?" Donny laughed.

"I don't know, I guess I was blessed with some kind of gift," Rick replied. "The pretty boys and fly guys look at me and say, "How can she be with that big lip nigger?" And sometimes, I wonder myself. Then I realize it's my game. It's not about the car I drive, the jewelry or clothes I wear. It's about me and that makes all the difference in the world. I know when I first meet a woman if she belongs with me or not. The funny thing about it, she knows it too."

"You should be a pimp then," Jesse said.

"What? And give up this grand lifestyle that I have come to know?" They all laughed at how Rick said it.

"Look at them pimpin' niggers; Silky and K.C.," Rick said. "They pop shit about that little two or three hundred thousand they clock a year. Imagine Jesse, how could you live on such a little bit of money?" Rick continued joking. They broke up with laughter.

"We live the true American dream," Rick stated. "An apartment to die for, money, dream cars, and the best clothes. We also had our choice of the most beautiful women in the world, not for business but pleasure. Now you tell me, what more could a 22-year old black man ask for in this country of hopes and dreams." They broke up again with laughter.

Crime had come over to join the merriment. They were kickin' it live. The laughter was sincere. The enjoyment was felt by those who join the group of men by the music machine and by the women who watched the men at play.

Rick sat in the black Eldorado parked just off the corner of 104th street Columbus Avenue. He watched the people who milled around on Columbus Avenue between 104th and 105th street. Then he saw who he had been searching for. He watched him as he crossed Columbus Avenue to come on the same side of the Avenue where he was parked. When he crossed 104th street to walk right in front of him, Rick turned the car engine on. Rick waited until Robert was between 104th and 103rd street with nowhere to run if he tried before calling out to him.

"Robert, yo Robert!" Robert had not expected Rick to pull up on him and like a con man true to his game, a smile came over Robert's face to ease the surprise of being caught off guard.

Rick pulled the car over on 103rd street right in front of the project police station. Once Robert reached where the car had stopped, Rick told him to get in. Soon enough Robert had closed the car door and Rick pulled the machine back into traffic.

It was a bright sunshine day but the bitter cold still tore at you.

"Yo Robert, I've been looking all over for you. I want to get your version of what happen to my money before I make my decision as to what I should do." The black machine cruised down Columbus Avenue as Robert ran his spiel on Rick.

"Look, you and James, not to mention the other motherfuckers I tried to do something for, all run the same bullshit. You are telling me it's James fault that my money got fucked up. He says you are to blame. Either you are taking advantage of our friendship or you think I'm a punk and you can just take my money."

"It's not like that Rick. Things just went wrong. James didn't know how to handle it," Robert defended.

"I don't want to hear that bullshit. You think I can take that bullshit story uptown to pay the man with. He wants his money and if I don't pay him he will kill me. Do you think I'm going to die so you motherfuckers can spend my money like it's yours. I gave you a shot, the money you fucked up, I could use to take care of my family. You put my life in danger and you take food out of my child's mouth. Not to mention the story you gave me like I just came off the farm!" Rick was furious. "Donny told me that all of you weren't shit. I've known you just about all of my life and I figured because I came off that you could too. But Donny was right and you proved I was wrong. I want my money and if you want to get on some crazy gangster shit, that's what we will do,"

Rick pulled the machine over on 102nd street Amsterdam Avenue.

"So when am I going to get my money?" Rick asked Robert again.

"Give me a little time Rick; I'll get your money together. I will see you in a few days for sure," Robert said as he got out of the car. Robert stepped quickly across 102nd headed back towards Columbus Avenue. Rick knew that he would have to hurt Robert to get that little bit of money from him.

Rick sat there quietly in the car reflecting on the events that were now taking place. He reached inside of his leather coat and felt the butt of his weapon that hung in its holster. Rick knew that he would not kill Robert or the others for such a small amount of money. Rick knew his share of the profits had all just about gone down the fucking drain with his so-called friends. As near as he could figure it, it had to be 10 to 12 thousand lost out of his share. That would be the only way to keep the books right and to keep Donny from finding out what a fool he had been to trust them.

Rick knew he could not kill them for the money, but the rage that filled him because of the betrayal was enough to push him over the edge. Rick decided it was best he put the gun away before someone got seriously hurt.

Rick was ready to go, but every time he asked Sean he said no. It was cold and Sean was bundled up so tight he moved like a robot. Rick picked up a hand full of snow and hit Sean with it, then ran a few feet to get out of Sean's reach. Sean threw as much snow as his little hands could hold. Sean could not throw the snow far enough to hit his father. They played in the snow white beauty of Central Park as if they were the only two people in the world.

Rick's thoughts weighed heavily on his mind. It had been almost three weeks since Jesse said they could get the two keys. Rick still hadn't collected the money owed by his so-called friends. It was time to pay the bills again; at least he still had a few more days before they were due. With no money coming in, the lifestyle he had come to love ate away at the money he and Donny had stashed away.

The panic that now swept through the dope trade was new to him. It was hard to believe the people he got the dope from couldn't find any. Rick knew his trip to the Shalimar tonight would be the same as the others for the past few weeks. Jesse would tell him that he just spoke with someone about getting something, not that he hadn't. It just seemed that when they met at such and such place at whatever time, it was the same old story. And for good reason Rick didn't think things would be any better tonight.

Sean and Rick sat at the dining room table, drank hot chocolate and read the children's books Rick had brought. Sean was pleased to show his father he could write his name. Rick on the other hand, was amazed that in Sean's tiny finely carved body there were the complete workings that would guide him on the path to become a full grown man. Sean's mind was eager for knowledge.

The phone's ring interrupted the serenity of the apartment; Rick pulled the receiver from its cradle before it could ring a second time.

"Look, I'll come by in a few minutes," Donny informed Rick.

"Yeah, that's cool, who have you got with you?" Rick asked.

"I'm by myself, who would I have with me this time of day?"

"Knowing you, it could be anyone."

"Later. I'll be there in a few," Donny then hung up the phone.

Donny sat at the table with Rick and Sean. Donny had taken on the task of helping Sean with his studies.

"If this goes on much longer, we will have to cut some of the stashes loose," Rick said.

"It should be about to break," Donny replied. "I was at the Fast Track last night and that's all anyone talked about, the panic."

"Something got to jump off or we will fuck up all the money we have stashed away," Rick said.

"Yeah, I know what you mean. I blew 32 hundred last night. After I got skied the fuck up I don't know where the money went."

"It's fucked up. Just to fuck around at the Shalimar, stop off at Small's or Mr. Welles you can blow hundreds. Don't mention the Fast Track or the Piggy Back, you can blow crazy G-money," Rick added.

"Shit, you can loose millions at those spots. You remember two weeks ago, Skull dropped 350 thousand one night than came back and dropped another half million the next night?"

"You are right about that my brother," Rick agreed. "I took 50 dollars out the other night and swore that was all I would spend. Shit, I ended up getting five hundred from Jesse and he hit me with a quarter of blow. We live a lifestyle so extravagant most people outside of the game would never understand how we spend so much money doing nothing. It's alright, though. As long as we are clocking, but right now we are not clocking."

"I took Joyce with me to the Fast Track last night and she kept dropping lugs about you Rick. She talked on and on about all the shit you've got and how fly you always are."

"Yeah, so what about it?" Rick asked Donny.

"I think she wants to give you a play. I'm just about finish with her so if and when she gives you a play, don't you let me be the cause for you not taking it."

"I'll keep that in mind," Rick replied, and they gave each other five in agreement.

The crowd at Smalls' Paradise had just begun to thicken. Rick informed Donny that he was ready to get out of there. The two men stepped from the bar onto the crowded sidewalk; it held a winter display of fashion wear. Singers, movie stars, hustlers, pimps and players all had come together to enjoy the festive winter nightlife at the popular nightspot. Jimmy Castra had a group of females in a trance standing under the bright lights that lit up the corner of 135th street 7th Avenue.

Skull came over to speak with Rick and Donny.

"That's a badass pair of boots Jimmy Casta has on," Skull stated.

"He's doing a show at the Copa," Rick replied.

"What, has he got a new record out or something?"

"Nah. He's doing the same old shit. They quickly lost interest in Jimmy Castra and got to talking about what was on all of their minds. This panic had everyone looking high and low to score."

"Something going to jump," Skull agreed and said,"Look around, everybody that is somebody is here tonight. Check out the man, you know when the boss is on the set something has got to be in the works. Nicky said he may be getting a little something also. He's got a good connection, not as good as the boss but we may be able to get some work."

Jesse joined Rick and the others as they kicked it about the problems they faced with no product.

"You know the feds knocked all of them guineas last month?" Jesse commented. "You do remember that shit Ricky, it was on TV and in all the papers."

"A hundred motherfuckers knocked at one time," Skull said.

"Nothing but a show for the public. All of them was out on bail the next day. The papers didn't say shit about that," Jesse said half joking. "But it makes their bosses a little nervous. So they put all the shit back in the closets and stopped all shipments coming in off the farms until they can see what's what."

"I want to let you know that everything looks alright," Jesse said, trying to assure his crew. "The boss has found one of those guineas who are not afraid to move. The boss made a deal, we all have to put up X amount of money. The boss has got to pay cash with the way things are now and you know he is not going to use his own money. I am getting ready to take care of B.I. now, I should be ready to hit everybody with a little something around five or six this morning. I don't know where the drop is going to be. If you are going to be out, you know how to find me or one of my Lieutenants. One of them will be able to tell you when the drop is going to jump off," Jesse stated.

Rick felt relieved and could see the relief written on the faces of the others.

"It's about time," Skull responded, "A few white boys get busted and all of Harlem shuts down, that's crazy."

'Look, its 12:30, I'm going home, it's too cold for me just to hang," Rick told the others.

"What are you going to do Donny?" Rick asked.

"I don't know yet," Donny replied. "I'm just going to see what jumps off."

"Well I'm out of here," Skull told them. "I've got to get ready to put this work out."

"I'm out of here too, I've got business to take care of if you want that thing. Later," Jesse said.

"Yo Donny, I'll be back out around three-thirty or four. Where do you want me to meet you?" Rick asked.

"I don't know," Donny replied.

"Fuck it. I'll catch up with you somewhere. Later."

Rick could hear the music coming from the apartment as he got closer to the door. He didn't think anyone heard him when he unlocked and opened the door. The apartment was full of familiar faces, not that he wanted to see them in his apartment, sniffing his blow and smoking his reefer at this hour. Rick saw Jenny sitting in the corner with Thad. She hadn't realized he'd come in. How cozy they looked sitting there. Rick knew Thad was fucking her, not that it mattered to him. Their relationship was just about at its end once again. Faye spotted Rick and shouted in her surprise, "How are you doing Rick?" Rick thought that Faye must have really thought him to be stupid. The way she greeted him was to tip Jenny off that he had come in unnoticed. Rick was disgusted with what he saw and Jenny's melodramatic act when she greeted him.

"Where is Sean?" Rick asked Jenny.

"He's in his room," Jenny replied. Rick walked away without saying another word to anyone. Rick knocked on his son's bedroom door before entering. Rick found Sean watching an old movie on television and joined him on his bed.

"Hi daddy," Sean greeted his father with smiling eyes.

"Hey little man, how are you doing? Is it alright if I watch TV with you?"

"Okay, daddy." Sean was a baby in most people's eyes, yet Rick spoke and treated him as if he were much older. The dog had come to the end of the bed and sniffed at Rick, using his head to get under Rick's hand so he could be petted.

"Come on Sean, get dressed, we are going to take the dog for a walk."

Sean held the dog by the short leather strap on the choke collar. Rick had not bothered to put the muzzle on the dog because of the late hour. They walked two blocks over to Broadway. Rick brought four cups of hot chocolate from the Spanish store on the corner of 94th street. When Rick came out of the store, he saw Lefty talking to Sean.

"Yo, what's up Lefty?"

"Ain't nothing, I'm on my way home. I told Gloria that I was only going to be out for a few hours, that was two days ago. So where you headed?" Lefty asked.

"I'm taking my man to Riverside Park so we can let the dog run around." Lefty didn't bother to ask about the late hour for walking the dog, he understood Rick's lifestyle fully, only because his lifestyle basically mirrored it.

The dog ran wild in the snow. Rick had pushed aside some of the snow that covered the bench and he and Sean sat drinking hot chocolate as they watched the dog play. Rick knew his mother would be awfully upset with him if she knew he had her grandbaby out this late. Rick thought back to the few brief moments he got to spent time with his father as a child and how special they seemed. Rick looked at the sparkle in his son's eyes and the smile that lit up his whole face. The way the young child emulated his every movement, and Rick knew these were the most precious of all moments. Rick thought about getting out of the drug trade. He wanted to buy a house with some land, open a business that he could live off for the rest of his life. He wanted to get a nice place for his mother also. Somewhere quiet and peaceful, something she could handle the expenses if anything ever happen to him. He wondered how much money he would need, a million, maybe two or three. Rick pictured the money he and Donny had stashed away, nearly four hundred thousand free and clear. Rick figure it would take another two years and he would be out of the life.

Rick yelled, "Yo!" and the horse size dog leaped over a pile of snow then plowed into another pile. The dog's white spotted body made it almost impossible for him to be seen. Rick yelled once more and Sean echoed his father's yell. The dog came faithfully to his master's side.

"It's time to go little man," Rick told Sean.

Rick told Sean to let the dog go when the elevator doors open. It was the devil in Rick that made him do it. Rick knew the dog would run and jump up against the apartment door scaring everyone inside. Rick heard

Jenny screamed not to open the door and let the dog just run in and Faye echoed Jenny's plea. Sean had a big smile on his face and Rick laughed.

"Scared daddy," he said.

"Yeah, they're scared to death." Rick and Sean both laughed.

When Rick entered the apartment everyone moved to the furthest end of the living room away from the dog. Rick took the dog straight to his bedroom and closed him in. Sean was right on his heels.

"It's time for you to go to bed young man and get some sleep. Don't turn the TV on."

"Okay daddy, good night!" Sean responded. They gave each other five and Rick said good night as well.

Rick was taking a shower when Jenny came into the bathroom. She stood there and waited for Rick to step out.

"Are you going back out Rick?" She asked.

"Why?"

"Because you never stay home anymore and I want to know," Jenny answered.

"Let me explain something to you, we might as well get it straight now," Rick said with a little more anger in his voice than he wanted to express. "I know you are fuckin' that little nigger in the living room. Don't stand there looking so surprised at what I just said, and close your mouth. I know you can put on a better act than the one you are now Lady. I'm not mad."

"See, I knew you didnt care about me," Jenny interjected.

"Shut up and let me finish talking!" Rick harshly said. "I'm not mad, its' your pussy, give it to whomever you want. But think again if you really belief I'm going to sit around and get high and party with you and your friends. Especially since they all know about your thing with Thad. You and them got to be crazy to smile in my face and laugh behind my back. Only now the joke is on you and them, I am not that fool. When I'm not around you jump in that niggers arms and be acting like that's how it's supposed to be. You really must have thought I was stupid but the last laugh is on you Miss. For all of your cheating and sneaking behind my back I always knew. I just didn't give a fuck because the only thing you can give me is some pussy. Now I don't even want that."

"You've got another woman!" Jenny said in anguish, "So don't act so righteous."

"Yeah, that is true but there is a difference. I never brought her here to fuck her in our bed. I have never brought her in your face. I have never acted like she is just a friend, like you are some stupid bitch who could not see pass go. Your stupidity is beyond anything I could imagine. For you to believe I was so blind I couldn't see what the fuck you are doing. Tears now, and what are they supposed to mean? You can go back to your company; I don't have anything else I want to say. Besides, I have to get dressed, I'm leaving. By the way, I will call you and let you know what time I will come by to get my things."

Rick sat in the warmth of the car and looked the block over. He had hoped to see one of his workers or Donny. The late hour and bitter cold had 102nd street empty of all life. Rick drove through the block towards 8th Avenue; he saw Tonya and Latisha standing in the lobby of building 15 and half, just across the street from 9 the dope building. Rick blew the horn and they ran and jumped in the car.

"What the fuck are you doing standing out here this late?" Rick asked, as if he didn't know.

"We are trying to get high," they both responded.

"Who's got dope in the block?"

"Prince," Tonya replied, but you know how he is. You have to lay up with him before he will get you high."

"You can always buy it," Rick responded to Tonya's comment.

"We don't have any money," Latisha said.

"We were hoping someone would turned us on. When are your people going to have something?" Tonya asked.

"I don't know," Rick answered. "Have either of you seen Donny come through the block tonight?"

"No."

"Here's twenty dollars so you can get high and get something to eat,"

Rick said. "I've got to go take care of something."

They thanked Rick with smiles on their faces that reached from ear to ear.

Rick sat waiting for the traffic light to change on the corner of 102nd street, 8th Avenue, and he wondered how Prince could have some dope. Rick drove the car in and out of traffic on the streets of Harlem in search of someone from the crew and now he knew why Prince had dope. The panic was over. Rick could feel the vibrations of the streets and saw the evidence of it in the movement of the people who moved through the cold weather at this early hour.

Rick parked in front of the Shalimar, it was closing time and just about everyone had already cut out. Rick did not get out of the car; he blew the horn to acknowledge the few men and women who stood in the cold before getting in their cars' to drive off. Rick headed straight for Mr. Welles where he found Willie double parked in Jesse's black Coupe Deville.

"What's the good word?" Rick asked Willie.

"Everything is everything," Willie replied. "I need to talk with you." Rick got out of his car leaving the engine running and climbed in the car with Willie.

"So what's up Willie?" Rick asked.

"Jesse told me to let you know that you could get the two keys but I was only to give you one tonight. I'll give you the other one in a few days. We are just going to hit everyone with a little something now."

"Okay, that's cool with me. What time is the meet?"

"Let me see where I can fit you in." Willie pulled a sheet of paper from his coat pocket with list of names written on it. "I'm busting my ass Rick, we've got so many people to hit that we are making three or four drops this morning. I'm going to put you down for the second drop, meet me on 117th street between Park and Lexington at 6:30 a.m."

"Cool. Have you seen Donny, by the way?"

"I saw him about an hour ago, he was with Joe Frog. They were going to the spot on 112th. You know the two, always on the prowl for freaks."

"Did you tell Donny about the drop?"

"No, when I saw him I didn't know what was going to jump off."

"Alright, later Willie. I'm going to try and catch up with them to let Donny know what's up."

Once Rick arrived at the after spot he knew it was crowded by the number of cars double parked outside. The tiny smoke filled room was packed just as Rick knew it would be. Rick found Donny seated at a table in the corner with Joe Frog and several other hustlers. There seemed to be at least two women seated at the table for each man. Rick made room at the table for himself. Joe Frog passed the blow to Rick and he took a social hit before passing it right back.

"Yo Donny, I need to talk to you for a moment," Rick said. Both men excused themselves and went outside.

"Damn, that fuckin cigarette smoke was killing me. Anyway, everything is alright. I just left Willie, he's going to give us one key now and the other key in a few days," Rick informed Donny. "Since you are skied I'll make the meet. I'm going to cut half a key and hit our workers sometime before noon today, so you can hang out."

"Okay, that's cool with me," Donny replied. "I'll meet you at your house around one o'clock this afternoon."

"No, meet me at my hide away crib. That is where I will be living from now on," Rick said.

"You and Jenny broke up again." Donny responded, more of a statement than a question. Rick did not respond to Donny's comment.

"Look, I've got about an hour to kill before the meet, so I'm going to get something to eat," Rick said. They gave each other five and said later.

Rick drove downtown to the all night dinner on 33rd street 8th Avenue. Rick sat at a table in the restaurant with Prince. Prince happen to be the only Puerto Rican pimp in New York City so he claimed, and very successful.

"So what's been happening?" Prince asked.

"Ain't nothing." Rick replied, What's been happening with you?"

"You know how it goes with this pimpin.' A fellow got to stay down on his game."

"Not only with the pimpin'."

"Check that snow piece at the counter. The way she's been eyeballing you Rick, don't you think it's time to get paid."

"I'm a dope kid. Besides, I don't have the time to break her right now."

"Can you break her?" Prince challenged Rick.

"You just want to see if I got it down the way you gave it to me. You want to know if my game is still tight or if I'm slipping," Rick laughed. "Look, I've got half an hour before I have to be somewhere. I'd say it takes me less than 15 minutes to break the bitch," Rick boasted. Rick raised his hand and snapped his fingers.

"Say Ms. Lady, your place is right here," pointing at the seat in the booth next to him. As she gracefully eased from her seat at the counter Prince whispered something to Rick.

"She's interested but can you break her?"

"Say girl, the way you been looking at a fellow kind of makes him think you like him or something. Because you lookin' but it don't really mean a thing" Rick told her. "Now if you really like a fellow, then you would set it out." Rick was speaking her language, and he spoke it with that New York confidence.

She took the seat next to Rick sliding as close as possible. She opened her purse and pulled a large roll of bills out and placed it in Rick's hand. Rick put the roll of bills in his pocket without giving it a second glance.

"Look girl, this money ain't no promise to my pimpin. This money only gets you an opportunity to show me what you can do and if I am going to allow you to get with this pimpin. What are you called?" Rick asked her.

"Precious."

"Precious, we shall see just how precious," Rick stated. "Okay Precious, who were you with?"

"I was with Pretty Ed out of San Fran."

"Okay baby, I've got to call him and give him the news. I've got to let Mr. Pretty Ed know that you are with real pimpin now. Come on Precious, we are going to take a ride. Oh, and Mr. Prince, I'm game tight," Rick said with a big smile.

"I'll get with you later Prince," Rick said as he made his way out of the restaurant with Precious.

Rick started the car and he felt the pressure of time. He had to be at the drop in less than 20 minutes. "Look here Precious, you and I have a lot of talking to do. But right now I've got something very important to take care of. I have a suite at The Americana Hotel and I'm going to drop you off there. When I finish my business I am going to get back at you."

"However you want it daddy," she replied.

Rick parked the Caddy under the Park Avenue train trestle and walked across 117th street, it was 6:25 a.m. Rick was relieved when he saw familiar faces waiting for the drop.

"My brothers!" Rick greeted them.

"What's up Rick?" they replied. The excitement of, along with the anticipation and relief filled the moment.

"Man I'm glad to be getting this work."

"I know what you mean," Turk responded.

Rick leaned back on the sofa, his feet resting on the coffee table. Donny sat in the armchair lost in the world of soap operas on channel 7.

"Yo Donny, how can you watch that bullshit?" Rick asked not really looking for an answer.

"These are the shit," Donny replied.

"You know what I find funny? A few days ago I was with Reggie and Jesse in front of their building. They were kickin it about some bitches. I mean they were really into it so I am wondering who these bitches are. Then I find out they are talking about some damn soap opera hoes. All of you motherfuckers watch that bullshit. My mother and sister are hooked too."

"Oh shit, I almost forgot!" Rick said out of nowhere. "What's the number to the Americana?" Rick asked Donny.

CHAPTER NINE

Pimpin' Hard

R ICK DIALED THE number and waited for the hotel operator to answer.

"Yo Donny, I knocked a piece of snow last night, fine bitch. She's staying at the suite. I was supposed to call her at one o'clock; I hope she didn't break out. Yes operator, ring me suite 2454 please."

"Hello," Precious said in a soft sleepy voice.

"Precious, it's me Rick. Everything alright with you?" Rick asked her.

"Yes daddy, I was watching some television and resting. I'm going to get with you in a few, have the hotel send someone up to do your hair and nails. Order yourself something to eat from room service and charge everything to the suite," Rick informed her. "By the way, what size dress and shoes do you wear?"

"I take a 5/6 in a dress and a 6 1/2 shoe," Precious answered.

"I will be there in a minute."

"Okay," she replied so soft and sweet.

"What's up with that?" Donny asked once Rick hung up the phone.

"Ain't nothing, I was sitting in the restaurant after I left you at the spot and this pretty little white girl fell in love with a fellow. She gave me 23 hundred choosen money. So, if she's not going to be a problem, you know. If I don't have to stay down on her then she can pay a fellow."

"Here's the list of what I put out," Rick informed Donny. "It came to 20 thousand. I put half a key of pure in the safe with our money. Every time I look at that money it makes my dick get hard. That night I collected the 50 G's; I took it with me to Shemika's apartment. That money gave me a rush. I spread it across Shemika's bed, and you know. The prettiest sight I have ever seen was Shemika laying naked on top all that money."

"You're a funny motherfucker," Donny said, and they both laughed.

"Check this Donny, I'm going to wait for my sister to come home. Hopefully she will be here soon. She's at a rehearsal for a fashion show she's going to do. I want to ask her about a good woman's store where I can buy Precious an outfit for tonight. After that I going to the hotel and get some sleep before I take her out."

"You can handle everything tonight. The dope is already cut, all you have to do is make up the packages. Everybody should be finished and ready for something new by 10 o'clock tonight. Anyway, that's what time I told the workers to meet you at the bar," Rick informed Donny.

Rick hadn't thought much about the way he was dressed until he spotted the security team. They were white, one man, one woman, a loving couple that followed him around Saks Fifth Avenue. It was not that he was dressed poorly, white Pro-Ked sneakers, black pants, shirt and short black leather jacket, Harlem to a T. Rick knew if he were white and dressed the very same way the floor manager would be assisting him with his shopping.

Rick found the floor manager and asked that a sales person assist him with his selections. She was a pretty thing and richly dressed to match the décor of the store. Probably from Queens or Staten Island, Rick imagined. Or maybe she was from out of town and just here to knock down the doors at one the modeling agencies, she had kind of look. Rick flirted with her as he made several choices in dresses, suede and leather jackets and shoes. Rick also picked out accessories to go with each outfit. Rick made several selections for himself, all the while, the security team kept a close eye on him. Rick made remarks of it to the sales girl who attended his needs, it turned her face red with embarrassment. The security team should have realized by now that he was not a booster. Perhaps fake credit cards kept them on his trail and they needed to see how he would pay for such expensive merchandise.

The cashier rang up 27 hundred dollars in total sales. Rick pulled a five thousand dollar roll of hundred dollar bills from the inside pocket of his leather jacket. Rick could see the anguish written on the faces of the security team as he taunted them with the sight of all that money. Rick placed a folded 50 dollar bill in the sales girl's hand.

"I can't accept this," she started to protest.

"Look, I know with what they are paying you, you can use it. Besides, your charm and kindness goes beyond what the job calls for."

Rick placed the boxes under his arms and held the shopping bags, one in each hand. He walked directly over to where the security team stood and addressed them. "You dime store detectives have been following me for an hour. You've watched me from the moment I came into this store. What is it with you two? Don't you think a black man has enough money to shop in a store like this? You watched me and couldn't see that white bitch in the mink coat loading up. There was no lady in mink," Rick had just said so to add insult to their wounded pride. "Oh, before I leave don't you think you should check the money I used to pay for this stuff, it may be counterfeit." Rick said to further fuck with their heads.

Precious jumped up and down in sheer delight, then came over and sat on the bed next to Rick.

"Thank you daddy for all the gifts you gave me!" She got up and went to stand in front of the mirror again to admirer her new outfits. With rollers in her hair she tried on each outfit and asked Rick's opinion on how she looked in each. Rick knew by her reaction to his generosity, that her performance at work would replace all the money he had just spent.

Rick understood from the way Precious had chosen him it must have been all work and no play with Pretty Ed. It was for sure that Pretty Ed did not take the news well that he had been knocked for his bottom bitch. When Precious had once again stripped down to her panties and bra, Rick called her to come and sit on the bed next to him.

"Look here Precious; it's time for you to take a step up in your hoeing.

I know a thoroughbred like you brings ones' and twos' a night. Now that you are with me you've got to understand it not about playing a street game. It's about what you and I are going to be to one another so that we can get ahead in this man's world. I will show you life as you never dreamed it could be."

Rick noticed the blushing red color Precious' skin had turned and the far off look that had come to her blue eyes. Rick knew the look and realized the orgasmic state that now swept over her mental being and every fiber of her body. Rick knew her hopes as they called out to him.

"It is rare, Precious, that a man finds a lady that is indeed himself," Rick whispered softly in her ear.

Precious brought her head to rest on his knee, he ran his fingers through her hair as he continued to speak. "It is in you that I see a reflection of all that life was ever meant to be. You were a lost soul that awaited the hand that would guide it. I want you to know Precious, when you chose me it was the right choice. Look at me, if you can see no further, than you will know that all I have said is true."

"Look here Precious, I want to get some sleep and you've been in this hotel room since early this morning. If you want to take a walk or see a movie you go right ahead, but please be back so you can wake me at 10:30. All I need is four or five hours of sleep. When I wake up, I will take you out to dinner."

"I don't want to go out now, I will stay in until you are ready to take me out," she insisted. Precious massaged Rick's neck and back until he fell asleep.

Rick awaken, slowly easing his eyes slightly open. Precious was sitting on the bed naked watching him, thinking he was still asleep. Rick did not move or give any indication that he was wide awake. He watched Precious as she stared at what she thought was his sleeping form. The expression on her face was like that of a mother who had just seen her newborn child for the first time. Rick turned on the bed as though he were doing it in his sleep. His hand came to rest on her legs, which were tucked beneath her. Rick stroked her thigh as he pretended to be coming alive from a deep sleep.

Precious slid into Rick's embrace and he drew her close to him.

"I hope you are ready girl, because I going to show you the life like you have never seen it."

"I'm ready daddy," she replied.

Rick's head was resting on the pillow at the back of the tub. The soap bubbles covered him up to his neck. Precious climbed into the tub straddling him. She washed Rick's body with loving care, stealing a kiss whenever she thought her timing was right. Precious pulled the bath tub plug and turn the shower on. They both stood to rinse the soap off.

Rick was naked, laid across the bed and watched as Precious tried on several outfits to see which pleased him. Once he had decided which he liked best for tonight's event, he got up and placed his black pleated pants across the bed. Rick looked at the black suede shoes with the gray lizard skin bow tie across the front that sat on the table next to a pair of black full alligator shoes. Rick also considered a pair of black and gray lizard skin shoes. Rick laid his jewelry out as Precious took her hair out of rollers. Rick chose the black full alligator shoes to drape himself in all black. Rick knew his outfit would match the black mini evening gown and red fox jacket he had chosen for Precious to wear. Rick also knew these outfits would further claimed to the fact that Precious was now with him.

All eyes fixed on them as they walked across the lobby of the Americana Hotel. Precious turned in surprise and looked up at Rick as the chauffeur open the door to the Cadillac stretch limousine.

"I told you Ms. Lady, it's time for you to take a step up in life."

They rode in the quiet splendor of the limo, the soft sounds of Sam Cook's velvet voice eased them into a tranquil state of mind as he sang, *"I was born by the river... in a little tent, and just like the river I've been running ever since. It's been too hard living but I'm afraid to die... because I don't know what's up there beyond the sky, but I know a change is going to come, o--h yes it will"*.

Rick placed his hand on Precious' thighs, which were crossed. Precious opened her thighs slightly so Rick's hand could come to rest between both her thighs, then she laid her head to rest on his shoulder.

Precious stared across the table into Rick's eyes. She could careless that Mr. & Mrs. Dustin Hoffman along with dinner guests were at the next table, or that the room was filled with celebrities. Rick felt good like a man in his glory and his confidence was felt by Precious in every word he spoke.

The La Martinique dance floor was crowded and the music moved the people to its beat. Rick checked his watch to be sure of the hour then led Precious by the hand off the dance floor. They stood at the coat room waiting, Rick's demeanor had turned ice cold and Precious felt the danger he now radiated.

Rick said nothing as they sat in the limo. When Rick told the chauffeur to take them to 49th street between 8th and 9th Avenue, Precious shifted stiff in her seat. She knew the address well and now she understood the change in Rick's demeanor.

Rick told the chauffeur to pull the limo onto the freight elevator and blow the horn twice. The elevator came to a stop on the third floor and the limo pulled off into what could have been the world's largest store for luxury cars.

Rick followed Precious' eye movement as they walked across the garage floor. Rick knew Precious would be searching for Pretty Ed's car, but never once did he let her know he had pinned her unconscious action. Rick knew now that Pretty Ed was not inside the afterhour's club.

Rick entered the elegant room with the mink draped over his shoulder and Precious on his arm. Rick sized the large room up quickly and eased into a vantage point. Rick sat Precious next to him where she could see everyone entering the club and where he could watch her eyes without her knowing. Rick ordered Dom perignon and spoke with several of the players he knew and a few he didn't know as they passed his table. Prince came over and took a seat at the table with Rick and Precious.

"My brother," they greeted one another. Count and Albert, two pimps out of Los Angeles joined Rick at his table, each with their bottom bitches. Rick ordered several more bottles of champagne, but he never took a sip.

Albert told some bullshit half ass pimp tail about stealing bitches that some jive time want to be pimps brought back from Minnesota. They all laughed and joked and were sincerely having a good time. The champagne and blow flowed freely. Rick passed on everything.

Precious looked up just as Pretty Ed entered the club and Rick noticed the change in her body language. At the same time, Pretty Ed had also spotted Precious. Pretty Ed stepped to the table in such a manner that everyone at the table became silent. The silence swept the room. Rick knew this was going to be a test to see whose game was the strongest.

Pretty Ed who was known for his vicious style made the first move. With total disrespect for Rick and the other players at the table, Pretty Ed spoke directly to Precious. "You had your fun bitch with this wannabe pimp? Now it's time to come the fuck on home where you belong."

Rick said nothing as he sized Pretty Ed up and everyone else waited to see what Rick's move would be. Pretty Ed was confident that he had the situation under control and began a verbal assault on Rick. Rick still had not said a word, he just looked on as Pretty Ed ran his mouth.

What Rick really wanted to do was kick Pretty Ed's little faggot ass but that would be totally out of character for a man with his style. Rick stood slowly, he let the mink fall from his shoulders.

"Mr. Pretty Ed," Rick addressed him. "So, you come over to my table, you insulted me and my lady in front of my friends."

"Bitch ain't no lady, she's a hoe and she belongs to me." Pretty Ed spat out. If you don't know a hoe from a lady than give the bitch some money so she can pay me." Pretty Ed was dressing Rick down.

"Okay Mr. Pretty Ed, it's about the pimpin. Look around you, these are pimps and players. I don't know what the fuck you are," Rick responded.

"Let me lay it out for you Mr. Ed," Rick said with venom in his every word. "I'll give you five minutes with the bitch, if you can come up with her she's yours. That's what the pimpin game is about Mr. Ed." Rick deliberately said in loud voice for all to hear. The crowd echoed Rick's sentiments. Rick had made a strong statement and Pretty Ed had his back up against the wall. If he took the five minutes and blew he knew he would loose his stable of other hoes'.

Rick knew any man who was backed into a corner was dangerous. Rick knew also that he had to crush his opponent mentally.

"Check this Mr. Pretty Ed, I broke this bitch, are you going to stand here in front of all these people and tell me you'll accept a hoe hoping she'll get some money or do you have a stable of broke bitches? What kind of pimpin is it that you do Mr. Pretty Ed?" The crowd laughed and Rick knew he had shamed Pretty Ed. He also knew that Pretty Ed would be making his move some time right about now to save face.

"You ain't no pimp nigger, I ain't never heard of or seen you before!" Pretty Ed said, his voice cutting through the silence of the crowd.

"You're right, you ain't heard of me but I still peeled you for your bottom bitch," Rick stated.

Pretty Ed was infuriated, "You faggot motherfucker, and you won't be leaving here tonight with that bitch!"

Just as Pretty Ed and two of his riding partners made their move pulling guns, a man stepped from the crowd and placed a 45 at the back of Pretty Ed's head. Another two men pulled modified M-16's from under their coats. The crowd stepped back, a deadly silence filled the room.

Rick's man with the 45 on Pretty Ed's head patted him down and removed a 25 automatic from his inside coat pocket.

"You are a very stupid man," Rick said. "You see, I knew you were a got damn fool so I came ready. You want to be on some stupid shit, so I had to get on some real gangster shit. I'm telling you straight up Mr. Ed, this bitch is mine and if you ever get in my face about anything they won't be able to find you or your faggot friends. I'm here, just like these other good people to do a little socializing and kick the pimpin. Now, you are welcome to stay and do the same or you can make it a night you will regret for the rest of your short life."

The crowd parted like the red sea as Pretty Ed and his two remaining hoes along with his riding partners turned to walk out. The crowd remained silent for a brief moment that seemed like forever. A voice was heard coming from the crowd; "Nigger weren't really no pimp, no how." Then another voice broke the silence, "Gorilla pimpin nigger don't know shit about the game. You give pimpin a bad name!" The crowd came back to life and the night went on and the legend of Rick's pimpin was born.

Rick's gunmen eased out almost unnoticed. Rick's attention returned to Precious and his friends at the table as they kicked it about the sporting life. Several players stopped by the table to acknowledge Rick's pimpin. Rick could tell by the looks he received that some of their hoes were ready to make him their choice.

Rick excused himself from the table and walked over to the bar acknowledging all who greeted him in the fame of this night. Rick spoke with a brown skin kid who sat at the bar unnoticed by just about everyone. When Rick returned to the table, he told Precious that it was time for them to go. He said 'later' to his friends.

Rick told the chauffeur to drive over to Madison Avenue than up to 97th street, then to come back over to Fifth Avenue and back down to 85th street and to park in front of the museum. Once they had reached their destination Rick got out and walked over to the man who stood at the foot of the museum steps. This was the same man he had spoken with at the bar in the after hour spot just before leaving.

"Hey Tony," Rick greeted him.

"Rick my man, did you like the way my people worked tonight?"

"Yeah Tony, everything was cool."

"So you alright now? Or do you want to keep one of my people with you?"

"Nah, I'm alright, so what you want, for me to take care of the bill now or what?" Rick asked.

"Come on Rick, we grew up together; I know you're good for the money. I'll catch up with you in the projects, enjoy the rest of the night, business can wait."

"Okay my brother. You want some of this blow?"

"No, I'm going home my wife is waiting. Besides, I've got to go to work in another three or four hours."

"Okay Tony, later." They gave each other five.

Rick climbed into the limo and watched Tony get in the rented car with two men inside. As soon as Tony pulled off two other rented cars followed, each with three men in them. Rick knew Tony would come well prepared to take care of business. Rick had always known that about

Tony since the days when he had been warlord in one of the neighbor-hood gangs.

Rick asked the chauffeur to drive slowly down Fifth Avenue and to pull over once they reached 71st street. Rick and Precious got out and Rick told the chauffeur to follow as they walked. It was a cold winter night though they paid little mind to it. Rick stopped and looked at the high rise buildings that lined one side of Fifth Avenue.

"You see these building Precious, in them live some of the riches peo-ple in the world. They sit in their fancy apartments and look out over the beauty of Central Park. What makes them so different from the people on the other side of the park where I come from? These people here make the laws that we break. They own the factories where our parents earned a living so that we survived. One word from anyone of these so called movers and shakers sets the moral standard for others to live by. Yet they think nothing of meeting women in your line of work in some out of the way place. They give you two or three thousand dollars to piss and shit on them for 45 minutes. Their wives chase a dream of a young black stud that has nine inches or better. They suck a black man's dick behind close doors like it is the salvation of their life. But they have the nerves to look down on him in a social setting. These people are the fantasy of every poor man, woman and child on this planet. It is them that motivate us to do what we do." Rick placed his arm around Precious' shoulders and resumed a slow stroll down Fifth Avenue.

"You know Rick, you are the first man that I have ever felt I could re-ally talk too. You make me feel so at ease with myself. It's like I can tell you what I feel and you will truly understand," Precious said in a soft child like innocence. "Oh, I do understand. If we are to be anything to each other, each must understand the others needs," Rick said sincerely. We must also share the same dreams and have trust in one another."

"My real name is Rita Brogan," Precious said as if a great weight had been lifted from her shoulders.

"Rita, I am pleased to know you," Rick smiled.

"I come from a small town in Oklahoma," Precious continued to say.

"Choctaw Oklahoma, the kind of place where everyone knows everyone and their business. When I was a younger I always dreamed of becoming a fashion model. My father's brother would bring me all of the latest fashion magazines and tell me that I was just as pretty if not prettier than the models in the magazines. He would encourage me and tell me when I got older I should give it a try. When I turned about 11 or so, he started to touch me. He was my own uncle! On my thirteenth birthday he fucked me. Some birthday present, huh? This went on until I made up my mind to run away. I ran to California in search of my almost forgotten dream. Here I was, 15 years old, when I ran into a so-called pimp who said he'd show me the good life. The only good life he knew was shooting up the money I brought home."

"Then, then came Pretty Ed with his sweet talk, nice house, car and clothes. I was with him from the time I was 16 up until yesterday when I saw you in that restaurant, I am 21 years old now. I have been selling my pussy for what seems like all of my life. I made millions for Pretty Ed and hated every minute of it. For the first time in my life, I don't mine selling my pussy and I am going to make plenty of money for you Rick. I will do whatever you tell me, Daddy and be happy while I am doing it."

Rick and Precious walked bound by the words they spoke. Before either Rick or Precious realized it they had walked the 20 or so blocks to the hotel. And once again the steel gray dawn rose over the city to greet Rick and those who shared a similar passion for a lifestyle. The nightlife known only to those in New York City.

The group of young men stood on the building next to the Oasis. Their conversation was serious. The bosses were awaiting another shipment of tragic magic. There was enough of a supply to last for the next week or so, hopefully. They all hoped something would jump off in that time.

Rick and Donny join the group of men on the stoop. They greeted each and started to talk business.

"Yo! I'm not going to be able to give you that other key right now," Jesse told Rick.

"Damn! I wish I had known that about two days ago. I've been giving my workers loose dope when I should have been baggin it up," Rick sighed.

"I'm sorry, it's not going to fuck you up or anything right?"

"Nah, everything is cool," Donny responded.

"I've got money for you in the truck of the car," Rick informed Jesse.

"You finish the whole package?"

"No," Donny answered. "We've still got more than a quarter key of pure left."

"That will hold us for a few days if we bag it up," Rick said.

"By that time I should have something else," Jesse assured Rick and Donny and the rest of the crew. "By the way, yo Ricky. I heard you are pimpin' now."

"No, not really. I've got this pretty little thing that likes a fellow that's all."

"What kind of money you get from that shit?" Jerome asked.

"Check this out, she's only been with me three or four days and she gave me sixty-five hundred."

"That's not bad," Jesse said.

"I know but she's busting her ass to show me what she can do," Rick told them. "And besides, I can't really get with it at the moment. I've got to show on the set so those other motherfuckers know she's with somebody that is somebody. A few days ago I got into it with the fool I copped her from. It's a different kind of lifestyle. I either have to get all the way down with the pimpin and give up scrambling or figure out a way to make them both work. But it's for damn sure I am not going to give up scrambling."

Donny and Rick sat in Mr. Welles, it was noticeably empty. Then again, it was much too early for the hustling crowd to be drifting in.

"I spoke with the lawyer today," Donny said.

"Yeah, so what's the story?" Rick asked.

"He thinks he can get me in an out patient drug program."

"That beats the fuck out of jail, don't it?"

"Yeah, it's funny though. I kicked on my own and now the courts' want me to go to a program for treatment. In fact, I had kicked before I got busted. The only thing good about it is that we caught a break with no jail time."

"So Rick, what's up with Rita?" Donny asked.

"The lawyer has taken care of the lease on the apartment and I spoke with that Italian kid Vinny down on Mulberry street. He made an appointment for Rita to see some big shot bitch named Blanche. Blanche runs a house that deals with the UN crowd and the high rollers on Madison Avenue. So everything looks good," Rick said.

"Once Rita is set in the apartment and she'll start to work in a day or so. She will make just as much if not more turning one trick as she did from turning five or six. It's costing a small fortune to hook up her apartment, plus new clothes and the whole shit. But it's worth it. It works out for me too. Now that she's not on the streets I don't have to show on the set for the jokers to see. She's got her work cut out so she can meet payment on all of the bills, but I know she can handle it."

"Check this out Donny," Rick said, "Let's bag up that eight."

"Okay, that's cool with me," Donny replied. "You want to do it right now?"

"No," Rick replied. "I was going to do it in the morning and get Tonya and Latisha to help."

"You ain't slick Rick, you just want to get your dick sucked."

"Nah, I'm not fuckin with them like that. But you know what beats the fuck out of me? Their mother doesn't like me. She thinks I'm the cause for them fuckin around. If it wasn't for me both those bitches would be selling pussy on Broadway somewhere just to take care of their habits. Shit, it was my money that paid for the program Tonya was in," Rick said.

"Yeah, I know that," Donny commented.

"That bitch only lasted two day in the program," Rick continued. "She came back with that bullshit story about the counselor being on her back, two fuckin days! Can you believe that shit, Donny? The way she cried and begged for the money to get in the damn program I really believed she was with it."

Rick sat in the comfort of the upper eastside apartment; he liked what Rita had done with it. He also liked the way Rita fit it or it fits her. Rita looked good prancing around in the lace teddy and high heel shoes as she fixed him a sandwich. Rita had killer legs and a fat ass.

"Yo girl, you sure you ain't got no black in you?" Rick teased.

"Not that I know Daddy," she replied and asked,"Why?"

"Your ass girl, in all of my young life I ain't never seen a white girl with an ass like yours. Come on, you can tell me, your great granddaddy or something was black," Rick joked. Rita blushed and made sure the view of her ass was even more tantalizing as she strolled over to the refrigerator to get him something to drink. Little did she know that it was really her legs that were driving him crazy.

Rita waited patiently for Rick to finish eating before she eased on the sofa next to him.

"Daddy."

"Yeah?"

"Daddy, I've got this trick, he owns a modeling agency." Rick sat up and used the remote control to turn the sound all the way down on the television.

"I know this is going to be good girl or you wouldn't be taking so much time to tell me about it, so go ahead, and talk."

"He told me I would make a good model. Is he for real or does he just wants you to bring your prices down for him? I think he is for real Daddy."

Rita got up and ran over to the cedar desk in the foyer and brought a manila envelope back. "He wants me to sign this contract, but he said to have a lawyer look it over first."

"So what's the catch?" Rick asked. "I know there is something you are not telling me woman."

"Well," Rita hesitated, "He wants me to be his mistress and go to Paris with him. That's where his modeling agency is," Rita said in a whisper that Rick could barely hear.

"You have only been in this apartment for a month or so, whose going to pay the rent on the rest of the lease, in case you have to come back here? I don't want this place."

"Daddy," Rita cut in, "This could be the one break I need to realize my dream of becoming a model."

"It's not that girl, you've got to make sure everything is on the up before you go running off," Rick told her.

"Then I can go Daddy?"

"I didn't say that. Once all the details are worked out and everything is everything, we'll see. You know that if you go it will be goodbye for us."

"No it wont Daddy, I could never say goodbye to you."

The cool spring night showed very little intention of turning into anything other than more cool nights. Rita sat close to Rick as the car glided along the Grand Central Parkway headed towards Kennedy Airport. Rita was going to Paris and two nights ago they had made love for the first time, which led to two days of uninterrupted bliss. Rick could still hear her whispering, "Rick, I love you. You have made me what I am and have given me more than I had ever hoped for from any man. You have my love and undying affection".

Rick threw the coins in the box at the toll booth on the Triboro Bridge. The empty echo sound made by the coins going in the machine reminded him of the emptiness he felt for a woman who had shared a brief moment of his life. Rick put on a tape by Gene Chandler, "A Man's Temptation", and he thought she was truly a man's temptation. Rick listened to the words that seemed to go right to the center of his emotions as he worked the luxury machine in and out of traffic headed west going across 125th street. *"One more time to test the will power of the,* Gene Chandler sang. *This feeling that I hold now... just won't let me be.* Rick's feelings swept over his entire being, this woman he thought. *Sing it, Gene. ... won't leave me along... she's going to ruin my happy home... with a man's temptation".* How smooth and easy Gene's voice sounded. *Well I've got another back home... who is the beat in my heart. I never thought no one else... could tear us apart. To each other we had been so true. Until along comes a lover like you... with a man's temptation. I know I've got to be strong... I've got to fight this all alone. So afraid for what I must do... I've got to curve my wants for you... well I've got a feeling telling me... let your heart be your heart be your guide".*

"Gene Chandler, you are a bad motherfucker!" Rick said out loud and wondered why Gene had dropped out of sight.

Rick lost all thought of Gene Chandler but still felt the emptiness of Rita's absence as he pulled the machine in front of the Shalimar. Rick was greeted by as he greeted the crew.

"Yo Jesse, Willie, Crime, what's up?"

"Ain't nothing Rick," they replied.

"Yo Jesse, what do I owe you?"

"Forty-five thou," Jesse said.

"I've got 50 in the truck, so take five G's off my next bill. I can still get the three joints?"

"Yeah, but I'm going to give you one now and the other two as soon as I get the new thing. I should have it by day after tomorrow. Anyways, before you finish the one joint you will have the other two."

"Okay that sounds good to me," Rick replied. "What time is the drop?"

"Meet Willie at 3:30 on 144th street Amsterdam, there is a bar right on the corner," Jesse informed them.

"Yo Jesse, has Donny been up this way?"

"No, but he must be going to show because that Spanish girl Joyce is inside waiting on him," Willie told Rick.

Joyce sat at the bar laughing with Leechie and Rick knew that Leechie was trying to get her to go off with him. Rick walked over and sat down on the stool next to Joyce, she turned placing her hand on his leg.

"This is who I've been waiting for," Joyce told Leechie. *Me?* Rick thought, *why?*

"Do you know Rick?" Joyce asked Leechie.

"Yeah, we know each other well, what's up Leechie?" Rick said.

"Ain't nothing my brother," Leechie replied.

"You seen Donny?" Rick asked them both.

"No, not tonight," they replied. Rick got up to leave and Joyce asked, "Are you going back to the projects?"

"I can give you a ride home," Leechie said. Rick did not respond to Joyce's question. Rick waited to see what Joyce would tell Leechie. Joyce politely informed Leechie she would be riding with Rick. Rick told Leechie later and walked out of the bar. Rick told Joyce he would let her know when he was ready to break out. Rick was talking with George Fulellen when Joyce came out side. "I'm ready whenever you are," Joyce told Rick.

"Yo Rick, what's up with that?" Willie asked, "You cutting in on your man Donny?"

"We're partners," Rick replied. "And sometimes we share."

Rick waited for the light to change on 110th street 7th Avenue. He was going to take the drive through Central Park to 59th street to save time. He wondered where Donny could be as he listened to Joyce giving him every opportunity a man would ever need to make a play for a lady.

"Look Joyce," Rick finally said, "I'm going to give you a shot for us to really get tight. I know you can dig where I'm coming from but right now I've got something that need to be taken care of. It's important that I find Donny."

Rick looked everywhere he could think of in Manhattan to find Donny. It was getting late so he decided to try the Motor Inn in the Bronx, no Donny. Damn, he needed the fuckin keys before he went to the drop.

"Joyce I've got a little problem right now so I'm going to drop you off at your building."

"Maybe I can help if you tell me what the problem is."

"You just may be able to help at that. Who's in your apartment right now?" Rick asked her.

"No one, my father is spending the weekend with his girlfriend."

"Okay, that's cool." Rick said more to himself than Joyce. "I need to bring a package to your house for a few hours. Is that all right with you?"

"Sure it is," Joyce replied. "If you walk me up I will give you the keys so you can let yourself in when you come back."

Rick looked down at the brown bag on the coffee table. He looked up to catch a glimpse of an old movie on television, and across the living room to where Joyce sat in her panties and bathrobe. Rick really wanted to get some sleep but he dare not because of the package. He didn't really want to get skied even though it would help him stay awake.

Rick studied the frustration on Joyce's face as he opened a bill with some blow in it, he took a hit. He laughed to himself, never had he seen a woman worked so hard trying to entice a man into her panties. '*Woman*,' he thought, *if you want me to fuck you so bad just come right out and ask me to fuck you instead of playing this bullshit game with me.*

Rick took another hit then called Joyce to come sit next to him. He got an eye full as she rose from her chair. The naked beauty of her thick shapely legs set in motion a feeling deep in his loin. The creamy tint of her skin color highlighted the contour of her legs and it was all over for him.

It was 7:30 in the morning when Joyce came back from the restaurant with breakfast for two and Donny in tow. "Look who I found," she proclaimed.

"Yo, what's up Donny? I've been looking all over for you!"

"I stayed with Mia last night. That is the last place in the world I would have thought to look for you," Rick said.

"Sit down my brother we've got business to talk about. Will you excuse us?" Rick told Joyce.

"I will go watch some TV in my room while you talk business," Joyce nodded.

"I see Joyce finally gave you some," Donny commented, "She terrible ain't she?"

"Yeah, but I served her. Anyway, we've got more important things to talk about. I've got one key in that bag and Jesse said we could get the other two later."

"We can put half of this out today and the rest day after tomorrow," Donny suggested.

"Okay, that's cool. So are you going to take care of putting it out today?"

"Yeah, I got it. Besides, you made the drop so the least I can do is handle this. What are you going to do?"

"I'm going to stay here and get some sleep. You can pick me up around one, okay?"

"Yeah, that's cool. I should have the work out on the streets by then. But you going to sleep don't fool yourself. You know you are going to tap that ass again."

"As good as Joyce slings it I may hit it one more time before I go to sleep." They both laughed.

Rick leaned against the fence of the playground area next to his mother's building. It was a cool spring night. He was kickin' it with Benny and William. He also wondered where Donny could be. It had been two days since he last saw him at Joyce's house. He knew, though that Donny must be alright. It was just this morning that Donny had collected the money and given out a new package to the workers. Rick thought that he most likely was laid up in some hotel with a new freak or an old one.

Rick had that eerie feeling he always got just before an ambush or being hit by a rocket attack. He displaced his feelings, however, as being too much blow.

"Check this out," Rick said, "I've got to go take care of some business. I will see you after it's done."

"We'll ride with you," William said.

"Nah, I can't take you with me. I should be back in about two hours. If Donny shows up, tell him I went uptown to pay some of our nut."

The knot tightens in Rick's stomach as he sat in the car watching the building. He wondered if the police had the apartment staked out. He didn't trust the superintendent of the building or his bum ass son. They may have set him up with the police. Whatever it may be, he felt the danger. It had all of his senses on high alert.

CHAPTER TEN

Take The Money and Run

RICK OPENED THE glove compartment and hit the switch to release the truck lock. He stepped quickly to the rear of the car and lifted the lid of the compartment that held the spare tire. Rick took a look around before taking the 45 from the compartment and placing it in the waistband of his pants.

Rick took the steps of the old tenement building slowly, working his way to the third floor. He listened closely for any sign of trouble before inserting the keys in the locks. He closed the door behind him and pulled the 45 from his waistband. He got down low and began to work his way through the apartment in the dark. He checked the living room, working his way to the far corner. Once he reached the corner, he got even lower, then hit the light switch on the lamp turning it on, then off, as fast as possible. Once he was sure the living room was clear, he worked his way in the dark towards the bedroom. He was now one hundred percent sure that something was wrong.

Rick pulled the hammer back on the 45 and started a slow, deliberate crawl across the bedroom floor. He used the cocked 45 as a probe to check under the bed and behind the curtains that hung over the window. He worked in the darkness checking the bathroom and kitchen. Still uncertain as to what the problem may or may not be, Rick worked his way back to the bedroom. In total darkness he made his way over to the night table. He took the lamp from the table and placed it on the floor. Rick used the bed for cover before hitting the lamp switch. The bedroom lit up and alarms went off in Rick's head. His eyes focused on the closet doors, the one place he had not checked. At this moment, the doors of the closet seemed to be ten times larger in the image of his mind.

Rick swung the doors to the closet open, the bare emptiness of the closet made his bowels loose to the point where he almost went in his pants. The shock of the empty spaced clouded his vision. The eerie reality, the electric shockwave swayed his body back and forth. The pain of reality knocked him to his knees.

Rick peered at the gaping hole in the rear of the closet wall and at the space where the safe once stood through the water in his eyes. He leaped to his feet and raced out of the apartment. He ran down the stairway touching only one step of each landing. Rick made his way to the basement in record time. He banged on the superintendent's door screaming, "Open the door you motherfucker!" When he received no reply to his ranting and raving, he blasted the three locks that held the door with the 45.

Rick, in all his frustration, spent all of the rounds, and then threw the 45 up against the rear basement wall. Rick raced through the basement alleyway and got back in his car. He peeled out and had to stop for a red light behind another car at the corner. Rick blew the horn franticly to the other driver to pull over and let him pass. The other driver became aggravated and started to yell out the window at Rick. Rick stepped out from the car to approach the other driver. However, once the other driver got a look at the expression on Rick's face, he pulled right over.

When Rick was a block or so away from the Shalimar, he stopped the car and doubled parked between Lenox and 7th Avenue on 121st street. Rick needed a moment to get his composure back. He also need to clear his head so he could think. Suddenly, Rick just realized that he had not locked the apartment door. *'What the fuck, the only thing left worth shit was the T.V. and stereo.'*

Rick broke out in a cold sweat and was finding it hard to catch his breath. He hit the switch, rolling all the car windows down and laid his head back on the seat's headrest. His response to the situation was more out of anger than any other emotion. *How could this be happening, it's the worse nightmare come true. Maybe Donny had moved the safe*, he thought. It was just a wish and dream to bring some sense to the madness going through his head.

Four hundred and thirty thousand dollars, plus a half key of pure. What the fuck are we going to do now? Oh shit, the other stash, just maybe, Rick thought. He turned the machine on and pulled off. He stopped at the Shalimar for a brief moment to speak with anyone he saw from the crew. He found Willie.

"Yo Willie, have you seen Donny?"

"No, not for a few days," Willie replied.

"If you see him, tell him to find me because we have a problem. Tell him that it's an emergency."

"What's up Rick?"

"I'm not sure," Rick replied, "because I don't know how bad it is yet. All I do know is that we just took a hell of a loss."

"Have you told Jesse about it?" Willie asked with concern.

"Nah, you are the first person I've talked to since I found out the bad news."

Rick pulled the machine into the block, the street was quiet. A few people milled around, nothing seemed to be out of order. Rick took the steps slowly to the top floor, not really sure of what he would find.

The apartment was in order, so Rick opened the cabinet draw and found the days receipts. The attached note indicated that it was 12 thousand dollars. Rick picked up the phone and dialed a number.

"Hello Ma."

"Yeah Ricky," she replied.

"Sorry to wake you Ma."

"That's okay, I was just sitting in the chair, and you know me. I'm supposed to be watching TV, but I was sound asleep."

"Ma, do me a favor please. Look out the back window and see if Benny and William are out there. If they are, tell them not to go anywhere, I am on my way."

"Okay, hold on for a minute while I go check for you." Rick heard the click of the bedroom receiver when his mother picked it up.

"Hello, Rick?"

"Yeah Ma, I'm still here."

"I told them what you said."

"Okay Ma, thank you."

"Are you coming here tonight Ricky?"

"I don't think so."

"Okay, be careful then and I will see you tomorrow."

"Okay Ma, good night."

Rick led his two friends to the basement were he retrieved the 45.

"We will come back for the super," Rick told his friends pointing at the door where he had emptied his gun earlier. They took the steps quietly making their way to the third floor. Once they had reached the apartment door, Rick pushed it open.

"Damn Rick," Benny said, "you must have been in a big rush not to have locked the door."

"I told you I broke the fuck out in a rage."

All three men drew their guns, not really certain as to why, maybe, only because of the suspense this moment held. Rick turned on the lights and the three of them checked the apartment out. They stood in front of the closet, their eyes glued to the handy work of the intruder or intruders.

"That's where the safe was bolted to the floor," Rick informed them.

"Whoever did this knew they had plenty of time to work," William said as he checked the bolt holes.

"Who live in the apartment next door?" Benny asked.

"No one," Rick replied, "it's been vacant for as long as we have had this apartment."

William aimed the flashlight beam through the hole in the wall and around the empty room of the other apartment. The room was cluttered with junk and it was easy to see the fresh prints in the dust were the safe had been wheeled across the floor.

"Benny you go around to the front of that apartment, me and William will go through the hole in the wall," Rick commanded. William and Rick checked the empty apartment carefully before they opened the door to let Benny in. It was clear to them all that the safe had not been opened in this apartment. The dust trail showed the safe being wheeled out the front door.

"It had to be the super." Benny said. "The locks on the door are not broken."

"Or, it could have been his punk ass son," Rick said.

"Well let's go find out," William suggested.

They listened closely for any sounds of life coming from basement apartment before knocking on the door. When they received no response, William kicked the door trying to push it open. The door held fast by one of the three locks still in place. The other locks had been blown off by Rick's gunfire.

"Stand back!" William warned and opened fires on the remaining lock. The door flew open from the impact of the shot. Rick and Benny rushed the apartment with guns drawn. They found the apartment empty, but the tools that lay in the center of the kitchen floor were enough evidence to convince the trio that they had found the guilty party.

"Let's get the fuck out of here!" Benny said, "Someone may have called the cops because of the shots."

"Let's tear the place up before we leave," William said.

"Nah," Rick replied, "Look in all the drawers. Take all the pictures, letters, bills, and any addresses you can find." The three men filled a medium size cardboard box they had found with all the items of interest.

The red light flashed in the front window of the dark green Plymouth Fury. It was the police pulling them over. Rick brought the machine to a stop just off the corner.

"Yo William, Benny, just show them your badges. Get out and do it, don't let them walk up on the car. They might start asking questions about the stuffs in the box."

Once Benny and William showed their badges, the plain clothes cops eased off.

"Is the driver a correction officer?" asked the slightly built white police.

"No, he just got out of the army. He took the test at our suggestion and is waiting to be called."

"You know why we pulled you over?" the other officer asked.

"No," William replied.

"You ran a red light back there."

"I'm sorry; I honestly did not realize it," Rick responded.

"I'm going to let you go being brothers under the badge. Be careful and watch the lights."

Benny and William sat in the living room. The TV was on, however, they paid no attention to it as they went through the contents of the cardboard box. Rick was in the kitchen talking on the telephone. He hung up and took the 12 thousand dollars from the draw. Rick peeled off two thousand; he made two rolls out of the remaining 10 thousand placing a roll in each jacket pocket. Rick walked into the living room and took a seat with his friends.

"What's our next move?" William asked.

"I don't know yet," Rick replied. "I've got to think about it. Did either of you come across something I can use to find these motherfuckers?"

"We don't really know. There are some addresses that can be checked out. The Bronx, lower Manhattan, plus one address from Shelby North Carolina, where ever the fuck that is," Benny said.

"We can try to match some of these females picture with the addresses we found in Manhattan and the Bronx," William told Rick.

"At least we've got something. Now I've got to give Donny and Jesse the bad news. Here, this is for you," Rick said as he handed each man a thousand dollar roll of bills.

"What's this for?" they both asked.

"It's for your assistance with the police and your other help tonight."

"Come on Rick, what the fuck's wrong with you man?" William asked. "We helped you because you're our man. Take this money back," and they both handed him their roll of bills.

"Since you came off Rick, we ain't never wanted for nothing," Benny said.

"You need help now, so whatever it's going to be we are down with you. Ain't that right William?"

"That's right," William responded.

"Okay, if you won't let me give you this money at least take a hundred a piece to cop something to eat with or buy some bullets."

Rick and Jesse sat on the rail of the building just across the street from Jesse's mother's building as they talked. Benny and William sat in the car parked right in front of Jesse's mother's building waiting on Rick and Jesse to decide that the next move would be.

"Damn Ricky, I don't know, that's fucked up. I'm having some money problems myself. But I will do the best I can for you. Give me what you can on what you owe and I will give you another package when I get the new thing," Jesse said.

"I'll give you this ten thousand, plus the five that makes 15 thousand. So we owe you another ten thousand," Rick explained.

"Where's Donny?"

"I don't know! I haven't seen him for two days."

"You don't think he had anything to do with this?"

"Nah, half the money was his anyway and I trust him with my life. I am more worried about the super and his son having knocked him off because he was in the apartment. Besides, I know that it was the super and his son working this by themselves. You still want to go over there and take a look at the place?" Rick asked Jesse.

"I don't know Ricky, the way you said you shot the place up it may be crawling with cops right now."

"Who's going to call the cops," Rick said, as more of a statement than a question. "Certainly not the super."

"Yeah, you are right about that. Alright, I'll ride with you."

Rick and Jesse climbed in the back seat of the car and Benny pulled off. Rick gave Jesse the ten thousand once they where rolling. They came to a stop where they could sit and watch the building to make sure it was safe. William got out and went to check the building to make sure it was safe so that the others would not be walking into a trap.

"Everything is cool," William told them when he returned to the car. "The super's apartment is the same way we left it."

Jesse and Rick stood looking at the space where the safe once was.

"Damn Ricky, why did you have all of your money in one place?"

"We were waiting for our new safe to come. You know it has to come from Japan," Rick replied. "It's going to take a pro to open the safe them mother fucker stole."

"Yeah, that may be true Ricky, but you know them motherfuckers got that safe some where in Long Island or New Jersey where they can work on it."

"Well, I'm going to find them even if it takes a lifetime," Rick proclaimed.

Rick and Donny checked every address they had found amongst the papers taken from the super's apartment. Donny had finally shown up. He had been lying up with a new freak. He was just as shook by the bad news that would forever change their lives.

Rick and Donny sat in the shadows so as not to tip their hand. Their endless search had become more frustrating as the days went by. Rick knew from the search and destroy mission in Vietnam, that the enemy could be most elusive.

"Look here Donny, we've got to put this search off for awhile and get down to our other business. These motherfuckers will show up, but right now we have to get bank. We started with nothing before so we can do it again. Right or wrong, we can do this shit again my brother," Rick stated, trying to convince Donny in the spirit of the moment.

It was a cool damp spring night. It had been raining off and on all day. Rick had not seen Donny for a few days but he knew he had been hanging out with Joe Frog. Rick had spent the day with Shemika, mostly passing time in her apartment. Now he was waiting at the Shalimar for Jesse to show. Something felt out of place. Rick had come to know this feeling well, he just could not pin point what was causing it at the moment.

Jesse pulled up, double parking in front of the bar. He and Willie both got out of the car. Jesse, walking passed Rick asked if he had any of the money he owed. Rick, barely had a chance to answer before the doors closed and both Jesse and Willie went inside the bar. *Damn, I wonder what the problem could be?* Rick thought to himself.

Jesse came back out of the bar and asked Rick to step off to the side so they could talk.

"Who picked that last package up Ricky, you or Donny?" Jesse asked.

"I picked it up. Why?" Rick responded.

"That makes you responsible for the money then," Jesse told him.

"Hold it, you know that Donny is my partner, so we both are responsible for it. I don't see what the problem is. You know we are good for it."

"When was the last time you saw Donny?"

"I don't know. It was maybe yesterday or the day before, why?"

"You sure you didn't see him today?"

"What's the problem with Donny? You said we could give it to you when we got the other key." Rick was puzzled.

"I saw Donny on the Avenue this morning in front of Nat's bar."

"So?"

"I sent my man over to tell him that I wanted to speak to him about the money. His message was like *fuck me, I'll get my money when he gets it,*" Jesse's statement took Rick by surprise.

"What?" Rick was speechless. He did not know what else he could say. "I find that hard to believe. Maybe your man got the message wrong."

"It's not important, but I am getting a lot of feedback from the grapevine, Jesse continued. "Donny feels like because he made money for me that he shouldn't have to pay this nut because of your problems. There are too much talks on the streets for everybody to be lying. Your man is letting motherfuckers who don't have nothing to do with our business souped him up. I want you to find Donny and meet me later so we can talk about this other package." Jesse told Rick.

"Yeah okay, that's cool," Rick replied.

Rick looked everywhere he could think of to locate Donny, sometimes just missing him by a few minutes or so. Rick ran into Jesse again before he had a chance to see Donny.

"Yo Ricky, where's your man?" Jesse asked.

"I ain't had a chance to see him yet," Rick replied. "Look Jesse, I don't know what the problem is with Donny, if there is a problem. I don't know how all this shit even came about anyway. But I want to get it straighten out so we can get back to the business of making money. Can you dig it? I'm going to find him and we will meet you at the Shalimar tomorrow night," Rick informed Jesse.

"Yeah okay Ricky, that's cool with me. Later," Jesse said.

It was a cool rainy morning; Rick sat half-heartedly watching Good Morning America on TV. Rick heard Donny calling him and he stepped to the window to let Donny know he would be right down. The two men greeted each other warmly but there was iciness in the air.

"Jesse wants to talk with us before he gives us another package," Rick told Donny. "I told Jesse we would meet him tonight. Jesse is mad because of some bullshit rumors he's been hearing. He wants his money before we get another package."

"Look Rick, Jesse has got us on hold. I know for a fact that he has given out packages since we took a fall."

"How do you know that?"

"Willie told me. We made a lot of money for Jesse. Shit! He should never put us on hold. Especially since we caught a bad break. Jesse is acting like if we get work his money won't be good. Anyway, Jesse said he was going to give us three keys, but he only gave us one! So when he gives us the other two keys, we will pay him what we owe," Donny boldly stated.

"He doesn't see it like that," Rick said. "Jesse wants his money because the rumors make him look like he is soft. Whoever you have been kickin it with, they really supped it up and that has got him mad. They are telling Jesse that you said *fuck him; he'll get his money when we get it.* Besides Donny, it don't really matter how much money we made for him, we made money and that is what the game is all about."

Come on my brother, just think how crazy your supposed message sounded to Jesse," Rick went on. "Just imagine if one of our workers sent us a message like that."

"That's not the message I sent!" Donny defended himself. "Anyway, Joe Frog asked me to get with his crew. Joe Frog's crew is getting plenty of money, so I am seriously thinking about it. So Jesse will get his money, he don't have to worry about shit."

Rick and Jesse sat on the stoop next to the Shalimar, their conversation was a serious one.

"Did you tell Donny I want to see him?" Jesse asked.

"Yeah, we kicked it around this morning."

"So what's it going to be?"

"We've been with each other little more than a year. We've made money and had some good times together as well."

"But what's that got to do with the money you owe me?"

"It doesn't have nothing to do with it. All I am saying is let's not let a misunderstanding ruined a good business relationship and our friendship. You were willing to give us another package until you heard some shit about what Donny had supposedly said. What I am saying is if you don't want to give it to me and Donny, then why you don't just give me a package. I will be responsible for it. I will also pay the 10 G's we owe," explained Rick to Jesse.

"If I give it to you Ricky, you alone will be responsible for it. I don't want to hear any stories about your partner."

"Look Jesse, you give it to me and you will get all of your money."

"I'm going to do that for you Ricky, don't fuck me around," Jesse warned him.

Rick lay across the bed; he and Sean shared a pillow as they watched television. This was the first time he had been back to the apartment since him and Jenny had split up, though he had spent time with Sean.

"Rick," Jenny said as she took a seat on the edge of Sean's bed. "Sean wants another dog." Rick and Sean looked at each other before Rick replied to Jenny's statement.

"He had a dog, you got rid of him!" Rick said.

"That was your dog, he was much too big for me or Sean to handle. The man from the ASPCA even had trouble with him. I want you to get Sean a nice puppy," Jenny requested.

"Is that right?" Rick asked his son. "What kind of dog do you want Sean?"

Sean got up and ran over to his toy box, he just threw his toys out of the box until he found his ABC book.

"This is the dog I want daddy," Sean said pointing to a picture in his book.

"That's a German Shepherd," Rick said to Sean. "Okay my man, I'll get you one next week."

"Rick, then get the dog for Sean and not you," Jenny told him. "Don't bring some big monster here like you did before." Rick rolled Sean over and they wrestled on the bed. Rick playfully bit Sean on the nose and let Sean pinned him down to win the match.

"See Ma, I beat daddy!"

"Ah… I think you broke daddy's arm. Look Jenny, Sean broke my arm." Sean's eyes' look so sad and Rick felt bad.

"Come on Sean, you've got to take daddy to the hospital."

"It's not broke daddy," Sean said.

"Yes it is," Rick teased. "You have to drive daddy to the hospital. Can you do that for daddy?"

"Yes, come on. Ma, I'm going to drive daddy to the hospital.

"Okay, get your coat while daddy waits for you."

Once they got outside Rick handed Sean the car keys. Sean ran over and opened the front passenger door. Sean climbed on the seat and stood behind the stirring wheel.

"It won't go daddy," Sean said much to the delight of his father.

"Well, I guess you better let me drive my arm feels better now."

"See, I told you daddy, your arm would get better."

Rick drove to 102nd street and parked in the horseshoe. As he and Sean walked through the projects they ran into Irma.

"Hello Rick, and Sean how are you doing?" she said. "Come here Sean and give me a kiss." Sean was always ready to give a pretty lady a kiss, as was his father. Irma picked Sean up and kissed him several times on the cheek.

"He's getting so big and heavy!" Irma said. "Well Rick, don't I get a kiss after all this time?"

Rick kissed her and took Sean from her arms at the same time.

"It has been a long time," Rick said. "Where have you been?"

"In the Bronx, I was staying with my father," Irma answered. "I just moved back in with my mother a few days ago.

"Yeah? Did your sister come with you?"

"No, she's going to stay with my father until her baby is born."

"Where are you living?"

"I don't really know," Rick replied.

"I heard you and Jenny got married."

"You heard wrong. Jenny and I are not even together." Rick's statement seemed to brighten Irma's smile. "I've got to go now Irma, but I will be seeing you."

Rick made several calls and read his telephone messages. Sean ran between his grandmother's bedroom playing with her and the living room to play with Jeff.

"Yo Rick, are you going to leave Sean here tonight?" Jeff asked.

"No, I'm getting ready to take him home."

"Damn, you don't even let him spend the night anymore."

"I've got to many things to do now Jeff, to let him stay overnight. Once I get things in order he can stay over more."

Indeed, Rick had a lot to handle. The full responsibility was now his to bear. In another hour or so he would be picking up his first solo package. He knew too, that the rumors were eating at Jesse. He figured if he could get the package, rock it and pay Jesse before him and Donny ran into each other that everything would be cool.

Rick stopped at Carvels' on Broadway to buy some ice cream for Sean and Jenny. Jenny was on the phone with her friend Denis when Rick rang the doorbell. Jenny let them in and went back to talking with Denis.

"Jenny!" Rick yelled, "I'm leaving!" Jenny told Denis that she would call her back later and came to find out why Rick was leaving so soon.

"I thought you were going to spend the night," Jenny questioned.

"No, I can't. I've got some very important business to take care of," Rick said and kissed them both before he left.

The twilight stillness of the street had a macabre effect of eeriness on them. Rick cruised along Central Park West up to 110th street. He was relieved once he was out of the peaceful dreariness of his neighborhood. Yet he found the streets of Harlem contained the same eeriness on this cool damp spring night. Rick thought of the monster, Frankenstein, as he made his way up to 7th Avenue. Rick remembered the first time he had seen the monster on television, he was around 3 or 4 years old. He had sneaked out of bed late one night at his uncle's house in New Jersey. It must have been 10 o'clock when he peered around the corner at his cousin, Charmaine, who was watching television in the living room. The deep suspense-filled sound of the announcers' voice made him focus on the black and white picture of the TV screen. As the scene unfolded, a very young Rick became loss in the drama. So much so that he thought he was in the church as the coffin slowly began to open and the hand of the once dead Frankenstein came into view. The mourners who had come to pay their last respects all fled leaving him alone in the church. Or, so it seemed to Rick, a child who had seen his first monster. It was something he had not forgotten. That feeling, not quite as intense as those from Vietnam, but nevertheless had set the mood for tonight.

Tonight as Rick sat waiting for the light to change, he looked over 7th Avenue and all of his senses came into play. That same feeling when he saw the monster Frankenstein for the very first time and just like the first time he had been in an ambush in Vietnam.

Why? Rick asked himself. 7th Avenue seemed to be a distant world and he is a stranger. 7th Avenue seemed to become a world that he was no longer a part of. The glazed wet green of the tree leaves set against the dark wet gray of the tree trunks, and the cold faded gray color of the sidewalk matched by the cardboard emptiness of the tenement building that lined the Avenue were a sharp contrast as to the life he had come to know.

This picture of nothingness, what did it mean? Was he taking on too much responsibility by going into business alone? Was his vision a warning to back off? Whatever it was, it was eating at him this very moment. Rick felt no danger, but he knew something was not right.

Rick saw Jesse sitting on the window's edge outside of the Shalimar. The look on his face increased Rick certainty that something was wrong. The danger alarm warned Rick to leave, while his nerve told him to face the problem whatever it may be. Jesse only said two words as Rick approached him. "Donny's inside." Rick knew what the problem was and why he felt the way he had on his way here tonight. "Yeah? So what?" Rick replied, "What's it got to do with our arrangement?"

Donny sat at the bar. He and some pretty thing were having drinks on Jesse. The boss himself sat at a corner table with his usual entourage. The boss and Rick spoke briefly before Jesse came into the bar. Jesse went straight to the back and spoke with Willie. Willie came and told Rick and Donny that Jesse was ready to speak with them. Along with Rick, Donny, Jesse, and Willie, a small group of men stood in the rear of the Shalimar for what seemed to be just another business meeting.

Rick sensed that this was no ordinary meeting. His skin crawled and he had a knot in his stomach, the same kind he always feel before an ambush in Vietnam. Rick now realized what he had been feeling all night. However, it was too late now. He had already walked into a trap. The only thing left for him now was to see how it played out.

Quick as a flash, the short black object hit Donny in the head. Donny screamed in agony as he flew backwards through the swinging double doors. The impact of the blow sent Donny rolling under the metal table and up against the rear kitchen wall. Jesse was on top of Donny like stink on shit striking him with a blow to the head and body. Rick was held at bay with the threat of gun played by two of the crews.

The Billy-club thuds echoed throughout the bar. The boss and his people came in the back to see what the problem was just as Jesse came out of the kitchen. Jesse walked towards Rick as though he were about to repeat the same. The boss walked over and placed his hand on Jesse arms, the one which held the Billy-club, before Jesse could make a move. The boss told Jesse to hold it and asked what the problem was. Jesse told the boss that they owed money.

Glenn broke through the swinging doors of the kitchen and grabbed

Donny in the collar.

"Get the fuck out here!" Glenn screamed at Donny as he pushed him up against the wall next to Rick.

"You ever have any problems with them about money before?" The boss asked Jesse.

"No," Jesse replied.

"Then just take their jewelry, furs or a car to cover your losses."

"You do have some valuables?" The boss asked Rick.

"Yeah, I've got a few. Yo Jesse, I thought we had an agreement! I was supposed to get another package to work off what I owed, so why the change now Jesse?"

"Your man's got too much mouth," Jesse replied. "So what are you going to do about the money Rick?"

"I'll give you few pieces of jewelry."

"Put Donny in the bathroom until we get back," Jesse told Glenn. "BJ, you stand guard by the door, and don't let anyone go in," Jesse ordered.

Rick, Cisco, Willie and Glenn stood outside while Jesse and the boss spoke inside. Jesse came out of the bar and told Glenn to get Donny out of the bathroom.

"Yo Ricky, this is what I am going to do," Jesse said. "You meet me in the morning with the jewelry so we can see what it is worth."

"That's cool with me," Rick replied.

"Yo Jesse!" Glenn yelled out from the doorway of the bar, "He ain't in there!"

"Get the fuck out of here! How the fuck did he get out?"

They all went to check the bathroom, but there was no Donny.

"How did he get out of here?" BJ wondered out loud. "The only window in the bathroom was six inches long and four inches wide. It was for sure he didn't come out this way!"

"Damn, that nigger must be Houdini's brother," Glenn commented.

Book Two

CHAPTER ONE

The Man's Hustle is Gone

IT WAS A hot summer afternoon, everyone was mostly indoor as the high noon sun baked the projects in its blazing rays. Rick laid languidly on the sofa in his mother's apartment. Rick paid little or no attention to his man, Moon, who was lost in a game show that played on TV. These days, all Rick did was watch day time television, going outside only when the blazing sun had set in the western sky.

Rick rarely ventured outside of the projects. He spent most of his time sitting on the benches just in front of his building. A few months had come and gone since that bizarre night at the Shalimar, when his world had been turned inside out. Rick had sold all of his jewelry to pay Jesse and still he came up 25 hundred short. Donny had gotten away by squeezing through the bathroom window. It was Willie who had told Donny about the window. The window was a feat of magic that no one can figure out to this day. As great as Donny's escape was on that night, he had not managed to escape the long arm of the law. The judge had decided that it would be best if Donny were placed in a drug treatment program for the next six months to a year.

Rick had thought back over the events of the past year many times. Like a needle stuck in the crack of a record, over and over the same thoughts played. It had been an incredible year by anyone's standards.

The heights they had reached were the stuff legends are made of, Rick and Donny, every poor man's fantasy. Their downfall had become a trip into the twilight zone. Other than just a handful of people, no one really knew what had caused Rick and Donny's downfall. If you listened to the rumors, the streets told a thousand one different stories.

Rick showed no signs of depression due to the heartbreaking madness that had befallen him. His attitude reflected a belief that he was content in just saying 'fuck it' and anyone who choose to look down on him. After all, he had been to the mountain top and how many people can say that?

Gone from Rick's life were his so-called friends, the ones who used to beat a path to his door. Gone were the greetings from the dope fiends who he saved from crawling in someone's window for money just to get high. Long gone were the dope fiend bitches that did not have to turn a trick on any given day because Rick had thrown them a bag or two.

The people who whispered the loudest about Rick's misfortune were the ones he had given plays too. They whispered because he had given them product and they fucked the package up and still owed him money. It was as if he was watching a cartoon each time he saw any of them.

Rick's wardrobe still reflected the status quo, a man of success even though it hung in the closet. The women who were sincere about him stayed in his corner. However, he found no pleasure in playing the mating game. Every now and then he would snatch up one of the project freaks, taking her to a rooftop or an upper floor in one of the taller buildings to suck his dick. He no longer found a challenge in women other than the few minutes or so to relieve his sexual tension.

Rick's routine had become craved in stone. He stayed up all night hanging out in the projects and slept the hot days away. Occasionally he would cook dinner or run errands for his mother. Other than that his days held no importance. On this day, however, his sister called from work to let him know she wanted to talk to him when she got home.

Rick asked his sister what the problem was and she sensed that her brother felt something was wrong.

"I need your advise on something that came up," she said reassuring him. "I've got to make a decision by the end of the week."

"Okay, I'll be here."

They sat in the living room talking, sister and brother. Moon had cut out just after Pam came in from work. It was also time for the rest of the family to start drifting in. Rick enjoyed talking with his sister; she had her special ways that always made you feel good about yourself. Their conversation today was on a serious note. She wanted his opinion and advise on a career move she was thinking about.

She told her brother that her agent informed her he could get her the centerfold for Playboy magazine.

"Do you think I should go for it? She questioned her brother. "Would it be a good move for me to make?"

"Do you want to do it?" Rick asked.

"Yes, in a way."

"So, I don't see were there is a problem if it is something you want."

"I asked you because you are my big brother and I want to know how you feel about having your sister all naked in a magazine everyone will see."

"Shit, I'd be proud, ain't none of these motherfuckers going to put a dime in your pocket. All they do is wish that your life is going to be worse then theirs, so they can feel good about themselves. So it doesn't mean shit what anyone outside the family thinks," explained Rick. Pam leaned forward and kissed Rick on the cheek thanking him.

"So, when are you supposed to do this?" Rick asked his sister.

"I don't know, the agent said he would let me know by Friday. That is, if I want to do it in the first place. They said I would be paid 15 hundred and that just don't seem like enough money," she said more to herself than her brother.

"I am almost sure Playboy pays ten of thousand dollars for a centerfold," Rick commented. "Your agent is trying to beat you out of 85 hundred, sis."

"Are you sure?"

"I'm not sure if it is 10 thousand but I am damn sure it's more than 15 hundred. You want me to pay your agent a visit? I'll teach him a lesson so he knows that he can't beat my sister."

"No, I don't want you to get yourself in any trouble. But if you are right I won't be working with him again," she informed her brother.

Rick felt a sense of renewed life. He knew it was due to the talk he had with his sister. He felt good knowing that she still thought enough of him to come ask him for advice. Admittedly or not, he thought himself to be a failure. When in truth, he had come off the mountain top to be just another young black man lost in the concrete jungle of New York City, like so many others.

Rick's pride in his sister caused him to hold his head high as he strolled through the projects. He stopped in front of 840 and took a seat on the end of the bench where a group of people had gathered to pass away the evening hours. Rick had known each of these people most of his life. Michael Terrel, Shep, Junie, Bertha, Susan, Sam, Jou-ju Beamon, Freddy and Gail. Junie, Jou-ju and Bertha greeted Rick with a friendly smile. The others made a conscious effort to display indifference.

Shep pulled Michael and Sam off to the side and whispered to them about some scheme he had come up with to get over in the dope game. They spoke loud making sure Rick could hear every word they spoke. It was obvious that they were putting on a show for his benefit, trying to belittle him. To further try and rub dirt in Rick's face, Shep flashed a roll of one dollar bills like it was G money. They fronted like they were about to cope a key of dope.

Rick laughed to himself and thought, '*What stupid motherfuckin' clowns you all are. Three bum ass wannabe motherfuckers buying 65 dollars worth of dope. You ain't me and Donny. I know you won't have enough money to cop tomorrow. You clowns are talking that partner shit like you really are so fuckin fly. If you are all you think yourselves to be like that then you can pay me some of the money you owe me. Nah, I bet that thought never crossed your small thinking minds. Fuck them,*' Rick thought with contempt.

'*I'll sure be glad when Benny and William get off from work,*' Rick thought. '*My true friends, Moon, Benny, William and Lefty. It didn't matter to them if I am rich or poor, they still hang tuff.*'

CHAPTER TWO

Fools, Oh How They Lie

RICK AND MOON sat on the barrels in the small playground area next to Rick's building. It was a beautiful summer night that brought into play a relaxing state of existence for the two men. Rick felt as though a heavy burden had been lifted from his shoulders even though nothing had changed his fallen status in life. For the first time in, who knows how long, Rick's face held a smile. Rick and Moon kicked it, not about anything in particular, but like it was life's greatest pleasure to sit on the barrels and enjoy the pleasantries of the summer night in New York City.

Rick and Moon watched as Shep, Sam and Michael crossed 102nd street Columbus Avenue, along with some of their flunkies. They walked as if they owned the world. *'Fuckin jokes all of them,'* Rick thought to himself. Nonetheless, he greeted them warmly, as did Moon. Michael pulled a roll of bills from his pocket and called for one of the flunkies with them to run an errand. "Anybody else want something from the store?" Michael asked.

"Nah," they all responded.

"Yo Rick!" Shep called out,"We just left Jesse. He told us to tell you that you don't owe him anymore money. But, he didn't ever want to see you again in life. Ain't that right?" Shep asked his little group of hypocrites.

"Yeah," they replied in harmony.

"Yeah, he said straight up that he doesn't ever want to see you again in life," said one kid that Rick didn't even know of.

"I told him not to worry though," Shep said. I let him know that we were taking over down here and that it would be business as usual, only under new management." Rick laughed to himself at their attempt to rub shit in his face. How serious they thought themselves to be and at the same time, they are the biggest fools he had ever seen.

Moon did not take their comments as lightly as Rick did and exploded in rage.

"You punk ass motherfuckers ain't never going to come off like they did! He should be kickin off in your asses for all the breaks he gave you and you all fucked up. If any of you faggots don't like what I just said, I'll fuck all of you up. Go ahead, say something!" Moon challenged them. They all stood silent.

"Yeah, I didn't think so!" Moon roared at them. "Come on Rick, let's get the fuck out from around these punks!"

Rick and Moon walked the projects kickin' it.

"Yo Rick man, you shouldn't take that shit from them. After all the plays you gave them they should be kissing your ass."

"Check this out Moon, I don't give a fuck about them or what they think. The shit them cartoon ass motherfuckers be poppin' don't mean nothing. It's an act to make themselves feel important and I'm not going to feed into it. To me, they are a joke," Rick responded. "They try to rub shit in my face but my silence doesn't give them the satisfaction they want."

"All summer they've been talking to get that money shit," Rick continued. "They were copping the same amount of dope for months. They never have correct money and all they are buying is 65 fuckin dollars worth of dope. They flash their little bank rolls on us for me to see like they are really coming off. So, if I wake them up by kickin' the real deal I may have to do something to one of them when they realize whose really laughing at whom. Anyway, I must be real important to them if they are going through so many changes to impress me. So, every time they put on one of their little shows like they're coming off, I just laugh to myself."

"Yeah, I see what you mean Rick. The real joke is on them," Moon nodded. "Yo Rick, what are you going to do right now?"

"I don't know. Why, what's up?"

"My woman will be getting off from work in another hour or so and I'm going to meet her in her projects. So you want to hang or what?"

"Nah man, I don't feel like going all the way down to the Amsterdam Projects. I think I will come by Lefty's house and hang for awhile there. C'mon, I'll walk you to the subway."

Rick sat in the basement apartment kicking it with the slim brown skin brother Joe, whom Lefty had introduced to him and stepped out to take care of business. Lefty's three year old son, Kip, joined Rick and Joe in conversation. At his young age, Kip was real smart and the spitting image of his father. Kip reminded Rick of his own son, Sean, who was a few months older. Rick and Lefty often took Kip and Sean out with them.

"You look like you play ball," Joe said.

"Yeah," Rick replied. "But to be honest, I haven't played for awhile. What about you?"

"I play. I would like to play some while I'm in town."

"Where are you from?"

"I'm on the road so much now I don't really know where I'm from anymore."

"He's a singer!" Kip told Rick.

"Yeah, you sing huh?"

"Yeah," Joe replied. "We are starting to do a little something in the business."

"Yeah, who do you sing with?" Rick was curious.

"I'm the lead with the Deltones."

"Shit!" Rick was about to say something but he hold himself because of Kip.

"You're coming off. I've got everything you've put out!"

"I'm glad," Joe smiled. "We need the money." They both laughed. Lefty rejoined them and the three men left together for a nigh out on the town after stopping by Rick's house so he could change.

Rick, Lefty and Joe stood in front of the club on 23rd street Fifth Avenue. Billy Underwood came over to where they stood and Rick introduced everyone.

"Wood, this is my man Lefty, he's getting married this Sunday. And this is Joe, he is the lead singer with the Deltones."

"Glad to know you both," Wood greeted them. "Here Rick, take these VIP tickets. These will get you in and free drinks for you and your friends. I would like to talk to you later Joe, if you don't mind. And congratulations Lefty," Wood said before stepping off.

"Sure my man," Joe replied.

Rick walked few steps with Wood.

"Damn Wood, you are coming off with this dance thing," Rick said.

"Yeah, it's coming together," Wood replied. "The twins and I put this one together. The next few, I will be giving on my own."

"Where?"

"Manhattan Center, but I didn't bring any flyers. I don't want to disrespect my working relationship with the twins. We are cool and all but people get funny if they think you are cutting them in or out," Wood said more for himself than Rick.

"I can dig it. I'll kick it with you later," Rick told him.

It was hot, the sun set high in the sky on this Saturday morning. Rick, Lefty, Moon and Benny were trying to figure out where they would play ball today.

"I can't go too far," Lefty told them. "I have to pick my tux up no later than 3 this afternoon."

"Where from?" Benny asked.

"On 125th street between Lenox and Fifth."

"Don't worry about it. I'll drive you there."

"In that case, why don't we check out 77th and Riverside Park, there's always plenty of good runs there."

The trio sat in Benny's blue Oldsmobile 98 while Lefty went into the tux shop. The mood of the three men was light, though Rick felt uneasy. Rick did not want to come along. But time had been short and they wanted to catch the store before it was closed.

When Lefty went out from the store, it was clear, you could tell by the expression on his face he was a happy man. It also showed by the bounce in his stride. His enthusiasm caught on and lifted the spirits of the other men in the car. They were as happy for him as he was for himself.

Benny pulled the car into traffic and stopped for the red light when he came to the corner of 125th and Lenox Avenue. Benny made the left turn on the green light and headed down Lenox. Rick saw the black Eldorado earlier when it crossed 125th while they waited for the light to change. Rick knew it was Jesse behind the wheel and hoped he'd be long gone by the time they made the turn. Lefty mentioned the beauty of the black machine as they pulled behind a few cars from Jesse's.

Rick was like "That's Jesse's car, just the man I didn't want to see."

"Nah, that's not him," Benny said. "That's my man Billy and his little brother."

"Only Jesse would have a car hooked up like that!" Rick said.

"I bet that's my man," Benny insisted.

"I don't want to bet shit!" Rick shot back. "I don't want to see Jesse right now and I know that's him driving that car."

"That's not Jesse!" Benny said as he pushed the gas pedal to the floor. Benny pulled alongside of the black machine so abruptly that it startled its two passengers.

Jesse eyed the passengers in the blue Olds 98, his face took on a big smile when he spotted Rick in the backseat.

"Yo Jesse, pull over!" Rick yelled out. "I need to talk to you." Jesse pulled the black machine over near the corner of 123rd and Benny pulled in behind him.

"I know who the fuck I owe money to," Rick told Benny as he was getting out of the car.

"It's a good thing he didn't want to kill you," Lefty said, "or we all would be shot the fuck up."

"Shit, I could have sworn that was Billy," Benny said.

Rick stood on the curb and watched Jesse as he approached walking in the street. Rick was about to go into a speech when Jesse extended his hand to give him five.

"My brother," Jesse greeted him. "I have been looking all over for you Ricky. Didn't you get my message?" Rick was dumbfounded by Jesse's greeting and when he began to speak he was cut off by Jesse.

"Look, you don't owe me anymore money. Come uptown tonight and I will give you a package. Can you handle an eight?"

"Yeah," Rick replied.

"Good, I'll start you off with that." They gave each other five and said later. Rick was stunned momentarily by the circumstances of the event that had just taken place. He just stood there and watched Jesse as he drove off.

CHAPTER THREE

Back In The Game

THE SUMMER NIGHT was cool compared to the blazing heat that had baked the city earlier that day. The humidity that had caused everyone's clothes to stick to their skin had disappeared with the sunset. Rick sat on a car at the corner of 118th street on 8th Avenue. This was the first time he had really been back uptown since that troubled night at the Shalimar. He watched the busy bee movement of the crowded street. *'Something never change,'* he thought to himself. Most were scheming to see how they could or would get over. Some dope fiends nodded out, bouncing back into a standing position just before their legs gave out. Funny how they never seemed to fall, as if falling would end their lives and to the few whom fell, it seemed their lives were drained away by an overdosed.

Nights spent on Harlem street corners in the summer are festive times. Every corner has its own charm, a lifestyle that makes it different from any other corner in Harlem or any other place in the world for that matter. If you know how to read the streets' every pleasure known to man can be found in the concrete jungle that made up of Harlem.

Tonight Rick felt alive, it was the beginning of a new chapter in his life or the end of his life all together. Was Jesse ready to put him down again or was the offer of a package just a ploy to set him up to be killed?

Rick's demeanor was calm, his mind raced though he did not feel an existing danger. However, the move he made now was for added insurance on his safety and life.

No one paid any attention to Rick as he nonchalantly switched positions in the car. Rick was not aware of how long he had been there when he saw Skull coming up the block towards him.

"Yo Skull, what's up?" Rick greeted him.

"Ain't nothing Rick," Skull replied. "My man, where the fuck have you been?"

"I've been chillin."

"I heard you had taken a fall and about the shit that went on that night at the Shalimar. You should have came and talked to me."

"I was fucked up, plus I still owed Jesse a nut. So I was just going to give the life up and say fuck it. Then I ran into Jesse and he told me the nut was squashed."

"You should have sat down and talked with him a long time ago," Skull responded. "Shit, you and your man made a lot of money for him. I don't like the way your situation was handled, but everybody does business their own way."

"Anyway, that's why I stopped by tonight. I'm supposed to meet Jesse at the usual time and place. Have you heard any talk on the streets about me?"

"Nah, I ain't heard nothing. If you have any doubts, take my lieutenant with you and see what's what. Yo Henry!" Skull called up to the second floor window of the building on the corner of 118th street 8th Avenue. When Little Henry appeared in the window, Skull signed him to come down. As Little Henry approached the two men, he recognized Rick at once.

"Oh shit Rick!" Henry said.

"What's up Henry?" Rick greeted him back.

"Ain't nothing."

"How's Ma, Sis and the rest of the family?"

"Everyone is okay."

"Yo Henry, I want you to hang with Rick until he cuts you loose," Skull informed him.

"That's cool with me," Henry responded.

The magical illusion, the power, the star studded glitter, the splendor of a New York City night held Rick spell bound as he stood in front of the Shalimar with Little Henry. Rick was greeted casually by the patriarchies of the fast life. It was clear that everyone had grown light years since he had last seen them. Rick could smell the money, the power. The evidence of success was written on everyone. The jewels were worn sparkled in the city's night lights. The clothes they wore would lead to the reputation for black men in Harlem and New York City being the best dressed in the world. The lines of double-parked cars outside of the bar were the toys they played in. These machines were changed by the men who drove them just like any ordinary man would change his socks. They drove cars for going to the playground, to shoot baskets, or just cruising the streets in the day light hours. One car for cruising at night, one for moving the products and yet another to show the world how fly one had become. 'Yes,' Rick thought to himself. He was ready to take this step on his own.

The stone cold beauty of the black women who gathered to be around these rich and powerful youth showed the blessing of a race graced with pure beauty. From the deep dark chocolate colored skin of an Amazonian girl in a raw silk mini-dress, to the crème gold colored sister with the curvaceous behind in hot pants. These women were a kaleidoscope of sex, beauty, and color, and there for the young and powerful to enjoy.

Willie pulled the black Cadillac Coupe Deville into a vacant space in front of the bar. Rick had been at the Shalimar for almost two hours before Jesse finally showed up. Rick could also see the stress on Jesse's face as he and Willie approached the bar where Rick and Little Henry stood. Jesse greeted Little Henry and Rick. As Jesse turned to walk away he told Willie to tell Rick what happened and then he disappeared into the bar.

"Yo Rick, we ran out of work. We just finished making up packages and didn't have enough to take care of everyone."

"So when are you going to have it?" Rick asked.

"I don't know, but Jesse said to give you some money to handle your business. Take this five hundred and check back in a few nights," Willie said and gave Rick the money. "If you need more money before we get work, come to my block and let me know."

"I should be okay. I can get setup with this," Rick said.

CHAPTER FOUR

Getting Ready to Play Again

AS RICK CLIMBED the back stairway of the Castle Hotel, he held a large brown shopping bag tightly in his hand. He watched the white bitch that was getting her ass felt by a trick that couldn't wait till they reached the room. Rick smiled at her when she glanced over her shoulder to see who was coming up the steps behind them. Rick had seen her around many times and knew she worked the stroll on 92nd street Broadway. It was clear that the old white trick that felt her ass was not from the neighborhood. As it turned out, they had the room right next to his.

Rick could hear through the wall how she was playing the trick for more money as he set about getting ready to take care of his own business. The damn walls of the hotel were so thin, Rick thought he could hear the trick entered her in his imagination. Yet, his sexual excitement was real. As it always was when he handled a large amount of drugs or money. It was a reminder of the many times during a fired fight in Vietnam how his manhood always came to life along with every nerve in his body. Rick moved the bed to block the door of his room and could hear her coercing the trick to cum quickly and at the same time making him believed that he was a great lover.

Rick had been working the mountain of dope for some ten hours. The early morning hours had long since past the noon and evening hours. Rick was beat. He had bagged and tapped the whole eighth. He breathed a sigh of relief as he placed a rubber band around the last half. He was now approaching a twenty-four run with no sleep. He contemplated his next set of moves. *Should I give out samples then go in and get a few hours sleep, or stash the dope and go right to work?*

Rick turned the sound up on the television and stretched out across the bed. He was too tired to get back up and change the TV channel to a program that interested him. He reached over, picked the telephone up and placed it on the bed beside him. He dialed a number and listened as it rang several times before it was picked up on the other end.

"Hello."

"Hey Cheryl, yeah it's me. Meet me at the Castle Hotel, I'm in room 324."

"Alright Rick, I'm on my way."

"Okay, on your way here stop by and get me something to eat."

"What do you want?"

"I don't know. Make it a fried chicken sandwich on a roll, soda and some kind of cake with icing. Yeah, that should do it. Cheryl, try to get here as fast as possible!" Rick hung up and dialed another number.

"Hello Ma."

"Yeah Ricky."

"How you doing Ma? Look here, I won't be coming in for a few days or so. Everything's is cool. I just wanted you to know so you wouldn't be worried."

"Okay baby, you take care."

Rick laid across the bed on his stomach. Cheryl straddled him while she massaged his back, neck and shoulders.

"You know Rick, I could very easily slip out of these clothes and give you something that will really relax you."

"Yeah, if we do that I would never get my business taken care of," Rick replied.

"You've always got an excuse for not giving me some," Cheryl responded, a bit angry. "You feel me up, get me all wet and ready to be fucked then stop. You ain't shit Rick. You know that's some dirty shit to do to me."

"Yeah, but you love it," Rick teased. "Get off of me. I'm ready for you to cut out anyway. I'll take you downstairs so you can catch a cab. Put the package away and get your ass right back over here."

"Okay. How long do you think it will take for you to get rid of all this?" Cheryl asked.

"Why?" Rick replied, trying not to let his voice reflected the concern he felt by the question.

"I just wanted to know how long I will have to sit in this hotel room alone."

"You won't be alone, I'll be in and out and I am going to take a break to get some sleep."

"Big fuckin' deal, I get to watch you sleep," Cheryl stated more to herself than Rick.

"Watch your mouth girl," Rick said to keep her in line.

"I'm sorry," Cheryl meekly apologized like a small child. "But it's the truth Rick."

Rick stepped quickly with Cheryl as they made their way down the back stairway of the medieval hotel. Rick could heard someone coming up the steps in front of them. It was his neighbor of the last 10 hour or so with another trick. She had been busy throughout the early hours of the morning and it appeared as if she was trying to get a jump on the night time traffic. Rick smiled as they passed one another on the steps. However, she did not respond. Her movements were short, jumpy and quick. The gaze from her eyes was ice cold. Rick realized at once, it was the same hurried movement he had seen a million times before. The pale color of her complexion, the watery look in her eyes and the cold stare told it all. She was sick and needed a fix badly.

Rick hailed a cab on the corner of Manhattan Avenue on 106th street. He kissed Cheryl as though they had just finished making passionate love. Then he watched as the cab made a u-turn and headed across 106th street towards Columbus Avenue. Rick took a deep breath and looked around. In a hundred years nothing had changed, Central Park still stood as the dividing line separating the rich from the poor. The tenements that lined the streets of the west side bustled with those still in search of their dreams and those lost in a dream of no hope.

While the majesty of the high rises on the east side stood picture post-card beautiful. The east side is also where the merchants of the poor men's fantasies and dreams sat secured in the dwellings of their own creations. *'Low life motherfuckers,'* Rick thought, *'You sell the fantasy of the American dream but you make it impossible for a man of color to reach. It is you who has created the need for men such as me. For two dollars I sell the answer to a bro-ken men's prayers. So great is their disillusion with life they come to me by the thousands… and still you are not satisfied. You send your hounds to hunt me insuring that I know only limited pleasure from a dollar with the hope that I never learn its true power. I know you Mr. Insurance Company owner and you Mr. Politician, through your multi-conglomerate corporations you take your share of each bag I sell. You hide your dope profits behind your saintly reputa-tions of American success and respectability. I laugh but I want to cry, the more things change the more they remain the same,* Rick thought.

Rick passed the same trick he had seen when he was on the way out of the hotel with Cheryl. The trick did not seem to be pleased and Rick could smell the fear he generated making his escape. The thought of fucking had made him a brave man on the way in, now he jumped at his own shadow. He had spent twenty dollars for less than five minutes of so-called pleasure. Rick had known all along that he would get a rush job. The only thing a sick dope fiend bitch would have on her mind was to get high.

Rick caught her just as she removed the key from the lock on the door. He grabbed her by the arm spinning her so she came face to face with him. He could smell the stink of her dope sickness mixed with the odor of her sex play.

"Say Miss, I've got just what you've been looking for," Rick said.

"Not right now handsome, I've got some business to take care of. I will be glad to play with you when I get back."

"I've got just what you need," Rick eased two bags out of his pocket and placed them in her hand.

"How did you know?"

"I've been around. Anyway, take them and let me know how you like it."

"What are they? Nickels?"

"Nah, they're deuces. I've got big habits."

"Deuces won't do nothing for me," she complained.

"After you do those, we can talk about more. But for right now I want to know how good it is."

"Okay, come in with me while I do them."

"No, no, you go ahead, I'll be next door. Knock on the wall when you are finished and I'll come over," Rick said.

When she opened the door to let Rick in, she still had the needle stucked in her arm. She was so high that she could barely stand up. Stumbling over her feet she made her way back to the bed. *I've got the monster bag*, Rick thought. *It's time for me to get money*. Rick pulled the needle from her arm and threw it in the trash along with the other shit she used to get high. He lifted her legs onto the bed and she threw her arms around his neck.

"Come on daddy, make love to me." In her dope induced state she rambled on,"This is the best dope I've ever had. Are you sure they were deuces? They were bigger than any nickels I have ever copped. I know what you did, you made those up just for me so I would give you some of this sweet thing."

"Sure, that's what I did. But look at you, how you going to give me some when you're fucked up like that?"

"Don't worry about it, daddy. When I'm high that's when I make it real good." Rick removed her arms from around his neck and stepped back.

"You know daddy, if I had known you had dope I would never have got beat this morning. That's why I had to turn another trick. They told me they had good dope but it was only baby power." Rick knew the story well. "If you were white you needed someone to cop for you. That's what always made whitey easy prey for the rip off artist."

Rick picked her key up from the small table next to the bed and told her that he would be back later. Cheryl exited the stairway as Rick locked the door behind himself.

"So that's it!" Cheryl said, "She can get some but I can't."

"You know how stupid you sound girl, and what makes you think all of a sudden that you can question my actions. You must have lost your mind, woman. If you think you've got your senses back we can get out of this hallway," Rick stated.

"It shouldn't take me long to get this off," Rick told Cheryl. "I know it's a monster because that bitch next door damn near O.D. on the two sample bags I gave her."

"Do you always have to say bitch?" Cheryl asked.

"Why, you don't like that word? That's the word my old man used to make me feel like shit when we were together. He kept calling me a no good worthless bitch. I don't use the word that much, but check this. I'm going to teach you to love the word," Rick told her.

"Oh really? I can't wait," Cheryl replied.

"Look, I'm out of here, you know the routine girl. Don't open the door for anyone but me. In a half hour call the room next door to make sure that bit—, girl is alright. I don't want her to die on me," Rick reminded her. "You better make that every 15 minutes until you are sure she is okay."

Rick walked along Central Park headed down to 102nd street. He had twenty half loads tucked in the waistband of his pants and used his shirt to hide the small bulge. He sat on the bench and looked across into 102nd street, watching carefully to see who was doing what. When he was sure of what he wanted to do and had made sure the people he wanted to see were in the block, he crossed 8th Avenue. Rick walked up to the few people who sat on a car in front of building 9.

"So what's up?" Rick asked. Their subtle and indifferent response was just what he expected. It did his heart good to know that they would soon sing another tune. Rick caught a glimpse of Peggy standing on the stoop of number 9 from the corner of his eye.

"Peggy, take a walk with me," Rick called her. They walked arm in arm towards Manhattan Avenue as he explained what to be done. "So get three other girls to run customers and I'll give them a sample now and pay them when I'm finished."

Rick gave each of the four women two bags each, but Peggy tried to play for more.

"Look, you go do them and I'll meet you back here in ten minutes," Rick said. I'm just going to walk around until you are ready to run me customers. Hurry up and do your thing so I can get busy." The three women couldn't wait to break for the building to get high. Peggy stayed close to Rick.

"Aren't you going to try the thing?" Rick asked.

"I only skin pop, so I can wait," she replied. "I'll walk with you and get high once we are finished if that is okay?"

"Yeah, let's go."

"I don't want to stand in the block if I am not working," Rick told Peggy.

So they walked down Manhattan Avenue to 100rd street where the Avenue ended. Undecided where they should go from there, they walked over to Central Park.

"Come on, we can walk around the lake and come out through the 103rd street exit," Rick suggested. Rick pulled the bundle of halfs from the waist-band of his pants and handed it to Peggy under the cover of darkness.

"This is how we will work it," Rick informed her. "I will keep two halfs with me, you sit across from me with the rest. That way when I need more I can signal you. You place two halfs on the bumper of the car, I pick out and walk away. I will ease over and pick them up and I won't have to worry about the police running up on me."

Rick and Peggy sat on the bench looking into 102nd street from the park side.

"What the fuck are they doing?" Rick asked, not really looking for an answer. "They should have been finished. Come on girl, let's see what the fuck is going on." Rick raced up the steps of building 9 with Peggy following him behind. In the hotel-like lobby of the building, Black Margaret, Cookie and Betty nodded in a dope fiend stooper while a small crowd questioned where they had copped.

"We had Rick's thing," they responded to the intense questioning of the crowd.

"Rick? Shit, when did he put something out?" someone asked.

"He just came through a little while ago with samples."

The crowd turned all at once when they realized Rick was standing there.

"Rick! You got any more samples?" the crowd asked.

"Nah, but I've got deuces." Before he could say more, he was on the corner while they began to push money at him.

"Give me five, give me two. Can I get a play, I've only got three fifty?"

It took Rick just a little more than ten minutes to knock the twenty halfs. Peggy walked with Rick over to Manhattan Avenue. "Tell anyone who want to cop, that I will be right back," Rick informed Peggy.

Rick threw the money on the bed; he counted out twenty-five singles stuffing them back into his pocket. He felt really good, alive and wide awake.

"Cheryl count this money for me, and then put a rubber band around it." Rick playfully rode Cheryl's ass as she bent over the bed counting the money.

"There you go again Rick, feeling me all up. If you are not going to finish what you started then I wish you wouldn't do this to me."

"You know you love it girl and besides, you just may get what you want. Look, I'll be back in half an hour or so," Rick told her.

Rick made his way along Central Park again with twenty halfs in the waistband of his pants. Rick sat on the bench to make sure everything was on the up before he entered the block. Peggy was waiting for him as were a couple dozen customers. He had the best dope out and his bags were three times the size of anyone else's. For a few dollars, Rick had given those in search of their dreams more than their money's worth. Rick had made eight or nine trips back to the hotel in the last hour or so. Things were going good. Black Margaret handed him a ten dollar bill and asked for five bags. Rick gave her a strange look.

"You are going to get paid in a little while, so why are you copping now?" Rick asked.

"It's for Michael and Sam," she replied. "They didn't want you to know. So the big time dope dealers have come to me after all the shit they popped. I thought they had dope?"

"Their dope ain't shit. They fuck over their bags so bad that no one who knows them will cop their product."

"Okay, after you take them this get Cookie and Betty and meet me in 101st street," Rick said to her.

Rick gave Black Margaret, Cookie and Betty one half load each plus fifty dollars a piece. Rick gave Peggy two halfs and a hundred dollars after the other three women left. They were as happy as jay birds on a Sunday morning in summer and promised undying loyalty. Rick took a seat on the stoop and Peggy came to stand in front of him. She placed her foot on the first step of the stoop so she could straddle Rick. Rick's eyes followed the shape of her thick hairy legs, up and along the shape of her hips. He played pass the full view she displayed under her short skirt and his eyes came to meet the warmth of her smile. Rick's fingers played the hair on her right calf, sending a chill through him. He had known Peggy since elementary school where she had grown from a fat kid into a beautiful woman. How long her beauty would last was only a question of time now. As long as she skin popped she would be alright. But just as he was a man in search of his dream, she had become a prisoner of hers. It was for sure it wouldn't be long before she started to get off.

"Hey Rick, are you going to be busy for the rest of the night?" Peggy broke the silence. Her sexuality was reeking and a blind man could see what she had on her mind. Rick leaned forward running his hands along her leg, up and under her short skirt, stopping only before they reached home. Rick could feel the heat of her passion on his hands.

"I know what you are saying and I know it's got to be good as hot as it is. There is nothing I would like better than to have those big brown hairy legs wrapped around my back. But I need to get some sleep, plus I still have a few business matters to take care of before I do. I'll be back out here sometime later today. So if you want we can work the same way, only we don't need the other three girls. By the time I get back everyone will know that I've got the monster bag."

Rick used the key to open the hotel door, Cheryl followed him in. The girl next door sat straight up on the bed when Rick came to stand next to it. She was still somewhat high and coming out of a dope induced sleep. It took her several moments before she realized where she was and what had happened.

"I just wanted to make sure you were alright before I cut out," Rick said.

"You're the one I got the dope from. I've never had dope that good before. You got anymore?" she asked. She turned around to get out of bed giving Rick a full view between her legs at her bare pussy. Then she noticed Cheryl standing by the door and pulled the sheets over to cover herself.

"Hi," she said, still half asleep, to Cheryl. "I didn't realize you were standing there."

"That was obvious," Cheryl replied.

"Your man has got some good dope."

"He's not my man."

Rick jumped in the conversation before Cheryl's temper got the best of her.

"Look, I don't even know your name," Rick said.

"Patty."

"Okay Patty, if you want to cop let me know now because I'm cutting out."

"You got the same thing?"

"Yeah, so how many you want?"

She reached in her bra and pulled out several crumbled twenty dollar bills.

"You got enough to sell me a half load?"

"Look, you tell me what you want, don't ask me what I've got," Rick scolded her. She fumbled with the bills for a few moments trying to count in her drugged out-state of mind. Rick became impatient and took the money from her hand.

"Look girl!" Rick barked, "You've got 85 dollars here. How many do you want?"

"Can I get three for 75?"

"Yeah, that's no problem. Cheryl, let me get that from you." Cheryl pulled her dress up and removed a small brown bag from the waistband of her panties.

Rick took the bag from Cheryl and dumped the contents onto the bed.

"You sure this the same dope?" Patty asked.

"Look girl, I'm not in the mood to play silly games with you. If you want it, buy it. If not I'm ready to cut out," Rick scolded her once again.

"It's just that I've been beaten so many times."

"If I wanted to beat you, I could have done it when you passed out. But because I am a gentleman, this is what I'll do. Pick any three halfs, open one bag from each. If you don't like the count, you keep the three bags and I'll give you your money back."

Patty picked out three halfs pulling a bag from each.

"Damn," she said, "these are bigger than the other bags I got from you. Are you sure this is dope?"

"Look bitch, I told you I ain't got time for your fuckin games. Taste the shit and see for yourself!" Rick screamed on her. She took a match book and folded it into a quill taking a one on one from each bag.

"It's dope," she declared. "If you sold your product where I come from, you could get twenty dollars for one of these bags."

"And just where do you come from?" Rick asked her.

"Bergen County, New Jersey."

Rick sat at the dinning room table, on one side he stacked the remaining halfs, on the other side he had counted out and arranged the bills in piles of numerical order. Rick was beat, he stretched, leaning against the back of the chair. It had been an action packed 48 hours. Rick reflected on what he felt the future now held in store for him.

Rick drifted off into a dream-like state of existence, he could see Cheryl when she stepped around the corner into the dining room. He did not know if she was real or a dream. She wore a lone sheer negligee and under it, a red silk G-string with matching bra. The high heel sandals made her short thick muscular legs seemed longer than they were.

Cheryl came and stood behind him. She massaged his neck and he knew it was not a dream. "Damn, that feels good," Rick told her.

"Well if you like this, you haven't seen anything yet," Cheryl confidently stated. "Come on, I ran a nice hot bath for you."

The soap bubbles formed a mountain in the tub that was a relaxing picture of pure delight. The reflecting light from the swaying flames of the candles danced across the bubbles like children at play.

"Nice Cheryl, you're working hard for what you want."

"It's not work. This is how I get my pleasure as you will soon see." Rick removed his clothes and eased into the hot water. He laid his head against the rubber pillow and let the heat of the water soothe his body.

Cheryl took Rick's clothes and left, promising to hurry back. Rick could hear her foot steps on the hard wooden floor; the music became clearer as she got closer. Cheryl sat the speaker right outside of the bathroom door. The soft music created a serene atmosphere as the flames of the candles swayed to the gentle rhythm of the music. Cheryl removed her negligee and placed two large throw pillows at the base of the tub. She came to rest on her knees beside the tub, lit a joint and placed it in Rick's mouth. Eddie Kendrick's of the Temptations sang Heavenly. "Marking Eddie," Rick whispered, "this is heavenly," he said to Cheryl.

They smoked the rest of the joint without uttering another word. Cheryl got a large washcloth and bar of soap from the cabinet under the bath room sink. She used them to massage and bathe Rick. She used her hands with the soap to bring life to Rick's manhood. She was careful not to arouse Rick to a full erection.

Cheryl pulled the bath plug and the water slowly drained. She got up to get a new toothbrush and razor from the medicine cabinet.

"Would you like me to shave you?" she asked.

"No, I don't use razors. I like magic shave but the toothbrush is cool."

"I must remember to get some magic shave." Cheryl turned the water on in the tub, adjusting it to the right temperature. She got in the tub and stood over Rick's legs and drew the shower curtain close. Rick got up to join her, they embraced and their tongues played. Cheryl used her foot to push the shower knob in. The large shower head bathed them in its soothing rain like mist.

Rick leaned against the edge of Cheryl's bedroom doorway. He had been in her bedroom many times and it had never looked this way before. "Seductive". Gone were the pastel colors that covered the bed, pillows, window and other furnishings. The music was soft. The glow from the candles gave the bedroom a nice warm feeling. The black satin sheets were turn back and the bedroom setting was picture perfect for a romantic seduction. Rick laid a pillow against the mirrored headboard. Then he leaned back on the pillow pulling the satin sheet up to his waist.

Cheryl came into the bedroom with a tray, glasses and cold drinks. She had also changed into another sexy outfit. The burgundy lace teddy clung to the curves of her shapely figure. She sat the tray on the table next to the bed. Her sexual prowess had long since stirred his animal lust and he wondered how much more there was to this lady. A question she was about to answer for him.

Cheryl climbed onto the bed and eased into a stance as if she were a cat staking its prey. Her smooth cat like purrs was hypnotic. She inched forward moving closer to Rick, Rick did not move. Their eyes met, locking them into a trance-like state. She leaped at Rick; he slid under her lunge, rolled to the end of the bed and came up into a cat like stance of his own. Their eyes were once again locking them into sexual heat. Facing off they jockeyed for position and crawled in a circle on the bed. She purred, he snarled and pawed at her like a lion. She rolled over and kicked the high heel mule slippers from her feet. She stretched her leg reaching for him, using her foot to rub his side. He snarled and she was quick to respond leaping into a stance for attack. He went limp to lull her in. She crawled over to cuddle and he used his body pinning her to the bed. She struggled to free herself, only to become more entangled in his grip. They had not spoken a word and they played their game as though it was second nature to them.

Cheryl laid submissively beneath Rick. He used his teeth to pull the teddy down to her waist. He slowly worked his way back up her soft body to play with her small firm breast. He straddled her, holding her firmly between his arm and legs. He nibbled at one then the other of her nipples. She closed her eyes, bit her lip, yet she did not move. He sat up and slowly removed the teddy down her thighs. Cheryl brought her legs up to her breast and Rick slid the teddy off. Cheryl spread her legs bringing them out and around his body. He used the movement of his body to guide himself home. Slowly he worked himself in and out of her. He teased her with his slow driving pace. She purred in his ear. He held her bound to the bed with his elbows limiting her movement. Her frantic grasping and movement told the story of her passion. Cheryl's desire at the movement drove her to try and make Rick go deeper and at a faster pace. Rick would not allow her to do it. She worked hard at her pleasure and her cat like purrs came from deep within. Rick whispered in her ear. "Tell me what you are?"

"I am whatever you want me to be," she grunted out. "Please tell me Rick, what do you want me to be for you? Tell me and I am her." Rick did not respond. He slowly stabbed at her using himself as a weapon. He trusted hard and drove himself all the way into her. Cheryl screamed with pleasure.

"You are my bitch," Rick whispered in her ear. He drove himself harder and deeper into her.

"Ah yes! I'm your bitch. Yes, yes!" she cried out. Rick used long slow stabbing drives to open her up. Each time he drove home she cried out, uttering *I'm your bitch*. Rick felt her orgasm as her body trembled beneath him and she screamed with pleasure. This was the first time Rick had really enjoyed himself with a woman in a long time, a very long time. All the frustration and tension of the past few months melted as the sensation of his climax neared.

Rick sat quietly in back of the Shalimar, he did not want to move around because the large bundles of money would be seen by everyone. Things had gone well for him the past few weeks and he was very cautious of and with his new success. He knew now more than ever that his future depended on how he and he alone handled the business. Rick sat there studying the beauty of the fashion plate females who graced the bar by their mere presence. He did not want to say anything to them as long as he had all this money bulging from his pockets and the waistband of his pants. That would make him like all the rest who played from behind the power of the dollar. His rule when it comes to woman, it would always be about him and not the image of his success.

Rick watched her moving among the crowd. She was tall, lean and oh-so elegantly dressed. Black alligator shoes, tailored silk slacks with an off setting gray silk shirt. Her diamond studded Cuban gold bracelet sparkled in the dimmed lights of the bar. It took a knowing eye more than one glance to know she was not a man. Bernadette was jubilant in her movement. He watched her as she played the part that fit her so well. She thrilled the ladies with her charm. Don Juan would have been proud. She worked her way over to Rick's table, offering to buy him a drink.

"I'll take an orange juice," he told her. She signaled for a waitress to bring an orange juice for Rick and a rum and coke for her.

"Damn Bernadette, you look like the cat that swallowed the canary."

"Yeah, I feel pretty good. We just got back from Pittsburg. Michael and I just picked up our new cars today. We both are doing a little celebrating," Bernadette told Rick.

"Yeah, I can dig it," Rick responded to her enthusiasm.

"Come outside and check them out."

"Not right now Bernadette, I've got all this money on me."

"It's cool, you can check them out when your business is taken care of," she said.

"You know Rick, a lot of people sleep on you."

"Sleep on me how Bernadette?"

"The way you ease in and out. You always come up with the baddest freaks and you do it on the downlow, real sneaky like. I know being a woman myself, I can see it in you."

"It took me a long time to master a technique where I could look at a woman and know her to become a part of her emotional state of existence," Bernadette told Rick as though he was becoming part of some secret. "But it seems to come so natural for you Rick. You're not what anybody would call a ladies man but you get what you want from the ladies. That look in your eyes say something to them that makes them understand, you know how to touch their deepest emotions whatever they may be. Yeah Rick, we've got to hang out one night and see what we can come up with. I know some underground bars where the women go both ways."

"Okay Bernadette, that sounds good to me."

"Yo Ricky!" Jesse called him from the front doorway of the bar. Rick excused himself from the table and started to walk out.

"Shit, I see why you didn't want to move, you've got fuckin money everywhere," Bernadette gasped.

Rick climbed in the front seat of the car with Jesse.

"So what's up my brother?" Jesse asked.

"Everything is cool. I've got all the money with me," Rick replied. "Would you believe I couldn't find a paper bag to put it in? I didn't want to walk into a store with all this money showing."

"I don't need a bag anyway, just put it in the glove compartment and under your seat," Jesse told Rick. "Check this out Ricky, I'm not going to give out any work tonight. Every motherfucker and his brother is making a drop tonight. That's too much shit on the streets for me to be making a move. So meet me tomorrow night, 9 o'clock at the News Café. Everything alright with you?" Jesse went on to ask Rick. "Is that a good time or what?"

"Yeah, that's cool," Rick replied.

"You need a ride or what?"

"Yeah, drop me off at my mother's. I need to get some sleep. I'm supposed to come by Shemika's house but if I do that I know I won't get any sleep."

"You know Ricky, you surprised a lot of people when you came up with her. She's a good girl and she never gave nobody a play when you were fucked up. She even stopped coming around. I don't know how you do it. I see you ease in and out with bitches that won't give a rich motherfucker a play."

"I don't know, lucky, I guess."

Rick heard the phone ring just as he was about to stick the keys in the lock. He rushed to pick the receiver up before his mother woke up.

"Hello," he said.

"Rick?"

"Yeah Jenny, what can I do for you?"

"You said you were going to give me some money for Sean."

"You calling here this time of night to ask me about money? You didn't even know if I was here."

"So?"

"Look, I'll bring you some money tomorrow."

"Can you bring it now?"

"I'm tired. I'll see you in the morning."

Rick stumbled out of bed making his way to the living room to fall back out on the sofa. He grumbled at Jeff who was sitting at the dining room table reading the Daily News and having breakfast. Jeff mumbled, the kind of greeting that showed their closeness. Yet, at the same time it would have been misunderstood by an outsider.

"Yo Ricky, they had a big bust last night. A shoot out with the police and the whole shit. It's on the front page and three or four pages inside."

"Where did the paper say it happened?" Rick asked.

"Uptown somewhere on Amsterdam Avenue," Jeff replied. "You may know some of these people. A police car pulled up behind a late model black sedan on the corner of 146th street Amsterdam Avenue. They say the occupants of the car, fired several shots and speed off. The police returned fire, knocking out the back window of the car before it got away. The paper also says a number of other suspects fled on foot with the police giving chase. One police officer chased a suspect across 145th street from Amsterdam Avenue, tackling the suspect to the ground on St. Nicholas Place. The officer had at first believed the suspect to be a man. He was shocked to find out it was a woman. I bet that was some crazy shit!" Jeff explained then read the names of the arrested to his brother.

"Yeah, I know all of them," Rick responded. "I was with Bernadette and Michael at the Shalimar last night. They had just picked up their new cars. They wanted me to hang but I cut the fuck out."

"It's a good thing you did or I would be reading your name here instead of telling you about it." The two brothers had a good laugh, they laughed together a lot. "Ma would be all upset if your name was in the paper for this shit and I'd be telling her not to worry because you could handle it."

Rick got up and went in the kitchen to use the phone.

"Hello."

"Yeah Jesse, it's me."

"What's up?"

"Did you read the paper this morning?"

"Yeah, that's some crazy shit!"

"Is everything cool?"

"Everything's okay, meet me in front of my building at 3 o'clock this afternoon."

"Cool my brother, I'll see you later," Rick said and hung up.

"Daddy, daddy!" Sean called his father. Sean was happy to see Rick, running to him and jumped into his arms. Rick kissed him on his cheek and they gave each other five. The people passing on the street watched as they played on the corner. A silver haired white lady stopped to comment.

"He's a happy child," she told Rick, "and he takes to you. You have to be his father."

"Yes I am," Rick replied.

"It's easy to see that you love each other. You have to take good care of him," the old woman told Rick. Jenny approached them carrying clothes in a plastic cleaners' bag over her shoulder.

"This must be your wife," but before Rick could answer she had started to speak to Jenny. "You take care of these two men of yours," the old woman told Jenny. "I've lived a very long time and in my life I have only seen a father and son as close as them a few times. It's a precious thing," the old woman repeated over and over again as she walked away.

"What was that all about?" Jenny asked.

"I don't know, maybe me and Sean reminded her of someone from her past."

"Oh," Jenny responded, tip toeing to kiss Rick on his cheek. "Rick are you going to stay with me and Sean for a little while or do you have to leave?"

It was a beautiful summer afternoon, a gentle breeze blew through the leaves of the trees creating a music all of its own. Rick sat on a piece of cardboard with his back against a tree. Jenny sat between his legs with her head resting on his chest and she felt the familiar touch of his hand on her thigh. They both watched as Sean played mountain man on the rocks. Central Park was a relaxing place to while away the afternoon.

"Look at me daddy! I'm all the way up here! Come up here with me daddy," Sean called his father. Rick eased around the rock and climbed it with the same deadly silence he had used so many times in Vietnam. Before Sean knew what was going on, Rick had picked him up and was playfully biting him on the neck. Sean laughed and fought with his father trying to get away.

"How did you get up here, daddy? I didn't see you."

"That's my secret for now," Rick teased. "I will teach it to you one day."

"Hey daddy you still going to buy me a dog?"

"Sure, you still want the same kind of dog?"

"Yeah, those are the best kind of dogs! My friend has the same kind of dog I want. He named his dog Midnight. When are you going to get the dog for me? Ma said that I should have a puppy but I want to get a big dog so I can ride him like a horse."

"Like a horse, huh? Well I think you're going to get a puppy so you can watch him grow up and you have to take good care of him."

"Okay daddy, when am I going to get my puppy?"

"Sometimes this week. Come on, it's time for daddy to go to work."

"Where do you work daddy?"

"I am an independent businessman. I buy large amounts of product and sell it to small businesses who sells it to different people."

"That's good daddy, I'm going to be a businessman just like you when I grow up."

Rick stood on the corner of 111th street 7th Avenue with several other members of the crew. They kicked the events of the night before and what they had read in the news paper or had seen on television. No one knew for sure how it would affect their business or if it would bring any repercussion from the police. All Rick needed now was to have the police crack down when things were starting to go so well. They all waited patiently for Jesse. He was the only one who could tell them if it would be business as usual.

Boo was the first to see Jesse's black coupe exited Central Park on 110th street 7th Avenue. He pulled up at the curb alongside them.

"Yo, yo, what's up?" he greeted them. Willie nodded his head to acknowledge them before removing a large shopping bag from the trunk of the car to disappear into Jesse building.

"Check this out," Jesse told them. "Everything is still on for tonight. So meet me at the News Café like planned. Anybody needs some money or what?"

"Nah," they all replied, "everything is cool."

"Yo Ricky, you hang tight."

The others got in their cars and drove off.

"So what's up Jesse?" Rick asked.

"Ain't nothing, come upstairs."

They sat in the bedroom Jesse kept at his mother's house.

"So what's up with Bernadette and them?" Rick asked.

"They're alright, I just came from court."

"I didn't know they were down with you."

"They're not, they are with my man's crew. I didn't know if he would need some help with their bail or what. So I took some money down to the court just in case. The whole shit ain't about nothing. The police admitted it could have been the car backfiring. The news media blew the shirt all out of proportion. The judge set the bail at 25 hundred for each of them. So that's like 10 or 15 thousand, so my man can handle that. The DA is running an investigation to see what the fuck did jump off," Jesse explained.

"No shit! The papers made it seem like the Vietnam war took place on a Harlem street corner," Rick responded.

"They don't give a fuck. All they want to do is sell papers," Willie commented.

"It's all about money and the truth has nothing to do with it," Jesse agreed.

"Especially when it comes to black people," Rick added.

"Yeah, they paint us as an evil people shooting at their good white cops," Jesse nodded. "Check this out Ricky, I'm going to give you your thing now, so lay for awhile okay? Willie, take that money and put it away and call me when the thing is hooked up." They laid back in the comfort of Jesse's bedroom knocking out a couple of quarts of grapefruit juice while watching 'It Takes A Thief.' When Alexander Monday made a smooth move, they gave each other five in agreement that they both liked his style.

The bedside phone rang and Jesse grabbed the receiver before the first ring was completed.

"Yo, okay cool," Jesse said into the receiver then hung up. "Ricky, that's Willie. He's downstairs with that thing."

"When do you want to see me with that?" Rick asked.

"Make it in a couple of days. You coming back uptown tonight?" Jesse asked.

"Nah, I don't think so. By the time I hook this up and get something out, it will be early in the morning," Rick said.

"Okay, later my brother," Jesse said as he let Rick out the front door of the apartment.

Rick sat on the chair on one side of the bed. He filled the small envelopes from the grayish white mountain of dope that laid in the center of the bed. Tonya and Latisha sat on the other side of the bed. Tonya folded the bags and Latisha taped them. Rick had grown fond of using hotels to bag up his packages. The larger the package being bagged up, the more exclusive the hotel. It seemed safer to rent a hotel room or suite to work out of. It was for sure no more apartments where the only occupants were his dope and money. He felt better paying someone's rent plus a few hundred dollars thrown in each week for pocket money. It made sense to him that there was always someone standing guard on his product for added insurance.

The Americana Hotel on 7ᵗʰ Avenue in midtown Manhattan was plushed, had security and ordering from room service was convenient. Rick had rented one double room with two beds and a suite with sitting room. After they finished work, Tonya and Latisha would share the double room because once again their mother had thrown them out for getting high. If it had not been for him giving them work, they would have been selling their precious bodies a long time ago just to take care of their habits. They were at the stage of the game where the drugs had not dogged their bodies. In fact, if you did not know they got high you would never be able to tell. Two short toy-like brown skin beauties, Latisha being just a little taller than Tonya. If their looks alone could earn them a dollar, they would be well off.

Hustling was hard work; cutting, bagging, getting the product to the streets and running the street crew without them getting robbed or arrested was a lot for one man to handle. Rick knew he would soon need a partner or lieutenant to help with the responsibilities or his growth would become stagnated. *Who?* he wondered. *Who could he trust?* His thoughts drifted as his hands continued working the mountain of dope. He stared off into the distance, lost to his thoughts. He noticed but did not realize what they were doing when Tonya and Latisha looked at one another then at him.

"Why are you looking at us like that?" Tonya asked. The sound of her voice brought him back to the reality of his surroundings.

"I was just thinking and I was not looking at either of you," he replied.

"You sure had a strange expression on your face," Latisha told him.

"It made us nervous," Tonya added.

"Why?"

"We thought you may have been having one of those Vietnam flashbacks we have heard about on television," Tonya said. "You looked like you were in another world and who knows what you were thinking about when you look like that," Latisha added.

"Well you don't have to worry, I am not going crazy and kill you or anyone else," Rick reassured them. "There was an important question that needs an answer so I was searching to see if I could come up with the solution."

Rick sat in his mother's apartment while she played with the German Shepherd puppy he had got for Sean.

"He's going to love this puppy!" she said. "You've got to watch Sean with this puppy Ricky. You have to make sure he does not hurt this puppy. Sean is a ruff little boy," she went on to say.

"Yeah Ma, I know. Anyway, once you tell Sean something he listens. All I have to do is tell him how to take care of the puppy and it will be alright."

"Yo Rick, you going to be around later?" his brother, Fred asked.

"I don't know. Why, what's up?"

"I need to talk with you about something."

"I'm coming back after I take the puppy to Sean so we can kick it then."

Jou-ju knocked on the door just as Rick opened it.

"Yo what's up?" Rick greeted him.

"Ain't nothing," Jou-ju replied. "Yo Rick, did your brother talk to you about that yet?"

"Talk to me about what?" Rick was puzzled.

"We want to do something but I will let Fred run it to you."

"He just told me he wanted to talk to me about something, so that must be it."

Sean was one happy little boy. He chased the puppy around the living room. The puppy did not like to be manhandled and sought safety under the sofa. Sean called to him but he stayed hidden in the safety of the dark under the sofa. Rick sat on the leather easy chair watching Sean trying to coax the puppy from under the sofa.

"Come here Sean, I need to talk to you."

"Okay daddy. My puppy, he won't come out."

"That's what I want to talk to you about. Come here." Sean ran and jumped on his father's lap.

"That puppy is a baby, you can't play with him like you did my big dog, understand?"

"He's not a baby daddy. He's a dog, my dog."

"That's right, a baby dog and you have to take good care of him until he grows up. If you play with him like you just did, you could hurt him real bad and he could die."

"I won't let him die, daddy. He's my puppy and we're going to play all the time."

"That's good, my little man. You take care of him, and you and him can be friends and play for a long time. You take care of him now and he will protect you when he is big."

THAT NIGHT

"Yo what's up?" Rick greeted Pee Wee and Freddy.

"Ain't nothing Rick, how's everything with you?" Pee Wee asked.

"Everything's cool."

"I've been hearing good things about you, Rick."

"I'm trying to do the right thing for myself," Rick told him.

Pee Wee was a soft spoken man, 6 feet 2 inches tall, lean and athletic looking. Pee Wee had been drafted to play professional basketball along with his teammate Bobby Danridge from Norfolk State University. Bobby Danridge was playing forward with the Milwaukee Bucks, while Pee Wee had turned down the Chicago Bulls offer to play for them. Rumor had it that he turned down 130 thousand dollar per year. That was a lot of money for any player in the early 1970's. Pee Wee's aura and outgoing personality demanded that he be treated like a superstar, even by those who did not know him. If he was not the flyest Blackman, or the flyest man alive there could only be one other to equal his status. That had to be New York Freddy Myers who stood like a carbon copy right next to him. Both were successful businessmen, whom rumored to keep several apartments just for their clothes. For anyone whoever saw them more than twice in one day, that rumor was not hard to believe. They changed outfits and cars several times a day. Black women, Oriental women, White women, Latin women from around the world all came to be on the arms of Pee Wee, as did singers and movie stars. His charm rewarded him with his pick of the most beautiful women in the world.

The blue Cadillac Brougham with white interior and roof, pulled up and stopped in front of Small's Paradise. The driver hit the horn several short blast. Pee Wee excused himself and went to take the seat next to the driver. Rick and the driver's eyes met and locked, yet neither spoke. Jesse came out of Small's to stand alone side of Rick and New York Freddy, only then did Rick brake off his stare. He had been determining not to let the driver forced him to look away.

"That old man is a fly motherfucker," Jesse said. "He and his partner Brown who owns that clothing store House Of Styles are killing them. But it's so hard to talk with them. They don't fuck with just anybody. I'm surprised to see him up here."

"Yeah, so that motherfucker is coming off," Rick said thinking out loud.

"Damn straight," Freddy replied.

Rick leaned back to enjoy the comfort of the ride as he and Jesse headed up 7th Avenue.

"Yo Ricky, there goes that fly old man again. He always has some bad freaks with him," Jesse told him.

"Yo Jesse, pull alone side of him. I want to ask him something."

"What makes you think he's going to kick it with you?"

"He's my father."

"Get the fuck out of here!" Jesse was shocked and it was clearly heard in his voice.

Jesse pulled along side of the blue machine and Rick hit the switch to roll the window down so he could signal his father. His father broke out of his gangster lean to roll down his window and speak with his son.

"How you doing young man?" Rick's father asked.

"I am doing okay, so what's up with you?" Rick asked.

"I'm taking it slow, how's the family?"

"Why don't you call and find out."

"I've been meaning to do just that."

"Yeah, well you take care of that and you can let me have one of those girls with you. I'll take the one sitting in the back against the far door, the red bone."

The young lady shifted in her seat and the bewilderment could be seen on her face, as if asking what *the fuck is going on, who is he?*

"Aren't you going to introduce me? Or maybe you don't want them to know I'm your son."

"It's not that," Rick's father responded. "You didn't give me a chance too."

"I'm Rick," Rick said to the four females in the car. "And you, Ms. Lady can hang with me any time," signaling out the Redbone woman in the rear.

"Where are you headed?" Rick asked his father.

"We're going to get some chicken from the chicken-man," his father replied.

"That's where I'm going. Well, not really, but to the Shalimar to hang for a minute. I thought the chicken-man was closed at this hour," Rick said to his father.

"He's opening for me," Rick's father replied.

Rick sat on the barrel next to his building talking with his brother, Fred. Rick was going over his plan to expand his output. Fred listened closely to all the details of his brother's plan.

"Why are you going to give him dope?" Fred asked his brother. "He's only going to fuck it up."

"Yeah, I know. That's why I'm giving it to him. Each time I make a drop, I plan to give something to one of those motherfuckers who talked shit about me. They popped that garbage about how they would come off if someone gave them a shot," Rick continued to say. "They have the balls to get in my face and talk shit about how they knew I would get back on my feet and the whole shit."

"That's still no reason for you to give them a package," Fred said.

"Yes it is, because once they fuck up like we know they will, they will never be able to ask me for anything again in life. I'm killing two birds with one stone. You never know when one of them will drop a dime on you or set you up to be robbed. By giving them a package to fuck up, they will say I did the right thing by them. Also, they won't be able to pop shit because everyone will know they fucked up and couldn't make it in the game. So, for the few dollars in product I give them its' worth it to shut their mouths and shame them at the same time," Rick explained.

The two brothers sat at the dinning room table enjoying a light summer meal and conversation with their mother. She was happy that her children got along so well.

"Ricky, I forgot to tell you when you came in a little while ago but you got a phone call from Rita. She said that she was at Kennedy airport. The reason I forgot to write it down was, your father called right after I hung up with Rita. Did you see him last night?" she asked.

"Yeah, I saw him," Rick replied. "He said he was going to call and see how everyone was doing."

"That's not why he called. He was more interested in how I was raising you."

"What? That's none of his damn business!" Rick said in anger.

"He wanted to know what kind of people I let you run around with."

"What did you say?"

"I asked him how he knew what kind of people they were."

"He's got a lot of shit with him. I bet he didn't mention that one of my friends got in his car."

"You know Rick," Fred jumped in, "He must still think you are 12 years old."

"No shit."

"That was the last time he came around playing that father role," Fred laughed. They joked about his millions of broken promises. It was funny to them now but as mere children they were heartbroken.

"That's one thing I told Sean, when I thought he was old enough to understand. That I would never make him a promise I could not keep. And that he could always come to me for any reason at any time," Rick added. This set their conversation to a serious note.

"That's what I always told all of my children, that you could always come to me," their mother said.

"Yeah Ma, and we are glad you did," Fred said.

"But it's just not the same, a boy should be able to sit down and talk with his father," Rick added. "Even though we do talk about everything in this family. There is some advice that only a father should give his son. I am not talking about sexual advice."

"Yes, I do understand and I told your father that his sons would never forgive him for that," his mother agreed.

Rick pulled the power blue Cougar over at the phone booth on the corner and told his brother that he would just be a minute. It was a hot morning and one could tell the sun would be blazing later on, driving most everyone indoors. The phone rang three or four times, Rick had grown impatient listening to it ring.

"Hello, New York Hilton, one moment please. Yes, how may I help you?"

"Yeah, give me room 1620."

"Hello," Rita said. "Yeah, this is Rita."

"Hey there, it's me Rick!"

"Hi daddy, I missed you."

"Is that right?"

"Yes, when can I see you?"

"I'll pick you up around 9:30 tonight."

"Daddy, I haven't seen you in along time. I have so much to tell you! Don't you want to come by now, daddy?"

"I'm busy right now. We can talk all you like when I see you tonight."

"Okay daddy." Rick hung up and got back in the car. Rick and Fred smoked a joint and talked as they rode. Their conversation was light as they enjoyed the freedom of this type of lifestyle.

Rick doubled-parked the Cougar between Amsterdam Avenue and Broadway on 79th street, right in front of the Only Child Restaurant. Rita had tried to get him into bed the moment he stepped in her room at the Hilton. She had aroused him to the point of no return and it took all that he had to stop himself from sexing her. He knew from experience he could build her passion and lust to the point of boiling just by making her wait. Thus giving him more pleasure when they did play. He toyed with her all the way to the restaurant. The Only Child was the first restaurant of its kind in the new age of New York. Dimly lit to the point of almost being to dark, the décor was simple. The music set to be soft so it wouldn't disturb one's conversation. The unique style set by this restaurant was your choice of being seated inside or outback on the patio. They had chosen to sit under the plastic bubble that shielded the patio. The five or six tables had been arranged to provide intimate conversation without worry of being overheard by others. The food was excellent, soul, and no pork. The restaurant was geared more for the bourgeois whites who like black food and music. It was a place where hustlers and players of more reserve chose to be.

"Europe was great. It was that asshole with his kinky shit that fucked it up. He got me work with Vogue and commercial works on Paris television, but mostly I did runway work," Rita started the conversation. "I had to work so damn hard to satisfy his kinky sexual habits, it became almost impossible to please him. That's when he started to tell me about things I never imagined to be sex. The man is sick and his wife is down with that sick shit. She is the reason I left. I withdrew when she wanted me to get down with animals. Her thing was to suck my pussy after I had several men cum in me. He liked to watch her eat me while someone fucked her and it could be a man or dog. They used me as a hoe. So I decided if I had to sell my ass, I was going to be paid cash. Daddy, they had me on some real bullshit. They would get me jobs modeling and I would bust my ass doing the assignments. Then I would have to put up with their kinky bullshit because I am supposed to be grateful they got me the jobs. Fuck them!" Rita said angrily.

Rick did not interrupt Rita. He listened to all she had to say. He knew she needed someone to unburden herself on. When the meal came they enjoyed it in silence. Rita had coffee with dessert, Rick had milk.

"So tell me. What are your plans? I spoke with Blanche and I am having lunch with her tomorrow."

"So you plan to become a working girl all over again?"

"No, I have other plans. The few dollars I saved while in Paris will cover the cost of getting set up in a nice apartment. I figure if I turn one or two tricks a week for Blanche, I can hit all the modeling agencies by day."

"Working for Blanche, I won't be pushed into making the wrong career move. You know I am a good model, daddy. All the photographers that I worked with told me I was a natural. The whole thing with the modeling business is who you fuck. So daddy, I have made up my mind that I will fuck for cash and work hard for my fame."

"I see you have got it all together Young Lady."

"No, its' you who showed me how to get it together, daddy. You gave me the strength to know who I am. When things got bad and I was fed up with the bullshit over there I remembered all the times we sat talking. In your words, I found the confidence to look within myself and push on."

"Is that so? And all the time I thought it was my pretty faced you liked," Rick teased.

"Ah daddy, it wasn't your face, it was that body I was after."

"Is that so? Well, we have to see what can be done about that," and he signaled for the check.

The crowd overflowed from the basketball court onto the sidewalk. Earl Manigault had brought fame to the ball court on 99th street Amsterdam Avenue. Today was the first of the semi-final playoff games in the basketball tournament sponsored by Nicky Barnes. Rick stood there with Sean sitting on his shoulders along with the locals and others from around the city that had come to watch the game. He would be playing later on that afternoon. Rick watched Joe Lewis worked magic on the court with his jump shot. Instant two points every time he released the ball. Rick remembered when they had played ball one summer during his first year of high school. The Church Of The Masters had taken several teams to Colorado to play ball. They were delighted at how the crowd cheered their moves and jumping ability. The one thing the crowd never failed to marvel at, no matter where they played was the smoothness of

Joe's jump shot, and today he was throwing them down with the same ease.

Rick had fixed Sean something to eat and when he came out of the shower, Sean was waiting for him to refill his plate.

"Daddy, can I have some more beans please?"

"Damn my man, you really must like them," Rick said. They both had the same taste for vegetarian beans, and ate them with just about every meal. They had become the joke of the family; like father, like son, beans and more beans. Rick grabbed the phone pulling it from the cradle before the first ring was complete.

"Yo Rick, it's me, I'll be home in a few minutes."

"Everything's cool?"

"Yeah, everything is cool," his brother replied.

Rick and Fred sat in the living room laughing as Sean played with his uncle.

"So Fred, we can take care of that after the game tomorrow?" Rick asked.

"You must have won your game today," Fred replied.

"Yeah, it was a good game."

"How much did you score?"

"I think I hit about 25 and I threw it down three times."

"How many times did you fall and bust your ass?"

"I didn't fall one time."

"Get out of here! Do you expect me to believe that?" Fred joked.

"Okay, I fell one time," Rick copped out.

"I'll go for that, but one time is still kind of hard to believe. I remembered Jeff told me one time that he and his friends used to go watch you play just to see how many times you would fall. And they would have bets to see who would be the closest. You fall in slow motion like in the movies," Fred teased his brother.

"That's because I jump so high, when I get pushed in the air I relax so I don't get hurt when I come down," Rick explained.

"I don't care why you do it. It looks funny as a fuck!" Fred laughed.

"People come from all over just to watch you fall."

"Nah, they come to watch me bust a motherfucker ass, the falling is a little something extra they get along with the show I put on," Rick proclaimed.

Rick and Crime stood in front of the Shalimar talking with Flat Top, Guy Fisher and Frank James. All around them splendidly dressed men talked in small groups and the women as always were every man's fantasy. This night like any other was business as usual and everyone enjoyed the gaiety of the night.

"Yo Crime, tell Jesse I'll see him some time tomorrow," Rick said.

"What's up?" Crime asked. "You know Jesse is going to show in a little while."

"I've got this girl waiting on me. It's 2 o'clock and she gets off from work at 2:30 tonight.. So, I'm going to break out so I can get her."

"Okay, my brother."

"Later Guy, Frank, Top," Rick said.

"Yeah, later Rick."

Rick eased the car up around and along the hilly streets that made up the drive through Central Park. He listened and sang along with the music blared from the car's sound system. The cloud of smoke from the reefer was swept away when he hit the switch to lower the window. Rick caught the light to exit Central Park on 59th street 7th Avenue, only to be stopped by the red light on 57th street. Rick eyed the few people who strolled along on this summer night. *Tourists*, he thought to himself.

Rick worked the car across the Avenue, around and back up 59th street 5th Avenue to double-park in the shadows of the trees lining Central Park East. The Plaza Hotel stood as a grand reminder of the elegance of New York's past. The few horse carriages that lined the park side just in front of him, were a strange sight in modern New York. Nevertheless, Rick knew the stage coachmen were awaiting the lone millionaire to exit the Plaza Hotel with sweetheart in tow for that romantic late night ride through the gentle quiet of a Central Park night.

When Rick saw Rita, he stepped out from the shadows and went across 59ᵗʰ street. Rita only saw him when he was about to step from the street onto the sidewalk. Rick could see the sparkles in Rita's eyes as she raced down the front steps of the Plaza to throw herself into his arms. They embraced and Rick looked from their embrace at the beauty Rita had been standing on the steps with. His eyes followed the shape of her slightly bow legs and up the short skirt that fit so nicely showing the curves of her body, then back to her legs. It was not until Rita broke their embrace and called her friend did Rick noticed her pretty face. She was a stunning beauty and his eyes followed the stride of her legs as she made her way to where they stood.

"Rick this is Jacqui, Jacqui this is Rick." She offered her hand and he took it.

"Please to meet you," Rick sincerely said.

"I am pleased to meet you," Jacqui replied. "Rita has told me so much about you that I feel I already know you."

"Rick, if you have the time would you take Jacqui and me to get something to eat?" Rita asked.

Rick found a nice quiet candle lit restaurant in the village, not to far from where Rita had rented a loft. They were enjoying the pleasure of one another's company. Each was sincere in stating their feelings and oblivious to all that was around them. Jacqui was warm and outgoing. She and Rita joked about the trick they had just left at the Plaza. He had taken them to dinner and a show on Broadway. The sex was so so and did not get them off. Two thousand dollars a picce for several hours work. "Where else but in New York," Jacqui joked.

"Where are you from Jacqui?" Rick asked.

"Texas, Corpus Christi," she answered.

"I've been there, nice little town. I've been all through Texas; Temple, Waco, Houston, Dallas, plus some places so small I can't remember their names."

"That's Texas alright," Jacqui laughed, "small hot towns not worth remembering."

"So why have you chosen to grace our city?"

246 PRISONER OF DREAMS

"I want to be an actress. During the day I take acting lesson."

"Ah, I see now why you and Rita get along so well. She's going to be a top fashion model and you an academy award winning actress. Just don't forget me once you both are famous."

"You know I could never forget you daddy," Rita purred.

"You know Rick, Rita has told me if it wasn't for you she would still be standing on a corner selling her pussy."

"Maybe, maybe not, that's something we will never know the answer to. But I would like to think I helped in some small way."

"She also told me that you were good in bed."

"Is that right?"

"She's like my sister, daddy and I shared everything with her," Rita said. "She knows my thoughts, feelings and my dreams, daddy."

"Since I have been in New York, the only men I have been with are the ones who pay to be with me," Jacqui sadly said. "My sex life has been all business."

"Sex is 90 percent a thing of the mind," Rick responded. "Most people find pleasure in the mechanics of sex never to find the key that opens the door for their true sexual gratification. A man in satisfying himself must understand first that his pleasure really comes from pleasing. Not only in what he gives, but to truly know what a woman's pleasure is and not what he thinks it is. Most men think that some magical power is to be found in their dick. They believe that sex makes them strong when in truth it makes them weak. Once a man realizes that the power of sex is in the mind he has found the magic that makes for unbelievable pleasure. I myself find my pleasure in the response I receive in waxing a bitch's ass. So if that makes me good in bed, then I'm great. No, I'm only kidding about the great part," Rick laughed.

"Well Rick, I will tell you this," Jacqui said. "You have impressed me and as a free thinking woman you have captured my mind and soul. You have stimulated a desire in me of wanting to know more about you."

"See, I told you Jacqui, he is the kind of man every women needs to know," Rita jumped in.

"If you ever want this body Rick, it goes with my free spirit and is yours for the asking," Jacqui offered.

"So that's it!" Rick joked. "You two have plans for passing me around!"

His remarks caused them all to laugh. At this moment they shared an unmentioned bond of togetherness, a kind of oneness.

It was a humid summer night, Rick stood on the corner talking with Crime. He watched Jenny sitting in the comfort of the air-conditioned car.

"Look Crime, I'm pumpin 24/7, and it was my brother and his man that got me over the hump."

"Yeah, I know," Crime replied. "Jesse was talking about you last night. But that shit with you giving those suckers dope to fuck up is crazy, Rick."

"If you really want to know the truth about it, I could have killed them all without a thought. If I was like some of the others' who came back fuck up from Nam I most likely would have. You'd be surprised to see how easy it came to me once I looked at the first person I killed."

"That was different," Crime said. "You didn't know who you were killing and they were trying to kill you at the same time."

"You're right in that part, my man. I didn't know why I was killing them other than to stay alive. But my so-called friends put my life in danger and that is enough reason enough to have killed every one of them."

"So why didn't you kill them?"

"Hatred, pure hatred. My hatred for them was so great that killing them would have held no satisfaction for me. My greatest satisfaction comes from knowing they ain't shit. I gave them work, they fucked up so they know they ain't shit in their own minds. Every time they have to face me, it's more salt in the wound. I don't say shit. I just act like everything is everything. I listened to their bullshit and it would have been nothing to kill anyone of them with ease. But they just ain't worth it," Rick explained.

"I wanted them to live, to see this day," Rick continued. "I'm back on top and they still ain't shit. Besides my brother, killing them wouldn't have got me my money back either. Look, I've got to break out. I'm going to take my son's mother home and get shit ready for tonight. I'll catch you later, my brother."

Rick eased the car into Central Park on 110th street 7th Avenue, up the hill and around to the west 106th street exit. Rick pulled along side of a gypsy cab to wait on the red light to change before exiting the park. Midway through the block on 106th street, between Central Park and Manhattan Avenue, he noticed a yellow cab with the driver's side door wide open. It was parked in the middle of the street in front of the Castle Hotel. Rick felt the chill of danger as it crept from his feet towards his head. Then an image played back to when he had exited the park. The man standing in the middle of the street that he had only acknowledged in his subconscious, waving his arms like he had gone mad was the cab driver. A momentary thought, he must have been robbed. Then Rick's attention focused on the late model black Mark IV. The broken door window on the driver's side was slightly open. And there was Melvin, his arm hung lifelessly in the sleeve of his black silk suit jacket. His head laid against the headrest as though he were asleep. A thin stream of blood poured like a waterfall from his left ear.

"Damn, Melvin!" Rick said out loud but to himself. It was not till Rick had spoken Melvin's name did Jenny noticed his body and began to scream.

"Shut the fuck up! You want people to see us?" Rick scolded Jenny. Rick slowed the car to a crawl as he passed in order to get a better look at what had happened to Melvin. Rick sped up and caught the light climbing the hill to Columbus Avenue. He made the turn on Columbus Avenue and headed downtown.

"I'm going to take you straight home," Rick told Jenny. "I've got some things to take care of."

"What about Sean?" Jenny asked.

"He can stay at my mother's until later."

"No, I want him to come home now. I don't want to stay in that apartment by myself after seeing that!"

"What? You didn't even know the man! So why should it bother you?"

"It's not everyday that people see dead body on the streets and it scares some of us," Jenny said trying to be at ease. "Look Rick, just because you are used to seeing dead people laying around in Vietnam and it does not bother you now. It's still a shock to me. So, please stop so I can get Sean."

"Okay, so when he comes in tell him to wait on me because I am on my way up. Tell him its important, thank you," Rick hung the phone up in his mother's bedroom and joined the others in the living room. Jenny was telling them what she had seen.

"Jenny!" Rick yelled, interrupting her in middle of a sentence. "You think what you saw is something to talk about?"

"I'm only telling the family," she replied. "God Rick, you're always on some top secret garbage."

"Next, you will be telling Faye and who knows who else. You think this is a game? People hear you talking about being one of the first to see the body, next thing you know the police will come around asking questions. You don't know who killed him and if word gets around someone may think you saw something that you didn't or shouldn't have. Talking could be the cause for you to end up with a bullet in your head Ms. So keep your mouth shut please," Rick said.

"Don't be so ruff on her Ricky," his mother defended Jenny.

"Ruff? This is not a game, Ma."

"I know Ricky, but you didn't have to come down on her like that." Rick caught a glimpse of Sean from the corner of his eye. He noticed how Sean's eyes darted back and forth between each person as they spoke.

"Yeah, okay Ma, we can talk about this later. Come here Sean, I want to talk to you." Sean ran and jumped in his father's arms. Rick told his brother Fred that he wanted to speak with him in the back bedroom.

Rick sat Sean on the sofa bed to watch television while he spoke with his brother. They both stood in front of the bedroom window. Rick put his arm around his brother's shoulder and spoke just above a whisper in his ear.

"I don't know what's going on yet," Rick said. "I just called Jesse house but he wasn't in. I told his mother if he came in to ask him to wait for me. I didn't know Melvin well but he was getting money. He used to hang with Frank Matthews some times. I'm not sure if he was down with

Frank or what. It may have been a hit on Melvin because he owed money. Or, it could just some bullshit. Whatever the fuck is going on I don't want to be in the middle unless I know who the players are. I wouldn't normally be alarmed about a situation like this but I saw the body. The killer could have still been on the set and recognized me or my car. For these reasons alone I've got to find out what is what," Rick informed his brother.

Rick stood quietly on the stoop of the building next to the Shalimar. The crowd was a bit smaller than usual. When Shemika drove up Rick noticed her warm smile and it eased the intensity of danger he felt. He watched the titillating beauty of her stride as she made her way to where he stood. Shemika tiptoed to kiss Rick and he felt the softness of her body push the hard gun holster up against his rib cage. He knew she had felt it by the way she stepped back and the sadness that now showed in her eyes.

"I'm moving a lot of money tonight, it's just for protection," Rick lied. "So don't worry." He did not like to lie to her of all people.

"How did…?" she started to say.

"It's written all over your face, even though you tried to hide your surprise when you felt it." Rick kissed her softly on the lips and her tongue quickly found its way into his mouth.

"What are you trying to do girl," Rick teased.

"Nothing that you don't want to do," she seductively replied. "But you have to work so I guess I will turn the air-conditioning up in the car to cool it off."

"Lucky air-conditioning," Rick joked. Shemika hit him playfully on his arm in response to his smart remark.

Jesse pulled the black Lincoln Mark IV to a stop in front of the bar and blew the horn to get Rick's attention.

"I've got to go," Rick informed Shemika. "If you don't have any plans for later I will come by your apartment in an hour or so."

"You promise?" she asked like a small child.

"I'm coming by if you are going to be home."

"I can't say for sure what time though. Okay Rick, I will wait on." Shemika kissed Rick and told him to be careful as she walked away.

Rick bent over to speak to Jesse through the passenger side window.

"Get in," Jesse told him.

"I'm dirty," Rick replied.

"That's alright, I am too." Jesse eased the car back into traffic and they made their way up 7th Avenue.

"So what's up?" Rick asked.

"Ain't nothing, I've been in Brooklyn all night with them Guineas taking care of business," Jesse replied. "So why are you strapped, you got a problem or something Ricky? My mother told me you called and needed to see me about something important. If you've got a problem we can go take care of it right now."

"Nah, I don't have a problem. I don't think I have a problem."

What is it then?"

"You know Melvin?"

"Which one?"

"The one who has the black Mark IV like this one."

"Yeah, he's my man. Well he's not really my man, we are just alright. He's getting money too."

"He's dead."

"Get the fuck out of here!"

"Yeah, and I stumbled up on his body. That's why I am strapped. I don't know if the motherfucker who killed him saw me or what the fuck is going on. So I got my shit with me to be on the safe side."

"Where did all this take place?" Jesse asked.

"He was shot in the head. He parked across the street from the Castle Hotel down my way," Rick informed Jesse. "He was dead when I got there, but the blood was still running from his ear. He couldn't have been dead more than 10 or 15 minutes, if that long. Looks like whoever hit him put the gun in his right ear. The impact blew him up against the driver's side door and his body broke the window," Rick explained what he saw earlier.

"Damn," Jesse stated more to himself in disbelief than a response to what Rick had been saying. "You tell anyone else about this?"

"Nah, I didn't want to invite trouble."

"It had to be his crew business or someone tried to rob him. There are no problems on the streets that would cause us to go around shooting each other. At lease that I know of," Jesse added. "You know what I'm saying Ricky?"

"Yeah, I can dig it."

"Look my brother, can I drop you off somewhere? I want to check on a few matters and I'll get back with you later my brother."

"My car is back at the bar, so you can drop me off any place where I can catch a cab easy," Rick said.

"Where are you going to be, at your mothers or home?"

"Call me at Shemika's."

It was five in the morning when the phone rang waking Shemika after she had just drifted into a post sexual sleep. Rick turned the sound down on the television while she spoke on the phone.

"Here, it's for you," she said, "It's Jesse."

"Yo my man, what is it?" Rick said into the receiver.

"Ain't nothing, everything's cool. There are a lot of rumors being kicked around. But it doesn't look like nothing big is jumping off. You can relax and hang loose my brother. Do thing the way you feel comfortable with them Ricky. Meet me in front of my mother's building tomorrow afternoon at one o'clock," Jesse said.

"Okay, later." Rick said and hung up.

Rick reached over Shemika to place the receiver back in its cradle on the bedside table. He could feel the warmth her naked body generated and the smooth softness of her skin. He bit her tenderly on the neck and ran his hand down her back and over the curve of her ass. His hand lingered on her ass, tracing its shape. His hand seemed to have a mind of its own as his fingers found their way between her legs. He buried his finger in the wetness of her womanhood. She rolled over opening her legs to his touch, only to question his actions.

"What's going on Rick?"

"I am trying to enjoy the wonders of your body," he responded.

"It's more than my body that has you excited, I know you Mr. Talley. The way you fucked me tonight, I know it was more than the passion of the flesh that drove you to sex me like that. I can feel the change in your touch now, the burning intensity, the all consuming passion. Don't get it wrong Rick, I really enjoy it too when you get this way. I enjoy the way you make me feel whenever you sex me. But the way you sexed me tonight was like you had something extra built up deep within you. You know what I am trying to say Rick?"

"Yes, so it seems you really do know me, Ms."

Jesse pulled the black machine over between Morningside Park and Manhattan Avenue on 116th street. He called Cisco who sat on a car, parked on the shady side of the street.

"Yo what's up Jesse, Rick," Cisco greeted them as he crossed the street.

"Ain't nothing," both replied.

"Melvin's funeral is tomorrow."

"All that shit we have been hearing about how fucked up Melvin's face is bullshit!" Jesse told Cisco.

"How do you know?"

"My man here saw the body."

"No shit, Rick!"

"Yeah, I stumbled onto his body, he was still in his car. They said his whole head was blown off and that he was so fucked up they weren't going to open the coffin," Cisco told them.

"That's bullshit!" Rick responded.

"Did you read what the papers said," Cisco asked them.

"Yeah," Jesse replied.

"I read that shit too," Rick added.

"The papers said they found ten thousand in his apartment. The police had no idea of who he was or what he was into. They had no record of him being involved in any wrongdoing. When they asked his wife what he did for a living, she told them she didn't know. All she knew was that he paid the bills on time," Jesse said.

"That's the way it's supposed to be," Rick agreed. "He did the right thing by keeping her in the dark."

"When the investigation is over, she will get that money back," Cisco added.

"That's bullshit!" Jesse bellowed. "Them whitey's are going to keep that money."

"On what grounds, though?" Rick asked.

"Because they are white and they want to."

"You've got a point."

CHAPTER FIVE

Look Again
Just Another Part of The Game

SITTING QUIETLY AT the far end of the bar, Rick watched the middle-aged white man's image in the mirrors that lined the wall behind the bar. Rick noticed his salt and pepper afro and thought it to be overstated. Tuesday's was the happening place for the so-called 'Jetset whites' who walked on what could be called the wild-side of life. Along with their six figures jobs, a line of coke every now and then, as well as the misuse of what they thought was a hip term, Rick was intrigued by a world that exposed the raw side of its nature to him. The strange reality of it all was, Rick knew he was much too fast for their porcelain world of make to believe. So on occasions, when he wanted to escape the madness from which he made his living of, he made rounds in the clubs where you were judged only by your ability to pay.

Rick would never forget the first time he had come to Tuesday's. He had chosen a spot at the rear of the bar where he could sit and view the movement and mixture of the crowd. That's when a pretty statuesque blond in a black gown that was cut shockingly low in the back approached him with a drink in hand.

"You look like you are a dangerous man," she said as she approached to bait him. "Are you dangerous," she whispered.

"That depends on just how dangerous you would like me to be," Rick replied. She took him to her Park Avenue penthouse and he showed her how dangerous he was in bed. Much to her delight.

After Rick had served her and she was completely spent and recovering from being fucked crazy, she told Rick that she was an actress on an ABC day time soap opera. Rick's indifference to her status in life infuriated her. So much so that she now wanted more from him than he was willing to give. She had become the victim in a game where she was used to setting the rules. Rick was always willing to play and they never knew until it was too late. The danger they sought in him was not what they expected when he changed the rules of the game by leaving them, so that they wanted more of him. And that it came when it was too late for them to do anything about it.

Rick stood grooming himself in the mirror of the club's restroom. There had not been much going on tonight and he decided he would try one of the underground clubs. Rick noticed the change of atmosphere once he stepped out of the restroom. His eyes once again caught sight of the slim middle-aged white man with the salt and pepper afro, or was it the two beauties that attended his needs like slaves. He watched as the two beauties wiped and mopped his face and clothes. "That low class bitch didn't have to throw a drink in your face," one of the beauties said.

Rick paid his bar tap and exited the club. He walked over to the Avenue of the Americas. Midway between 58th and 57th street, he heard the wailing of a female who sounded as though she were in a great deal of pain. As he approached near the sound, her cries seemed even more agonizing. At this late hour, the Avenue of the Americas was a lonely deserted stretch of emptiness for as far as the eye could see.

Rick noticed four men standing in a semicircle around a mailbox where the wailing appeared to be coming from. Three of the men had on business suits and their style of dress told him that they were most likely from out of town. The fourth man had on work clothes and Rick guessed that he had just gotten off from work in one of the large hotels in the area. Rick stepped in between two of the men, they looked up for a brief moment before returning their attention back to the pretty young girl who sat on the ground and cried.

Rick knew she was not one of the many crazies that ran loose on the street of New York by the way she was dressed. At first, he thought her to be a hoe. This area is known for high-priced call girls. Upon closer inspection, he knew this was not the case. Her expensive tailored clothes, she had manicured hands and in spite of the mascara that ran down her cheeks because of her tears, there was freshness about her beauty.

"Are you alright?" Rick asked her. His question seemed to make her cry even more. Rick squatted and took her hand. "Come on, get up and let's get ouf of here." All life seemed to have been drawn from her. Her limbs hung lifelessly as he tried to lift her. "Come on now," Rick coaxed, "it can't be that bad."

Once Rick had managed to get her on her feet and to sit on the hood of a car, the four men disappeared into the shadows of the lonely street. Rick placed his hand under her chin to force her to look into his eyes. She fought his attempt. Rick talked on, his gentle manner seem to ease her pain and her breathing return to a normal rhythm.

"So, do you want to talk about it?" Rick asked her.

"That motherfuckers…" she bellowed, not yet fully in control of her emotions. "He invited me out for drinks and he had those cheap bitches with him!"

"Who are we talking about and where did all this take place?"

"It happened in Tuesday's and the motherfucker is Bob."

"Is he tall and lanky with salt and pepper hair?"

"Yes, that's him! Bob Stone. Do you know him?" she asked, her eyes searching for comfort.

"I don't know him personally, but I know who you are talking about though," Rick responded.

Rick took the handkerchief from his suit-jacket's upper pocket. He held her chin in his hand and wiped the black mascara from around her eyes and off her cheeks.

"I can do that," she weakly protested.

"Now would you deny me the chance to show that chivalry is not dead? Would you like to go back to Tuesday's for a drink or some other place?" Rick asked.

"No, no thank you. I would like to go home. I have to work in the morning," she politely rejected the offer.

Work? Rick thought, *where would a lady like this work?*

"Work, and just where do you work?" Rick asked.

"I make commercials. Maybe you have seen them on television. I am the "Charlie Perfume Girl."

"Yes, I've seen your work. They are better than some of the programs they sponsored."

"Why, thank you."

"So Ms. Charlie, what do I call you?"

"My name is Maggie."

"Well Maggie, it's nice to meet you. I'm Rick."

"I would like to thank you Rick for being so understanding".

"It's my pleasure," he replied.

"If you will help me once more, I would like to catch a cab home," she told Rick.

"That is my car parked across the street, the black one on the corner. I would be more than happy to drive you home," Rick offered her.

She made small talks as Rick worked the car along Central Park West. He listened as she made herself to feel at ease with him, inviting him to a place where she needed someone the most at this moment in her life.

Rick pulled to a stop in front of the tall white building on 72nd street between Columbus Avenue and Central Park West. The doorman rushed to open the car door. She backed him off with a wave of her hand.

"Is this your apartment building?"

"No, it's Bob's," she replied. "He has this place and a mansion on 5th Avenue."

"So where do you live?"

"I live in Missouri with my parents on a farm. I fly in once or twice a month to work. I stay with Bob while I'm in town. I don't know why Bob does this to me," she said more to herself than Rick. "He knows I have to work in the morning. Now the make-up man has his work cut out for him. What really has me so upset is the way I change his dirty diapers when he wants to play his kinky sex games. I don't get anything from the way he like his sex other than the pleasure of knowing I pleased him, and I only do it because I love him. Bastard, this is how he repays my love."

"How old are you Maggie?"

"I am 20 years old. Don't tell anyone, everyone thinks I am 17. That will give me a few more years to work in the business. Rick, I want to thank you for being a friend. You are a good man." Her words caused a pause in time. They leaned towards one another, their lips met. A brief kiss filled with electricity to seal the bond of understanding.

"Rick, if you want to get in touch with me, leave a message with the doorman here or come by the agency. It's on 53rd street Fifth Avenue."

"I know where it is, I've been there many times."

"I'm only going to be in town long enough to finish these commercials. I want to get the fuck away from Bob as soon as I can." She opened the door, leaning over to kiss Rick at the same time. He watched as she made her way into the lobby of the building, disappearing from sight. Rick sat there a few moments more, contemplating his next move. He looked at the clock on the dashboard, it read 2:15. It was still early, enough time to find actions somewhere in the Big Apple. *Let me go by my mother's house first, I don't feel like this suit and tie any longer.*

"Ricky, Jesse has called here several times tonight looking for you."

"I'm sorry he woke you, Ma. Did he say what he wanted?"

"He said to call him at his mother's house. He said he would be waiting on your call," she informed her son. "It sounded like it was important Ricky. Is everything alright?"

"Yeah Ma, everything is alright with me."

"Well, I'm going back to bed. Would you call him so I can get some sleep, please."

"Yeah ma, I'm going to call him right now."

The phone rang just as Rick was about to lift the receiver from the cradle.

"Yo."

"Ricky, I told you about saying 'yo' when you answer the phone!" she scolded her son.

"Okay Ma."

"Okay my foot! You do what I told you to do!"

"Okay Ma. So what's up Jesse?"

"How much money can you get hold of right now?" Jesse asked.

"I don't know. I've got six G's on hand. If you can wait until 9 or 10 o'clock tomorrow morning I can get more, a lot more," Rick explained.

"No, come to my mother's house, bring the six G's."

"Alright, I'll be there in 15 minutes."

Jesse was standing outside of his mother's building when Rick pulled up. They greeted each other.

"So what's up?" Rick asked.

"Freddy and everybody who went to Atlantic City is busted," Jesse informed Rick.

"What? Get the fuck out of here!" Rick said in surprise. "What are they busted for?"

"I'm not sure. Cisco said something about murder when he called. I want you to ride down with me, Ricky."

"Who else is going?"

"I don't know. I think Black Donald is going so he can bail the people in his crew out. You got that money with you?"

"Yeah."

"Here's the key, put it in the trunk." Rick opened the trunk to find three cardboard boxes filled with rolled up knots of money held by rubber bands. The sight of all that money brought tears to his eyes.

"Damn Jesse, how much money is this?"

"It should be 680 thousand with your six G's."

"Do you think the bail is going to be that much?"

"I don't know. I sure hope not. I don't want my money tied up in court while the case is ongoing. Yo Ricky, we can cut out as soon as Skull brings me the 25 G's he said he had. He should be here in another ten minutes," Jesse informed Rick.

CHAPTER SIX

Jersey Shore

THE FLOAT OF the Lincoln Town car through the tranquil beauty along the Garden State parkway made the trip to Atlantic City an easy drive. They had been to Atlantic City many times. Yet neither had any idea as to how they would find the court house.

"Pull over Jesse, we can ask that cop how to get to the court house. If he doesn't know, no one will," Rick joked.

"Excuse me officer!" Jesse called him. "Can you tell me how to get to the court house?"

"Yes Sir," the officer replied. "It's two blocks over this way, you can't miss it once you make the turn at the corner."

"Thank you," Jesse replied and drove off in the direction the officer had pointed them in.

"You hear that shit Ricky, the police said sir. You never hear that shit from the police in New York."

"I know what you mean. The police in New York draw their guns and call you nigger if you ask them where St. Patrick's Cathedral is." They shared a good laugh about the rudeness of the New York City police.

They spotted Black Donald and his woman at the same time they did the court house. Greetings were exchanged and they got right into the business at hand.

"We have been inside already," Black Donald said. "They haven't started to call cases. No one could tell us anything either. They said we had to wait until the court docket is made up. It should be ready by 9:30 or so they said," Black Donald added.

"Court don't open until 10 o'clock," Black Donald's woman informed them.

"So we have about two hours to kill," Rick commented. "So what do you want to do Jesse?

"We have to ask around and find a lawyer that worth a dime to handle the arraignment. We need a good lawyer if the only thing he can do is get bail set," Jesse stated.

The one story "A" frame buildings that housed the bail bondmen's and legal firms around the court house were closed at this hour of the morning. So everyone decided to have breakfast at the all night dinner across the street from where they stood.

They sat quietly in the back of the dinner. They listened as the waitress and short order cook spoke about the big arrest. When the waitress brought their orders, Rick used the opportunity to question her knowing she would be willing to tell all she knew.

"Yes, some fellows from New York rented the Motel New Yorker," she said. "Every damn room for one big party, they sure must have a lot of money to throw away. But it wasn't really a party if you know what I mean. More like one of them there sex orgies," she whispered. "Seems they came down on a chartered bus and a lot of fancy cars, yeah that's what I heard. Money, drugs and naked people all over the place is how I heard."

"Lord, what this is world coming to," Rick said in his best southern accent. He could see the others holding back their laughter.

The court room was crowded, it seemed that every law enforcement officer who was not on duty this day had come for the arraignment. Extra chairs had been placed in front of the fourteen seat jury box for all the defendants. The court was a buzz when the bailiff called order. The men defendants were brought in, in different stages of dress and undress and placed in the jury box. They numbered so many of them it over flowed into the seats set up in front of the jury box. The women, some with blankets wrapped around them were placed in the first two rows of seats in the spectators section.

The district attorney stated his name for the record and the attorney for all the defendants did likewise. The attorney for the defendants informed the court that he had been hired by friends of the defendants. The district attorney begin, "A young man has been murdered. We have a full confession, witnessed and signed. We believe that this pretty much covers the most unfortunate circumstances that took place early this morning," the DA stated. "We have 22 men and 39 women who were at the scene of the crime. They played no part whatsoever in the most serious of the crimes. Nevertheless, they were charged with several misdemeanor counts. Lewd and lascivious conduct I believe are the charges." The DA's office wished to pursue, the attorney for the defendants stated,"You're Honor; my clients were arrested in the privacy of their motel rooms. Whether their rooms were wide open or locked should have no bearing on the fact that the state of New Jersey has violated each and every one of my clients constitutional as well as civil rights."

"Gentlemen, I have no wish to prolong this matter," the judge interjected. "Of the most serious crimes committed the killer has confessed to the murder which does not implicate anyone of the other defendants. Nor has he made any statement to the fact that they had any knowledge of the crime before or after the facts. Therefore, I am releasing all 61 defendants on 250 dollars bail. I will set a court date of 90 days from this date for a hearing on all related charges. Let me forewarn all the defendants, if you do not show up for your court date, the court will take your absence as a guilty plea. In that matter the court will confiscate bail as payment of your fine."

CHAPTER SEVEN

Women Power and Women

T HE COOL NIGHT air was a disappointing reminder that the cold north wind would soon be arriving in the city. Rick stood quietly on the corner of 116th and Manhattan Avenue, in front of Mr. Maynor's grocery storing with Cisco and Underwood.

"Yeah," Wood stated.

"Get the fuck out of here! It don't seem like no five years," Cisco said.

"When you see Tito Johnson, you ask him," Wood replied. "I bet he can tell you to the minute how long he was down."

"Yeah, I bet he can," Rick commented. "I saw Tito last night but I had to make the drop so I didn't get a chance to kick it with him."

"He's stepping already, come home and jump right in a new Tornado, black and white joint," Wood added.

"Yeah, he has always been a bad motherfucker," Cisco agreed.

"So what's up Wood, when is your next show?" Rick asked.

"I'm working on something with Black Ivory and the Emotions," Wood replied. "If everything goes as plan it will be next month."

"Shit, I'll buy my own ticket but I still want a backstage pass. The Emotions are some of the baddest bitches on the planet," Rick commented. "Shit I'm going deep in my closet." They stayed on the corner joking, laughing, and giving recognition with the high sigh to friends and associates who drove by. The business hour was nearing; they greeted each other goodbye and eased into the darkness of their own private business worlds.

Rick sat quietly resting on the sofa in the living room of his mother's apartment. She was in her bedroom watching television, most likely she was sound asleep. When his brothers came in, they would play the parkers Brothers game Trouble for pocket money and smoke a few joints. They would place the folded bills under the cardboard box in case their mother woke up. She would not be happy about them smoking and gambling.

The phone rang twice before Rick was able to grab it and he knew for sure that his mother had fallen asleep.

"Hello," Rick said into the receiver.

"Hello, is Rick there?"

"This is he," Rick replied.

"Hi Rick, it's me Jacqui. I'm having a celebration party tomorrow just for Rita and I. We would like you to be the guest of honor. We want to go out to dinner around 8:30 and to a private party afterwards. Can you make it?"

"I don't see a problem, what are we celebrating?"

"It's a surprise. I haven't even told Rita what we will be celebrating. I want to tell my two favorite people at the same time. So Rick, can you be at Rita's around 7:30-8 o'clock?"

"Yeah, I'll be there."

They played a dollar a game, Rick Fred and Jeff. They laughed and ooo-ed like madmen when the die in the bubble popped on a number that would send one of them back to home base. Rick kept watching on the time so he would not be late for the meet. They had played nine games by the time the hands reached the hour for him to leave. Rick had lost eight games and his brothers did not miss out on the chance to rib him. It took all of a second to get serious once Rick picked up the bag with the money in it. Jeff went in the back to let his mother know he was going downstairs. One by one Rick and Fred followed suit. Once outside, Rick spoke briefly with Fred before they headed off in different directions.

The cab pulled over blocking Rick's exit from the parking space. Jenny leaned forward sticking her head out of the cab's back window.

"Rick, I need to talk to you."

"I've got to go Jenny, people are waiting on me."

"It's always something, you never have time for me or Sean."

"Look girl, you show up from nowhere, in who the fuck knows how long and expect me to jump. You must have lost your damn mind. Yo cabbie, you want to move your fucking cab so I can get out?" Rick yelled.

"Rick, I need to talk to you!" Jenny insisted. "It's important."

"It will have to wait. I'll call you in a couple of hours," Rick said.

Rick turned into the Harlem River Motor Garage. Jesse was already in the back office waiting on him. They greeted each other warmly and Rick handed Jesse the bag of money.

"Yo Ricky, I want you to ride with me," Jesse said. "I have to meet Guy Fisher and Nicky at the Hubba Bubba."

"What's up?" Rick asked.

"I'm fucked up on the quinine tip."

"If they don't have any I'll speak to Jerry tomorrow. I'll go by his drug store and see if I can catch him. If I don't catch him, I'll leave word with his wife for him to call me."

"I forgot all about him!"

"So how much should I crack for?"

"I need five hundred pounds or better. You made whatever deal you can but I want a sample before I buy. A lot of quinine fuck dope up," Jesse remarked.

Jesse sat in the far corner of the Hubba Bubba social club talking to Frank James and Guy Fisher. Nicky had yet to show on the set. Rick was at a table near the front exit sitting with Thelma. Rick took a hit and offered one to Thelma. Thelma declined Rick's offer and politely excused herself from the table. Rick leaned back against the wall and moved his head to the rhythm of the music.

Nicky entered the Hubba Bubba, and you could feel his power over take the room. The massive bulk of Big Tyrone, Nicky's lieutenant, dressed to the nines was an impressive sight. But it still made Rick wonder why any woman would want either of them for anything other than their money and power.

Two beauties rushed into the arms of Big Tyrone and Nicky stopped to speak with Thelma at the bar. Nicky excused himself from Thelma and he and big Tyrone went and took seats at the table with Frank, Jesse and guy. *The generosity of women,* Rick thought. *Strange to say the least.* It's amazing the men they choose to give themselves to and the reasons they do it. Rick knew Big Tyrone was a trick, it was written all over his face. Why else would any woman want him, if were not for his money. He could use his power to attract woman, but he had none. All he had was money, a lot of money, which he spent like the trick he was. Never once did he realize money and power are not the same. On the other hand, Thelma showed a genuine affection for Nicky. And, his power was the big attraction for this short middle-aged balling ex-dope fiend who had become king of his own mountain.

Jesse and Nicky walked over to the table where Rick sat.

"Yo Ricky, stay here for me, I've got to make a run," Jesse said. Nicky greeted Rick then signaled for Thelma. Jesse told Rick to wait at the club for him to come back.

"That's' cool with me," Rick replied.

"Anything you want Rick just ask for it, it's on me," Nick stated.

Rick sat and talked for what seemed like hours with some pretty young thing he had no idea of who she may or may not be, nor did he care.

"So how are you and Shemika doing?" she asked. Rick knew his facial expression had not given him away. Nevertheless, she went on before he could answer her. "I've seen you with her at the Oasis. It must be love. I have seen you ease in and out of a number of places with delicious ladies on your arms," she seductively stated. Rick said nothing but wondered what all this was leading too. "One day you and I have to take one of those beauties off some place and share her." Her statement did not surprise Rick.

"So what else is on your mind?" Rick asked. Rick knew the answer to the question before she replied and stated that just may be possible.

The steel gray dawn rose over the city like a curtain being drawn to let the sunlight through a window. The chill of the early morning had caused them to step quickly, not to mention the contents of the shopping bags they each held. Once inside of the apartment with the last of the shopping bags they relaxed a bit.

"Yo Jesse, do you still want me to crack on Jerry for that quinine?" Rick asked.

"Yeah, you can never have too much quinine. Someone in the crew may need some, shit anything can jump off. Let's put this shit away and break out, I want to find a freak to suck my dick."

"That sounds good to me. I know where two bad freaks live not to far from here," Rick said. "What time is it anyway?"

"It's 6:35," Jesse answered. "Yo Ricky, check this out, I don't want to get any of those freaks from the spot who want to hang out and sniff. I just want a bitch to suck my dick and step off."

"What's happening down your way with the freaks?"

"That is where the two I told you about live."

"Hello," her voice came sounding so sweet over the telephone.

"Yeah Jenny, it's me Rick. What did you want to talk to me about that was so important?"

"Can you come by?"

"It's 7:30 in the morning and I've been up all night girl. I want to get some sleep."

"You can sleep here and Sean will be happy to see you."

"Okay, I'm going to stop and buy breakfast. I will be there in 20 minutes so do you want me to bring you anything?"

"Bring me and Sean whatever you get for yourself."

Sean was happy to see Rick and after he finished his breakfast he climbed in bed right along with his father. Sean turned the television to the Little Rascals and shook his father's shoulder to get his attention so he could watch with him. Jenny came into the bedroom to change and get ready for class.

"Didn't I tell you about changing your clothes in front of Sean? He's getting to big to be seeing you with your shit all out. Ain't that right Sean?" Rick asked.

"So where am I supposed to get dressed?" Jenny asked.

"Try the bathroom or make sure Sean is in his room. Right Sean?"

Sean still did not answer his father or have any idea what he was talking about. Sean was more interested in what Stymie was doing on television.

Jenny left to get dressed in the bathroom and when she returned to the bedroom Rick and Sean both were nearly asleep.

"Rick, Rick," Jenny softly called.

"Yeah, what do you want Jenny?"

"Don't forget, I need that to pay for my school trip."

"I said I'd bring it tonight, didn't I?" Rick shouted at her.

"You know how you are when you get busy," Jenny responded. "Sean, give Mommy a kiss before she goes."

"Leave him alone, you see he's asleep."

"I can't leave without kissing him and you."

The black three piece suit was tailored to perfection. The diamond studded white gold bracelet and matching pinky ring sparkled in the light of the night.

"You look good Rick," Jenny commented. "But there are other colors besides black. It must be one hell of an evening you have planned."

"I'm having dinner with a few friends," Rick replied. "Look, before you start asking a lot of questions that you are not going to get answers to, here is the money you asked for your trip. I've got to go. People are waiting for me. I will come pick Sean up the day after tomorrow if you don't have any plans for him."

Rick smoked a joint on his way to the village. By the time he had reached Rita's loft he was good and high. The sleek black limo parked in front of Rita's loft caught Rick's eye but he did not give it a second thought. Rita and Jacqui both were dressed in black stockings, open toe high heel shoes and guarder belts. Jacqui wore a lace G-string, Rita did not have on panties. They giggled and laughed a lot. They greeted

Rick with sloppy wet kisses. He knew they had been smoking reefer and drinking.

Champagne, Dom perignon sat on the glass coffee table in the living room area.

"I see you ladies have gotten started already. We really must have something to celebrate," Rick said to no one in particular.

"You look like you have done a little celebrating yourself," Rita commented.

"I smoked a joint on the drive down, nothing special." Rita took a joint from the band of her stockings top and lit it, passing it to Rick.

"You can smoke this while we put our gowns on." Rick took one pull and snuffed the joint out in the ashtray on the coffee table. He turned the music down on the stereo and the sound up on the television to watch the channel 11 news.

Rita was the first to step from behind the oriental print silk screen. She modeled her black floor length sequence gown, which had a split that rose from the floor to the top of her hip. The gown was also cut breathtakingly low in the back. Rita struck a number of poses met to arouse. Rick could see that Rita still did not have on panties. Rita took a seat beside Rick and planted another wet kiss on him pushing her tongue deep into his mouth.

Jacqui wrapped her legs around the oriental print screen. She slithered around the screen into a squatting position, giving Rick and Rita a full view of the goodies between her legs. Rising from her squatting position Jacqui turned on her heels and peered over her shoulder at Rick and Rita. Jacqui's black sequence grown was neatly rolled up to her waist. She did a pirouette dance step and sashayed over to where Rick and Rita sat. The gown fell freely down her waist as she stepped. It came to rest at mid-thigh when Jacqui came to a halt just in front of them, she spun, looked over her shoulder at them and Rick notice for the first time that her gown was also cut dangerously low in the back as well. Jacqui bent from her waist with her legs spread as wide as the short dress would allow. Looking between her legs at them Jacqui teased,"Rick you are going to have the time of your life tonight."

The limo came to a stop in front of Mr. Chow's on East 57th street. The valet opened the limo door and Rita stepped from the limo in a setting of glamour, pure Hollywood. She held Rick's arm as they awaited Jacqui's performance exiting the limo. The few people on the plush eastside corner all took notice. The grace and beauty of the trio was of success, power and a mixture of Hollywood production.

All eyes fixed on them as the maitre' D led them to their table. The whispers became louder, *Who are they?* The wine steward stood table side ready to pour the champagne as per instructions. "Come on," Rita coaxed, "What are we celebrating Jacqui?"

"As soon as the steward is finished pouring I will tell you. Let's drink a toast to success and the future," Jacqui said as she lifted her glass. Their glasses clicked in mid air over the table. Rick wet his finger in his glass to taste the champagne while Rita and Jacqui sipped theirs.

"Well, here we go. I am so excited, I just got a part in a new television series!" Jacqui informed them. Rita squealed with delight at Jacqui's news. The patrons of the restaurant looked around to see what all the excitement was about. Rick congratulated her.

"So tell us the details! I want to know everything!" Rita said in excitement.

"Well I got a call from Jay Bernstein, he's a producer who making a name for himself in the entertainment business. He told me about a new hour long drama that is scheduled for next fall. He sent the contracts out my carrier and I had your lawyer, Rick, looked them over. It looks like my career is going to get started at long last. Look out world, here comes' Jacqui," Jacqui said proudly.

"Sounds good to me," Rick said. "If this guy Jay is in California how did he find out about you?"

"I was at a party given at Sotheby's by the Ross'. You know one of those painting show where a lot of famous people get drunk and talk shit. Anyway, I was with this trick that passed me off as his girlfriend. He introduced me to Mr. Bernstein. We made small talks and I told him who I was studying acting with. It turns out my instructor is a friend of Mr. Bernstein. He called my acting instructor to see if I had what it takes to handle the part. That's how he found me and knows what I can do as an actress."

"That's good Jacqui, I'm happy for you. But, does he know about your other occupation?" Rick asked.

"It came up in our phone conversation. It seems the asshole I was at the party with is known for passing call girls off as his girlfriends. Jay told me not to worry about it, it would be our secret."

"That's good, at least you don't have to live in fear of him finding out," Rick said.

The music rocked the walls of the loft. Rick sat watching Rita and Jacqui stripped to the beats of the music.

"This is the best private party I've ever been to!" Rita cooed as she danced to the beat of the music.

"That's right Rita," Jacqui said. "And Rick, I did promise you the time of your life tonight." Rick took several deep drags on the joint and fed himself hits from the crystal ashtray filled with cocaine.

Rick walked over to the reel tape deck and hit the stop switch bringing the room to a sudden stop.

"Now that you two have stripped down to almost nothing, I want to lay back and enjoy the beauty of your bodies," he stated. "And for me the best way to do that is when the music is soft and easy. Dance for me, but make it slow and easy. You ladies listen to Mr. Willie Hutch. He's going to make it alright. Willie's ruff and easy sounding voice rang out, *I choose you girl... and I'll tell you why. No longer do I have to shop around*". Rick took a seat on the sofa and sang along with Willie, *"I choose you Rita and you Jacqui, and I'll tell you why"*. Jacqui and Rita moved slow and easy, and as one, arousing Rick as well as themselves. By the time they had undressed him piece by piece the Moments were well into singing *"Sexy Mama"*. Their sexual performance was well choreographed. It was a performance by people in *lust* and in love.

CHAPTER EIGHT

Making Money for The Man

RICK AND JESSE sat in the Lincoln Town car parked just off 145th street St. Nicholas Avenue. The weather was pleasant for this time of year. Willie pulled in behind them, got out of his car and climbed in the back seat of the Lincoln.

"Yo, what's up Jesse, Rick," Willie greeted them.

"It's alright," they both replied. Jesse pulled off, turning left headed north on St. Nicholas Avenue.

"So what's it going to be?" Willie asked Jesse.

"I'm going to drop you off on the corner and drive around the block. I want you to bring me the two Macy's shopping bags with the money in them. They're in the bedroom closet. I'll pull in, in front of the building when I see you coming out. I don't want to park this car in front because it may draw attention on us," Jesse explained.

Rick and Jesse sat quietly. They had parked near the corner. They were alerted, looking for any sign of trouble. Their pistols were tucked neatly a way and could be reached in a split second.

"There he is," Rick said. Willie stepped between two cars parked in front of the building. The Lincoln was there to meet him.

"Check this out Willie. I'm going to drop you off on the corner. You can take a cab back to your car, okay? That way I can get right on the

East river Drive," Jesse informed him. "I don't want to drive through the streets with two million in the car."

"That's cool with me," Willie said.

"Yo Willie, make sure you meet those people for me and collect that money."

"Okay, my brother."

"I'll meet you at the Shalimar around 12:30 tonight."

"Do you want me to bring that money too?"

"Yeah," Jesse replied. "Yeah, that will work," Jesse said more to himself thinking out loud.

The black machine kept a steady pace going down the East River Drive, across the Brooklyn Bridge and along the quiet back streets of downtown Brooklyn. Jesse pulled over at a corner phone and got out. When he returned to the car he opened the passenger door and told Rick to move over and drive.

"Ricky, stay on this street for the next three blocks," Jesse instructed. "Drive slow. I don't want to miss him. Okay, I see him, pull over here."

Jesse stood in the shadows of the building talking with the middle-aged white man for 15 minutes or so. They both came to the car, Jesse got in the back, and his guest got in the front with Rick.

"Yo Ricky, make a right turn at the corner and just drive. We're going to ride for a minute."

The middle aged white man was dressed casually and had what must have been a three karat diamond pinky ring on his left hand. He did not speak to Rick, he sat sideways in the seat speaking with Jesse. The graying of his temples gave his strong facial features a rather distinguished look.

Jesse passed the shopping bags over the front seat and they were received as though they were simply groceries. Rick kept a watchful eye on a car in the review mirror. It appeared to be following them, he said nothing to Jesse.

"Okay that takes care of my bill with you," Jesse said.

"You can pull over here," the white man said, speaking to Rick for the first time.

"You can give me a call sometime during the middle of the week," the white man informed Jesse. "I should have what you want by then."

Jesse and the connection both stepped out of the car at the same time. Jesse got in the front with Rick and the connection got in the car Rick had seen following them in the review mirror.

Once back in Manhattan, they dropped the pistols off. They both breathed a sign of relief. Their mood lightens, the car stereo pumped the music out and they began to feel more like themselves.

"Yo Jesse, you know carrying a gun and doing this shit some times reminds me of being in Vietnam," Rick said.

"Damn, that's right. I keep forgetting you were in Vietnam."

"Check this out Jesse, when we were in Brooklyn. The car that picked up the connection, I spotted it in the review mirror when we pulled off after the connection got in with us. I didn't say anything because I was waiting to see what was going to jump off."

"You've got good instincts," Jesse smiled. "That's one reason I trust you with my life. But that Vietnam shit you went through, I don't think I could fuck with it."

"You could handle it, it's all in what you tell yourself it is," Rick said. "Check this bullshit out, Jesse. I've listened to a few people who came home and told their war stories. They'd be kickin' it to people who didn't know shit about Vietnam, they'd be making themselves up to be something they ain't. Then when I get to kickin it with them and they know I knew the deal. Shit, it became a whole another story. Especially when I wouldn't co-sign that bullshit they be running. When I was in training, before I went over I heard all the war stories from the career sergeants that were supposed to get us ready to do battle. I found out later that those stories were all real bullshit. I met one brother when I was stationed in Maryland, he had just come home from the Nam. He was the only one who told me the real deal. He said I would have some good times and that I would have some real bad times. He also told me that the bad times would be the hell I could never imagine. He said the good times would be like heaven because of all the deaths and destructions going on around me. But one thing out of all he had told me that really stuck; he said to count myself lucky if I made it back alive."

"Yo Ricky, did you kill anyone while you were over there? I don't mean if you just shot out in the field and then went out there and found bodies. Can you actually say you saw someone you shot and killed?"

"Yeah, I can say that a hundred times over."

"What was that shit really like Ricky?"

"The best way I can tell you is like this."

CHAPTER NINE

The Vietnam Story

THE EARLY MORNING light rose over the tops of the rubber trees. The air was cool and it would not be long before the jungle would bake in the hot sun. "C" company of the 11th Armored Calvary, The Black Horse Regiment set in the clearing. They were a picturesque view nestled between the jungle and rubber plantation. It was like a reminder of the covered wagons of the old west sitting in a circular formation. On each vehicle a guard manned a 50 caliber machine gun that sat behind a six foot by three foot armored shield.

In the distance, the sound of a helicopter could be heard, the noise of its engine was breaking the silence of the early morning. The helicopter sat down in the center of the circle as the sleeping men came to life. The mess crew rushed to remove the hot food from the helicopter. Within minutes the chopper was airborned and "C" company was busy getting ready to move out on the day's mission.

The lieutenants and sergeants from each of the three platoons went to be briefed by the captain in his tent on the day's mission. "Gentlemen, this is our operation for today." the captain went on to explain,"First platoon to stand down and guard the perimeter. The second and third platoons will be ready to move out at 08:30. Everyone take a good look at this map. We will line up here; second platoon on the left and the third platoon on the right. We will move through the Michelin Rubber Plantation going north for six miles. From there we will make a north east turn and begin to break jungle. The rest of our squadron, A, B, and D companies will be moving in this direction working their way towards us. Five companies from the First Infantry Division will be working in a south east direction coming towards us also. They will be starting at this point on the map, 20 miles to our north. Colonel Patton believes that if the intelligences reports are correct that the Third Battalion of the North Vietnamese Army is somewhere in this area. Our hope is to catch and trap them between us and the Big Red One. Are there any questions? That's all then gentlemen, get your men ready and good luck."

The sergeants spoke on their vehicles head sets briefing the vehicle commanders on the day's mission. At 08:00 the roar of the vehicle motors being started could be heard for miles as they broke the silence of the early morning. As each vehicle moved to take its place online, a vehicle from the first platoon took its place on the perimeter. The distance between the vehicles became greater but the circle was never broken.

The third platoon lined up with the 90 millimeter cannon of the M-48 tank at front. Two APC's fell in line behind the M-48 tank, then a Sheridan tank behind the APC's. Three more APC's came on lined followed by another Sheridan tank, one more APC, then another Sheridan, and an APC to bring up the rear. The second platoon took the same order ninety feet or so to the left of the third platoon. Taking front and center was another M-48 tank. The tanks appearances were monstrous and menacing. The captain's APC took its position between the two columns formed by the second and third platoon.

At 08:30, "C" company roared into the jungle. Each man was poised behind his gun shield, his finger on the trigger of his 50 or 60 caliber machine gun. Each man's eyes locked to every inch of his firing lane. Their underarms wet, and their stomachs tied in knots. Everyone knew An Loc was a dangerous place and that the Michelin Rubber Plantation was the worse place of all.

The sunlight broke through the leaves silhouetting the men and vehicles as they moved along the rows of the rubber trees. The noise of the vehicles was deafening, yet here was a deadly silence. Five miles and two and a half hours into the mission "C" company came to a stop. The vehicles tuned into a 45 degree angle, each column facing out while the three M-48 tanks remained facing forward. The captain spoke to his lieutenants over the head sets. "We have another mile to go before we begin to break jungle again," the captain informed them. "We will rest here for ten minutes while I check the positions of our other forces."

Positions checked the vehicles pulled back on line and moved out. The vehicles came to a halt once again when they reached the point where the jungle met the rubber plantation. Breaking jungle is hard work; it takes its toll on men and vehicles. The men pulled their gun shields slightly in getting a firm grip on their weapon so as not to allow the vines of the jungle to pull them loose or out of firing position. The three large M-48 tanks crushed the jungle in their paths. The rest of the vehicles made their way over the roller coaster like path of crushed jungle.

In the silence of all the noise everyone heard the hollow whistle. Then the muffled sound of the RPG, "boom". A twilight moment of stillness, a moment paused. Then in a split second and with one swift movement, sixty-nine men all pulled their triggers at once. The thunderous sounds of so many weapons going off at once sent vibrations through the earth. The rocket and machine gun firer seemed to come from the tree themselves. Turning into a 90 degree angle 23 vehicles laid down a base of firer. The thunder of the 90 millimeter cannons rocked the jungle. The vehicles moved back and forth in a short pattern so they were not a sitting target.

The sound of bullets bouncing off of his gun shields sent a sexual charge through Rick's body. Two rockets hit the center tank, it broke into flames. The first Sheridan tank in line from the third platoon pulled up in front of the burning tank. The medics were rushed to pull the wounded men from the burning tank. Rockets knocked out three APC's, one from the second platoon and two from the third. The captain was on the radio to headquarters. Working two radios at once, the captain spoke with the lieutenant of the third platoon while he talked to headquarters. "Get that artillery working!" the captain ordered his lieutenant. "No sooner," said than the lieutenant signaled Rick his M-60 machine gunner.

Rick went to work. This was not new to him, just another one of his duties. "Fire Base One, Fire Base One, this is Charlie Company, do you read me, over?"

"Charlie Company, this is Fire Base One, we read you loud and clear, over."

"Fire Base One, we have been hit hard, over."

"Charlie Company to Fire Base One, we've got a firing mission for you- over."

"Fire Base One we need 155's, over." Rick located their position on the map and called it in to Fire Base One. "Fire Base One to Charlie Company, we are going to mark your perimeter with smoke, over."

"Fire base One to Charlie Company, smoke is on its way."

Meanwhile, "C" Company had taken heavy casualties. Over the noise of the firer fight you could hear the whistling of the 155 smoke shells and their pops as they exploded marking the boundaries of the perimeter.

"Charlie Company to Fire Base One, fire for effect, out." The sound of the 155 shells whisking over head, then the loud crackling sound as they hit earth and blew pushed the men of "C" Company to fight with renewed hope.

Fire Base One pumped more than a hundred shells around the perimeter blowing jungle and body part everywhere. Still "C" Company was under heavy fire. The dead and wounded laid in the center between the two platoons. The captain informed HQ that they needed reinforcements. "D Company is two miles from your position, they are on the way," HQ informed the captain. When "D" Company came within a half mile of "C" Company they were ambushed. "D" Company suffered heavy losses in the ambush. This was it; two companies of the Black Horse Regiment had ran into the main body of the Third Battalion of the NVA. Both companies were fighting to keep from being over run. HQ informed both captains that the Big Red One was at the moment airlifting in three companies of infantrymen.

In the meantime "C" and "D" companies called for air support. The tactics were quickly worked out. F-14 jets will bombard the two outside positions of each company while Huey Cobra helicopter gun ships lay down a base of fire until the jets get there. "Once the jets get there, the Cobras will fire support for the jet," Rick worked the radio to make sure everyone understood the tactics.

In a matter of minutes the Huey Cobra gun ships arrived, six in all. They broke off into groups of two to fly in a circle diving formation. One was diving and firing while the other climbed. The first one laid down a line of mini-gun and rocket firer. The Cobra gun ship's firer was so rapid that it appeared to be a red laser beam. As the diving gunship started to make his climb, his partner began his dive spitting 40 millimeter rockets. The bone chilling crackle of the rockets sent jungle and bodies in all directions. The Cobras took up three positions around the two armor companies; still there was no sign of any real damage being done to the NVA. They had dug in well.

The F-14 jets came in low, skimming the jungle tree tops. The four birds made several passes over the tree tops. On their third pass they began their climb and broke off into pairs. The helicopter gun ships hovered high in the sky waiting the F-14's diving runs. Once the jets started their circular diving patterns the gun ships resumed their firing mission. The gun ships worked the areas between the two armored companies. The majesty and beauty of the jets diving, dropping their pay load was reassuring to the men fighting on the ground. The napalm and fragmentation bombs began to take a toll.

The M-48 tanks pulled back and began to knock out a clearing for an LZ. The captain of "C" Company called for med evacuation choppers. The helicopter gun ships laid down heavy firer around the landing zone. The med evacuation choppers were in and out with the wounded and dead in minutes.

The Cobra gun ships came in close and dropped smoke and laid down a base of firer as a shield to cover the choppers of the Big Red One. Each company of infantrymen took up positions between "C" and "D" companies. They moved up and into position behind their M-16 and M-60 machine gun firer. The men of the Big Red One got pinned down my firer from the NVA. The fighting was intense and the darkness of night began to push the light of day aside. The Black Horse Regiment had already been in battle for some 10 hours. Time passed so quickly it seemed like only 5 or 10 minutes since they were first hit.

As the night had set in, the U.S. forces formed a large circle. The jets had long since left to be refueled and rearmed. The Huey Cobra helicopter gun ships were on their way back to base camp. In their place the sky was lit up by flares from the 155, bringing to the night sky the effect of day. The American forces continued to fight firing their weapons throughout the night.

The pop of the 155 flares could no longer be heard. In the silence of the night the Black Ghost appeared. Puff The Magic Dragon began his assault. The AC-47 gunship and its mini-guns put on a laser light show of power and destruction as it flew around the perimeter of U.S. forces. The men on the ground fought long and hard throughout the night.

At the first sign of daylight Puff The Magic Dragon fell silent. The men on the ground half heartily open cans of C-rations while still under firer and fighting back. They ate and fought on so they would not be over run.

The first to reappear in the sky were the Huey Cobra gun ships. They took up firing position in the sky and the U.S. forces came back on line. At this time they were joined by the rest of the Black Horse Regiment. "A" and "B" companies had worked their way through the jungle during the night. The infantrymen of the Big Red One spread out and took up positions between all of the vehicles.

This battle would go on the same way for the next five night and six days. When it finally ended, there were 14 dead Americans and 33 who were seriously wounded. The body counts of the NVA numbered in the hundreds. The rest fled and the wounded were dragged off into the jungle.

CHAPTER TEN

Street Wars

THE PHONE RANG several times, Sean raced over to the table and picked the receiver up before it woke his father.

"Hello," Sean said into the receiver. Sean eye's lit up when he heard the voice on the other end. He liked to talk on the telephone.

"Yeah, it's me Jesse, is that you Sean?"

"How are you doing Jesse?"

"I'm okay Sean, is your father there?"

"He's asleep. I'll wake him up for you. Daddy, daddy! Jesse is on the telephone."

"Yo Jesse, what's up?" Rick said.

"Hey Ricky, your son is something else. He be kickin' it like we be hanging out or something."

"Yeah, he's my main man," Rick said with pride.

"By the way Ricky, have you been out this morning?"

"Yeah and I took care of that. Everything is cool. So what time you want me to meet you?"

"I'm at my house in Westchester. I'm going to my mother's for dinner so I'll meet you after the Eyewitness News."

"Cool," Rick replied. "Jenny is on some kind of modeling assignment for Essence magazine and I don't know what time she is going to show back. If she's not back by 5 I'll be at my mother's house, that way I will have someone to watch my little man until his mother comes to get him. You can pick me up at my mother's house."

"Okay Ricky," they both said later and hung up.

Rick held Sean on his lap and every time Sean dried his cheek, Rick would give him another big sloppy wet lick.

"Stop daddy!" Sean protested, hitting his father with his fist.

"Ricky, why don't you stop teasing that baby!" his mother yelled at him.

"Ah Ma, I'm only playing with him."

"Grandma, make daddy stop or I'm going to beat him up!" Rick, his mother and Jeff all broke up with laughter at Sean's bold statement. Sean's big brown eyes beamed with delight to know he could make them laugh. And to know he could make them laugh always brought the clown out in him.

"Let me hold him," Jeff told his brother just as the phone rang. Jeff grabbed the receiver, "Hello."

"Yes, hello. Is Ricky there? This is Jesse."

"You don't have to say who you are, I know your voice," Jeff said. "Hey Rick! It's for you, Jesse."

"Sean, go play with your Uncle Jeff while daddy talks on the phone."

"Come here you little rascal," Jeff called Sean, handing the phone receiver to Rick.

"Yo what's up my brother?" Rick said into the receiver.

"Ain't nothing," Jesse replied. "I'm going to watch Tricky Dick's new conference right after the news, then I will pick you up."

"Sounds good to me."

"Hey Ma, you know only you and Jesse calls Rick, Ricky," Jeff said. Jeff playfully marked his brother's name, "*Rick-y*, like he's a little baby. He is my baby, like all my children are my babies." Sean ran over to where his grandmother sat and asked,"Am I your baby too Grandma?" She bent over and kissed him on the cheek,"Of course, you are my baby too."

"Grandma watch this," Sean said. Sean cocked his head to the side, rolled his eyes back in his head and did a peacock stroll across the living room floor.

Sean marked his father's name the same way he had heard his Uncle Jeff do just a few minutes before. The little showmen knew how to get a laugh.

"Hey little man come here, you want to watch the new with daddy?" Rick and Sean were so close, most people could not believe how the young child emulated his father. Sean climbed onto the sofa next to his father and crossed his short legs.

"Mama are you going to watch Tricky Dick's new conference?" Rick asked.

"Do I have any choice Ricky?" she replied. "They put that mess on all the channels and nobody really wants to hear that baloney anyway. They take the Jefferson's off for that junk."

"Today Tricky Dick is going to talk about Vietnam, so I want to hear what he has to say," Rick told his mother.

"As the President of the United States, it is my duty to inform you the American public that for the first time in the history of the Vietnam war, American forces have crossed the Cambodian border. The American forces have gone 22 miles inside of Cambodia to a place known as the Fish Hook. There they have encountered heavy fighting against the North Vietnamese regulars." Rick sat in disbelief at the president's statements. Rick was visibly angry at the lies being told by the President of the United States. Rick's family could see the bewilderment written on his face.

"What's wrong daddy?" Sean asked. The anguish could clearly be heard in Rick's voice,"He's lying and everyone will believe that bullshit because he is the President. The people in America are fools! They are no better off than the people in some illiterate third world country. For all their education and sophistication they are so easily misled."

"Don't let it get you so upset," his mother told him.

"Yeah," Jeff cut in, "you're home, forget about that now."

"Grandma why is daddy mad?" Sean asked.

"Ask him baby," she told Sean with the understanding that only a grandmother would have.

"Daddy what's wrong?" Sean was confused by the tension in his father. Rick reassured his son and continued to speak. His voice was low and still filled with tension as he spoke.

"I can remember so clearly as if it were yesterday," Rick responded. "We had been briefed the night before. We knew we would encounter heavy fighting. You could feel the tension in the air that morning as we moved out on a search and destroy mission. The ambush came without warning as they always do, but we were ready for it. There were a lot of us killed that day and many more wounded. In a way I was lucky. I was amongst the first of the wounded to be airlifted out. What was that Ma, two years ago they came in the middle of the night to tell you I had been shot." It was more a statement than a question for his mother to answer.

"Yes Lord and it scared me to death!" she replied. "I was glad your sister and brother were here, I don't what I would have done if they were not."

"That was 1969," Rick remembered,"and the place damn sure was the Fish Hook, 20 to 25 miles inside of Cambodia."

Rick and Jesse leaned back comfortably in the large leather seats of the black Eldorado as it floated down Columbus Avenue. The mood of both men was subdued.

"Yo Ricky, did I give you your Christmas dope?" Jesse asked.

"Christmas dope?" Rick asked.

"Yeah, I gave everyone half of what they cope as a Christmas present."

"Nah, you missed me."

"I'm sorry my man, I knew I had forgot one or two people. But how could I forget you, my main man? So when I get my next thing I will hit you with a little something extra."

"Sounds good to me," Rick replied to Jesse generosity.

"How much dope were you copping at Christmas?"

"Just a key."

"So that means I have to give you half a key. That's yours Ricky, you won't have to give me a dime for it. Yo Ricky, Tricky Dick talked plenty of shit about the war tonight didn't he?"

"Yeah, but he's a lying motherfucker," Rick was still furious.

"How so Ricky?"

"This motherfucker got on national TV and told the world this is the first time in the war that American forces were fighting in Cambodia. I was in the Fish Hook and I've got the holes in my body to prove it. Anyway, that's not really what has me fucked up. It's the way things are done that fuck me up," Rick explained.

They came to a stop for a red light on Columbus Avenue and 66th street. A blue and white police car pulled along side of them.

"Check them out," Rick commented. "They look at us like we are not supposed to be riding in a car like this. The disgust is written all over their faces."

"Fuck them police," Jesse responded.

"Like I was saying, let me hip you to how they do shit. When I came home from Nam I was sent to Fort Knox Kentucky. I was assigned to the 198th Light Infantry, a training outfit. At the time I had only been back from Nam like 40, 45 days. One morning while we were working in the motor pool this sergeant gives us this bullshit speech. He told us, *'For you guys who have not been to Vietnam, I have to train you so you will be ready when your time comes. For you guys who have just come back from Vietnam, I must reinforce your training so that you will always be ready. You never know when the country will be calling you to fight again.'* So I'm thinking to myself this sergeant is a real asshole just like the damn fool who told him to retrained us so we will always be ready. Here I am fresh from the jungle and ready to kill anything that moves in the shadows. So the government gives me a refresher course in killing and turns me loose on the streets of America."

"Another thing that fucked me up was the shit that jumped off when I got out of the army," Rick went on to say. "It made me realize that the people in position to help me get started thought I was a piece of garbage for going to Vietnam."

"Them whitey's were on that protest shit, free love and some real crazy shit," Jesse said.

"Yeah, I can dig it, it was them who got a lot of us killed. Send a man to do a job with one hand tied behind his back. Anyway Jesse, before I knew what I wanted to do I went to the employment office to see about a work. I was sitting in this office talking to some square ass whitey. He asked me what am I qualified to do. I told him that I just got out of the army. He looked at me like so fuckin' what. Then asked me if I went to

Vietnam. I told him like my answer was going to help me get a job. One bullshit question after another this whitey asked. *Did they teach you any type of work skills?* Now I was getting upset with this whitey's attitude. So, I told him yeah, *they taught me a work skill. I can cut your fuckin throat and leave you for dead and no one in this office will hear shit.* You should have seen how red this asses' face turned." Rick and Jesse both had a good laugh at the thought of how the whitey looked.

"Then this fool goes into this stiff business attitude, like I got this crazy nigger in my office and I don't know what he might do. He pulled out one of those computer sheets with job listing on it. He said, *well, I have several openings that may interest you. There's a dish washing position at the Brassrail restaurant and a garage job parking cars on west 47th street. Each of these jobs pays $110.00 per week.* He informed me like I should be impressed by the money. I asked him if he was crazy and he said, *I am sorry Sir but that is all we have for a man with your job skills.* I got up and started to walk out. He looked at me like *you will be back when you can't find anything else.* He was right about one thing, though. I got the same response everywhere I went. It was like I was being paid back for something I had done wrong. Like I was a monster and going to Vietnam was the worse crime I could commit. I believe they would have spit in my face if they didn't think I would go off and kill them. It's fucked up, you risked your life for a whole year because this government sent you to war. Then when I come home they want me to wash dishes or park cars for $110 a week. The government had no kind of job training programs to get me ready for the world. Oh, yeah hold on for a minutes Jesse, they did have one program for us. They retrained us how to kill so we would always be ready," Rick said.

"Maybe they wanted you to become a hit man for the CIA," Jesse said jokingly.

"Fuck them, that's why I pump this product. I make more in a day than I would make in a year on that dish washing job they wanted me to take." They gave each other five in agreement and laughed as good friends do.

"You know Jesse, there are two things about the war that stand out in my mind and I will never forget them. One happened in the rainy season.

We had been out on a search and destroy mission and all week long we had run into heavy fighting. On this one particular day it was real quiet. The rainy season was a miserable time. You were wet night and day. Five inches of heavy red clay stuck to your boots and the whole shit. It felt like you were carrying a ton of shit around with you. You get your food and just as you sit down to eat it started to pour. The can of food you were eating from filled up with rain water. Sometimes I'd get so mad I would just threw my food away. On this day it was raining harder than usual when the lieutenant brought the mails around. I was sitting inside my ACAV truck trying to stay dry while I reading my mail. I must have read the letter he gave me a thousand times before I really realized what it said. It was from my woman and she told me that I had a son. That news reinforced my belief that I would make it home alive. Man was I happy, I told the crew in my truck then walked around the perimeter in the rain and mud, to tell everyone else."

"Jesse, do you remember this Spanish kid named Ortiz who played ball with us at school? He was from the lower eastside, you know him, I just can't think of his first name right now. He used to go with that girl from my projects, tall and pretty, called Jackie. She also went to Commerce with us."

"Nah, I don't remember him. Anyway my brother, finish kickin it."

"Yeah, Ortiz was in my platoon. I went over to his truck and we kicked it for hours on how it was going to be when we got back to the world. What we did that night is something you don't do while you are in the jungle. But that night we really had something to feel good about. Just imagine Jesse, all week we had been killing people and then I get this news about new life; my son's life. The birth of my son made me feel so full of life and my man was happy because I was happy. I will never forget the feeling of knowing I help give life to a child, especially after facing death everyday."

"The other thing I remember about Vietnam was when I was on my way home. I was one happy motherfucker. The night before I was to leave our basecamp to go to Long Beach it got hit with rockets. This was only the second time in a year that our base camp had been rocketed. Shit was blowing up all around us for most of the night. That morning when Ortiz walked with me down the dirt road which led to the tiny airstrip we counted the rocket holes in the ground. I realized then I had to get out while the getting was good. I didn't want to leave my man. But, he had 45 more days to go. I had only two days left in the safety of Long Beinh."

"Once I got to Long Beinh, I seemed to be in a state of shock. It was like I could see what was going on around me yet I was not apart of it. My body was going through the motions but my mind was lost to and in a place that was beyond anything I had control of. I didn't remember the plane ride back to the states either. I remembered stopping at the airport in Japan to refuel the plane. I don't know how to explain it, Jesse. I had this eerie lost in space kind of feeling. I kind of remember being in the airport terminal. There was this one guy and his family who was kind of curious about why there where so many soldiers in the airport. I believe he was from England or some place because he had one of those accents. He came over and asked me some questions. I was still in this twilight zone state of mind. You know Jesse, till this day I can't remember what the fuck he asked me and to be truthful, I didn't know what my response was to him either. But I will never forget the expression on his face as he rushed his family away from me."

"What the fuck did you say?" Jesse asked.

"I have no idea," Rick answered. "I do remember when we got to the customs in San Francisco I was ready to kiss the ground."

"Why?" Jesse asked.

"I don't really know, I guess because I had just come back from a living hell. I know unless you have been through it you could never really imagine how fucked up war really is. I do know, I was in a rush to get home and it took hours to be processed through the army base. To me it seemed like a life time, even more time than I spent in Vietnam. I was just ready to get back to New York and my people."

"At the airport I was a nervous wreck, jumpy and I couldn't stand still. I was talking to the receptionist at the ticket counter and she told me there were no flights to New York until 7 o'clock the next morning. I almost blew it Jesse. I could not imagine fuckin' around in the airport all night. I was ready too run across country. I had so much built up energy locked up inside of me that it was ready to go off like an atomic bomb. I guess it was written all over my face because the receptionist stepped back from the counter. I mean she stepped all the way back and was looking for help. These brothers that I had kicked it with at the army base came over and asked me what the problem was. So I ran it to them and they told me to chill. We started walking around the airport kickin' it about everything we had gone through. They told me they had to cut out when they heard the announcement for the flight to Philadelphia. I got on the plane to Philadelphia with them. Anything was better than standing around the airport in California."

"When the stewardess announced the time and weather in Philadelphia saying how hot it was, me and the two brothers had a good laugh. We joked about freezing to death in the 78 degree temperature. You know Jesse, of all the deaths and destructions I had witnessed and been a part of, I got the strangest feeling when I stepped off of that plane onto the runway in Philadelphia. I watched the wives, girlfriends, mothers, son, daughters and fathers of the returning soldiers crying and rushing to throw their arms around whoever it was they were there to meet. I got this eerie feeling that froze me dead in my tracks. I could feel it as it rose from my feet up and throughout my whole body. It felt like it went out the top of my head. It was as if I could see this feeling's invisible form drift of into the sunlight. And only after it had left my body and disappeared in the sunlight was I able to speak or move again. All this couldn't have taken more than a few seconds. And it seemed that it happens to the other two brothers standing right next to me. We looked at each other for a split second with bewilderment. It was the strangest thing I have ever felt. Once I was able to speak again I told the two brothers and we just looked at each other in silent agreement as we watched the happy reunions. *You know a lot of us didn't make it back*, someone said. It could have been me who said it or one of the other brothers. We just looked at one another and we knew we had a lot to be grateful for."

CHAPTER ELEVEN

Donny Back on The Block

THE WEATHER WAS brisk, Rick stood at the intersection of Columbus Avenue, on 102nd street. The night sky had come early as it always does for this time of year. Rick was surprised to see Donny standing directly across the avenue. *Had Donny been gone for a year already? Impossible, more like six months,* Rick thought. They met in the middle of the street, shook hands then walked back to where Rick had just been standing.

"So you home for good or what?" Rick asked Donny.

"Nah, they just gave me a 4 hour pass," Donny replied. "Besides, I've got Scram Jones here with me." Rick hadn't noticed the baby-face kid who stood 50 feet behind Donny. He thought the kid was waiting for the bus. After all he was standing at the bus stop.

"So Donny, when will you be out for good?" Rick asked.

"I've got five months in so I should be getting a week long furlough soon. If everything goes alright with the furlough, they may cut me loose when I go back to court."

"Sounds good, maybe you can make it out before next summer," Rick said. "Things are going pretty well for me, so let me know what's up when you get out for good."

"Yo Rick, I've got to cut out before Scram Jones writes a bad report about me standing on street corners."

"Okay, my brother you be cool."

CHAPTER TWELVE

Foolish Try
The Following Spring

RICK PULLED THE black Eldorado into 102nd street. Paul Lewis yelled down at him from his fifth floor apartment window in building 9. "I'll be right down Rick!" Paul said. Paul Lewis had a Popeye the Sailorman figure. Dope had taken a terrible toll on his arms and legs. He had been a good worker once upon a time for Rick and Donny. He had no choice but to be on top of his game. His dope habit was so big that the only way he could support it, was by selling drugs. He couldn't rob or burglarize because his body would not allow it. Rick remembered the last time he had brought Paul the package. It must have been last summer or sometime around that. It was around 6:30 or 7 in the morning, Rick made the climb up to the top floor of building 9. It was his practice to take Paul his package before going in. Paul would have his money counted out so all he had to do was to step inside the apartment door and collect it. However, on this particular morning Paul was dope sick and in desperate need of a fix.

Rick sat on the living room sofa while Paul got the dope ready to shoot. Rick had never seen a needle and syringe that large. Paul could not find a vein in his arms or legs to get a hit. He had burnt all of his veins out from years of abuse. Paul was now actually lifting scabs on the abscesses to find a flow of blood. Paul ran over to where Rick sat and asked if this one sore had a flow of blood under it. The sight of it turned Rick's stomach queasy. Rick swore this was the last time he would ever set foot in Paul's apartment.

Rick knew why Paul had been trying to get in touch with him. But Rick had no idea what Paul thought he could do to help him. When Paul exited the building, Rick signaled him to get in the car.

"Hey Rick, how you doing man?"

"I'm alright Paul, what's up with you?"

"I need a package."

"You can forget that."

"For old time sake. Please Rick," Paul pleaded. "I came to you because you are my last and only hope."

"Look Paul, the word on the streets is that there is a contract on you. The rumor is that you beat Jimmy Terrell for a hundred and seventy-five thousand dollars. I know that for a fact that you took that bitch Carole to the Bahamas. You laid up on white folks beaches like you were the King and Queen of England, but you didn't think about me when you were spending Jimmy's money. To top it off, you come back home and fucked up a couple other people's packages. Now you are cracking for a package from me. Just what is it that you think I can do for you Paul?"

"If I can get some work from you I can pay some of the money I fucked up."

"That's game Paul. You're in the hole about 210 thousand. You could never even imagine getting enough dope from me to pay any part of that nut," Rick said trying not to show his anger and contempt for Paul trying to play him like a sucker.

"Well, maybe you can talk to Jimmy and ask him to pull the contract. You know Rick, give me some room to work with so I can pay him his money."

"You really must be crazy or think I am crazy. How the fuck am I going to ask Jimmy some shit like that? He may kill me for getting in his business!" Rick said in disbelief.

"He ain't going to do nothing to you and you know it," Paul responded.

"You're up there every day, they know who you are."

"I'm nobody. I'm a worker just like you used to be. And you can believe this Paul that I am not going to get on anyone's bad side when it's not my business. The best thing I can do for you is give you this five hundred so you can buy a bus ticket out of town. Buy the ticket and two hundred in dope and try another town. Better yet, try a program and kick. Clean up your act Paul, because there's nothing else I can do for you. So you want this five or what?" Rick asked.

"Yeah Rick, you leave me no choice."

"Let me tell you something Paul, you take this money and don't leave town because you owe me five hundred. Do you understand what the fuck I'm saying?" Rick knew Paul would use the money to get high and try to hide in plain sight.

"Yeah Rick, I got you."

The half million dollar home sat in the center of two acres of land surrounded by a red brick and black wrought-iron fence. Jesse, his son and daughter plus Rick sat on the porch watching the Italian gardener doing his work. The maid served the two adults iced tea. She served the kids cookies and milk.

"Yo Jesse, when I cut out I want to take the black Lamborghini."

"Sure my brother, no problem. I'm driving the burgundy Corniche anyway. You can keep the Lamborghini for as long as you want my brother," Jesse said.

"Excuse me, Sir," the gardener interrupted. "I would like to show you what I have done so far."

Jesse listened as the gardener explained what had been done and what still needed work. Both children stood quietly by their father's side listening to the gardener speaking. Their eyes widen when Jesse pulled the roll of bill from his pocket to pay the gardener for his labor. Children, any and all of them always seem to pay close attention when adults talked about or handled money.

"You know why I sit out here with my kids and watch the gardener work?" Jesse asked Rick.

"Not really," Rick replied. "But I know there is a lesson in it for the kids."

"That's right. When they grow up they won't have any fear of white folks. They will always remember whitey as people who did works around the house for their father. Now don't get me wrong. There's nothing wrong with the work the gardener does. He makes an honest living and has nothing to be ashamed of. I want my kids to grow up with pride in them. They will see the world differently from the way we did. I also do not want my children to go through what I did to make a living. I'm going to pay for their college education and when they finish college I'm going to give them 250 thousand a piece. I figure, by the time they graduate from college they will know what they want from life. That's why I work so hard. I appreciate the rewards that my lifestyle has afforded me and it was the right choice for me. But I want my children to have a better choice than the one I had."

"I can understand where you are coming from," Rick nodded.

Jesse and Rick sat and watched Jesse Jr. riding his sister around the yard on his mini Ferrari.

"You know how much that toy car cost me Ricky?"

"About 3 G's?"

"Ten thousand."

"No shit!"

"Yeah, my wife took them Christmas shopping last year on 5th Avenue. You know that place, FAO Schwarz?"

"Yeah, I know it."

"When he saw that car, that was all he talked about for weeks. So I got it for him. It makes me feel good to see my children so happy."

"I know what you are saying. There is no pleasure greater than seeing your kids happy," Rick agreed.

"I don't buy them everything they want because I'm not trying to really spoil them. But as long as they do the right thing, I will make sure they are rewarded."

"Look Jesse, it's time for me to break out," Rick told Jesse. They walked over to the four car garage and Rick removed the "T" top from the Lamborghini.

"Jesse you coming into the city tonight?" Rick asked.

"I'm not sure yet. Why, what's up?"

"Ain't nothing. I'm going out to the Hamptons myself. I met this bad girl from Spain. She rented a beach house for the summer so I'm going to hang for a few days with her. Besides, I don't want to drive this car in the city. You know the police will stop me every two or three blocks," Rick said. Jesse knew that after all, they were his cars and they both were young black men in America. .

Rick found a parking space in front of Leighton's clothing store on west 47th street, Broadway. The people on the street stopped to stare at the Lamborghini and him. Rick rushed from the cool of the car to the cold air-conditioning in the basement shoes section of the luxury men's clothing store. The sales clerk came over with a rush to serve Rick. He had been shopping in this store since Jr. high school. Back then he would place a pair of shoes on layaway. Today he had already selected four pair of reptile skin shoes.

Rick caught a glimpse of a light skin kid from the corner of his eye who had just come into the shoe department. He had a chocolate brown beauty with him. They walked over to a rack of shoes that lined the far walls. Rick tried on another pair of burgundy alligators and walked over to where the couple stood, checking the feel and fit of the shoes.

"Say my brother, has it been so long that you have forgotten who I am?" Rick asked. The gentlemen turned to see who it was speaking to him. His voice filled with the pleasure of recognition, "Rick!"

"What's up Mike," Rick greeted him. They gave each other a hug and laughed.

"Man, it's been a long time!" they almost said it at the same time.

"What's been happening?" Rick asked.

"I've been making a living," Mike replied. "Damn Rick, you are still a fly dressing motherfucker."

"That's the New York in me."

"Rick, let me introduce you to my lady. Cheri, this is Rick, Rick this is my lady love Cheri."

"I am pleased to meet you," Cheri said. "Mike has spoken about you and Sonny so much that I feel like I know you both."

"How is Sonny?" Mike asked. Mike noticed the change in Rick at the mention of Sonny's name.

"He passed away a while back," Rick sadly said.

"What?" Mike responded in disbelief.

"Yeah man, he's gone."

"I am sorry to hear that." Rick could see Mike was shaken by the news of Sonny's passing and it didn't make him feel good to bring it up either.

"It's a terrible loss to us all."

"How did it happen?"

"I'm not sure what was wrong with him. He died in the hospital," Rick said. "So Mike, what have you been doing?" Rick asked trying to change the subject.

"Right now I'm getting ready to make this movie called Superfly."

"Yeah, you're a movie star now. I always knew you would be famous," Rick joked.

"Nah man, I've just got a small part," Mike laughed. "But I'm going to make it take me to bigger and better things. You should come down to where they are shooting. There are parts still open for a fly motherfucker like you, Rick. They need people who can dress up the set and as fly as you dress it wouldn't be no thing."

"It sounds good but that not what I want to do. So you still living in the city or what?"

"Nah, I moved to California. Cheri and I have a nice little place near the beach. It's a whole 'nother world."

"I've been out there a few times on business. How long you going to be in New York?"

"Just until they finish shooting my part."

"Call me and we can hang out, I'm still at the same number," Rick said.

"If I had known that I would have called you a long time ago! You have had that number for a long time and I was sure it would have changed by now."

"No it's the same, so call me. Let me pay these people so I can go. I don't want to get caught in rush hour traffic on the parkway."

"Okay my brother, it was good to see you again," Mike said.

"Same here and it's nice to have met you Cheri. Stay in touch Mike," Rick said as he headed up the steps.

CHAPTER THIRTEEN

Things Never Seem to Change

RICK AND DONNY walked across the Douglas projects by way of 102nd street, headed towards Amsterdam Avenue.

"Yeah Rick, I really like her," Donny said. "She's not like the other woman I've had."

"Irma is fine and she's a good girl," Rick agreed. "Let me ask you this Donny. Is she really different from the other women you've been with or is it you that has changed?"

"I'm not sure Rick. All I know is that I want this thing with her and me to last."

"Well, if you both feel the same way you are headed in the right direction."

"How are things with you and Jenny?"

"Off and on as always."

"You should try and make things work between you and her."

"You really must be in love, Rick teased at what Donny just said.

"No its' not that. You have a son with her. Sean is a good kid and he's my man."

"So what the fuck has that got to do with me and Jenny? Sean and I will always be good and cool. I am always going to look out for him because he is my son."

"How's business my brother?" Rick asked.

"It's cool, I'm taking it slow and easy," Donny replied. "I've only been on the streets for a few months so I'm playing it safe."

"If you've been on the streets for a thousand years with things the way they are now, you would have to take it slow and easy."

"Come on Rick, let's go get a hit from Lefty."

"Yeah, that sounds good. I see Debra sitting on the bench and nothing goes better with coke than Debra," Rick commented.

THAT NIGHT

Pee Wee and Freddy sat at the bar in the Shalimar talking with two very beautiful women. When Rick approached them Pee Wee, forever the gentlemen, introduced Rick to the ladies then excused himself so he and Rick could talk. They talked basketball, clothes, cars and women.

"I was at a dinner party last with Gordon Parks and a few friends," Pee Wee said.

"They are making a movie about the drug game in New York. It's a small movie but it sounds like it is promising."

"What's the name of the movie?" Rick asked.

"Superfly."

"No shit! I ran into a kid I knew from high school who is going to be in. In fact he went to high school with you, light skin kid named Mike. Anyway, he has a part in the movie and asked me if I wanted a part."

"You going to get down or what?"

"I told him no, I'm not with it."

"It could be a break for you to do something else good for yourself, Rick."

Shemika came into the bar with her girlfriend and caught Rick's attention before he could reply to Pee Wee's statement. Rick signaled her to come over.

"Hi Rick," she said and kissed him on the cheek. "Hello Pee Wee, how are you doing?"

"I'm fine Shemika. Don't I get a kiss from my baby sister? Rick is not going to say anything he is too much a man to let a kiss between friends mean anything," Pee Wee teased.

Jesse came in, greeted everyone and asked Rick to excuse himself so they could talk.

"Yo Ricky, here's your 5 hundred back. Al didn't have that much blow at the moment."

"Damn," Rick said as he took the knot of money from Jesse.

"I got a quarter from him and that was all he had. We can sniff it together."

"Cool my brother, good looking out."

"What do you want to do for the rest of the night?" Jesse asked.

"I don't know, Shemika is going to hang with her girlfriend. Pee Wee and Freddy have those two bad ass freaks with them so you know they are going to break out. I could ask Shemika to cut her friend loose but that won't be right. What are you going to do Jesse?" Rick asked.

"I was just going to hit the spots until I came up with something."

"If you don't mind the company I'll ride with you."

"Yeah, that's cool my brother."

They had two rooms right next to one another in the Bronx River Motor Inn. They sat in Jesse's room sniffing and watched Belinda go through changes with Glenda popping shit about who was the biggest freak.

"Come on Belinda, I am going to give you a chance to show me what you are about," Rick said. "Later Jesse, when I'm finished with her I'll send her over and you can send Glenda my way."

"Don't count on it Jesse," Belinda said. When I get finished with him he won't have nothing left for that bitch."

"She talks plenty of shit doesn't she?" Rick said.

"But check this, I fuck a bitch like her all night and never bust a nut," Jesse said laughing.

It was a bright sunny morning, Rick had decided he had enough of the bullshit and was ready to break out. He knocked on Jesse's door to see what was up.

"Yo, what's up?" Jesse asked.

"You ready to break out?" Rick asked.

"Yeah, give me a minute."

"In a minute Rick, I can rock your world," Glenda purred.

"In a minute I can shower and dress to get the fuck away from you silly bitches."

"You're no fun!" Glenda teased.

"Whatever."

"You want me to drop you off somewhere?" Rick asked Belinda as he dried himself with a towel that was too small.

"I don't know yet. I have to see what Glenda is going to do."

Jesse came over with Glenda while Rick was still getting dress.

"What are you going to do?" Rick asked Jesse.

"I'm going to get something to eat," Jesse said. "Then I am going to drop them off."

"Alright, cool."

Rick could feel that something was not right. It bothered him all through breakfast and he let Jesse know about it after they had dropped the girls off.

"I don't know what it is, something is not right," Rick said.

"I'm going to check on my crew. I'll give you a call later."

"Okay my brother," Jesse replied. "If there is a problem get right back to me. I'll be at my mother's."

CHAPTER FOURTEEN

Busted, Busted, Why?

RICK SAT ON the rail in front of the Spanish store on the corner of 102nd street Manhattan Avenue. It was a bright sunny morning as he spoke with two of his workers. He had come by this morning to find out what time they would be finished and if everything was alright. Before the trio realized it, the police had them surrounded.

"Okay you niggers, up against the wall!" The police commanded with guns drawn.

"They are all clean except this one," the officer told the sergeant. "He's got a lot of money, must be 3 or 4 thousand dollars." The sergeant spoke with his men while another officer held the trio at gun point.

"Okay," the sergeant said, "You two get the fuck out of here. You Mr. Money bags are under arrest for sales." They handcuffed Rick and threw him in the back of the unmarked police car.

"I'm going to read you your right even thought I know you have been through this shit a hundred times," the slim white plain clothes officer said.

"No, I have never been arrested before," Rick answered them in no uncertainty. Rick's answer surprised the three police officers.

It's another busy day at Central Booking in lower Manhattan. It had taken Rick two days to get there from the 24th precinct. He also knew it would take another day or so before he would appear in front of a judge.

Rick sat on the floor handcuffed to a young Spanish kid who had stolen a 100 dollars worth of shirts from a department store. He watched the corrections officer finger printing some hoes who had stuck her hand in a trick's pocket while rendering her services. Central Booking was the melting pot where all crimes and criminals shared the same concrete floor and steel bars. This one for murder, that one for robbery, and across the hall for selling her ass.

Rick stood before the judge in the crowded court room. His appearance was more that of a bum rather than a man who had 32 hundred dollars in his pocket. Rick's lawyer argued that there was no reason for his client's arrest. The assistant of district attorney stated what he called facts. "This young man sells narcotics. The proof is in the large sum of money he had on him. We feel Your Honor, that we have enough evidence to get a Grand Jury indictment against Mr. Talley. The people also ask that a large bail be set because we believe Mr. Talley will flee."

"Your Honor, my client had never been arrested before. He is a highly decorated Vietnam War veteran. He has lived at the same address since 1957, more than half of his life. The A.D.A has no case against my client whatsoever. They want him held in jail while the D.A.'s office tries to make a case. For this reason your Honor, I feel that my client should be O-R-ed."

"Bail in this case is set at 35 thousand dollars," the judge ordered. The D.A thanked him.

Next stop for Rick and all those who could not make bail was Rikers Island. It was another hot summer night as the bus pulled up to the receiving room gate. It had been 5 days of sleeping on the floors of court bull pens, one inch thick dry baloney sandwiches three times a day. Rick sat handcuffed on the bus waiting to be told to step off. The bus had a real bad odor. Most of these men had not had a chance to wash for 3 or 4 hot summer days, some even a lot longer.

Rick did not realize the madness he was about to face, nor did he give it any thought.

"All right gentlemen," the fat black C.O called out. "Step off the bus and line up one behind the other. Once your cuffs are removed, listen for your name then give your address and go to pen number 5."

Rick was fortunate to be uncuffed first so he managed to find a seat in the corner of the pen. One by one they piled some 60 plus men into a pen that was built for only 25. The rodent and roach infested pen smelled of months-old piss that had baked in the sun. Human waste overflowed from the toilet. The sink was broken and littered with trash. Several men stood at the gate as if there were something to see. The floor looked like a jigsaw puzzle made of bodies as the men began to fall asleep from exhaustion. Rick sat calmly knowing it would not be much longer before he made the bail. One or two days at the most.

The receiving room ordeal lasted one and a half days for Rick. It was a simple procedure; he was given a number in place of his name. Stripped and checked for contraband. And he wondered what kind of man was it that made his living by looking up another man's ass.

Rick was placed in the housing area where every moment was filled with the uncertainty of what would happen next. He had a number of homeboys there and he was known by others as a scrambling kid. This could have meant trouble for him from those who thought they could pushed up on him. However, his movements showed he had no fear and that all comers would find trouble in this young man.

Like the days of old two groups of prisoners came to battle in the corridor on the way to the mess hall. A battery of C.O.'s dressed in riot gear, helmets, vest and carrying three foot long riot sticks appeared in minutes. The riot squad split the battling groups down the middle, breaking heads to bring order. Rick and several of his homeboys stood against the wall watching the action but ready to deal if any of it came there way.

Rick thought to himself, *dirty stinking mother fuckers throw me in the middle of this shit and I haven't done a damn thing wrong. Now I have to deal with these crazy fools who are trying to kill one another over a pair of sneakers.*

Rick laid on his assigned bed. He had been on the Rock almost five days. He had called home several times and he knew for sure that he was going to make the bail. It's just seemed like it was taking forever. He had even gone to the commissary that morning spending the maximum amount allowed. As if he was setting in for a long stay. He would call his lawyer later in the day to see if the grand jury had indicted him, but for what he could not imagine. The stupid police had not taken the money and they sure did not find any drugs on him or around him. There were no pictures of him making sales so how in the fuck could they indict him? But he knew it was the easiest thing in the world for the D.A.'s office to get a black man indicted.

It was nearly time for the noon meal. The cell block began to stir in anticipation of being let out for the slop they called food. "On the bail out, Talley, Ricardo 265-3984. Pack it up," the announcement came over the loud speaker.

"Yeah, finally." Rick sighed. "I'm out of here."

"Yo Rick," his homeboys called out from their cells. "You're out of here!"

They were happy to see him go, at the same time wishing it were them.

"Yo," Rick said. "Split this commissary between the crew. I will put some money in your commissary on the way out," he told one kid he had know most of his life. "All of you be cool, later."

CHAPTER FIFTEEN

Basketball Dreams
End of Summer

RIVERSIDE CHURCH WAS down one point with ten seconds left on the game clock. Mr. Loyche called for time out to set up a play.

"Eddy Ray, I want you to in bound the ball to Funny. Funny, I want you to drive to the foul line. That will cause them to collapse around you. Rick, I want you to play off of Funny in the corner the same way we practiced it. Either you or Funny will take the shot, lets go!" Mr. Loyche yelled. Funny took the shot from the foul line with four seconds left on the clock. The ball hit the back of the rim and bounced high. Rick leaped over the defending player Cool Breeze to grab the rebound and drop it in. Game. Riverside Church would play the Church of the Masters in the championship game.

Everyone was laughing and joking in the locker room. There would be another game later on that night. Some of these players from both teams would suit up together to play for Community Center 44 against Manhattanville Community Center.

"Rick," Mr. Loyche called out. "I would like you to stop by my office on your way out please."

"Sure Mr. Loyche. No problem," Rick replied.

"What can I do for you Mr. Loyche?" Rick asked.

"Come in Rick, have a seat. Have you ever thought about going to college Rick?"

"No, not really."

"Did you finish high school?"

"I got my G.E.D. while I was in the army."

"You are a bright kid and I think you can handle college. You know that I am in touch with quite a few coaches and scouts, both in college and the pros. I am also the lawyer for several of the biggest stars in the N.B.A. You've got what it takes to make it in the pros with a little work. You need the experience of college then you will be ready. I know of at least ten colleges that would jump at the chance to have you. I am not asking you to make up your mind this minute. Think about it and let me know one way or the other."

LAWYER'S OFFICE

"Look Rick, I will have your case disposed of. It was a bad arrest. I have a motion ready to file to dismiss the charges. I spoke with the judge and he is in complete agreement with me."

"What about the D.A.?" Rick asked.

"It's his job to make waves," Rosenburg said.

"The D.A. makes waves, you do your job and I have to pay the bill. Fuckin' cops arrested me and I spent five days in jail on some bullshit," Rick angrily said. "The judge says it was a bad arrest and I pay you 45 hundred to get me out of something I should have never been in, in the first place."

"Why does that make you so happy Ma?"

"Because it means you want to do more with yourself than just run the streets Ricky."

"Well I don't know what is going to happen yet. I've got a meeting with the coach at Pace University tonight and a meeting some time next week with the coach of St. Johns. To tell the truth Ma, I never liked school and I don't know why it would be any different now, especially since I don't have to go."

"It's a challenge Ricky. I went back to school to get my high education after 25 years."

"Yeah Ma, you did that so you could get a better job."

"Not only that Ricky, it also made me proud of myself to know that I could do it."

"It made me proud too Ma, but school for me at this stage of the game? It just doesn't seem to fit in my plans. I know it will take a lot of work for me to catch up. I remember how I played the company commander when I went for my G.E.D. while I was in the army. I took the pre-test and purposely failed so I would be assigned to school instead of the motor pool. After my first week of classes, they told me I would be discharged from the army in the next two weeks. I asked the instructor if I could take the real test because I was getting discharged. The captain who ran the school told me I was not smart enough to take the test and pass. I had to damn near beg him. It blew his mind when I got the highest marks ever scored on the base. Yeah Ma, I can handle college."

"Mr. Talley I have heard many good things about you,"Mr. Beard said. "We stress education at this University more so than our basketball program. Mr. Loyche has said that you can play in the professional ranks. He also believes you can bring national prominence to our University, Mr. Talley."

"I would like to think so," Rick replied to the praise which took him by surprise.

"You have been out of school for some time. You also did a bit in the service did you not Mr. Talley? Vietnam?"

"Yes and yes," Rick replied.

"Our education program is amongst the best in the country. Do you feel that you are ready for the commitment it takes to study at a University such as this one?"

"We won't know until I have tried, will we?"

"What I would like if it is alright with you, is for you to attend a Junior College this year. You know, to get your study habits together and that kind of things. I recommend that you take several courses at Manhattan Community College. It's a good school and I know the coach there. They have a good basketball team also. Then next year we will bring you back on a full scholarship. You think about it Mr. Talley and give me a call once you have made up your mind. I will walk you gentlemen to the door. The Knicks are practicing and the security around here is tight. I would not want the security personel to give my future star a problem."

Rick eased the machine onto the east side drive headed uptown.

"Yo Lefty, what do you think about the shit he was poppin?"

"Well my brother, he was more interested in your game than mine's. We both can get scholarships once they see you play," Rick said. "I don't know about that shit with Junior College. He picked Manhattan Community college of all the schools in the world for me to go to. That's where Jenny goes, I don't know," Rick thought out loud. "I've really got to give this a lot of thoughts."

"Why should Jenny make a difference?" Lefty asked.

"Of all the colleges in New York, I'm going to end up in the same one as my ex-girl. It will look like I am following her around. I don't know Lefty, I've got to think about this seriously. Then there is my mother to think about also. If I forget about going to school she is going to be disappointed, real disappointed. Well, I've got time to think about it before I make up my mind. Besides, I still have the interview with the coach of St. Johns."

"You could also take one of those out of town offers," Lefty commented.

"No, that's really out of the question, business," Rick responded.

CHAPTER SIXTEEN

All Star Game

❝ INTRODUCING THE STARTING fives for the Harlem Rucker's All Star basketball game. On the Red team we have Pee Wee (Stickman) Kirkland, Julius (Doc) Erving, Joe (Smooth) Lewis, Charlie Sweat and Lew Alsindor. Now for the Blue team, Nate (Tiny) Archiball, Orbee (Cool Breeze) Matthews, Rick Talley, Earl (The Goat) Manigult and Tucker the Green Giant."

Cool Breeze won the tip, tipping the ball to Rick. Rick let the flow of traffic passed him and moved the ball to the top of the key. Rick threw a bounce pass to Tiny on his left side. Pee Wee came up to guard Tiny. Rick dropped low to set a screen for Cool Breeze. Cool Breeze's jump shot off the pick from the corner was good for two points. Smooth threw the inbounds passed to Stickman, Stickman took the ball the length of the court. Tiny had came up to play defense on Stickman. Stickman shook tiny and laid it up between the Goat and Tucker. The Rucker's crowd cheered Stickman's break away lay-up. Tiny and the Goat walked the ball back down court after Stickman's basket. Rick and Cool Breeze set up low, Tucker posted up high on the foul line and Tiny passed him the ball. Alsindor played Tucker close. Rick took a quick step backwards on Charlie Sweat and Tucker got the ball to him. Rick put the ball on the floor and did a shudder step pass Charlie Sweat. Rick went up for the lay up, the air lane closed on him. Rick could see Tucker out of the corner of his eye and brought the ball down and around his back and under the arm of the defending players into Tucker's hands. A pretty pass made to look even better when Tucker took one step and threw it in on Alsindor. The crowd chanted, 'Tucker, Tucker.'

Doc received the ball at half court from Stickman and shook Rick and glided pass the Goat at the foul line and threw it in on Tucker. The crowd was on its feet, the cheers could be heard for twenty blocks. Smooth stole Tiny's in bounds pass and laid it up. The Red team put on a full court press with Stickman and Smooth playing the trapping lanes. Rick came back to half court to help out. Charlie Sweat tried to steal the pass the Goat threw to Rick. Rick caught the ball and spinned and had an open lane all the way to the goal. Charlie quickly recover from the missed steal, leaped to block Rick's shot. Rick did a 360 using Charlie's body in mid air to spin off of and throw it in. The crowd went wild.

Alsindor came down and posted up low on Tucker. Alsindor's hook shot was good for two points from the corner. The all star game had its first substitution, Herman Helicopter for Tucker on the Blue team and Larry Newbow came in for Charlie Sweat on the Red team. The game was an aerial acrobatic show with Stickman and Tiny Archiball running the lift off patterns for the high fliers. The Rucker's games are playground basketball at its best. Pro and college scouts had come from all parts of the country to watch these games. Many legends have been born from the performances in the Harlem Rucker's Basketball Tournament.

CHAPTER SEVENTEEN

College Games

RICK CLIMBED THE stairs and came to a stop behind a pretty, milk chocolate girl who stood in line.

"Is this the line for registration?" Rick asked her.

"Yes it is," she replied. *This could take a long time*, Rick thought.

"How long have you been standing here?"

"About twenty minutes."

"I better go move my car before it get towed or I get a ticket," Rick stated as an after thought. "Will you hold my place in line?"

Rick returned to find the line had grown. Rick excused himself to step in front of the couple behind the pretty chocolate brown-skinned girl.

"Did you find a parking space?" she asked Rick.

"Luckily I found one right on the corner of 72nd street and Broadway. If I had known it would be this much of a hassle to sign up, I would have had it done by now. By the way, my name is Rick."

"I'm Debra."

"Please to meet you, Debra. What courses are you going to sign up for?" Debra asked Rick.

"I have a list of classes that have been held for me by the basketball coach."

"Basketball? You must be good if they are holding classes for you."

"That may be, but the classes are the ones I need to transfer to Pace University next year."

"You have a nice car," Debra said as she eased into the soft leather seats.

"Yeah, I like it," Rick responded. "Look Young Lady, I'm going to drop you off at the West 96 street subway station, okay? I would take you home but I have some business matters to take of."

"I understand. Anyway, your wife or girlfriend dropped one of their earrings on the floor."

"It's not my wife's because I don't have one," Rick answered. "And as for my having a girlfriend, it depends on how you define the term."

"The way you act, your car, the clothes you wear say the term girlfriend means that you have more than one."

"No, it's not like that. Let me ask you a question, Debra. This is the start of a friendship, and I can tell that we can be good friends given the change. So does that make you my girlfriend or my girl friend?"

"You're good with words Rick, and as smooth as ice. My mother told me about men like you."

"How would your mother know about men like me?" Rick said to catch her off guard. "One day I will teach you about men like me and you will know the true story."

Rick stood on the corner outside of the student lounge talking with Bosco and Sylvester, two of his college teammates. Rick listened as his friends spoke, yet their words were lost to drift into space. Rick watched her as she moved back and forth between her girlfriends. Her smile was warm and he felt it across corridor. *Her figure had to be carved by the hand of God himself*, Rick imagined. He had lost all senses of where he was when Sylvester elbowed him snapping him back to reality.

"That's Debbie Burrell," Sylvester said.

"Yeah and she is one of the cheerleaders," Bosco added. "She also goes with that kid James."

"You're not talking about the same James that is going with Jenny now are you?" Rick asked.

"Yeah, that's him, it seems like you and him share the same taste in women," Bosco joked.

ONE MONTH LATER

'Yes, when you hear this song and you are the fifteenth caller you will receive two tickets to the premier of "Superfly". A limo will pick you and your guest up at your front door. You and your guest will also attend the private party after the show. You will party with the stars. I am Vaughn Harper for WBLS, your F.M. station in New York City, with the best sounds on your radio dial. More contests than any radio station in the nation.' Rick threw a cassette in the tape deck ending the onslaught of the hip sounds coming from the radio. All the stations sounded the same to him anyway. He knew the DJ, Vaughn Harper, or he used to know him when they played ball behind the Douglas Community Center. *That was a life time ago*, Rick thought. Without further thoughts, Rick turned the Caddy around and headed back downtown.

Rick pulled the mink jacket from the passenger seat, draped it over his shoulders like a cape then handed the keys to the garage attendant. He stood watching the midtown crowd. He enjoyed the beauty of the women who worked in the office buildings. Most of all he liked the way they stared at him. He read their body language and the look in their eyes revealed their passion. Or was it a question they were asking with their eyes? *Who is this young black man who dresses so divinely? And what is your fantasy?* He would ask himself about them. There were always one or two who sparked more than just a passing interest. Rick in all of his glory held no interest in those women who were not available at the moment for his pleasure. However, there were always the few who would take the afternoon off to play in a nearby hotel. A stolen moment of passion kept secret from their husbands or boyfriends, an afternoon of pleasure never to be repeated.

Rick crossed the street and did the one flight of steps to the main lobby of Manhattan College. He crossed the corridor to the stairway exit, going back down one flight. He was greeted by the males and females that lounged on the stairway. The back stairway had privacy and had become student lounge for the fast crowd. Some just came there to talk and catch up on what was happening while others smoked reefer and blew coke. A few sniffed dope on the down low.

Rick did not see any of the females he wished to take off. Even though he could see a few who were willing to get with him just because of whom he was. He really had no idea what it was he wanted as several females and males tried to entice him to hang with them at their stairway party.

Rick made his way back to the corridor and the student lounge. He took a seat in the rear where he could sit and watch the door at the same time but not be bothered by anyone. He saw her, as she entered the student lounge and he realized what it was what had brought him back to school on this day.

Rick walked up on her just as she was about to take a seat. He knew that he had startled her by the way she jumped.

"I did not mean to frighten you."

"Do you always move so silently?" she asked.

"Habit," Rick replied. "May I join you Ms. Burrell?"

"Yes, but I am only going to be here for about ten or fifteen minutes. I have a class in the Broadway building."

"I will walk with you if you don't mind. There are some matters I would like to talk to you about. In fact, if you like we can walk over to the coffee shop now. This place is much too noisy to carry on the kind of conversation I want."

"Do I know you well enough to have that kind of conversation?" she teased.

"That's what I want to talk about, the chance for us to know each other well."

The coffee shop was crowded and almost as noisy as the student lounge. Rick and Debbie took seats at a table with the large picture window and watched the bustling midtown crowd outside on the sidewalk. The waitress in her starched tan uniform came over to take their order.

"What would you like?" Rick asked Debbie.

There conversation was light and filled with a sense of understanding as they waited for their orders. Rick drank orange juice and watched her as she ate a tuna club sandwich.

"Please don't stare at me like that," she said.

"Why, does it bother you?" Rick asked.

"You make me nervous. It also makes me feel self-conscious about myself."

"You have no reason to ever feel self-conscious about anything."

"You know Debbie, as I sit here looking at you there are a number of questions that I find I must ask myself about you. To my eyes or anyone's eyes there is nothing on earth that can compare to your beauty. The warmth in your eyes invite me to reveal more of myself than I otherwise would. The look in your eyes tells me that you are a lady that I have longed to know."

Rick's voice was soft. The deep rich bass tone showcased the passion that burnt within him. His eyes told her a story of his sincerity as only he could write it. She relaxed and seemed to float on the smooth rhythmic ease his words brought on. They sat hypnotized by one another and it was clear that this would be more than just a passing fling for either of them.

"Will you walk me to class?" Debbie asked.

"It would be my pleasure," Rick replied. They strolled alone Broadway, stopping to look in the windows of clothing stores and bypassed the porno theaters and peek shows.

"Well, here we are," Debbie announced.

"What do you have planned for this weekend?" Rick asked.

"Depends on what you have in mind and what night of the weekend we are talking about," she replied.

"I thought I would take you out, let's say Saturday."

"The school dance is this Saturday and I have to be there."

"So we can do it together. I'll come get you around 10, if that is a good time for you."

"You don't have to drive all the way out to St. Albans to get me. I will come into the city with my sister and friends and you can drive me home, if that is okay with you."

"Okay, we're set. I will see you Saturday."

"How about tomorrow, Thursday? I don't have any classes on Friday."

"I have some things to take care that I can not put off."

"Okay then, Saturday it is."

Rick and Jesse stood in front of the Shalimar talking. KC pulled up in his custom made black Eldorado.

"How do you like that car?" Rick asked Jesse.

"I don't," Jesse replied.

"I don't like it either." A few of the females standing outside of the bar squealed and raced over to embrace KC.

"Check him out, the movie hasn't even opened yet and these silly bitches are going crazy for him," Jesse said.

"It's the posters and TV commercials and those damn ugly pictures of his car. Check this out, Jesse. He's pimpin, before the movie these same bitches were running for the hills to get away from him. They were scared to death that he would put them out there. Now all of a sudden pimpin is alright," Rick told him.

"You going to the premier?" Rick asked.

"Nah, I'm going to see it after it opens everywhere. I just don't want to hang with all those fake motherfuckers who think they know what this life is about. They'll be acting like they are coming off and they don't have a dime."

"I know what you mean. But I'm going just because it's a first. Besides, I may knock off one of those wanna-be movie star bitches. I'm gearing up for it, I had a black corduroy jacket with a horse shoe white mink collar made. I'm going to drape myself in white gold jewelry."

"Yo Ricky, I want you to design a mink coat for me. Something like you did for your man and them when we went to the Ali, Frazier fight at the Garden. Those were some bad motherfuckin' coats!" Jesse said. "Where did you learn to design clothes, anyway?"

"When I was 12, I worked in a dress store after school. I made 14, 15 dollars a week going around to the factories downtown picking up dresses for this store Richard's on Broadway and 109th. One place I used to make a lot of pick ups at had a furrier next to it. They hared the same loading dock. I always asked a lot of questions about furs. The old Jewish man who owned the place took a liking in me. Anyway, he taught me the fine art of being a furrier. I could always draw so I put them together."

"Yo Ricky, do you remember when we were at the fight how that bitch Diana kept looking at Pee Wee?"

"Yeah," Rick said laughing. Rick and Jesse gave each other five in agreement, and continued laughing together.

"Yo, yo Jesse, Ms. Superstar jumped over a row of seats and grabbed him by the arm when we were cutting out."

"Yeah, yeah, but check this out Ricky. She fell crazy in love with the way he looked!"

"She pushed people out of the way to get to him, remember Jesse?"

"Yeah, she told him, *'Damn Brother, you look so good I just had to take some pictures with you,'* Jesse reminded Rick. They laughed and felt good about the memories of the night they had shown the world there are many rich black folks in this world. Everyone wanted to know where so many elegantly dressed blacks had come from.

They had come from England, the South side of Chicago, the Bay area in Northern California, Compton and Watts in Southern California, Jamaica in the West Indies, Detroit and Africa. They came from all parts of the world to cheer on the fight of the Century in Madison Square Garden.

"Where are you going?" Claude asked Rick.

"I'm going to meet this girl from school. Why?"

"She must be special, that's all."

"What makes you say that?"

"The changes you are going through to get dressed. This is the forth outfit you've tried on!"

"Yeah, she is fine."

"So what's up?" Rick asked Claude.

"Ain't nothing," Claude replied. "I think I'm going to check out this dance in the village. I'm waiting on Larry Cherry."

"Look in my drawer and take some of that smoke. Roll a couple of joints for me too."

"Ricky!" his mother called from the living room. "Will one of you boys come answer the door?"

"Yeah Ma, I've got it!" Rick replied. "It's probably Stanly for me anyway."

"Or, it could be Larry for me," Claude said.

"Who is it?" Rick asked, peering through the peephole.

"Stanly, Larry, and Jenny!" they answered. *What the fuck?* Rick thought. Rick opened the door to find them all dressed to the nines. Stanly and Larry were expected. But, Jenny? All three kissed Ma hello.

"Yo Stanly, I'll be ready in a minute, go ahead in the back. You too Larry, Claude is in the room," Rick said.

"Jenny let me speak to you in the kitchen," Rick signaled her. "So Jenny, what brings you here tonight?"

"I came to see you."

"How did you know I would be here?"

"I took a chance."

"Well I'm sorry, I've already made plans. Stan and I are going to hang out."

"I didn't come here to break up your plans. I just came to see if you had anymore of that smoke and if you would give me a ride to the school dance."

"Yeah, I have some of that smoke, and yes, I will give you a ride to the dance. That is where Stan and I are headed."

Rick found a parking space right in front of the dance hall. Rick paid everyone's way in and Jenny excused herself stating that she had to meet some of her friends.

"I will see you later Rick, Stan," Jenny said. Rick listened to the music that the band played as he glimpsed at the trio of females singing on stage. He did not pay much attention to the females singing as he walked around the dance floor.

"Do you see the young lady you are looking for?" Stan asked Rick.

"No, she may not be here yet," Rick replied. They worked the crowded dance floor as Rick searched for her. Rick and Stan made their way within feet of the stage. Rick stopped dead in his tracks.

"Do you see her?" Stan asked again. Rick did not reply he just stood there watching the lead singer belting out a soulful dance tune.

Rick tapped Stanly with his elbow, "That's her." He motioned his head to point out the lead singer on stage.

"That's a beautiful girl," Stan said.

"Yeah, and she sings well too," Rick said more to himself than Stan.

Rick found a table near the stage where he could watch the performance of the band and really feel the stage presence of Ms. Debbie Burrell. Stanly ordered the drinks and checked to see which of the many women would be of interest to him on this night. The band ended their set to a standing ovation. The ladies thanked the crowd in harmony and informed them the next set would be in 15 minutes.

Rick waited for Debbie to join him at his table only to receive a message sent by the drummer to meet her on the balcony.

The noise of the crowd disappeared as Rick made his way up the back stairway. The scene played like a clandestine meeting from a best selling spy novel or movie. The balcony was deserted and surrounded the dance floor. Once Rick ascended onto the balcony, he made his way in the dimmed light as he listened to the faint sounds of the crowd below.

Debbie stepped from behind a curtain at the end of the balcony like the scenario of a good spy drama. For a moment they dueled, fencing, feeling one another out to where each felt comfortable in and with the situation.

"Why all the melodrama?" Rick asked Debbie.

"I saw you with Jenny when you came in. I did not mean to cause a problem for you."

"I have nothing to hide from anyone. Jenny and I will always have a relationship because she is my son's mother. What I do with her has no bearing on what our relationship is or will become."

"Debbie, I know your first interest in me was for revenge," Rick said sincerely. "Your man went behind your back to be with a women who is in your face every day. I know you were embarrassed to have Jenny fucked your man, not to mention the pain of betrayal."

"I felt more like a fool than anything," Debbie said, "and I must admit that's just how our relationship did get started."

"When I first saw you Rick, I had no idea what kind of man you were. All I knew about you in spite of the entire good thing I did feel, was that you were a way for me to get back at James cheating," Debbie told him.

"Let me tell you something Lady, for me it was the way you smile, the way you talk, walk, and your pretty legs that made me want to know more about you. But most of all it was the warmth in your eyes that made me want to truly be close to you. You wanting revenge made it easy for me," Rick responded.

"That day you and I talked in the coffee shop was when I knew you and I would become close. You made me feel like I never have before and I knew you were a man that I had to know," Debbie whispered ever so softly.

Rick took her by the hand and led her into his arms. They stared into each others eyes for what seemed like a life time. The desire of unknown passion held them bonded in a spell. Their lips met, his pleasure swelled within him. He knew truly that she was the kind of lady he had long to know. She leaned back and he watched the stars dance in her eyes. She whispered, "Rick, it's for more than revenge. It's all about you and me now."

It was a cold sunny day. Rick was enjoying the ride in from Westchester County with Sean.

"Daddy, how come Joy is my aunt and I am older than her? Pam is my aunt and she's a lady."

"That's a good one, my man. Let me see…"

When Sean was satisfied with his father's explanation he asked if he could go see grandma.

"She's not here, she went to Ohio with her choir to sing," Rick told his son.

"When is she coming back, daddy?"

"In a few days."

Rick wheeled the car across the 155th street bridge, around the loop onto 7ᵗʰ Avenue. He worked the car in and out of traffic headed downtown.

"Where are we going, daddy?"

"I'm going to Jesse's house. Where do you want to go?"

"To the movies or the circus."

"After I see Jesse we can go to the movies and one night when I get back from upstate New York, I will take you and Joy to the circus. How does that sound to you my man?"

"It sounds good, daddy."

"Yo, yo!" Rick yelled up to the third floor window.

"Yo, yo!" Jesse yelled back out of the window. "Come up!"

"Yo Jesse, I've got Sean with me so come down!"

Jesse and Rick greeted one another. Jesse went over to the car to talk with Sean who was sitting on the hood. They gave each other five and Sean's face lit up like Christmas tree lights.

Jesse put his arm around Rick's shoulders and they began to walk down 7ᵗʰ Avenue. Rick kept a close eye on Sean as he spoke with Jesse.

"I only want one joint this time," Rick said. "I will bring the money uptown tonight."

"Check this out, if you want an extra one on consignment you can get it," Jesse offered.

"No, not this time. I'm going to be at Syracuse University playing in this basketball tournament. I will be up there for seven to ten days depending on how we do in the tournament. If I take the one joint and put it out, by the time I get back my crew should be finished or just about finished. So it don't make scene for me to have one joint just sitting in the closet."

"That's cool," Jesse nodded.

"I've got these kids from Buffalo bringing you the money they owe while you are in Syracuse. If they give you all of it Ricky, call me. That way I can send them something new. Can you handle that for me Ricky," Jesse asked.

"Yeah, I got you, no problem."

"You sure?" Jesse asked once more. "You going to drive up?"

"Yeah, I already spoke to the coach about it. He said it was cool for me and my man on the team to drive up in my car. I would rather take the bus with the team and the cheerleaders. It's like four other buses going up also with the student body on them. I know they are going to be partying on the buses. But then if I take the bus I'd be fucked up on the move around tip with no car in Syracuse," Rick explained.

Book Three

CHAPTER ONE

Lost on The Mean Street

I T WAS A beautiful Spring day. Rick, however, was in a sober mood. He sat quietly on the sofa and watched the evening news. The ringing of the telephone broke the silence and eeriness he felt in the large empty apartment. Rick grabbed the receiver and then laid back down on the sofa before beginning a conversation.

"Hello."

"Yeah Rick, it's me Turk."

"What's up my brother?"

"You watching the news?"

"Yeah, I've got it on channel 7."

"Turn to channel 2." Rick used the remote control to switch channels. He caught the news announcer as he was just about to end a story. *'And law enforcement agencies have closed down what is believed to be the largest heroin ring to exist with the sentencing of its three leaders today in Manhattan Criminal Court.'*

"You hear that shit?" Turk Asked him.

"Yeah. They have been kickin' that shit all day. I was in court this morning so I know the deal," Rick went on to inform Turk.

Rick had sat quietly in back of the court room. He had gone unnoticed by all except Jesse. Reporters from every magazine and television station you could imagine filled the court room. Television crews stood outside the court room ready to interview the prosecutor and defense lawyers once they exited the court building.

Rick sat and listened with the others in the court room as the judge sentenced Jesse and two others to 5 to 15 years in a New York State prison for their participation in organized crime.

"It's been a ruff year," Rick said to Turk. "Hard times all around with people getting themselves killed and going to prison."

"There's no money on the streets either," Turk added.

"There's money out there. We just can't get it. Look my brother, give me a call in a few days. I've got some things to check out."

"Okay Rick, you be cool," Turk said.

Rick eased the car in and out of the streets which made up the section of New York known as Harlem. He watched the spring time crowd standing on the corners, in doorways and looking out of their apartment building windows. *Nothing for them seemed to have changed*, Rick thought. Little did they know though, it was for sure the underworld of New York would never be the same again.

Rick found who he had been looking for when he saw Crime coming out of Sylvia's restaurant on the corner of 127th street Lenox Avenue. He caught Crime's attention just as he was about to get in his car.

"Yo what's up Rick?" Crime greeted him.

"Ain't nothing Crime," Rick replied. "Let me talk with you for a minute." Crime climbed into Rick's car and Rick pulled off.

"So what's up Rick?" Crime asked.

"What happened when you asked those people about the product I want to cop?" Rick asked.

"They can't handle it, Rick."

"So it was game they were poppin?"

"I wouldn't say that. Things are so fucked up, no one really knows what is going to jump off. It's going to be a long hot summer. You've got a few people with products but nobody really knows where to get the mother-load," Crime explained.

"I'm not interested in the motherload," Rick said in subtle anger. "I just need a connection to keep my things going. Since Jesse got knocked, I've only scored twice and the product wasn't shit."

Rick pulled back along side of Crime's car.

"Yo Rick, things are going to get better," Crime said, trying to assure Rick.

"Yeah, I know my brother. They can't get much worse."

TWO DAYS LATER

Rick waited for the customers to filter out of the small corner drug store. When Jerry had waited on the last of them, he signaled for Rick to come in the back.

"What can I do for you Rick?" Jerry asked.

"I'm making the rounds to see what the deal is," Rick told him.

"It looks like things are going to be pretty bad this summer. If you can get your hands on anything, take it straight to the streets. Break everything you get down and put it on the streets so you can get paid," Jerry instructed Rick.

"It's that bad, huh?"

"Worse. If I can come up with something I will keep you in mind."

"Okay Jerry, I'd appreciate it."

ONE WEEK LATER

"It really is my fault Rick, I should have entered your name as a heart ship case in the upcoming N.B.A. draft. At any rate, you should be selected by one of the teams based on your play in the summer pro league in Los Angeles," Rick's agent stated. "The scouts from the Warriors and the Lakers have expressed an interest in you."

THREE DAYS LATER

Rick and Melvin sat in silence as the limo made its way along the Grand Central Parkway headed for the airport.

"I don't know," Rick said breaking the silence. "This trip is costing an arm and leg."

"You can handle it," Melvin replied.

"Yeah, that's what I keep telling myself."

"Look my brother, after you sign a pro contract you will be straight for life," Melvin said to ease Rick's mind. "In the meantime, let us enjoy ourselves."

"This trip is costing me plenty of money as well," Melvin remarked.

"Yeah, with one difference. Your company will write it off as a business expense."

"Well it is business because I am producing the movie. The house I am renting is for the parties I give to bring the right people together to promote the movie, etc., etc."

"Well I'm not producing no damn movie so why the fuck am I renting a house for five thousand a month?"

"Because you are with me, my brother and you have to maintain an image. Besides, when you knock off one or two of those little starlets where would you take them if not back to your big fancy house?"

"Whatever," Rick replied.

Girls Of The Big 10", the cover of Playboy magazine read and it caught Rick's attention. Rick selected it along with several other magazines, Times, Newsweek and Ebony from the news stand at the airport.

"Come on Rick," Melvin called, "They're boarding."

Melvin was almost as tall as Rick who stood 6 feet 4 inches tall. Both had milk chocolate complexions and if you looked close you could see Rick's freckles. Melvin had none. Whereas Rick was quiet and reserved Melvin was outgoing and always made him the center of attention. Their personalities made for a strange pairing, yet they had become good friends.

Melvin kept a steady conversation going with the stewardess in first class. Rick sat reading the Playboy magazine. Rick read the caption at the bottom of the page over to insure he had gotten her name right. He elbowed Melvin to get his attention.

"Excuse me," Melvin said to the stewardess. "What's up Rick?"

"Look at this girl. Now tell me, ain't she a fine motherfucker." Melvin took the magazine and studied the photograph Rick had pointed out. Then he looked at all the other pictures of females who were nude.

"I don't know about you, Rick. I think you came back from Vietnam with a screw missing."

"What? You saying that she is not fine?"

"No, it's not that Rick. All of these women with their shit showing and you bug for the one who has her clothes on. What the fuck is on your mind?"

"She's going to be my girl," Rick said assuredly as if had known her all of his life. Melvin looked at his friend in total surprise and disbelief, then back at the picture in Playboy magazine.

"Yo Rick, check this out, we are going to Hollywood. You will be driving a sex machine and living in a house in Beverly Hills. You are a star ball player and you dress your ass off. Not to mention women always talk about how you look so damn good. Some of the most beautiful women will be coming from all over the world to the parties I throw off. Given all this, why and what makes you consider her? How will you find her?"

"I'm going to write her a letter."

"Get the fuck out of here! She's going to get hundreds of letters if not thousands!"

"Yeah, but only one will be from me. Ms. Betsy Beutler and I were meant to be together."

The real estate agent was a tall statuesque blonde whom style of dress was pure Californian. The surprise and shock was written all over her face as Melvin introduced himself at the curb. Rick had noticed it before she was able to regain her composure. Nonetheless, she was still uncertain as to how she should handle the situation when the limo pulled away from the Los Angeles International Airport.

"I did not expect either of you to be so young!" the real estate agent stated.

"Or black," Rick added. She seemed to relax with the frankness of Rick's remark and he knew she was not a racist.

"You are quiet right," she replied to Rick's statement. "I am used to dealing with the more established named clientele of old money or their offsprings. It's not often that I get such young black clients whose names I don't recognize from the publicity mills."

"Well, you will soon know my friend's name," Melvin said.

"Is that so Mr. Talley? Are you an actor or singer?"

"No, I believe my friend is a bit premature. I'm out here to play in the summer pro basketball league."

"Well, I wish you luck."

"Thank you. Anyway you are more likely to hear about my friend here before you do about me. He's in the entertainment business."

"Is that so? Which end?"

"I am a producer and I am in town to put together the cast for my next production," Mel replied. "It's a film called *Black Silk.*"

Her eyes lit up and she shifted in her seat as if Melvin's statement sparked an interest in an undying dream she held of becoming a legendary actress in Hollywood. Even if it was just in one of the new low budget black movies.

TWO WEEKS LATER

The house was so big it was lonely. Rick stood in the solitude of the veranda transfixed by the breath taking view of the Los Angeles City lights below. He had a good game today, 20 points, three monster dunks and 10 rebounds. He strolled back into the bedroom where he had laid out his clothes for Melvin's party tonight.

She stretched in her sleep pulling the raw silk sheets over her naked form. Rick stood and watched her as she slept. She was an actress, like every other female who lived in this town claimed to be. She had been in several movies with parts too small to mention or remember. When Rick brought up that he needed to find the right pair of shoes to match his outfit for Melvin's party tonight, before he could blink an eye she had led him to a secluded spot in back of the upscale clothing store and was on her knees with his dick in her mouth.

She had also walked off her job as a sales person right on the spot to spend the rest of the afternoon showing him the kind of stores he liked to shop in. They had topped a late lunch off with a swim in his pool and a romp in his bed. She was good in bed and pleasing to look at with the kind of legs he liked to feel wrapped around his body, so he decided to take her with him to Melvin's party. She had surprised him when she said she knew who Melvin was and that she knew about his party as well.

Rick pulled the candy apple red Lamborghini to a halt at the gate and showed his invitation to the guard. He drove up to the front of the house where 20 or so valet stood. One rushed to open each of the car doors. Rick stepped from the car and looked around. He was impressed. Melvin had gone all out for this party. The other party had been good, but this one was special. Rick watched as the valet drove the candy colored sports car off to park it. Rick did not like the color, too loud, yet it seemed to draw women like nothing he had ever seen before.

Rick understood now why Melvin had to have such a large place. He had not rented a place just to stay in. He had rented a ballroom in which he could stay when not hosting a party. Rick found Melvin in a crowd of faces he recognized from the movies and television.

"Hey my man," Melvin greeted Rick.

"How are you Melvin," Rick said returning his friends greeting being a bit reserve.

"Who is that pretty lady on your arm?"

"Excuse me, Melvin this is Sherry Ann. Sherry Ann, this is my very good friend Melvin."

"Nice to meet you Sherry Ann."

"It's my pleasure," Sherry Ann replied. "I've been reading about your production in the trades."

"Oh, we have an actress on our hands Rick."

"So it seems," Rick replied.

"Come then, let me introduce you both around to the famous and not so famous."

"No, take Sherry with you and I will catch up with you both later."

Rick worked the crowd on his own and was more than a little impressed. He listened to Flip Wilson tell jokes to a group at pool side as others danced to the music that the band played. Rick found a quiet spot where he could view the mix of the crowd and not really be seen or bothered. The bitter sweet aroma of reefer filled the air. Rick watched the bartender formed piles of cocaine into lines on a silver tray. One by one, males and females stepped up to do a line. *'Only in California would anyone sniff like that'*, Rick thought.

Sherry Ann found Rick and she seemed to be pleased to be back in his company.

"Rick, don't go anywhere and leave me here," she said.

"Why? Aren't you enjoying yourself?"

"Yes I am, and Melvin has introduced me to some very important people. But all the people he has introduced me to I get the feeling that I am just another piece of ass by the way they look at me. Most of these people seemed so fake, it's something about them, I just don't know how to put it."

"Rick, please don't misunderstood what I did for you in the store today."

"What is there for me to misunderstood?" Rick asked cutting her off.

"I'm a good person."

"Have I treated you otherwise? Look Sherry Ann, relax and enjoy yourself. Make the best of this opportunity that you can. Go mix it up, see what real contacts you can make for yourself. I will be here when it's time for us to leave."

Rick took a hit from the bill, *'Now this is how you are supposed to sniff,* he said to himself. *What do you California dreamers know about sniffing anyway.*

"Hello there," the short balling middle-aged man greeted. "Would you care to share a little of that with a friend?" Rick passed the bill and the man in turn passed Rick a joint.

"Here light this up, it's the best money can buy," he said to Rick still purring a like a French hoe.

"Raymond, Raymond!" the short man called. "Come here please, Raymond." Raymond St. Jacques was standing pool side with Roscoe Lee Brown and a very pretty black female. Rick thought the female was Betty Davis, Mile's ex-wife, but he was not sure. She was a pretty work of art whoever she was.

"Raymond, looked at what I have found, isn't he gorgeous? Oh, excuse me. Do you know Raymond St. Jacques and Roscoe Lee Brown?" he asked Rick.

"I know them, but I don't know you," Rick told the short man. Rick did not bother to introduce himself to the short man.

Rick had met Raymond when he was filming *"Cotton Comes To Harlem"*, and Roscoe had been introduced by a mutual friend back in New York.

"Are you in the business or trying to break into the business?" the short man asked Rick. Before Rick could reply he went on as if he were trying to dazzle Rick with his importance. "I and some friends have invested in a movie that is about to go into production. It's being shot up in New York and it's called *"Hell Up In Harlem."* There is a small part that could make you a star."

"I'm not interested," Rick responded.

"What? You have to be kidding! Everyone in Hollywood wants to be a star and I am the one who can do it for them," the little man said in controlled anger.

"Thank you, but no thanks."

The more Rick resisted the offer of stardom, the more he was offered.

"I know your kind," the little man spat out. "You pretty boys with big dicks think the world is supposed to fall at your feet. I can buy your kind a dime a dozen." The others were shocked by the hateful outburst of the short man. Rick's eye's narrowed and the blood in his veins ran ice cold. The smooth easy tone of his bass voice reflected the anger of a man in full control.

"Let me explain something to you," Rick told the little man. "I don't know you and I did not ask you to come over here. You came over here with honey dripping from your pants and purring like a bitch in heat. You tried to play me like a star struck fool in search of a dream. Then when I tell you I am not interested in becoming your victim you insult me. You have nothing to offer me, especially at the price you are asking me to pay. You do not know me or how big or little my dick is, so it would be in your best interest to leave me the fuck alone before you find yourself with a problem you can't handle. Do I make myself clear?" Rick asked the little man.

When Rick was able to locate Melvin he was talking with Ike and Tina Turner, Berry White, Vonetta McGee and Jim Brown. Melvin introduced Rick to his guests then excused himself to speak with Rick in private.

"Yo Melvin, I may have caused you a problem. One of your guests gave me the come on and I had to set him straight."

"It's no problem Rick, this is a town where money talks and I'm the man with the money. If he gives you another problem let me know," Melvin said.

"Shit, the next time home boy sees me he just may run," Rick joked. They laughed and gave each other five. "Look Melvin, I'm going to find Sherry and break out. You wouldn't know where she is would you?"

"No, the last time I saw her she was going upstairs to smoke a joint with Sly and his wife."

Rick made his way in and out of the rooms on the upper floor of the large house. He was not surprised when he saw one of the young valets fucking an older woman draped in a pound of diamonds. The valet had her up against the bedroom wall. *Damn, she had on way too much make up*, Rick thought. Rick also wondered why they would not have at least locked the fucking bedroom door.

Rick was, however, a bit shocked to find the lead singer of a popular group on the toilet with one leg on the sink and the other on the tub with a long haired hippie-type between her legs. He ate her pussy while she shot what must have been cocaine into her arm. Cocaine was the only drug Rick could think of to make them that damn freakish. Neither he nor she bothered to look up as Rick closed the bathroom door. "You stupid motherfucker," he heard the lady said,"Didn't you have enough sense to lock the door before we got started?" Rick just laughed to himself.

The D.J. had the crowd jumping as Rick looked them over from the top of the stairway. The living room crowd swayed to the beat of the music and Rick could feel it taking him with the beat. He went over and took Tina Tuner by the hand, leading her to the center of the dance floor.

They rocked to the rhythm of the music, lost to the endless onslaught of the beats.

Rick could see Sherry Ann dancing with Jim Kelly as he peered over Tina's shoulder. Tina excused herself to rejoined Ike. Rick used the opportunity to retrieve Sherry Ann.

It was still early by Rick's standards. If he were in New York the people would still be on their way out to find the night clubs. At one o'clock in the morning the Pacific Coast Highway was a lonely stretch of road. The roar of the ocean as its pounding surf attacked the shore gave one the sense of enormous power being released. The surf dancing in the moonlight reminded Rick of a love story he had once seen in the movies.

Rick had never envisioned himself in this type of setting. He wheeled the sports car off the road into a wooded area. He worked the Lamborghini in and around the trees until it set perfectly to allow him the pleasure the view offered.

"It's beautiful," Sherry Ann whispered.

"Yes it is," Rick replied. "How long have you been in California?"

"Two years, two long years." Her voice reflecting the disappointment she felt. "Sometimes I just want to give up and go back home. But there is nothing back there for me. I've had some ruff times out here. This is a hard place for a woman alone."

"From what I saw tonight, it's a hard place for anyone trying to make it in the film industry. On the other side of the coin Sherry, as a man, there are those who want a man to play just like they want women to play. I found that out tonight when some two-cent producer thought he saw visions of stardom dancing in my eyes. This is a user town," Rick said.

"Hollywood is a strange town. All these powerless little people living in a world of fantasy. The belief they hold in themselves and their importance being larger than their screen image or the signs on their door. The people who control the real power in this town never show their faces. They don't need to, they make and break people and studios with a spoken word. As a woman Sherry, I am sure you know how this town runs. The people who make the movies for the power people want you to play before you get the part. Most of the time the under links use you up before you can show yourself to be a talent in the business," Rick went on to say.

"Let me give you some advice, Sherry Ann. I remember once Melvin and I was talking about all the beautiful woman that has come to this town. They have stars dancing in their eyes and we questioned: 'Why some make it while others or mostly don't?' A lot of talented people are overlooked. Anyway, to make a long story short; if you give up your pussy on a promise or the hope of getting a part you will be passed around until you are used up. If you tell the fools you are an actress and not their personal sex slave you stand a better chance of getting what you want. If there is a part that some asshole insisted you play for, tell him you want a sign contract first. I guess what I am really trying to tell you is *don't* make yourself a victim. You've got to set the standard by which your life is guided. The stronger you are, the sooner you will find your own place in this town."

A FEW DAYS LATER

Rick sat at pool side enjoying the view and a glass of fresh orange juice. Sherry Ann brought him the mail and said good afternoon. She allowed the robe she wore to slip from her shoulders to fall down around her ankles. Rick glimpsed up at her naked beauty just as she dove into the pool. Rick read the names of whom the envelopes were from and addressed to. Most of the letters were for the people who owned the house or had rented it before him. The one letter that beared his name had been a long time in coming. Yet, he always knew it would come.

The phone rang as Rick was opening the letter. He grabbed the receiver and placed it between his ear and shoulder to hold it in place while he read the letter.

"Hello."

"Yeah Rick, its' me Melvin."

"What's up my brother? Yo Melvin check this out, I got a letter from that girl in Playboy magazine."

"No shit, what did she have to say?"

"Let me see, she said that she found my letter most interesting and she gave me and address where I can write her from now on."

"Look Rick, if I had known you were really serious about getting to know this girl I could have called Hef for you. Look Rick, I can still make arrangements for you to meet her at Hef's house."

"No my brother, I rather do it my way. She and I have made our introduction and the rest is up to me to make sure it happens. Thanks for the offer my brother."

"Oh, I almost forgot what I called for. Are you free this Saturday night around 8?"

"Yeah, as far as I know, why?"

"I've got a dinner party I want you to check out with me. It's a power business meeting," Melvin added. "You can check out how the truly rich do business in this town."

"Am I supposed to bring someone with me?"

"No, you and I will show up together. I will pick you up around 7:15."

"Okay. Yo Melvin, you coming to my game tomorrow or what?"

"Yeah, what time do you play?"

"My game is at 3. I'm going to get there early and check out the other games."

"Okay, I'll see you there."

The limo rounded the circular driveway and came to a stop in front of the mansion. Rick felt really good. He had another good game the day before. Rick knew Golden State was interested in him and the Lakers were feeling him out. He had written another letter to Ms. Betsy Beutler. And, he was dressed to the nines for this occasion, black tux of his own design, raw black silk shirt, black suede shoes and a matching suede bowtie. Rick had accessorized the outfit with a white gold pinky ring with a 3 karat diamond and a white gold 3 strand diamond tennis bracelet. He and Melvin had smoked a joint on the way over. They both were ready for the world.

This place made the one Melvin rented seem like a shack. There were a number of limos parked outside. There was a silence that came from the house and it made Rick wonder. They were greeted at the door by the butler. The brightly lit rooms were richly done, however, not to Rick's taste. The producer and his wife greeted Melvin with a friendly smiles and handshakes. Melvin introduced Rick to them and he was received in the same manner.

Rick guessed his host to be in his early 50's but there was no way to really know. She was a beauty, well kept, making it impossible to guess her age. Maybe late 30's could be late 20's. He knew though, that she was at least ten years his junior.

Rick looked around the star studded room. He recognized Cheri Caffaro the B movie Queen. She was much prettier than in the movies, great legs. Joey Heatherton stood holding the arm of a gentleman whom Rick could not for the moment place a name with the face. Sammy Davis Jr. and his wife stood off to the side with Connie Stevens admiring a painting. The party was an even blend it seemed of producers, movies stars and television personalities, as well as a few of the old time ballad singers thrown in as a chaser. You could tell the real power people by the way the stars went out of their way to greet or speak with them, kissing their asses.

Dinner had been enjoyable and Rick listened to the stories he would never have read in the tabloids. A few of the guests had already left because of early morning production calls. Rick sat at the bar talking with the producer's wife. Melvin and her husband, along with a few other gentlemen had gone into the study to finalize a deal.

"You don't drink alcohol, Rick and you don't smoke cigarettes," she said seductively. "What bad habits do you have?" she asked in her softest honey sweet voice. She pushed a gold cigarette case across the bar towards him. "Perhaps one of these is to your liking?" Rick opened the gold case to find a vial of cocaine, half dozen joint and several white pills. He opened the vial and stuck the tip of his pinky in it, then rubbed the white power on gums and tongue. He knew at once the blow had been cut to the max. It was the same as all the blow he had come across since dealing with these Hollywood types.

"Here, try this," Rick said passing her the bill he removed from his inside tux pocket. "See the difference," he said once she had placed a small pebble of cocaine in her mouth.

"Yes, this is excellent!" she stated. "You must introduce us to your man."

They strolled along side of the pool and watched the city lights of Los Angeles dancing off in the distance. They smoked the rest of the joint as they continued their walk under the stars. Rick leaned against the wrought iron fence with his elbows resting on it. He looked out over the landscaping, taking in it beauty. She stood with her back against the fence and looked up at Rick. He passed her the bill with the blow. She used the long fingernail of her pinky to scoop up a hit. She fed him then herself.

"Is Melvin going to star you in his movie?" she asked Rick.

"No," Rick replied.

"Perhaps then my husband may have something in one of his productions for you."

"Thank you," Rick said politely. "I am not interested in becoming a part of the entertainment business by working in front of the camera. If I had been I am sure I would never have received so many offers," Rick joked.

"What is it that you do?"

"Right now, I am playing in the summer professional basketball league."

"You look very athletic. Are you any good?"

"I would like to think so. I've been invited to one camp and I have spoken with the scouts from other camps who are interested in me."

"I wish you luck," she said in a soft seductive tone.

Rick sensed the change in her persona. Why and what had brought it on he was not sure of. At first he thought she was just being entertaining because he was a friend of Melvin's. Then too, this was a bit much for a friend.

"I have a fantasy Rick," she whispered. Hearing her words he searched her eyes for an answer. If an answer were to be found in her eyes it was hidden beneath the cocaine and reefer glare that now filled them.

"Is that right?" Rick responded being careful not to show a change in his demeanor.

"Yes," she whispered stepping closer to him placing her hand on his chest. "My fantasy is to be make love to an athletic black man while my husband watches." This stunned Rick but did not move him physically or mentally. He gave her no indication one way or the other as to what he thought about her proposal.

Rick leaned forward to kiss her softly on the lips.

"Can you handle it?"

"There is no doubt that I can handle it. The question is do I choose to deal with it."

"Don't you find me attractive?" she asked, stroking his chest. "I want to feel your hard body against mine. I want to feel your blackness. I want to be able to see the contrast of your beautiful brown skin against the pale white of mine. I want to feel your hardness driving deep in me."

Rick could see the passion in her eyes now and he felt the heat of her desires as he ran his fingers across her back. She guided her fingers down and along the outline of the open jacket he wore. When her hands came to rest it was on his manhood. She felt his hardness and she wet her lips seductively using her tongue.

"Does it have to be with your husband watching?"

"Yes it does. As strange as this may sound I would never cheat or be unfaithful to my husband. If I were to satisfy my desires without him being there I feel that I would be cheating on him."

"Why is that so?"

"That's how it is for us. He's not gay and his tool works and we have wonderful sex together in private. Every now and then we like to add a little spice to our sexual pleasure."

"Oh, and tonight I am the spice," Rick said.

ONE WEEK LATER

Rick asked the gas station attendant if it would be alright to park the Rolls on his lot.

"Sure, but I am going to charge you for it," he replied.

"No problem," Rick nodded. He gave the attendant several small bills then walked across the Pacific Coast Highway. He knew it was too early for the games to start but he always came early. He enjoyed the quiet emptiness of the early morning on the beach. Laguna Beach was a beautiful stretch of landscaping. With its ice cream parlors, small shops, boutiques and restaurants it had a European flavor.

Rick climbed a rock and sat under the shade of a palm tree. He looked out over the ocean at the surfers riding the waves and at the sail boats a bit further out. Off to one side from where he sat he could see the basketball courts, and on the other side, the parking lot.

Shwinn Nader was throwing up hook shots on the court along with several other players. Bill Walten laid on the beach soaking up the rays. Rick knew there would be a lot of scouts out to see the games here today. He knew also that there would be a lot of good hard games, the best part.

Rick looked across the parking lot at the lone Volkswagen Bug parked in the shade of the palm trees. Dirty and filled with junk he had thought it to be abandoned. He saw her head when she sat up in the front seat and now he knew it was not an abandoned car. She laid back down to disappear from sight. Once again Rick focused his attention back to the basketball courts. A crowd had begun to gather. Rick looked back to where the Volkswagen was parked and saw the female leaning over the front seat going through the junk in the back. She grabbed something and got out and walked over to the red brick house that were the restrooms. At this early hour the restrooms were still closed, so she walled to the side of the building and turned on the water faucet and began to groom herself. Rick watched her as she tried to hide in the shadow of the building.

When she returned to her vehicle, she found Rick leaning against it. He knew his presences alarmed her.

"I'm going across the street to have breakfast, you can join me when you are done here," Rick said.

"Why?" she asked.

"For one, I don't want to eat breakfast alone. And, I am sure you have not had any other invitations for breakfasts this morning have you?"

She had a nice body, gorgeous legs. Her round face and crooked teeth were a part of her charm. It was her accent that gave her an allure of majesty. It did not surprise Rick at all when she said she wanted to become an actress.

"So Ms. Actress, what is your name?" Rick asked.

"Cynthia, Cynthia Murray."

"That is a pretty name, one that is meant to be on a marquee. By the way, my name is Rick."

"Thank you Rick, for inviting me out to breakfast."

"It's my pleasure."

"That's a nice bracelet, are those real diamonds?"

"Thank you and yes, they are real diamonds."

They talked on through breakfast and he came to learn from their conversation that she was not about to become a victim of the Hollywood mill. She was strong and determined to find success as an actress.

THAT NIGHT

Sherry Ann was pleased and overjoyed with the way the gown had turned out.

"I am going to be the envy of every actress at the charity event tonight," she told Rick. "Rick, you know you could make a name for yourself in this town designing gowns."

"I just do it for fun," Rick replied. "If I wanted to make a living at it the sharks would be out to cut my throat. Maybe in the future when I am more…. Nothing, I'm just not ready for it," Rick said to himself.

"I want to thank you again for letting me stay here, Rick."

"It's a big house. Anyway, there is nothing to thank me for."

"Yes there is. In two days I'm going to Italy to begin filming on location and do you think I would have got the part if it were not for you? You never put any demands whatsoever on me for sex, for helping me. You introduced me to Melvin, now as it's been said. The rest is history."

The telephone rang before Rick could reply to what Sherry Ann had just said. Sherry Ann answered the telephone, "Hold on one moment please."

"Who is it?" Rick asked.

"It's *Jacque*", Sherry Ann said.

"Hello legs, what's up?"

"I am doing just fine," Jacque replied at the other end. "I am sorry that I won't be in town for another few weeks. We are way behind the schedule on shooting so I am stuck. The studio just brought in a new director to finish shooting. Things are just a mess. Well, I don't know how much longer I am going to be out this way, Rick."

"If I don't catch you this trip then I will see you on my next one," Rick told Jacque. Besides, I see you on television once a week and you are always in the tabloids."

"It's not the same and you know it, Rick."

"Touché aren't we?" Rick teased.

"You are the only one I can relax with, let my hair down so to speak."

"What about all those guys I see you draped around in the papers?"

"Real funny, Rick. That's why I like you so much. You know how to let me be me."

"And all the time I thought it was because I made your panties wet."

"Ooooh, if you talk dirty to me like that I just may jump on the next plane out of here! Or better yet, maybe I can talk you into coming on the set so I can fuck your brains out," Jacque said in her most seductive voice.

"I wish I could but I've still got business in this town," Rick replied. "Call me in a few days and I just may be able to steal away, okay sexy?"

"That sound good to me." They both said goodnight and hung up.

"Rick, my escort should be here in a few minutes," Sherry Ann said. "His agent thinks we will generate a great deal of publicity by being seen together. I think it's a lot of bullshit myself. He's an upcoming actor, they say when his next film is released he will become a box office idol. The only reason they want him to be seen with me is because he is gay and they don't want any rumors to get started. You know Rick, it's that old fool public game. I would rather you took me Rick."

"I wasn't invited first off, and I am tired. I am staying in tonight and I am going to get some sleep for a change. You have a good time and I will see you in the morning," Rick said.

The shower had relaxed him as he laid naked across the large bed watching the overhead television screen. He dialed a number and listened as the telephone rang several times. The anticipation formed a knot in his stomach.

"Hello," her voice was soft, musical and a pleasure to listen to.

"Yes, Betsy- it's me Rick."

"Hello Rick, I was hoping you would call."

Their conversation was filled with a desire to reach out and touch one another. It had been this way since they had started writing. Their written words told of a longing to be together. Now the telephone had become the bridge binding them in a bond of trust and understanding.

Betsy had been a student at Purdue University when Playboy magazine decided to do a layout on *"The Girls Of The Big 10."* Of all the models chosen, Betsy was one of the few who would not disrobe for the camera. Her beauty was soft and innocent. Her dream of working with children was a reflection of her inner most beauty and charm. The numbers of state and other beauty contest titles to her credit were a tribute to her style and grace, and yet they could never be a showcase for the purity of her heart. In her search to become a model, she had left her hometown of West Lafayette, Indiana and now worked as a hostess for the Frontier Hotel on the Las Vegas strip.

"I will tell you what," Rick said. "After my game next Thursday I will drive out to Vegas. How does that sound to you?"

"It sounds like a dream come true," Betsy replied. The sound of joy could be heard in her voice.

"I am going to say good night because I need my rest, I have an early game tomorrow."

"Okay, good night Rick."

Rick caught the outlet pass just across the half court line. The only thing between him and the basket was the Detroit Pistons' George Trapp. Rick's head faked to the left and went around George to his right. Rick leaped just after crossing the foul line leaving George in his wake and threw in a one hand dunk that brought the crowd to its feet. George was trying to stop Rick fouled him. George complained to ref that Rick had pushed him to get by. The referee walked to his position under the basket and Rick sank the free throw.

The coach sent in a substitution for Rick. There were less than three minutes to play in the game. Rick sat on the bench laughing with the other players. Melvin called Rick from the bench and when he turned to see what Melvin wanted, two glamorous females blew him kisses. Melvin winked his eye. "Some guys have all the luck," one of Rick's teammates kid him.

Melvin introduced the two ladies to Rick as Connie and Joy. Connie was a tall dark skin girl who was just about as tall as him. Joy was around 5 feet 9 inches with a small waist and huge breast. Manicured and draped in diamonds their stylish sweatsuits told a story of their being two well kept woman.

The limo had cruised the Santa Ana freeway while they spoke of social events and business matters. Rick listened and said nothing. Melvin told the chauffeur to get off the freeway at the Hollywood Boulevard exit so he could pick up his custom made shoes.

"You looked fantastic out on the court," Connie said.

"Thank you," Rick replied.

"Check my man out here," Melvin said pointing out the window of the limo. They had come to a stop at the traffic light next to a gold colored Elcapalaro. The driver of the fancy car paid no attention to the limo or its occupants. He was busy schooling his lady.

"He's a pimp," Connie informed the others in the limo.

"I heard they make magnificent lovers," Joy added. "That's how they get the girls to work for them."

Too many movies, Rick thought and said nothing. Rick told the chauffeur to blow the horn and he lowered the window. The driver of the Elcapalaro looked over at the limo to see who was interrupting his conversation.

"What's up Count?" Rick said.

"Ricky T, my man."

"Pull over. I want to talk to you." The two machines pulled nose to nose in the parking lot of Denny's restaurant on Hollywood Boulevard.

They gave each other five.

"How long you been out this way?" Count asked Rick.

"Little more than two months, give or take."

"I just got back in town myself. I had these bitches on the road. I came back for *"The Players Ball."* What brings you out this way?"

"Basketball and business."

"Here's my number," Rick said. "Give me a call and we can get together later."

"Okay Ricky T.," Count nodded.

Connie and Joy were elated and watched Rick the whole time he spoke with Count.

"You are a fascinating man," Joy said to Rick.

"And a gangster too!" Connie added, her words reeking with an invitation for him to get to know her better.

"Put your panties back on ladies, Rick had got to save his strength to play basketball," Melvin teased.

Rick, we are going to cruise over to Catalina Island than down the coast to Mexico on the yachts. Come along with us?" Joy pleaded.

"It will be four days of fun in the sun," Connie added.

"My ex-husband has a 120 foot luxury yacht. As part of the divorce settlement I get to use it every so often."

"That depends on when we are talking about," Rick replied.

"In ten days," Joy answered in the hope that her timing was right.

"Sounds to me like the ship sail when I say go," Rick joked. "What you think Melvin?"

"You have to watch yourself with these two," Melvin warned Rick. "I've been on that floating bed with them. My shit was sore for weeks afterward." Both women playfully smacked Melvin on his shoulders.

"Yeah right, he loved every minute of it," Connie said.

Rick always felt a sense of importance when the guard waved them through at the gate of Universal Studios. The quiet business like atmosphere of the bungalows that housed the many production companies and offices of the writers who did the weekly television programs, Alfred

Hitchcock, Telly Savalas with their offices right of the main entrances.

This was not what Rick had expected a movie studio to be. Now, well, the whole business of movies and television is becoming clearer in his mind. Melvin's office was no larger or smaller than any other producers. His secretary was a petite Latin beauty with strawberry blonde hair and legs to die for. They played at each other every time he was in the office. He could have misused his friendship with Melvin to take advantage of her but for him it was never a consideration. Perhaps that is why they had become so playful. She knew and appreciated the fact that he never took advantage of the situation.

Rick did not like the way Connie and Joy ordered the secretary around.

"You two silly bitches sit down and be quiet!" he told them. "You are giving me a headache." They did not like being spoken to in that tone of voice or being told what to do, especially in front of Mary. Rick could see their jaws tighten yet they were obedient, taking seats on the sofa in the waiting room of Melvin's office. Rick winked at Mary and she smiled as a 'thank you.'

"I can't use any of these damn designs," Melvin complained. "Mary, get the designer on the phone, please. Tell him these gowns are not satisfactory and I need these to be in my office tomorrow at 10:30 a.m. with something better than this shit. I have to go over to Paramount, if I get any calls I will be back at four."

They all sat quietly in back of the limo. Connie and Joy knew not to say anything to Melvin when he had business on his mind. They knew as well, Rick was upset with them because of their treatment of Mary. Melvin sat looking at the 8 by 10 of the actress whom the gowns had been designed for. Then at the sketches the designer had sent to the office.

"How in the fuck can he think this way out that shit is going to work!" Melvin said out loud and to himself.

"Let me see those," Rick said. "This is what you see in Vogue."

"Yeah, I know. I could have torn pages out of a magazine myself and done better than this! It's damn sure would be a lot cheaper then what I am paying this clown," Melvin added.

"When is your deadline for having these designs finished?" Rick asked.

"I needed them yesterday!"

"Let me see what I can do for you. Call me tomorrow afternoon, I should be finished by then."

"A designer too," Joy said using the opportunity in the hope she could get back on Rick's good side.

Rick milled around the kitchen fixing breakfast for himself. The house was exquisite and yet he did not like it for some reason. He was ready to move into an apartment complex. He walked out to the pool with his breakfast tray. Breakfast, then start working on the designs for Melvin, all under the warmth of a southern California noon day sun. The ring of the phone was the only other sound on the planet to be heard besides his heartbeat.

"Hello," he said into the receiver.

"Yes, is Mr. Talley in?"

"This is he."

"Hi, Mr. Talley. I have located several apartments that I believe will be to your liking. When will it be possible for you to view them?"

"You can pick me up here tomorrow at one o'clock."

"That will be fine, Mr. Talley. Thank you and have a good day."

It took Rick little more than two hours to sketched 20 outfits, decided on colors and what materials would be best for each gown. He had designed the shoes as well, knowing that most outfits could be so easily fucked up if the wrong shoes were selected. He had chosen as well, what was to be worn under each outfit so that each gown would hang just right.

His work had surprised Melvin.

"This stuff is really good Rick! It's better than good! I didn't know you had it in you, no wonder you always dress so fly. If you want to work in this field I can make arrangements for you," Melvin added.

"Maybe in the future my brother," Rick smiled.

The dark night sky engulfed the desert and the road opened up under the headlights of the sports machine. Rick had his foot to the floor as he checked the performance of the machine as it ate up the road. It seemed as though the vehicle was barely moving at 140 miles per hour.

Interstate 15 was a lonely stretch of highway that woves its way through three states, California, Nevada, and Colorado. He had thought about flying to Las Vegas, but he wanted to see how the Lamborghini handled on the wide open road. At this speed, it would not take him long to do the four hundred miles or so.

The heat waves rose from the ground as the hot sun baked Las Vegas in its early morning rays. Rick pulled the Lamborghini up at the Dunes Hotel on the strip. The parking attendant opened the door of the car for him.

"Just put it somewhere up front for me, please." Rick told the attendant. "I am only going to make a phone call."

Rick could feel the sweat on the palms of his hands as he dialed the number.

"Hello," her voice was soft and sweet, echoed through the receiver.

"Yeah Betsy, it's me. I'm here."

"What hotel are you at?" she asked. The excitement and delight was felt in every word.

"I have not checked into a hotel yet."

"Alright, I am going to take a shower and get dressed. Call me back when you have checked into a hotel so I can meet you."

"Do you know where the showboat is?"

"Of course I do."

"Good, meet me at the Showboat in the casino."

"Okay Rick, I will be there within an hour."

Rick asked the desk clerk at the Dunes if he had a room available.

"Sorry Sir, we are booked for the weekend."

"Would you make a courtesy call for me, please?" Rick asked then handed the desk clerk a bill he had just folded. The clerk suddenly became more attentive. "And just how may I help you Sir?"

"Call a few of the major hotels on the strip and see who has a room or suite available, please." Rick knew he would be hard pressed to find a hotel room or suite on the weekend. He knew he should have made reservations during the week.

"I am sorry sir, everyone is booked." the desk clerk informed Rick.

"Try the Plaza downtown for me, please."

"I did Sir, they are booked as well."

"Thank you," Rick said and walked off. Rick tipped the parking attendant and drove north on the strip. He made a quick turn off the strip and stopped in front of the Flamingo Hotel, just across from Caesar's palace. He knew he would find a room in one of these smaller hotels. Not what he wanted but it was better than nothing at all. He took a room, showered and changed. He rushed because he wanted to be at the showboat before Betsy got there.

Quiet and relaxed, he sat in the Keno lounge of the Showboat Hotel. He eyed every beautiful female in anticipation of Betsy's entrance. Her hair flowed down and over her shoulders, bouncing in time to her movement. She seemed to be moving in slow motion. Her stride was graceful, her sophisticated look was alluring. Her eyes smiled when she saw Rick. They made their ways to one another, neither spoke, a brief kiss sealed their understanding. And oneness.

Rick took Betsy by the hand and led her to the parking lot where he had parked the car. They stood so close it seemed as if they were one. He ran his fingers through her hair as her head laid resting on his chest. He could feel the tender softness of her body and it excited him.

The air conditioner cooled the room and there was no sign of the blazing summer heat outside. The cool room seemed to intensify their passion, desire, and lust for one another. They made love, sweet and tender love. No others existed; their world was bonded by the walls of the room. Their only reality was the bed that embraces them and the pleasure of touch that sent a satisfaction throughout their bodies.

CHAPTER TWO

These Ain't No Ghetto Streets

RICK SAT QUIETLY in back of the limo. All he could do was think of Betsy and how they met. He knew that he would be going back to Vegas and that one day they would be together again. He also understood his deep feelings for her. The desire she brought out in him made it easier to take when Al Attles, the coach of the NBA's Golden State Warriors told him that he would not play for them this year. Al Attles words still rung heavy in his ear. "You have a strong game Rick, underneath you can't be stopped. Up front you need a little work. Going to Vietnam threw your development off. You are a good ball player and I wish that I had a place on the roster for you."

'Vietnam,' Rick thought to himself. *'I would have never imagined all these changes I would have to face because of Nam. I thought once I made it home that everything would be alright, no such animal. First, I couldn't get a job because of Nam. Now I learn that it has fucked up my chance for a career as a basketball player in the NBA. If all had been lost*, Rick thought, *Betsy sure made it seem alright.*

"Rick, Rick! Snap the fuck out of it!" Melvin broke the silence.

"What? I was just thinking!" Rick protested.

"It must have been one hell of a thought," Melvin remarked. "Could it be that your disappointment in not making the pros is greater than you realize?"

"I wasn't thinking about that. I was thinking of Vietnam and Betsy," Rick said.

"She must be one hell of a lady for you to be thinking about her now."

"She is special," Rick replied. "But I was really thinking about what Vietnam had cost me."

"It's a damn shame, the way you were treated when you came home. I remembered the stories my father told us about coming back after World War II. It was a big difference from the Vietnam War. But anyway, I am sure Connie and Joy will take your mind off of things," Melvin teased.

"Yeah, I know they will," Rick agreed.

"They are two of the freakiest women I have ever known."

"Yeah, I know what you mean. The last time I went out on that ship with them they did the real crazy shit. I woke up and Connie was sucking my dick. I rolled over so she could get at it and looked into the ceiling mirror to see Joy eating her pussy. The three days I stayed with them, I never got out of bed!" Rick joked. "They washed, fed and fucked me in bed. And when I was not fucking one or the other or both, they were fucking each other."

The two yachts were anchored off shore and Rick could see the people parting on both as they approached in the speed boat.

"Looks like the fun has already begun," Melvin said.

"These motherfuckers don't do nothing but fuck and spend money," Rick responded. "Oh yeah, and they sniff the worse fuckin' cocaine in the world! They are acting like they're sniffing the pure, pure." He and Melvin both had to laugh with that remark.

"The shit they sniff, I wouldn't even use as a cut," Rick joked. "Them freak ass bitches be hawking me for my shit. They always asked me where I scored. Score, I'm from New York, what the fuck does score mean?" Rick said laughing.

"It's good to see you laughing," Melvin said.

"You know something Melvin? I must have fucked, I don't know. Who really cares anyway. But I can remember seeing these bitches on television and in movies or on a stage some fuckin' were singing. And like every other normal man I fantasized about them. Now that I've had most of them, I am fucked up! Most of them ain't shit. Can't fuck, don't know how to suck dick. They are acting like you have received the greatest gift in life when they let you stick your dick in them. But after you get them off two or three times they be following you around like your dick is made out of gold."

"I fucked that silly bitch Sondra because she said any man that was not turned on by her, had to be gay. So I spun her around and bent her over the sofa and pulled her skirt up. I didn't even bother to pull her panties down, I just pushed them off to the side and stuck my dick in her. Her pussy is all wet and she was saying, *'Yeah daddy, give it to me.'* I got so mad with the stupid bitch that I pulled out and walked out the door on her. I just didn't like the way that bitch played me. Funny thing about it, she called me everyday for a week trying to get me over to her house to fuck her. I know millions of motherfuckers out there fantasizing about fucking her but I wouldn't fuck her if she was the last women on the planet."

"The one woman I really want to meet is Freda Payne," Rick said. "She's got to be the baddest bitch on the planet. Now she is truly a *"Lady of Class,"* Rick proclaimed. "That little fag producer whose shit I got in at your party for fucking with me was also at Raymond's party when I went last week. I asked Raymond if he could introduce me to Freda because she was in "Book of Number," with him. This little man cut in saying, *'I can introduce you. She and I are close friends.* I looked at him like, *'I told you to stop fuckin with me.'* He got my message and went, *no, no strings.* He got his phone and dialed a number, no answer. Then he gave me his office and home number and said I should call him. He will make an appointment for me to have lunch with her during the week. I know it's game so I didn't call because I don't want to be associated with his crowd. Especially with the way this town placed labels on people. This is a real cut throat dog-eat-dog kind of place. This movie shit, it's not for me," Rick told Melvin.

Rock stars, soul singers, movie and television stars, personalities, and just plain rich people all gathered to party on the two yachts. The booze flowed as did the reefer and cocaine. Half naked and naked men and women danced to the music, got high and had sex to the beats of the music.

Below the deck in one of the staterooms, women were having sex with women while people stood around and watched. In another of the staterooms, men having sex with men were being cheered on. And still in another stateroom a crowd stood around a bed to watch two couples going at it. One couple was in the 69 position while the woman of the other couple rode the large member of her partner to orgasm. Rick had stayed for a moment to watch the woman ride her man because she had real nice legs.

Rick went back up on the deck and found a quiet place. He smoked a joint and watched the stars dance across the night sky.

"May I join you?" she asked. "You seem to be the only one that knows how to really enjoy the peace of a cruise like this." Rick pointed to the deck chair and she joined him, stretching out on it.

"I did not realize how truly crazy these parties get. I had heard about the wild sex and wanted to have a look for myself, maybe join in. But this is a bit too much for me," she said.

"Is that right?" Rick responded. "I wonder is it going to go on like this for the whole weekend?"

"No, there is a beach party that will take place during the day and all of that nights. After the beach party a lot of these people will head back because of work schedules."

Rick recognized her voice and could not place it. She was refreshing to say the least. No make up and very, very pretty. Then he realized who it was who had joined him. She played the secretary and sometimes girlfriend of a detective on a very popular television program.

"Will you be headed back tomorrow?" Rick asked her.

"I am not sure," she replied. "It all depends on whether something of interest occurs to warrant my staying on."

"Maybe I will be of interest enough for you to stay," Rick said in his response.

"Maybe," she replied smiling.

The few tourists with hand camera clicked away as the stars and would be stars disembarked at the marina on Catalina Island. *They would have had a field day last night*, Rick thought, *if they could have seen the madness.* Those who had manage to be awake this morning would shop and do whatever else they liked before joining the others on the beach on the other side of the island. Gretchen and Rick were the last ones to exit the yacht. The others were still lost to the booze and drug-induced sleep from the good times they had all night.

They galloped side by side and rode the horses into the ocean to cool them off. Gretchen leaned over and kissed Rick and then she stood up on the horse's rear end and drove in the ocean. Rick joined her and they wrestled in the surf. The incoming tide carried them back onto the wet sands of the beach. The wet farmer's dress clung to Gretchen's body like a second skin. Her small, firm breasts protruded from the wet material. Rick peeled off his shirt and threw it further in onto the beach, and Gretchen did the same with her dress. She ran along the waters edge in her panties. Rick followed her. He grabbed her and threw her into the deeper water. He drove in and came up behind her.

"Two can play this game," she said laughing. They played until sunset and enjoyed the solitude of the beach. Most of all, they enjoyed one another's company.

They built a fire and sat under the stars. They could see the two yachts sitting off shore as the moonlight silhouetted them against the dark backdrop. The horses stood in the wooded area just off from where they sat on the beach. Rick and Gretchen made love under the stars. Rick had lost all thoughts of reality wrapped in her embrace. Putting aside the fact that he had to make a move soon or be stoned cold broke. If it were not broke, this was the closest he had come to it in a very long time.

NEXT DAY

The raw meat that had been thrown overboard had drawn a number of sharks to the area. They were in a feeding frenzy. The Mexican fishermen had a number of them hooked on their lines. Rick and Gretchen watched as one of the fishermen hooked a shark then hoisted it with a crane to the deck of the yacht. One of the fishermen cut the shark open and three baby sharks about eight inches long slid through the belly cut and flopped around in a puddle of blood and water on the deck. Rick asked one of the fishermen what they are going to do with the dead shark and the baby sharks. He informed Rick that the dead shark would be food to feed his family and that the rest would go to the other fishermen's families. He also told Rick that they would sell the baby sharks alive to make money to buy things they needed.

It had been a pleasant weekend and Rick had managed to stay out of Connie and Joy's grasps. He and Gretchen had also decided to spend their last night on shore in one of Mexico's finer hotels. In the morning they would fly back to the states; Gretchen to her boyfriend of many years and Rick to the business that he could no longer put off.

Sex, raw sex was always better when you knew there was no tomorrow. Rick and Gretchen spent the night exploring the many wonders and pleasures of good raw sex.

A FEW NIGHTS LATER

Etta James had the whole house rocking to her husky voice and soulful beats. "Come on Count, let's take a ride it's much too noisy to talk in here," Rick said. Count worked his Excalibur in and out of the quiet streets that made up Bel Air. The beautiful landscaped lawns and half million and million dollar plus home were signs of Count's success. Count pulled the machine into his driveway and shut it off.

"I don't know about this shit Rick," Count said. "Look, I'm straight up pimpin with no chaser and as you can see I'm on top of my game."

"I can dig it," Rick replied. "But you know this town and I trust you. This is a dangerous business and it's not for everyone. I have two or three choices and I am not sure which direction I will take. I am waiting for word so I know what is available. Once I know, then I will know how I want to move. I ran it passed you to see what you think and if those people are worth my setting up a shop."

TWO DAYS LATER

Rick and Melvin sat at pool side talking. There were several women who swam in different stages of undress. They played in the pool with Melvin's other male guests. Somehow a small pool party had gotten started but it was of no interest to Rick.

"I know the papers are ready but I am not sure if I've got the money to invest right now," Rick said.

"I tell you what Rick, we will make it a joint investment, *"Rick Talley Production Inc"*, and *"Citylights Production"*. We can play twenty cities, west and midwest, how does that sound to you? We can change the headliner every five cities," Melvin proposed.

"If we generate the type of money we are supposed to, we can play the east coast," Melvin added.

"I've got business in Las Vegas, I will let you know when I get back Melvin," Rick responded.

"Going to see that girl from Playboy?"

"No, she went back to Lafayette for a while. I've got to see some friends about business matters."

TWO WEEKS LATER

Rick sat in the parked car in front of Mr. B's clothing store on Freemont street. Chuck, a smooth talking well-dressed Italian kid came out and got in the car with him.

"How are you doing Rick?"

"I'm okay, and you?"

"Fine, just fine." Chuck had only been in Las Vegas for a year, maybe a little more, maybe less. Like Rick, he grew up in New York City.

"Look Rick, for the kind of move you want to make you will have to speak to my uncle. He owns the biggest Italian restaurant in Vegas, it's out on the strip."

"The fewer people who get to know one another in this business, the better it is." Rick said trying to make a point.

"I don't move that kind of blow, so we have to speak with my uncle.

Don't worry about it Rick, it's all for the good. Rick, can you give me a ride? My girl has my car."

"Sure. You drive," Rick said,"so you won't have to give me directions."

"This is a nice house," Rick commented.

"Yeah, it costs a fortune."

"Yeah, whom does it belong to?"

"Elvis Presley."

"Get the fuck out of here!"

"I wouldn't kid you."

One of the security people led them out to the pool. Rick took a seat at one of the patio tables while Chuck spoke with two men at the far end of the pool, seated at another table. Rick had a glass of fresh orange juice and watched a pretty young lady doing laps in the pool.

Rick was his usual quiet self on the drive to Chuck's apartment complex.

"You like that house?" Chuck asked.

"Its' nice but not the kind I would buy if my money was long enough," Rick replied. "Not even if that girl who was swimming in the pool came with it."

"That was Priscilla!" Chuck said as if that should mean something to Rick.

"Who the fuck is Priscilla?" Rick asked.

"Elvis' wife. The way those white girls passed out when you mention his name, I am surprised he could commit himself to one lady. He's got one hell of a piece there," Chuck said snapping his finger by shaking his hand.

Chuck's apartment complex had two swimming pools. The one which was enclosed behind a ten foot wooden fence was for nude sunbathing.

"Lynn and her girlfriend are coming over," Chuck said. "I am going too laid out here by the pool until they get here. After the ladies arrive you can entertain them while I go talk to my uncle."

"Sounds good to me," Rick replied.

Lynn and Cathy walked around in high heel shoes and smiles. They rolled a few joints and placed them out on the table where Rick laid in the shade of the large umbrella. They were ready to fuck his brains out because Chuck had told them the first day he had come to Mr. B's, that he was a good friend of his. "Always treat Rick with great respect," he had told both of them.

They played with Rick's manhood making it hard just so they could see how he was hung. Rick jumped in the pool to cool off and to get away from those two silly bitches. They were back at him once he got out of the pool.

It was around ten when Chuck returned, and the dark of nightfall had cooled the city which sat in the middle of the desert. Lynn and Cathy had grilled steaks and fixed baked potatoes on the BBQ grill. They have changed dresses because of cool night air, they ate, drank and smoked reefer.

"Did you ladies show my man here a good time?" Chuck asked.

"He did not want to do anything," Lynn said.

"What Rick? You turned down my hospitality?"

"It was two damn hot to be fucking out here in the sun. Anyway, the night is still young."

"You ladies go home and get dressed, Rick and I will take you to the midnight show at the Hilton," Chuck informed them.

Rick and Chuck sat pool side talking long after Lynn and Cathy had gone off to get dressed.

"I had a sit down with my uncle," Chuck said. My uncle's friends in New York spoke highly of you. They respect your ability as an earner and you as a person. You and I have known each other for a long time, and I think of us as friend. The little nickel and dime coke I move is not what I want to do. You know how it goes, half ounce here and there, no real money. I've got these kids on the north side, they cop once a week, and a few celebs who cop when they are in town to do a show. What I would like to do is for us to work together. I have my uncle's blessing to move as I see necessary. We can put together a working plan and after we cover our cost, we will split everything down the middle," Chuck explained.

"Give me some time to think on it," Rick replied.

"Sure. Let me get dressed for the show before the girls get back. Once the girls get here we can go by your place so you can change," Chuck said.

CHAPTER THREE

California Dreamers

COUNT BROUGHT THE Excalibur to a stop in front of the Roxy Club on Sunset Boulevard. There was a nice size crowd waiting to get in for Smokey Robinson's show.

"He should be here. Yeah, there he is," Count said pointing to the far end of the Roxy Club. They got out of the car and walked over to Albert who as always was on his game trying to catch.

The three men crossed the Boulevard and spoke in the shadows of the tall black building that housed Disco 9000 on its upper floor.

"It's no problem, you give the blow to the white boy, and he's our front," Rick said to Albert. "Imagine you driving through Beverly Hills with a couple ounces of blow in your car at three or four in the morning." They chuckled and Albert said, "Funny, but not really funny at all."

"I know why you want to deal direct Albert," Rick said. "You want to try for one of those rich white bitches. Forget it."

"I'm going to give you four ounces," Rick continued. "You won't find better blow on the planet. Step on an ounce at a time, hit in once. Frankie knows to sell it just the way you give it to him or he will be cut off. He's not going to fuck up because he wants to get money. Besides, with him having the best blow in town he gets a chance at some of that movie star pussy." They both laughed at the truth of the matter.

"It shouldn't take you any time at all to move eight ounces," Rick went on to say. "Especially when word spreads that there is a new sheriff in town. Every ten days I want to see you in Vegas. If things go as expected the meets will be once a month." Rick and Albert shook hands in agreement to their business arrangement and walked off.

"Rick, let's catch Smokey's show," Count said.

"Sounds good to me, but I'm not fuckin with that long line to see God," Rick replied.

"It's okay, my man is the manager and he will hook us up."

The crowd stretched their necks to see what stars were being given first class treatment as Count's man rushed him and Rick into the club.

Smokey blew the house away. Of all singers past and present, Smokey was the one that Rick would always enjoyed listening too. When he was down or in search of a difficult answer, it was the smooth rhythms Smokey generated that eased him.

On rare occasion when his company had stand downs from search and destroy mission in Vietnam, Rick listened to the ballads that Smokey sang and drifted away with thoughts of home. The madness of Vietnam was not so hard to take.

There was a beautiful brown skin oriental lady at the next table. She swayed with the beat Smokey belted out and it seemed as if he was singing, *A Fork In The Road*," just for her. At the close of the show, Rick used a quiet moment as an opportunity to speak with her. He shook open a napkin in a jester of chivalry for her.

"Let me wipe those tears away," Rick said.

"Thank you," she replied.

"Does Smokey always affect you in this manner?"

"You noticed?"

"It was pretty obvious to me what was going on. I don't think anyone else realized what was going on because they were caught up in the show."

"I'm Rick and you are?"

"Monica," she replied.

"Please to meet you Monica. Do you have any plans for the rest of the night?"

"I have to go home, I'm leaving back to the east later today." Monica answered.

"That's too bad. I would have liked the chance to get to know you."

"I'm sorry, maybe we will meet again."

"You going to hang out?" Count asked Rick.

"I don't know. It depends on what's happening."

"They are having a party for Smokey."

"No, I'm going to break out, I don't feel like a Hollywood party to-night. Besides, I have a few matters to take care of in the morning before I get ready to go back to Vegas."

The ring of the telephone woke Rick from a deep but restless sleep. He had no idea what time of day it could possibly be.

"Hello," he said, still groggy and half asleep.

"Hello Rick," she said.

"Betsy, am I in heaven or is it really you?" Rick teased.

"I see I woke you."

"What time is it Rick?"

"It's 9:30 your time."

"You called just in time or I would have overslept."

"I will let you get yourself together then."

"Are you going to be home tonight?"

"Yes."

"I will call you then so we can talk, okay?"

"Talk to you then," she said before hanging up.

ONE WEEK LATER
LAS VEGAS

Rick had settled into his new home, met the crew from the North side and was set to start pumpin 24/7. Chuck was pleased with the way Rick had reorganized everything.

TWO NIGHTS LATER

The four cars followed the white convertible Eldorado out towards

Boulder Dam. Rick pulled the Caddy off the highway and the other cars did the same. Chuck who had been waiting walked up to each car and handed each driver a large brown paper bag before stepping off. Chuck never said a word to any of the drivers. The men pulled back onto the highway and drove off as they each received their package.

Rick and Chuck climbed a rock for a better view of the wide open Nevada desert. Rick used a starlight scope to follow the cars as they moved along the highway and searched the sky for any sign of a police helicopter or plane. Having spotted nothing, Rick was satisfied.

"It looks good, see for yourself." Rick said, passing the scope to Chuck.

SEVERAL WEEKS LATER

Rick stood on the sidewalk outside of the Four Queens Hotel and Casino. He had two of the kids with him from the North side crew and one kid who worked the strip serving the celebrities.

"Where the fuck is Clifford?" Rick asked one kid from the North side crew.

"I don't know, he should be here soon, I saw him around ten o'clock tonight," the kid replied.

"What time is it now?" Rick asked.

"Twelve thirty one."

"Shit! If he's not here in ten minutes, I'm breaking out."

The red convertible Corvette stopped right in front of Rick. Clifford and two white boys got out and Clifford introduced them to Rick. The tall white boy whose hair and beard were a dirty blonde color had the same name as Rick. The other white boy, who was at least a foot shorter than both Ricks, was called Tony.

"These are the people I told you about," Clifford said. "They are good people. They have been copping since I've been moving. They want a pound like I told you."

"Drive over to the Plaza Hotel and park your car on the second deck of the parking lot," Rick ordered. "I will be right there." Clifford started to get in the car with the white boys when Rick grabbed his arm to stop him. Rick watched until they had driven to the corner to make the turn and come back down Freemont Street headed to the Plaza Hotel parking garage.

"You sure you know these people?" Rick asked cautiously.

"Yeah," Clifford replied. "They're good people."

Rick met the two men by himself in the garage of the Plaza Hotel. He had change the time of the drop for the others and phoned Chuck to say he would be by his house in twenty minutes.

"Rick, Tony," Rick said greeting them in the quiet second deck of the parking garage. "You got the money with you?"

"Yeah, you got the blow?"

"No," Rick said. "You give me the money and I will tell you when and where to meet me to pick up the blow."

"What?" Tony said, "That's not how we do business! I'm not letting my money go on no deal like that!" Tony protested.

"You give us the coke, we give you the money," the other Rick insisted.

"It too risky like that," Rick replied. "To much to loose, money and drugs at the same location at the same time. If something were to happen now for instance, we would only loose money. Or, if you give me the money and I put it away and something happen I will still have your money to return. But if we had everything in the same place at the same time, well. You can see for yourself that it is a hell of a loss," Rick explained.

"Yeah, but we don't know you," Tony said.

"You are right," Rick replied before Tony could say anything else. "So we do it my way or we don't do it at all."

"I guess we don't do business," Tony said.

"Later," Rick said and walked off.

"Fuckin' with that kid Clifford, could drive me to drink!" Rick told Chuck. "He brings me these two fools that think I am supposed to make special arrangements to sell them a pound of coke."

"Like we really need their business," Chuck added.

"By the way, Clifford is out for tonight's drop. I told him to meet me at the Frontier Hotel at 3 o'clock tomorrow afternoon," Rick informed Chuck. "I think he and I need to talk before we do any more business."

Somewhat satisfied with Clifford's explanation, Rick made arrangements for him to give Tony and the other Rick a pound of coke. As long as Clifford was responsible for the money and that neither Chuck nor he had to handle anything, it was cool. Rick walked over to the Circus, Circus Hotel and Casino from the Frontier. It was a longer walk than he had imagined in the hot mid-day sun.

Rick was greeted by one of the valets at Circus, Circus that ran little earns for him and Chuck.

"Hey Rick, how ya doing man?"

"I'm cool Billy."

"Check this out Rick. I've got to watch George Foreman's Rolls, he gave me twenty bucks to watch his car. I don't know why it's parked right in the fuckin' doorway," Billy joked. "But for twenty bucks, I'll stand here and watch it all day."

Rick laughed, not so much at Billy watching the car, more at the way he had said it. "Is Chuck inside?" Rick asked.

"I saw him go in and I didn't see him come out. So I guess he is still inside," Billy told him.

"Okay, thanks."

Rick found Chuck at one of the Black Jack tables.

"How you making out?" Rick asked.

"I'm up a few dollars," Chuck replied. "How did things go with you?"

"Everything is cool. We'll kick it around later," Rick told Chuck.

"Nah, let's go and have something to eat," Chuck said.

"Yeah, that sounds good to me."

Chuck drove over to the Hacienda Hotel at what could be called the far end of the strip. The Hacienda had the best food in town as far as they were concerned. They knew how to lay out a buffet. Rick and Chuck had chosen a table off to the side and out of the way.

"We will hit the rest of the crew tonight," Rick said. "You can take care of the white boy from Hollywood tomorrow. How's he doing?"

"He's coming along," Chuck replied.

"The drop tonight is not a big one so we can make it somewhere in town. We will give Clifford the pound for those two fly guy cowboys also.

He will be responsible for the money too. That just about takes care of everything."

"When do you think we should make arrangements to fly the next load in?" Chuck asked.

"After we make the next drop," Rick answered. "That way we can pay the rest of our bill and the money still on the streets will belong to us."

THAT NIGHT

Rick sat on the hood of the car and looked across the distance to where the Hilton Hotel stood in splendor. On this quiet side street, he waited and watched. His car was filled with the best cocaine in the world. He saw Chuck when he drove into the parking lot. The others pulled in behind him. Rick opened the truck and removed the black plastic garbage bag. Rick walked quickly with the plastic bag over to the trash can which sat near the foot path that was used to exit or enter the parking lot. The path was dimly lit; it was good cover for him to pass out packages as each man approached. Once he had given out the last package he threw the black plastic bag into the garbage can and breathed a sigh of relief.

Chuck came over and him and Rick spoke briefly. Rick had seen a beautiful sister as she exited her room in the small but nicely laid out motel.

"Excuse me Chuck, I want to see if I can catch up with that lady."

"Cool, I'm going in. My girl is upset with the time I've been giving her lately."

"Call me in the morning," Rick said, and they both departed.

"Excuse me Ms. Super-star!" Rick called out. She was still some distance from where Rick had called to her. Nevertheless, she did stop and waited for him to reach her.

"You were calling me?" she asked.

"Yes, yes I was."

"Do I know you?"

"That can be arranged." He found her question rather strange.

"You were headed somewhere?" Rick asked. However, before she could reply Rick had said,"mind if I join you?"

"No, I don't mind," she replied. "I'm going to the Hilton, I have to get ready for our show."

"Are you a singer or dancer?"

She was a tall lady with a medium brown complexion. Maybe 20, 21 years old. She was a very beautiful lady in every aspect.

"I am a singer," she replied. My group is performing in the main lounge."

"Should I know your group?"

"We do have a top 40 single and our album is doing well."

"What is your name?"

"My name or the group's name?"

"Both."

"I am Kathy, and my group is called "Love Machine"."

"Well Kathy, I'm called Rick, and I have heard of your group." They reached the Hilton before either of them realized it.

"What time is your show?" Rick asked.

"We have to do two shows tonight, one at 10 o'clock and then at midnight."

"I will have a front row table for the midnight show then. Then after the show maybe you will join me…" Rick started to say before she cut him off, "I have a boyfriend back home."

"I understand, I'm not asking you to run off and marry me," Rick laughed. "We can be friends. You are allowed to have friends, aren't you?"

"Yes."

"Okay, we will be friends then," Rick said with a smile. "I will see you after the show."

The cocktail waitress led Rick and his companions into the lounge. Rick was disappointed that the lounge was so empty. Yet he knew better than to expect more of a crowd on a week night. Rick watched the ladies going through a routine as they sang and danced on stage. The cocktail waitress had seated them center stage in front per Rick's request. Then he ordered the house's best champagne for his companions. All but a few tables in the room were empty. Still, Love Machine worked as though the house were packed.

J.D. tapped Rick on the shoulder to get his attention.

"Look whose coming down the aisle," he told Rick. Rick recognized the face. However, he could not think of the person's name.

"You know who that is?" J.D. asked Rick.

"Yeah, it's what's his name…?" Rick said.

"That's Billy Preston," J.D. said.

Billy Preston took a seat with a kid at the table right next to Rick's. Rick and his two companions had noticed the kid at the next table when they first came in. How could they have missed him? His metallic silver outfit, silver knee high boots and afro made him an attraction. "Dressed the way he was, he could only be a musician," Rick had said when he first saw him. Billy Preston proved Rick's thoughts to be right.

The cocktail waitress poured the champagne and was about to step off. Rick motioned for her and she came around the table to see what he needed.

"Give those two gentlemen a bottle of champagne," Rick said pointing to Billy Preston and his friend seated at the next table.

Rick lifted his glass of soda and nodded his head to acknowledge the gift of champagne when the cocktail waitress pointed in his direction. Billy and friend, Rick and companions, raised their glasses in a silent toast before turning their attention back to the stage show.

TWO DAYS LATER

Rick sat at the Black Jack table in the casino of the Hilton Hotel. He had always been what most would call lucky at cards. While in the army, there was a banned placed on him because company commanders had made it against the rules for other soldiers to play with him. Nevertheless, there were always the career sergeants who would team up against him. Not so much for his Spec 4 pay, more for the pleasure of being able to say they beat him. The results were always the same, Rick would walk away with each of their months' paycheck.

He laid the table and each time he beat the house, he thought about the twelve hundred he had spent for classes at the dealer's school run by the Lady Luck Casino. *Money well spent*, he thought to himself. It gave him an insight as to how things were done in casino gambling. The other

Rick tapped Rick on the shoulder, interrupting his concentration on the cards. Rick turned fully on the stool to speak with the other Rick.

"It looks like you are breaking the bank," the other Rick said.

"I'm doing alright," Rick replied.

"I'm having a little party at my house. I've got some of the prettiest girls you ever want to see just waiting to for as player like you."

" Is that right, if you've got all that waiting on you why are you here fuckin' with me?"

"I had some business to take care of, you know how it goes. Come on and hang out with me, you can gamble any time."

"Sit down Rick," Rick told him. The other Rick took a seat on the stool right next to him and he laid the table again.

"Will you bring a phone for me?" Rick asked the pretty Black, Black Jack dealer. She signaled to the pit boss for a phone.

"Damn, you are lucky!" The other Rick said to him because he had laid the table and won on all of the hands. Rick took the phone and placed the receiver to his ear while he laid the table once again.

"Yes operator, will you ring the Love Machine's dressing room. I would like to speak to Kathy please."

"Yes Sir, who should I say is calling?"

"Rick Talley."

"One moment please, Mr. Talley." Rick had won four out of the seven hands played this time. "Go ahead Mr. Talley," the operator said.

"Hello Kathy."

"Hi Rick. where are you?"

"I'm in the casino but I have to leave, something came up. If I am not back by your last show, I will call you tomorrow."

"Okay Rick, I hope you can make it back."

"We'll see," Rick said before hanging up. Rick asked the dealer to have the pit boss bring a tray for his chips so he could cash in.

"Have you got any blow on you?" The other Rick asked.

"I've got a little, why?"

"I would like to take a hit before we head to my house. Come on, let's go in the bathroom over here."

Rick passed the bill with the blow in it to the other Rick in the privacy of the bathroom. The other Rick went into a stall to take a hit, while Rick used the opportunity to freshen up. When the other Rick came out of the stall, he still had blow on his nose. He passed the bill back to Rick and used the mirror as a guide to clean his nose. Rick felt how light the bill was when he took it back. He opened it to see that more than half the blow was gone.

"You big nose motherfucker," Rick told him. "What did you do, sniff a gram up each nostril?"

"Don't worry about it, I've got plenty of blow at the house."

"I am not worried about it, you could have sniffed it all. I just want you to know that you are a big nose white boy and that if you didn't sell blow you could never support your pleasure." They both laughed.

"Did you bring your car?" The other Rick asked.

"Yeah, didn't you?" Rick replied.

"No, I never bring my car when I have business in these hotels."

The attendant brought Rick's car around to the front entrance of the Hilton. The other Rick gave him two twenty dollar bills for his services.

"That blow must have given you one hell of a rush," Rick joked.

"Why do you say that?"

"You gave the attendant forty dollars to bring my car out. Either you are feeling good or you are trying to impress me."

Rick, Tony, and the other Rick along with Butch sat on the huge sofa. Rick was impressed. This was one hell of a house. They passed the crystal astray with the cocaine between them. They smoked reefer, drank wine although Rick preferred not to drink it, and watched the women do a striptease. The music was too loud, or it just sounded that way because Rick was skied up. "Come on, let's go into the other room," the other Rick said.

This room was set up to play adult games. Nicely decorated with large throw pillows on the floor in place of chairs, the center of the floor was sunken and shaped in a circle, shag carpeting, plants, state of the art stereo system, television. The other Rick had lined the walls of the room with giant video games that he had specially to set the room off.

The music was softer in this room, as well was the lighting. Rick grabbed one of the giant pillows and stretched out on it. The women danced into the room. There were two women to attend Rick's every need, fed him blow as he called for it, rolled him a joint of some of the best smoke he had ever had. Lost to the pleasure these women provided, he paid no attention to what else was going on in the room.

ONE MONTH LATER

"Yeah Betsy, she's in this month's Essence magazine. This is the second time Essence has used her. She did the layout for black hair care, and one for black skin care. She has the whole page!" Rick boasted.

"You sound like the proud brother," Betsy teased.

"That's right, she is my only sister and I am proud of her."

"Rick, I've got to go to work. Call me tomorrow please," Betsy said.

"Okay," Rick answered before hanging up.

"Hello."

"Yeah Ma, it's me."

"Hi baby, how are you?"

"I'm doing okay. How are you and my sister and brothers?"

"Everyone is fine. They are all out at one place or another right now. Ricky, the FBI came here looking for you."

"What? What did they want?"

"They asked me if I knew where you were and what you were doing."

"What did you say, Ma?"

"I told them, yes I knew where you were and that I never ask you what you are doing because it is none of my business."

"Okay Ma, if they come back tell them to contact my lawyer and not to come to your home again. I've got to go now, Ma. So I check a few things to see if I can find out why they were looking for me. Tell everyone I said hello. Love you Ma."

"Okay baby, you take it easy now."

"Okay Ma."

Rick laid back on the sofa and tried to figure out why the feds would be interested in him. The more he thought about it the less he knew or could imagine he knew. He grabbed the phone and dialed a number.

"Hello Chuck, it's me."

"Yeah Rick, what's up?"

"What have you planned for tonight?"

"I'm taking my girl out to dinner then we will probably drive out to the lake. Why?"

"I need to see you for a few minutes. Meet me at the Plaza when you come from dinner, okay?"

"I'll be there around 10," Chuck said. They both hung up.

Rick and Chuck looked up from the table at the same time.

"Hey Tony, Rick," Chuck said to greet them. Rick just looked at them both and remained silent.

"Surprised to see you downtown," the other Rick said to both of them.

"A friend of our sings with Hucklebuck and the Soulsters, so we came down to see the show," Rick responded.

"I've seen their act and they are good," Tony said.

"So what brings you two down this way?" Rick asked.

"Business," the other Rick replied.

"Things are coming along for us," Tony added.

"I'm glad to hear it. I always like to see enterprising gentlemen like you doing good," Rick responded.

"We may be ready for the big time in a little while," the other Rick commented.

"I wouldn't know anything about that," Rick replied. "I guess that is a matter for you and your business associates to work out."

"I guess so," Tony said, a little furious at Rick's attitude. "Come on Rick, we have things to do."

"We must not keep the people waiting," the other Rick agreed. They both said later to Chuck and Rick.

"What do you think about those two?" Rick asked Chuck.

"I never really gave them much thought, why?"

"It's something about them, I don't know what it is. Let's get out of here. I know your girl is going to blame me for keeping you so long."

"As long as she has enough coins to keep the slot machines jumping she won't mind. I may have trouble getting her to leave now," Chuck joked. "Anyway Rick, I wouldn't worry too much about those people. If they really had anything they wouldn't have to ask your mother questions."

Rick stood silently in front of the Plaza Hotel and waited for the attendant to bring his car around.

"Come here!" he called to a bad-ass stacked white girl as she walked passed him coming out of the Plaza.

"What can I do for you?" she replied.

"I've seen you around and you bounce in and out of these casinos like you own them." Her reply was weak and a bit off handed.

"Is that how you talk to a man?" Rick asked, his tone was scolding her. Her demeanor became more attentive as Rick continued his conversation.

"Where is your man?"

"He got busted last night."

"So where are you staying?"

"I just checked out of here."

"What are your plans now?"

"I am just going to walk up and down Freemont Street to see what the game looks like."

"You can check your traps later; I've got something I want to kick with you," Rick said.

"Let me explain something to you, I don't turn tricks," she told him.

"I'm not looking to become a trick," Rick said cutting her off.

She looked Rick up and down and liked what she saw. She was careful before she spoke again.

"My thing is credit cards," she finally said.

"I don't know anything about them," Rick remarked.

"I can teach you and we can work together," she was quick to say.

The attendant pulled in front of Rick and left the car door open for him to step in. He gave the attendant a tip and asked him to put his car back.

"Come on," Rick said to her and slid his hand under her as they started to walk off.

They stopped for the light at the corner in front of the Plaza.

"You have a beautiful car and you are dressed real nice," she said to Rick. "The jewelry and clothes you have on, I can get free with credit cards. I only work with the gold cards. We were doing pretty well until we came to this town and Franklyn, Franklyn is my man. He got gamblers' fever. That's why he's in jail now, for using a card that should have been thrown away."

"Oh shit, what the fuck is going on?" Rick said, really surprised. He was shocked and couldn't believe his eyes.

"Is something wrong?" she asked.

"What the fuck are they doing in Las Vegas?"

"Who?"

Rick blinked several times to make sure he was not seeing things. He began walking towards them and the bus station. He said nothing and she followed him to see what the fuck was going on.

"What the fuck are they doing in Las Vegas?" Rick said to himself.

"Who?" she asked, but Rick did not answer her question. He just kept walking.

"Jenny!" Rick yelled.

"Rick!" Jenny replied before breaking into laughter.

"Hi Rick," Penny said. Jenny and Penny broke up with laughter. Rick and the white girl just stood looking at them. They had a tall white kid with them who said nothing as well. All three of them just looked at Jenny and Penny who were just bent over with laughter. When the two had regained their composure they introduced the white kid as David. David was someone who shared the ride from Salt Lake City and a few joint with them on the bus. Before anyone realized what was going on, the white girl had grabbed David by the arms and walked off.

"Why are you here?" Rick asked them.

"Aren't you happy to see me? I told my mother I would find you. I knew I would find you," Jenny explained.

"My mother said I was crazy and when I saw all of those lights as the bus came down the highway I begin to think she was right. I asked Penny how I was going to find you in all of those lights. I didn't know Las Vegas was so big. I thought it was two streets or something where people came to gamble. It's unbelievable! I get off the bus and here you are, the first person I see," Jenny told him.

"Now that I have heard your story, tell me why you are here?" Rick said once again.

"I wanted to see you, I missed you. And this was an adventure—setting out to find you."

"Where is Sean?"

"He's with my mother. My mother wanted Sean to stay with her so Joy would have someone to play with."

"Where are your bags?"

"In a locker at the bus station."

"Come on, I'll buy you both something to eat because I know you must be hungry."

Jenny and Penny walked wide eyed through the Plaza casino. Jenny grabbed Rick by the arm as he made his way quickly through the casino crowd.

"This is something else," Jenny said.

"Yeah it is," Rick replied.

The waitress led them to a table and both women talked on and on about the trip and the wonder of the only casinos they had seen in Las Vegas. The other Rick and Tony approached the table where Rick sat with the two ladies.

"Well, well Rick," the other Rick greeted. "I see you are in much prettier company now."

"How are you Rick, Tony," Rick responded.

"This is my girl from New York and her friend," Rick said introducing them all.

"Hey Rick, how much is a suite in this place?"

"I don't know," the other Rick replied. Why, what's up?"

"I'm going to get one for tonight."

"Let me take care of it for you."

"Nah, I've got it."

"No, no, I've got it. Come on Tony, let's go get our man here the best suite in the house."

"They sure made a big fuss about paying for the suite," Jenny said.

"Yeah, and I wonder what it's going to cost me later," Rick said thinking out loud.

"Look at him," Penny said. "He's so cute!" Penny was looking over at the gentlemen who were paying for a takeout order at the cash register.

"That's my man Stanley," Rick said. "He plays drums and sings with Hucklebuck and Soulsters."

"Ooooh, musicians eat your pussy real good," Penny gasped.

"Listen to her Rick. She's got it all wrong," Jenny stated. "It's the horn players who are supposed to eat pussy good.".

"No, I know what I am talking about."

"Both of you silly bitches shut the fuck up. I don't want to hear your bullshit about eating pussy and who does it best," Rick scolded them.

Rick called Stanley and signaled for him to come over.

"Stanley, I want you to meet someone." After Rick had introduced everyone, he told Stanley that Penny wanted to see how good he ate pussy.

"Rick!" Penny said in embarrassement.

"What? You were just talking about getting your pussy ate by musicians."

"Yeah, but I am so embarrassed," Penny said.

"Okay Stanley, I'll bring her by after the last show."

Stanley gave Rick a strange look but did not say anything.

"Okay Rick, I will see you and the lady after the show."

"I am so embarrassed! How could you do that to me Rick?" Penny whined.

"Yeah Rick, how could you do that to her?" Jenny added.

"Look, you were sitting here talking about how cute he is and how good musicians eat pussy, what the fuck. Either of you want to fuck him or you don't," Rick told Penny.

"I do, but you didn't have to do it like that!" Penny defended herself.

"Why, so you could play some silly game about not wanting to give it up before you give it up? You fucking women are something else! You want the dick but you act like we are forcing you to get it. You pop shit about women's lib…" Rick went on to say when Jenny cut him off,"Please Rick, don't get started." Before Rick could say anything else, the other Rick slid the key for a suite across the table.

"Enjoy yourself, everything is on the house,"Tony said.

"Okay, thanks." Rick replied.

"My pleasure," both the other Rick and Tony replied before walking off.

Rick and Jenny took in the shows on the strip and visited backstage so Jenny could collect autographs of the stars who played in these shows. They also saw several burlesque shows and went on outings at Lake Mead. Whenever Penny was not with Stanley, she joined them. It was a pleasant week. It's been a busy week. Rick had not realized how much time he had given to business matters until he had taken time off from them. Things were going well on the California end with friends and business associates coming from both coasts. And once again for Rick, the larger the package that they gave out, by street volume, they counted less money.

It was a typical summer morning in the desert of Nevada. Rick laid in bed and spoke on the phone with Sean.

"I don't know when I'm coming back to New York, Sean. How about you come out here to see me?"

"Okay daddy, when can I come?"

"Your mother is coming home tomorrow and she will want to see you and spend some time with you. What if you come out here in three weeks."

"Okay, daddy!" Rick could hear the excitement in Sean's voice when he told Joy he was going to see his father. Rick could hear Joy in the background laughing and the excitement caused by Sean's news in her laughter.

"Daddy can I call you tomorrow?" Sean asked.

CALIFORNIA DREAMERS   387

"Sure, you can call me any time you want."

"Sentimental fools both of you. You've only been in this town for a hot minute and you act as though you are leaving your birth place," Rick said to Jenny and Penny.

"Rick is just so cold-hearted," Jenny said to Penny.

"This is a cold world and the attachments I make are to people not things or places."

Rick drove into the parking lot of what he felt had to be the ugliest airport he had ever seen.

"If you want to know what cold is, take a look around this airport," Rick said to Jenny. "This is a cold ugly place. Slot machines all over the place, the color is drab. Just a big ugly place."

Penny said 'so long' to Rick and boarded the plane. Jenny lingered behind to kiss Rick and to share in the closeness of the moment. She boarded the plane and he could still feel her touch.

THAT NIGHT

Rick and Chuck went over the books and put together a plan to increase business. They had another hour before making the meet. Tonight's business was only to take orders and to collect the rest of the money owed to them.

They met the crew at the Tropicana Hotel and casino then drove to the outskirts of town by way of the Showboat casino. Rick wrote the orders down and Chuck collected the bags of money. Chuck wrote the names on the bags before placing them in the truck of his car.

Clifford laid behind after the other crew members had left so he could speak with Rick and Chuck.

"What's up?" Chuck asked Clifford.

"It's Tony and Rick. They want to buy ten keys," Clifford said.

"That's a big order. You got that money?" Rick asked.

"No, they won't give me that kind of money because they know I am just the middle man. They want to meet with you or Rick to make a deal."

"Get the fuck out of here!" Chuck said.

"No wait," Rick cut in. "Be cool Chuck, we will work something out. Tell them it takes time to put together a deal like that. But it could be possible."

"Okay, okay, I will let them know," Clifford said before he walked back to his car.

"What's up?" Chuck asked Rick. "I thought you were never going to go hand to hand with them."

"They are not right, I wanted him to take a message back to them like everything was cool. That will give us some time to figure out what the fuck is going on," Rick explained. "Think about it, what the fuck are they going to do with ten keys? They are coping a pound at a time now they want to up it to ten keys. Where the fuck are they going to sell it? I know they are cops, I've just got that feeling and I've had it all along. The question is, whose cops? I want you to check with your family, maybe they can find out who these cowboys are," Rick told Chuck.

"If we get lucky, they may just want to shake us down," Chuck said. "If not, we have to prepare for the worse."

"You see what you can do and I will meet you in two hours."

"Where?"

"Downtown, Binion's Horseshoe. I don't think we will run into anyone we know there."

Rick and Chuck started for the exit of Binion's at the same time a fool snatched a woman's rack of playing chips and raced towards the front door. A security guard pulled a 44 magnum from its holster. Rick pushed Chuck to the floor rolling him and Chuck under a crap table. People went flying everywhere. The security guard knelt on one knee, aimed and fired. The shot caught the thief dead center in the middle of his back. The impact knocked him through the glass doors breaking them into millions of tiny pieces. Women were screaming, some even fainted. Many of the men panicked, some grabbed their wives, girlfriends and their money trying to find cover. The security team working the casino brought order before total panic set in and chaos took over. Rick and Chuck walked out, stepping over the lifeless form.

"Can you believe that shit?" Chuck asked.

"I can believe anything," Rick replied.

Rick led Chuck to where he had parked his car on a quiet street just off of Freemont. They sat in the car talking for an hour.

"I'm going to ease everyone away from Clifford," Rick said. "I don't know how many of us he has trapped off with his bullshit. If we stall these people long enough we can collect all the money we have on the streets and close up shop."

"I don't know. What could they possibly have on us?"

"Don't you find it strange now that you can look at it? They have always showed up where we are, invited us to parties and introduced us to their funny time friends as people who make things happen."

"It is kind of strange, but they also got high sniffing that blow," Chuck replied.

"How could we ever prove they got high? Besides, cops get high, so what difference does it make?"

"We didn't talk business on the phone and they were never at any of the drops, and the money we got from Clifford is long gone. Still, I know they've got something," Rick thought out loud. "I can feel it. All we can do is take the necessary precautions to protect ourselves best we can. We have to avoid arrest and get rid of our books so the police won't find them."

"If we have made a mistake it's too late to change it now, all we can do is cover ourselves like you said," Chuck agreed.

THREE DAYS LATER

It was mid afternoon when Rick rolled over in bed, half asleep he began to trace the shape of her naked form. In his dream-like state, he tried to figure out who she was by the touch of his hand on her skin. She stirred under his touch.

"You sure know how to wake a lady," she said. Before Rick could say anything the ring of the telephone interrupted his train of thoughts. He reached over her to grab the receiver. He laid across her enjoying the feel of her nakedness under him as he spoke on the phone.

"Yeah, she is still here. Chuck said to tell you hello. She said hello back," Rick told Chuck. "Chuck said to ask you if you would like to go with him, his girl and me to catch Redd Foxx at Caesars tonight. Yeah? Yo Chuck, she said yes. Yo Chuck, you and your girl are taking it for granted that I am still going."

"What, yo Rick we have planned on going to this show for more than a month!" Chuck said.

"Yeah, I know, I am just not sure about what I am going to do. I'll see you at the store in an hour and we can talk about it. Later," Rick said before he hung up.

"Why don't you want to take me to the show?" she asked.

"It's not like that Kimberly, and you know it. I'm operating on moment to moment basis because of the things that are going on. So I can't promise you or anyone anything for tonight. If everything is cool we will see the show," Rick explained to make it clear.

"I understand."

"Good."

"I'm going to take a shower, are you coming or do you plan to stay in bed?" Rick asked, teasing her.

"I will take a shower with you then fix us breakfast before we go out," Kimberly replied in one of her sexiest tones.

Rick teased the sales girls in Mr. B's while Chuck inspected the merchandise the store had just received. Rick looked at the rack of suits that had just arrived and selected three of them for himself.

"Is the tailor in?" Rick asked one of the sales girls.

"Yes he is. I will get him for you."

"While she is doing that, you can help me select shirts and ties to go with these suits," Rick told the other sales girl.

The tailor measured Rick and went to work to have one suit ready for him to wear that night. The tailor had finished his work on Rick's suit moments before he and Chuck were ready to leave the store for the day.

Rick and Chuck loaded the boxes filled with money into the U-haul trailer.

"It's these one dollar bills that make this load so big," Rick said. "You got the list for what's what?"

"No, it's with the books in the house," Chuck replied. "I am going to keep all the paperworks in the car with us."

They made the drive north on interstate 15 without saying a word. Rick checked the map to ensure they were on the right course.

"You can pull over so I can get a better reading of our location on the map," Rick told Chuck.

"What time have you got?" Chuck asked.

"We will be there in plenty of time."

Twenty-seven miles north west of Las Vegas, Rick and Chuck waited for the plane to come into view. They had pulled the jeep and trailer into a cove out of sight from those who might be spying off in the distance.

Rick sat on a rock with the M-16 across his lap. He got a cold drink of water from the cooler at his feet.

"If this ain't some real Hollywood shit they'd never be," Rick said breaking the silence. "I could have never imagined myself in this kind of situation."

"Neither could I," Chuck replied. "It's an emergency so we had to take drastic steps."

"Well, I for one, will be glad when this is over."

The plane came in low, almost like a car as it made its way down the hard flat desert floor bed. Once the plane had come to a stop, Chuck ran over to speak with the pilot. Rick watched from his hiding place in the rocks and held the M-16 in the ready position. When he received Chuck's signal, he proceeded to climb down the rocks to where he was. Rick drove over to where the plane sat and they quickly loaded it with the cardboard boxes that contained with money. They gave the pilot the books and the plane took off in less than 15 minutes.

Rick, Kimberly, Chuck and his girlfriend Lorrie had the best seats in the house for the show in the lounge of Caesars Palace. The upcoming young female group was entertaining and had the audience wrapped up in their velvet harmony. Elvis and Priscilla Presley sat three tables away.

Chuck pointed him out to the ladies, but did not bother to call to him. It seemed that everyone had become aware of Elvis' presence. The people at the tables nearest him began to point and whispered. People who were further back climbed onto tabletops to get a better look at him. Like a wave rushing to the shore, the crowd was overwhelmed by their passion and efforts to get a glimpse of Elvis. Taking heed to the crowd's reactions to Elvis, the security personnel surrounded Elvis and Priscilla's table. Finally, Elvis could take no more of the disruptive crowd and signaled the security people and they ushered him out.

"That's a hell of a way for someone to have to live. The man can not go anywhere or do anything without causing bedlam," Rick said.

"He's used to it," Lorrie commented.

"Maybe, maybe not, who knows how this kind of shit effects him," Chuck added.

Redd Foxx had brought the house down and they had enjoyed his show. Now they had stopped of at P.J.'s to hang out and danced. Rick became distant, edgy.

"We can leave if you want Rick," Kimberly said.

"There is no reason for you not to have a good time because I'm in a bad mood," Rick told her.

"What's wrong? Is it something I have done?"

"No, it's not you baby. It's business." Rick knew by telling her it was about business she would not ask any more questions.

"Will you take me back to my apartment, please?" Kimberly asked.

What the fuck is wrong, Rick asked himself over and over again on the drive from Kimberly's apartment to his house. He parked across the street from his house and sat there to watch. *What am I looking for? You've got problems*, he told himself.

If you go in that house Rick, all hell is going to break loose. He started the car up and drove in one side of his driveway and out the other. He made his way across town where he kept an apartment. He felt safe because he was sure no one knew about this place. Not even Chuck. He parked the car two blocks away and walked the quiet dark streets back to his apartment.

Rick laid across the sofa with the light on dimmed and the sound of the television turned down low. The knock at the door startled Rick. He reached for his pistol then decided against it.

"Who is it?" Rick asked.

"I'm sorry to bother you," she said. "I am your neighbor from across the hall."

Rick peered through the peephole to find a nice looking red head in a bathrobe standing outside his door. Sounding relaxed, he asked,"What can I do for you?" without opening the door.

"My sink is overflowing and I don't know how to turn it off from underneath," she told him. "Would you please come over and see if you can turn it off?"

"Sure, just a minute. Let me get my shirt," Rick replied.

Rick peered through the peephole again just to be on the safe side. She was still there waiting on him. When Rick opened the locks and turned the door knobs, the warning alarms went off in his head. Danger! It was too late. Two police officers with nickel plated 45's in one hands and their badges in the other pushed their way through the door. They threw him up against the wall as several other officers rushed in.

"Rick Talley, we have a warrant for your arrest. You are under arrest for the sale and distribution of a control substance. You have the right to remain silent, anything you say can and will be used against you in a court of law. You have a right to have an attorney present during questioning. Do you understand these rights as I have read them to you?" one of the officers asked Rick.

"Yeah, I understand them," Rick said in a state of bewilderment.

"Do you have anything you want to tell us?" the officer asked in a demanding manner.

"No, I don't have anything to say at all."

Rick sat on the sofa with his hands cuffed behind his back. Several other federal and state police officers had begun to search the apartment. The lieutenant showed Rick a piece of paper and informed him that it was a warrant for his arrest.

"However, it does not give us permission to search this place. You wouldn't want to give us permission to look around," the lieutenant asked with a sly smile.

"No I wouldn't," Rick replied.

"By the way, this is a warrant for that too," the lieutenant said with a slight laugh.

"It gives us permission to search that big house of yours in North Las Vegas and your three cars. A little cooperation from you would make the rest of the night go a lot faster," the lieutenant said.

"We have been after you for some time now," a fat out-of-shape sergeant said to Rick. He had just come over and stood next to the lieutenant and stared down on Rick like he wanted to kill him.

"This is one we won't have to worry about again," the lieutenant said to the sergeant as he stared in Rick's eyes searching for any sign of weakness. "Yeah, we are going to put you away for the rest of you life boy."

The police tore the apartment up while Rick sat on the sofa and watched. All the police could come up with were two joints, a little more than five dollars worth of reefer, 750 dollars and a 38 caliber pistol. Each time an officer found one of the items they paraded it in front of Rick and threatened him with it.

"We've got your ass now boy," the sergeant stated with a big shit eating grin on his face. "It ain't no pretty women where you are headed," an officer said trying to rub the arrest in to make it hurt more.

Rick was sober sitting in the back seat of an unmarked police car. He watched the changing street lights play a song to the music in his mind, a sad song just for him. He knew also that he was being taken to his house on the north side. A number of patrol cars had joined them. Rick assumed to make sure he did not try to escape.

None of the keys Rick had on him opened the doors to the big house.

"You can give us the key," an officer informed Rick, "Or we can break it down."

Rick said nothing and continued to look straight ahead as he stood at his front door.

"You are a smart ass nigger aren't you, boy?" the fat sergeant said. "When an officer ask you a question, you damn well better answer it, got that shit nigger?" Still, Rick said nothing.

The officer hit Rick across the face with his hand radio drawing blood. Rick spit the blood from his mouth on the officer's pants and shoes. The officer brought the radio up and into Rick's gut doubling him over. The lieutenant rushed over to stop the officer from beating Rick. "That's enough of that! Out here," the lieutenant said, "besides, someone may see you."

Rick stood against the wall in the foyer with two officers guarding him. The other officers went about destroying the house more in jealousy than a search for money or drugs. The lieutenant and an officer brought two leather basketball carrying bags over to where Rick stood.

"How much money in these?" the lieutenant asked. Rick said nothing. "Where are the books, we know you kept records." Still, Rick said nothing.

"Get him out of here," the lieutenant ordered, "We've got enough." The lieutenant walked back into the living room to talk with the federal people. The two officers who had been guarding Rick took him by the arms and walked him towards the front door. The officer who had hit him in the face ran over to stop one of the officers from opening the door.

"Just one minute," the officer said. He grabbed Rick by the arms spinning him around. "Don't you know boy, niggers ain't supposed to live in a house like this."

Rick looked him dead in the eye and did not blink. Rick knew the look of cold hatred he found in the officer's eyes.

"You dope dealing niggers are the one's who are ruining this country for the good Christian white people." Rick could feel it coming and he braced himself for the attack. The officer hit him with several rapid blows to the head and face. Rick refused to go down under the officers' onslaught of blows. Infuriated by Rick's resistance, he picked him up and threw him to the floor.

"He attacked me! This nigger attacked me!" the officer screamed out. The officer beat Rick savagely and called for the other two officers to do the same. Rick was kicked and stomped by the other two officers while being hit in the head with the hand radio by some other officers who joined in just for the fun of it. Still Rick refused to cry out and fought against passing out.

"So you are one of those bad niggers, huh?" one officer said. But in his condition Rick could not tell which one it was. "Let's see how bad he is after we finish whipping his ass!" another officer said. Rick had passed the point of being able to comprehend what the officers were saying or doing to him.

The lieutenant ran back into the foyer from the yard and over to where Rick laid on the floor still being beat. "You men, stop!" he ordered. "What the fuck brought this on? Are you fools trying to kill him and get us all in hot water?" the lieutenant asked, not really looking for an answer.

"He attacked me," one officer said.

"Is that so?" the lieutenant said shaking his head.

"Yes sir," the other officers replied knowing the lieutenant did not believe them nor did he really care what they did to the prisoner.

"Pick him up and get him the fuck out of here!" the lieutenant ordered. "And sergeant, you ride back with the prisoner and make sure nothing else happens to him! Do I make myself clear sergeant?"

"Yes Sir," the sergeant replied.

Still in handcuffs, they marched Rick down the row of cells in the Clark County jail booking section. "You motherfuckers didn't have to beat the man like that one!" prisoner yelled out from his cell. "If you don't shut the fuck up we will be back to see you!" the officer scolded.

It was four o'clock in the morning and the other prisoners awoke after hearing the commotion. Bloody and in pain, Rick stood strong while they booked him in.

"You want to go to the hospital?" an officer asked Rick.

Rick refused to let them see any sign of weakness and replied no. The other prisoners cheered him on by yelling insults at the officers. Their cheers and insults to the police gave Rick the needed strength to push on.

One by one, they brought in the rest of Rick's and Chuck's crew. The

Clark County Corrections officers emptied the cells in the booking section just to house Rick and Chuck's crew.

The Drug Enforcement Task Force placed a long metal table in the center of the booking section. On the table they sat the two basketball bags taken from Rick's house. The table held a number of items taking from different crew members.

Clear plastic bags held large sums of money, brown paper bags also held large sums of money, and some small clear bags held reefer and another held cocaine, but each held less than an ounce.

Rick cleaned himself up as best he could in the sink in the corner of the tiny cell.

"They've got us all, except Chuck," J.D said. "I heard them talking about him while I was downstairs, they can't find him to arrest him. They are probably going to beat his ass real bad just because he was not at home or his girls for them to bust him."

"What did you do to make them fuck you up like that?" J.D asked Rick. "Did you shoot it out with them or what? The way you look Rick, it's like one of those ass whipping you get when you try to kill one of them."

"Nah, I didn't shoot at them. See that little motherfucker sitting over there in the corner at that desk?" Rick said pointing. "He doesn't like dope dealers and he hates blacks even more."

"It's a lot of racist pigs working for the police department out here," J.D commented.

"Not just out here my brother. This country was built on the white man's hatred of the black man."

The officer stood over the table counting the money they had gotten out of Rick's house. Three hours had past and they were just finishing up. Seventy-three thousand dollars came from the two basketball bags. Another hundred and eighty-three thousand dollars in small bills, singles, fives and tens where taken from the crew members when they were arrested at their homes. The police counted two-hundred and fifty-six thousand dollars in all. The police had also confiscated the crew's cars and jewelry.

398   PRISONER OF DREAMS

The police tried to have each of the crew to sign for the money, cars and jewelry taken from them. Each of the crew members told the police to fuck off and that they were not going to sign for anything. They each would state that, *'I don't know what the fuck you are trying to do, that money is not mine.'*

It was almost twenty-four hours before Rick and his crew were allowed to make phones calls. By that time, the judge had raised the standard bail for each man based on the written reports of the arresting officers. The bail was doubled and tripled what it would be for anyone else arrested for the same crime. The police and prosecutor used the 256 thousand dollars that was confiscated to influence the judge in setting their bail.

Rick's bail had been set at half a million dollars, and the other crew members bail ranged from 75 thousand dollars to 250 thousand dollar. Yet, none of them had been in front of the judge or spoken to a lawyer.

Rick spoke on the phone with his mother, she was not taking the news of his arrest well.

"Don't worry Ma, I can handle it," he said to reassure her.

"What is your bail?" she asked.

"I don't want to talk about it or anything that happened over the telephone." He knew that his conversation was being recorded.

"Ma, give me my father's telephone number. I have to call him to see what kind of help I can get from him."

"Hold on for a second baby, I've got it somewhere in this book. Okay, here it is, have you got a pen and paper?"

"Yeah Ma, go ahead." Rick wrote down the numbers. "Ma, I've got to hang up if I want to make another call. I am not sure how many calls they are going to allow me."

"Okay, I am going to pray for you and I love you."

"Love you too Ma, got to go now."

"Yeah, they want half a mill," Rick informed his father.

"That's a lot of money, have you tried to get it lowered?" he asked.

"I haven't been in front of a judge or seen a lawyer or nothing! The judge set a high bail on us based on what the police told the district attorney," Rick said.

"How did you get yourself in this mess?" Emory asked his son.

"That's not the question. it's how am I going to get myself out of it and how can you help me. The only two people I have spoken to since I've been arrested are you and Ma. I called Ma so I could let her know I am alright in case she had heard about my arrest. I called you because you are my father and I need your help."

"What do you want me to do?" he asked.

"Speak to your friends because I may need some help with the bail until I get to the streets."

"Okay, I will see what I can do for you. Be cool in there and watch your back." Advice coming from his father sounded strange to Rick. But most welcome because it was his father. Advice is something that Rick could only remember his father giving once or twice in his life. There was one time when he was going into the army, on how to watch his back with the racist crackers in the south. But he could not, for the love of money, remembered the other time. It was always about watching your back. *Watch your back*, father to son.

Chuck had surrendered to the prosecutor with his lawyer. Forty-eight hours had passed. His uncle had put his two million dollar home up as security for Chuck's bail. Rick had yet to call a lawyer. Rick and his friends were housed on the fourth floor of the Clark County jail. A place set up to house those with the most serious crimes.

Clifford had been arrested in a sweep and was released as soon as he had been booked. He was not brought upstairs to the holding cells or anything.

Rick leaned against the cell block walls as he spoke on the telephone with his mother. Nothing had changed and he reassured her that he was all right.

"Ricky, the FBI came by here again. They wanted to know if we going to bail you out. I told them that we don't have that kind of money. They asked me a lot of questions about your friends. I don't know how to deal with those people Ricky. I wish they would leave me alone."

"What did you tell them?"

"I told them if they want to know about your friends they should ask you."

"That is all you have to ever tell them Ma."

"Are you alright Ricky?"

"Yeah Ma, I'm alright."

"That's not what I heard. I overheard a conversation and they said that you had been beaten real bad by the police."

"You know them white boys can't fight, Ma. So don't listen to the rumors, okay?"

"Did the lawyer come see you yet?"

"No. Well, he will be there I was told. If you were told that then he will be here. Ma, I've got to go now and I am alright," Rick said to reassured his mother.

"I love you, Ricky."

"Love you too Ma. Say hello to everyone for me."

Rick sat across the table from the lawyer, wearing the county jail's gray jumpsuit.

"I was asked to look into your case by a friend of yours," the lawyer stated as he introduced himself to Rick.

"Who?" Rick asked.

"Chuck, do you know him?"

"Yeah, I know him."

"I wanted to make sure I was speaking with the right Rick," the lawyer said as he smiled.

"In the morning, my secretary will bring you a fresh change of clothes for the court," the lawyer informed Rick. "At 2 o'clock you will appear in court for a bail hearing. I want the bail hearing for two reasons. Of course one of the reasons is to get you out, and the other reason is to get a better understanding of just what they have on you."

"This is the strangest indictment I have ever seen," the lawyer continued. "They have Chuck for distribution of a control substance, and then you for a sale. They are saying you arranged for a sale of 1.5 million in cocaine. Then they say you made a sale for 40 dollars. I would like to see the expression on the jury's faces when the prosecutor tries to explain the difference between a million dollar sale one day and 40 dollars the next day."

"I see also that a small amount of marijuana and a pistol were taken from an apartment you were in. Also Rick, they say you had a large sum of money, two hundred and fifty-six thousand dollars if I am not mistaken."

"No, that is not right, I only had 70 thousand," Rick said. "How low do you think you can get my bail?"

"Considering the amount of money they found, I would say not much. How much bail can you make?"

"One dollar." The lawyer smiled and said, "I will see what I can do for you. See you in court tomorrow," said he said as he headed out the door.

Rick watched as the officer named John Buckley as he sat on the witness stand and testified that he worked for the Las Vegas Drug Enforcement Task Force. He outlined his contact and dealings with each of the defendants. When Rick's lawyer cross-examined him, his answers were not as precise.

"Let's go over it one more time officer, please," Rick's lawyer said. "You said that my client, Mr. Talley, sold you two grams of cocaine on the night of, at the Hilton Hotel. Did you place any money in his hand?"

"No," officer Buckley replied, barely audible.

"I have no further questions," Rick's lawyer said.

Rick's lawyer argued that a 500 hundred thousand dollar bail for an alleged sale of two grams of cocaine is beyond human decency. The prosecutor objected.

"Your Honor, he may have only sold two grams himself but he is solely responsible for the organization that distributed millions of dollars worth of this drug."

"Objection, we have no testimony of that nature here today."

The prosecutor asked that the bail be raised to one million dollars. Rick's lawyer asked that he should be released without bail.

"I do not understand why the defendant was brought before this court. If this case is as what the prosecutor would have the court believe, then the federal courts should have taken jurisdiction. However, since he is taken before me it gives little credence to the weight one way or the other and I shall proceed in that manner."

The Nevada State law requires on a sale of less than or a total of but not more than 28 grams, a bail of 20 thousand dollars. An unregistered firearm in a home is a misdemeanor, for which in this case I will set bail at 10 thousand dollars. On the possession of marijuana, which also is a misdemeanor, I will set the bail at 10 thousand dollars. On the prosecutor's other allegation, possession of cocaine, I will set bail at 20 thousand dollars. Bail for the defendant is set at 60 thousand dollars by order of this Court."

"Thank you, Your Honor," Rick's lawyer said.

A week had passed and one by one each of the crew made the bail. Rick and Chuck went to a meet that was held in secret with Chuck's uncle. This was the first time Rick had ever met the man.

"They have no real case on you or my nephew," Chuck's uncle said. "In our lives these kinds of things happened. Fortunately we are men enough to take care of them. Rick, you can trust this lawyer, he will take care of you and this thing will go away."

Rick sat in the reception area of the law firm headed by a senior partner, attorney Andre Gray. Andre Gray's assistant was the attorney who came to the County lock up and handled the bail hearing for Rick. Now Rick was set to meet with the brains of the law firm.

"You may go in now," the receptionist said to Rick. Rick pushed open the floor to ceiling oak wood doors that led to Andre's office. The huge office was impressive.

The office was tastefully done in modern provincial, Andre's desk sat straight ahead from the entrance. Off to one side a smoke glass and marble refreshment stand stood, and on the other side of the room sat a leather sectional sofa surrounding a glass coffee table.

"Rick," Andre Gray greeted him, rushing across the thick pile carpet with his arm attended to shake Rick's hand. "Come in, sorry to keep you waiting." He and Rick walked over to the leather sofa and took a seat. A hostess came from behind a wall panel that opened into another room.

Andre motioned for the hostess to come over.

"Would you care for something to eat or drink?" she first asked Rick then Andre.

"Nothing for me. Thanks," Rick said.

"Where have you been staying since your house and apartment have been confiscated?" Andre asked Rick.

"I have a suite at the Sands Hotels."

"Nice place. We are going to file a number of motions on your behalf. I want to stop this madness before this thing gets a chance to go to trail."

Andre Gray was a soft spoken man. He was younger than what most would expect for a senior partner, or a founder of such a successful law firm. His suits were tailor made and most likely hand stitched. His manicured fingers and custom made shoes spoke for his refine breeding. Rick pictured him at work in the court room pacing slowly back and forth in the silence of the crowded court room, only the whisper of his voice to be heard over the silence. He appeared trusting, he made you believe in what he was saying. Just the kind of lawyer Rick needed for this case.

"If I have to go to trial, this case could cost in the low seven figures. Are you in a position to pay my fee Rick? Should it go to trail?"

"At this point, I don't think so. You talking seven figures when you should just have come right out and said a million dollars," Rick said, a little angry.

"Well Rick, you have some very important friends who speak highly of you. I am sure things will work out for us both of us. For now Rick, just relax and we will handle things from here on out," Andre said with that jury winning smile of his.

Rick preached his sermon as he paced back and forth in front of his car. The desert sun set high in the sky and it was an unbelievably hot day. Chuck sat on the hood of Rick's car listening to what Rick had to say.

"People read that bullshit in the paper and believe that we have millions in bank accounts all over the world. Sure a lot of money goes through our hands. It would be nothing to say we handle a mill or two in a month's time, but it don't mean it goes in our pocket."

"What has got you so riled up?" Chuck asked.

"This lawyer, can you believe he said this case could cost me a million? No, not a million, he said more than a million. Who does he think I am? Where in the fuck does he think I will get a million dollars in cash?" Rick asked himself more than saying it to Chuck.

"Relax."

"Relax shit, this fuckin' case could break me. I am tired of busting my ass so other motherfuckers can walk off with my money! I am through with this shit. Once this case is settled with the courts, I'm out of here. Whatever money I can walk away with, that will be it. Fuck this business and all the bullshit that comes with it!" Rick said out loud and clear to drive his point home.

TWO WEEKS LATER

Rick parked his car on the street in back of the Mint Hotel and Casino. It was near dust as Rick made his way to the rear of the hotel. Rick held the briefcase firmly in his hand by its handle. It was in the dead heat of a late summer's day. This was Rick's favorite time of day, other than the night itself. The changing of the guard, the brief period before day becomes night.

Rick eyed everyone and paid close attention as he made his way across the lobby. He was not worried about being robbed, his concerns were more about the police catching him with a brief case filled with hundreds dollar bills.

Chuck opened the door after asking who. They smiled at one another and Chuck led Rick into the sitting area of the suite. The room was filled with smoke and there were two other men besides Chuck in the suite. They looked up when Rick came in but said nothing.

"Okay, I suppose we can get right down to business," Chuck said. "Rick, you did speak with the lawyer this afternoon?"

"Yeah."

"Did you bring the money, all the money?"

"It's all here." The other still said nothing, contented on letting Chuck run things. Chuck took the brief case from Rick and handed it to one of the two men. Chuck instructed him and the other man to take the money to his uncle.

"Okay Rick, I guess that takes care of everything."

"The lawyer knows how to reach me if he needs me to be in court," Rick informed Chuck.

"This money pays for any bills that may occur in regards to your case," Chuck said. "If anything does come up that more money is called for, I will handle it. So that's it my friend, come on I will walk you back to your car."

"You sure you won't change your mind?" Chuck asked Rick.

"No my friend," Rick replied shaking his head to reinforce his decision. They shook hands then hugged one another.

"It was a good thing we tried to do."

"Yes, it was."

"Any time you need anything, you call me."

"Same here." They both said good bye, neither having any regrets for the way things had worked out. It was business, simply the nature of the business they were in.

Book Four

CHAPTER ONE

Just Another Day, Another Dollar

RICK WAS LYING quietly on the sofa, he was almost asleep. He enjoyed being in the apartment mostly when Sue Ann was not there. Sure he liked her well enough. It was more his state of mind than anything she said or did. In the time since his return to New York from Las Vegas, he had done next to nothing. Unless you want to call sniffing coke and smoking reefer something.

Rick used every excuse in the book to celebrate; coke and more coke. And when he received the telegram from Andre Gray's office informing him that the case in Las Vegas had been dismissed, it set off for one long celebration.

Rick laid back in the quiet of the afternoon thinking, *this is not you. You had better get yourself together. You've got a son and family that loves you. You can not keep on this way much longer. It's time for you to make a move.*

Rick sat up and leaned back on the sofa. He ran his fingers through his uncombed hair and stretched. Then he got up and walked over to the full length mirror that hung on the closet door. He held himself at bay by placing one hand on each side of the mirror. He looked his reflection over and was disgusted with the mess he had let himself become.

Rick turned away from his reflection in the mirror and walked slowly down the hall, taking off his clothes, dropping them to the floor as he made his way to the bathroom to shower.

Rick turned the shower on and stepped into its hot needle-like spray. He tried to wash away all that troubled him. Today he felt that if he did not force himself to be faithful to whom and what he knew himself to be, that he would be lost forever.

Rick drove in and out of the blocks in search of no one in particular. The streets sang the same old song. He did not stop other than for a red light. He drove across the 155th street bridge into the Bronx. He had know idea what he was looking for, especially in the Bronx. Before he had realized it he had parked the car in front of Sue Ann's parents' home just off the Bronx River Parkway.

Sue Ann was a tall woman, 5 feet 10 inches, with thick muscular bow legs, and Sue Ann knew how to use her legs to please him. Rick remembered the first day he saw her outside of the student lounge at Manhattan Community College. Her milk chocolate complexion and curvaceous ass and those crazy bow legs told him that they were bound to become good friends. As it turned out at the time, she liked him right off. Little did he know back when that they shared a bed occasionally and one day they would share an apartment.

Rick walked over to the fence and the two Dobermans growled and barked at Rick's intrusion of their turf. Rick yelled a command and they eased off. Sue Ann and her mother came out of the house to see what had excited the dogs.

"Rick," Sue Ann said in her surprise. Sue Ann's mother yelled at the dogs to get away and they took off for the back yard.

Rick joked with Sue Ann's mother briefly before she went back into the house to leave Sue Ann and him to talk.

"There are some things I want to say to you," Rick said.

"Couldn't they have waited until I came home?"

"I hadn't planned on coming here. I was driving around, thinking things over, and I just ended up here. I took a good look at the streets of New York City to see if I still had a place on them. So I have decided what I must do."

"Does your decision include me?"

"That's why I want to talk to you." Sue Ann shifted uneasy in her seat and her body stiffened as though she were a fighter getting ready for a punch she knew was coming.

"Right now, it seems the only time we get along is when we are in bed. For two people to live like that is not fair to either of them. I have a lot of deep feeling for you. You are a very special lady and you are special to me."

"Say it Rick, don't play with my feelings like this."

"I want you to stay with your mother for awhile, okay? There are a few matters I must take care of and I don't want you to be sitting by the phone waiting for a call to inform you I have been busted, or worse, killed."

"Look Sue Ann, our relationship started out good and there is no reason for it not to remain on good terms. I want you to stay here because I don't want you to ever doubt me or yourself. I don't ever want there to be a question of what we are to one another. The things I have to do and the moves I make will keep me on the streets. You and I both know the games that the streets play." Rick leaned forward to kiss Sue Ann softly on her lips. "You are my girl and you will always be my girl."

"Then why can't I keep living with you?" Rick kissed her again and he felt her tears in the hair of his mustache.

"One day you will understand why this had to happened this way. Believe me Sue Ann, it's for the best."

Rick talked with Sue Ann's mother while she did the dirty dinner dishes. Sue Ann played with her baby brother in the living room while her father watched the 9 o'clock news on television. When it was time for Rick to leave, Sue Ann walked him to his car.

It was 11:30 at night, a warm summer night, a beautiful night Rick thought to himself. *It's time to get busy*, Rick told himself. The ride back into the city was filled with the excitement of his thoughts. Rick stopped at Smalls, Mr. Wells, and the Shalimar Also at the Baby Grand and Oasis. At each stop he asked for the players he believed could make it happen, and in the language of the streets, all knew that he was looking for work.

Rick saw Peppe and Crime standing in front of the Clinton Arms on 118th street, 8th Avenue, looking at a brand new car. Crime was inspecting

Peppe's brand new Mercedes 450SL. They laughed and joked and were happy to see one another.

"Yo Peppe, you learn how to drive well enough to own a car like this? We all know how you fuck cars up," Rick continued to joke.

"I'm surprised they allowed you to buy a car!" Crime jokingly said. "There has got to be a warning out in the city now." They all laughed at what Crime had just said.

"So how's it been going Rick?" Peppe asked.

"I'm making it," Rick said, "but I see you and my man Crime here are stepping."

"We're doing alright. Look, I've got to break out. If you need anything let Crime know," Peppe said.

Rick watched Peppe drive off before he said anything to Crime.

"So what's up?" Crime asked Rick.

"Looking for work."

"There's work but the product is fucked up. Sam is about the only one with dope and it ain't shit. I am having a hard time moving it over on the ave, so that should tell you how fucked up it is," Crime told Rick.

"Maybe you can give me a hand," Crime proposed.

"How my brother?" Rick asked.

"I want to put something in your block."

"It sounds alright to me. How much do you want me to move?"

"I've got two keys of that bullshit."

"Why don't you just give it back?"

"Look, no one has dope and when the fiends realize it they will buy this because they have too."

"Well my brother, I am not set up to move two keys. I will help you move as much of it as I can," Rick responded.

TWO WEEKS LATER

It was a hot humid summer afternoon and 8th Avenue was deserted for as far as one could see looking uptown from 110th street. Every now and then someone could be seen darting into a building or store. There was short money on the streets and combined with the unbearable heat there was no real reason for anyone to be outside.

Rick stopped the car on 114th street, 8th Avenue and blew the horn. The barmaid looked out of the window to see who it was. A few minutes later Crime exited Nat's bar and crossed the avenue to where Rick sat double parked in his car. They greeted one another before Crime came around to the passenger side and got in.

"You were right. This dope ain't shit! I'm selling quarters for half quarter money," Rick complained. He reached over and opened the glove compartment. He removed a neat stack of bills. "Here my brother, this is twelve thousand and I should have the rest for you by the end of the week."

"If you weren't my man, I wouldn't be doing this shit. I'm only going to make a few G's out of this for myself, if I am lucky. You should have given this shit back to them."

"I would have, but by the time I found out how fucked up it really was, it was to late. Check this out Rick, I've got a meeting with Michael and he is supposed to have something good. I am also working on something with Flat Top. So, hopefully I will come up with something that we can get money with," Crime said.

"Let me break out, I'll kick it with you later," Rick said.

THE NEXT DAY

Rick was asleep in the back bedroom and Jeff was asleep in his mother's bed. Rick did not hear the phone when it rang. Jeff stood in the doorway calling to him.

"Rick, what the fuck man! Did you die? I've been calling you for five minutes!" Jeff informed his brother. "Shemika is on the phone, I started to tell her I couldn't wake your dead ass up."

"Bring the phone in here for me," Rick asked his brother.

"Yeah, alright. When you finish bring it back in Ma's room because I am expecting a call."

"Hi Rick, its' been a long time."

"Yes it has. How have you been?"

"I'm doing okay. I just got back from England studying."

"I had heard you were away."

"Well, I am back and looking for work in the fashion industry."

"I just got back myself, I was out in California and Las Vegas."

"Who are you telling?" Shemika was just a little more than upset with Rick. "You go away for what you told me would be a few weeks and it turns out to be what seems like a life time!"

"Did you call me to fight?" Rick joked.

"No, I called because I would like to see you."

"How about tonight, dinner and a show?"

"That would be nice."

"Okay then, I will pick you up at eight. Where are you staying?"

"At my apartment and the phone number is still the same."

Rick had just crossed 111th street, 7th Avenue when he heard Herc calling him. He pulled over, doubled-parked his car. He got out and walked over to the stoop where Herc and several others stood.

"What's up?" Rick said greeting them.

"Ain't nothing," Herc replied.

"Check this out," Wayne said, "when are you and your man going to hit us with some of that money?"

"What?" Rick was puzzled.

"Yeah, when are you and Crime going to give us that money?" Kenneth asked.

"Hold on," Herc told them. "Rick doesn't owe us no money so don't be talking to him like that."

"You're right, sorry my brother," Wayne apologized.

"Yo, what's going on Herc?" Rick asked.

"Sam gave Crime two joints and he ain't turned in no money yet," Kenneth said.

"You know that product is going to move slow," Rick responded.

"Yeah but Rick man," Herc said, "at least the man could come around and say something."

"Come around, he's just two blocks away on 14th street," Rick said. "Give him time, he probably trying to get all the money together. I gave him twelve thousand yesterday…"Rick said before he realized the mistake he made with the slip of his tongue.

"You see Herc," Kenneth said, "he could have brought us that money."

"Herc, why are you worried about that money? You know Crime is a good businessman," Rick said. "Look, I'm breaking out, I will tell Crime when I see him to come in the block. Okay? Later."

Rick sat in the shade of the trees in front of his mother's building. He saw Irma when she came out of 840 pushing the baby stroller just across the way from where he sat. She must have seen him as well because she headed in his direction.

"Hello stranger," she said.

"How are you doing Irma?" he replied, kissing her softly on the lips.

"So this must be your nephew."

"Yes, that him, I'm just watching him while my sister takes care of some business."

"Where is Donny?" Rick asked.

"He won't be around until some time tonight."

"Tell him to come by my mother's tomorrow morning. I would like to kick some things with him." Rick and Irma sat on the bench talking about the old and the new. The five o'clock shadow closed slowly like a curtain being drawn, bringing a coolness to the hot summer day in the Douglas project. A silent reminder that it was near the dinner hour and also time to get ready for whatever the night would hold. Rick and Irma said so long with a friendly kiss.

Rick and Shemika stood outside of the Broadway theater looking at the publicity still promoting the play,"The Wiz." They enjoyed themselves and strolled along Broadway contented with the pleasure that they shared being in one another's company. The still shot of the Good Witch of the South stuck in his mind. If only it were better lighting than maybe he could identify who it was, and why this picture called to him.

They walked around to the corner up to 8th Avenue and stood with the crowd that had gathered outside of Studio 54.

"Would you like to go in?" Rick asked.

"For a little while maybe," Shemika said.

Rick called Mark, with his dirty blonde hair, standing guard as God of the entrance to Steve Rubell's kingdom. Rick whispered in Mark's ear and the door to Steve Rubell's kingdom opened for Rick and Shemika.

The celebrities were out in full force on this night. Rick stood at the bar next to Big John Tate and wondered why he was called "Big". Big John Tate as he was called stood at lease 2-3 inches shorter than Rick and they weighted about the same.

Shemika leaned with her back against Rick's chest as he wrapped his arms around her. Rick watched Marisa Berenson dancing with some little guy who must have had plenty of money. He was plain as day but he carried himself like all powerful men do. Rick also understood why Marisa had become so popular. Her true beauty was not captured by the camera. She was truly a very beautiful woman.

Halston, Bianaca Jagger, Andy Warhol, Liz Minnelli and Diane de-Beauvau sat at a nearby table. Rick had been intrigued by a photograph he had once seen of Bianca Jagger. His fixation for the sensual beauty of her face caused him to stare whenever he saw her, and lately he had ran into her at a number of places.

Jackie O was dancing with Sterling St. Jacques. It took a second glance before Rick recognized Jackie. She was much shorter than Rick had first thought her to be.

"Damn, look at her ass," Rick said out loud.

"What?" Shemika answered, a bit surprised at Rick's outburst.

"That's Jackie O, over there dancing with that black kid who happens to be Raymond St. Jacques' son. Look how big her ass is," Rick said playfully to Shemika. "She can't say she don't have no black in her. She has an ass just like one of the sisters. I know Kennedy was tearing that up!"

"You should be ashamed of yourself," Shemika teased.

"Why? Look at how her shit bounces as she dances. You know Kennedy was all up in that."

"Well, I tell you what Mister, let's go home and see how you can get all up in this."

THAT MORNING

Rick was on his way home from Shemika's apartment when he ran into Crime. They stood on the corner of 136th street, Lenox Avenue talking in the early morning hour.

"Yo Crime, what the fuck is going on with you? Herc and them are kickin' it like you are trying to beat them."

"I've got everything under control."

"Check this out, I told them I gave you twelve thousand."

"Good, at least they know I've got money and they will get off my back for a minute. I just need to keep them off my back for a minute more to work a few things out."

"If you need any help let me know."

"I got it."

TWO WEEKS LATER

Rick pulled to a stop on 116th street, between Manhattan and 8th Avenue. Rick called Dancing Deb who was standing on the stoop. Dancing Deb came over and got in the car with Rick.

"How are you doing Rick?" she asked.

"I'm okay Deb." Rick had known Dancing Deb since she was thirteen years old. Her baby brother Keith and his brother Jeff hung out together. Deb was about 5 feet 5 inches tall with shapely legs and a gorgeous body. It was her dancing that fine-tuned her body. Her crooked smile added to her charm and enhanced the beauty of her face.

"Deb, you seen Crime?" Rick asked.

"No," she replied.

"Damn, I wonder where he could be. I went to his mother's house in New Jersey and she hasn't seen him either."

"I don't know, but I do know that he has been doing the right thing for a lot of people who are fuckin' him over. They're running off with packages, money, just taking advantages of his good nature."

"Yeah, I know. People think he is fuckin' up. Look Deb, if he comes in the block tell him that I'm at my mother's house. Tell him that I am there waiting on a call from Jesse this morning."

"Yeah, how is Jesse doing?"

"He's okay. He's at Green Haven now. I'm getting ready to send him a package as soon as he tells me what he wants. You can give me some pictures to send him," Rick told Deb.

"That's a bet," Deb replied.

"Let me break out. Deb, don't forget to tell Crime what I said."

"Okay Rick and you can stop in the block later today for the pictures," Deb responded.

NEXT DAY

"I came here straight from the interview. I don't know what to do," she said, her eyes pleading for a response. "Tell me what I should do Rick?"

"Why?" Rick asked.

"Because I need to know from you, where we are and if our relationship can stand by me making this kind of move."

"After all this time, if you don't know, that nothing I can possibly say at this point would make a difference."

"You know what I mean, Rick."

"Yes, I do know. You want me to take you in my arms and say please don't go. To say please don't leave me because I need you here with me. To be truthful Shemika, those are the words that I am saying to myself, they are the words I feel."

Shemika ran across the living room and jumped into Rick's arms. Their lips met and he could feel the wetness of her tears on his face. Rick gently pushed Shemika back so he could speak.

"Shemika, I can think of no greater wrong that I could possibly do to you if I asked you to stay here with me. You have a once in a life time opportunity and it would be selfish of me no matter how I feel about you, to ask you to stay here."

"I understand, Rick. But I just don't want to loose you. Come with me to Houston," Shemika told Rick.

"What? Now what would I look like hanging on your coattail following you across country? What is there for me to do in Houston anyway? How long do you think I could sit at home waiting for you to get off from work? Besides, Houston is not that far. I can fly down and spend time with you," Rick tried to assure her.

"Tell you what we can do. After Pat Cleveland's party tonight we can go back to your house and I will help you pack. We will pack for two trips. We'll get your things ready for you to leave on Monday and we will pack for the weekend trip, I'm taking you on tomorrow," Rick told her.

"Where are we going?" Shemika asked.

"Anywhere you want as long as it is a place where no one will disturb us."

THAT NIGHT

Rick drove along Riverside Drive and came to a stop next to the big Mercedes.

"That's a mighty fancy car you've got there," Rick said to the driver. "What's up Joe L-e-w-i-s?" Rick said drawing Joe's last name out.

"Hey Rick, what's going on?"

"How are you Joe?" Shemika greeted him as well.

"How are you Shemika, I didn't recognize you at first."

"That's okay. I understand why, Rick always has so many girls with him," Shemika said playfully, but she was serious at the same time.

"Where are you headed?" Rick asked Joe.

"I'm going to that thing for Pat Cleveland," Joe answered.

"So are we. Let me find a parking space and I will see you upstairs," Rick said.

Pat Cleveland was a hometown girl from the Bronx. Tall, lean and beautiful, she had been the jewel of the Ebony Fashion Fair. She had moved up in the world of fashion modeling by working in Europe and with the named designers of the world and tonight's celebration was all about her.

The party overflowed into the corridor outside of her huge apartment. Everyone was having a good time. Rick had decided to leave early so he could spend time alone with Shemika.

"Yo Joe, I'm breaking out. I'm taking Shemika to the Castskills so I want to get an early start."

"Okay my brother, I catch you later." Joe said.

ONE WEEK LATER

Rick waited at the gate of Kennedy airport for the passengers to disembark. Betsy was one of God's most beautiful creations. Wherever she was, people turned their heads to look at her. All his life Rick had heard the expression, "She could stop traffic." But in his life he had only seen two of such woman; Shemika and Betsy Buetler. On at least one occasion, each woman had literally stopped traffic. The people passing by on the busy street stuck their heads out of car windows to get a better look at them. They couldn't have drawn more attention to themselves if they had been walking down the street butt ass naked. And today at the busy airport people stopped, stared, whispered and asked if she was a movie star.

Rick, Betsy, Sean and Sean's friend, Paul, took in the sights of New York. They saw all the places the tourists wish they knew about. Rick enjoyed being with his young son and his friend. Betsy enjoyed the two young boy's intelligence and marveled at how mature they were for such a young age. Rick just enjoyed being with them all.

It was a quiet morning and the snobbish atmosphere of the Ford Modeling Agency's outer office was not a place Rick cared to be. The receptionists looked over her glasses at him every few minutes. It was written all over her face, the contempt she felt. Betsy is a nice white girl and beautiful. Rick is black, dressed to the nines, a low life pimp. Rick understood how and why she could have thought this. Yet, it was not fair. You can't judge all by just a few. However, he still felt the snooty bitch needed to be put in her place and not to stereotype all black men. When Betsy came back to join him, they talked about him going to California to play professional basketball. The receptionist hearing this became more attentive and offered them something to drink. Rick just laughed to himself.

It seemed he was always saying goodbye and the only thing good about it was the love making the night before, so intense. Betsy was on her way to California after being informed by the Ford people that her look was much too sophisticated for the New York market. And Rick, he went back to dealing with the mean streets of New York.

THREE WEEKS LATER

Rick pulled over on 111th street, 7th Avenue and told Sue Ann that he would be right back. He ran across the avenue and up the steps of the corner building. He rang the door bell and waited to be buzzed in.

Rick sat at the table with Sam and watched as Sam poured the contents of the plastic bag onto a mirror.

"This is what I've got, it's good and you can get all you want," Sam informed Rick.

"I'll take a sample and if it's like you say, I'll take a key," Rick told Sam.

TWO DAYS LATER

Rick put the key and a half of cocaine in the safe.

"Check this out Slim, as soon as you finish with that blow you got from George, we can start to move the coke we got from Sam."

"Okay Rick, that sounds good to me."

ONE WEEK LATER

Rick went by Lefty's house to get his advice.

"Look at this, what would make it turns brown like this?" Rick asked.

"Synthetic," Lefty said. "It's a lot of this shit around. You have to be careful, I hope you didn't get caught out there with a lot of this."

"Enough," Rick replied.

"It's okay if you can move it in one or two days, maybe a week if you are lucky. Anything longer than a week and you've got problems," Lefty commented.

It was a hot day and Rick weaved the car in and out of the blocks. He couldn't find a soul. *'If he thinks I'm going to pay him for this shit, he's got to be crazy*, Rick said out loud to no one but himself. *'I should have known better after that bullshit dope he put out on the streets.*

THAT NIGHT

All the bars and known hangouts were deserted. Not a sign of anyone anywhere.

'What the fuck is going on?' Rick wondered. It did not take him much longer to find out. Crime had been hit. His body had been found at the Hunts Point Market behind the wheel of his car. One bullet to the head.

THE NEXT DAY

It was a bright sunny morning. The world awoke as it did every morning, and only those who knew the sadness caused by the loss of a friend saw it any differently. Rick dialed a number and listened as it rang several times.

"Hello Jenny, it's me Rick."

"Hi Rick, how are you?"

"I'm okay, I want to take Sean with me that's if you don't have any plans for today."

"No, we don't, Sean will be glad to see you."

"I will come by in an hour to pick him up."

"That's fine, I will have him ready."

As soon as Rick placed the receiver in the cradle it rang.

"Hello, I have a collect call from a New York State Correctional Facility," the operator said. "Will you accept the charges?"

"Yes operator, I will accept the charges."

"Yo Ricky, what's up? You alright or what?"

"Yeah, I'm cool."

"I just heard about Crime, ain't that a bitch?"

"Yeah man, I don't know what the fuck is going on. I'll be up to see you this weekend and we can kick it around. You want me to bring anything special?"

"Nah, just pick me up a few goodies at the store."

"Okay my brother. You be careful out there and I will see you this weekend."

Rick was glad that he had Sean. In Sean, he found the peace from the madness of his world. Sean's eyes smiled and Rick became lost in the joy for life they expressed. *If only the world were as pure as his smile*, Rick thought.

They had gone to the movies, lunch and went shopping. They roamed the theater district and looked at the marquees for all the Broadway shows. Once again, Rick found himself drawn to the publicity of the still photograph of Good Witch of the South in the play called 'The Wiz.' In the daylight he was able to identify who it was and now he knew why he was drawn to the photograph. He laughed to himself.

"Sean, look at this picture and tell me if you know who this lady is?"

Sean eyes lit up when he looked at the photograph. "That's Debbie!" Sean said laughing.

"That's right my man, that is Debbie Burrell. I didn't think you would remember her," Rick told his son.

"Let's see if Ms. Burrell is around," Rick said. The front of the theater was locked so Rick and Sean walked around to the rear of the building. The attendant on duty at the rear door told Rick that no one was around. Rick asked the attendant if it was possible for him to leave a message. "Sure young blood, I will put it in her mailbox." Rick thanked the attendant, then him and Sean left.

THAT NIGHT

Rick stood with Herc on the corner of 111th street, 7th Avenue.

"Look, I'm telling you. You can't get a dime for that bullshit coke," Rick said. "If you would have told me the real deal so I could have pumped it right away, you'd have your money with no problem. But no, you motherfuckers want to jerk me with your slick game."

"Look Rick, I'm not the boss," Herc said. "I'll tell Sam what you said but I know he don't want to hear shit about not getting his money. He wants his money and you have to pay. You see what happen to Crime?"

"What's that supposed to mean? Is that some kind of threat?" Rick asked. Herc did not reply.

FOLLOWING NIGHT

"Rick you got a call from Debbie, she said that there are two tickets at the box office for you at tonight's show," his mother informed him.

"Okay, thank you Ma."

Rick sat in the orchestra seats, Debbie and a few other female cast members waved to him from behind an enclosure. He felt like he was back in high school being watched by the girl he liked and her friends. They laughed and giggled before they ran off to get ready for the show.

Shining like a new car, Rick was dressed to thrill for this special occasion and he was enjoying the show. The show was excellent and Rick was amazed at the power of little Stephanie Mill's voice. After the show, Debbie came and got Rick so that he could wait backstage while she changed into her street clothes. Debbie introduced Rick to Stephanie and Jasmine Guy who had a small role in the play.

They sat in the lounge of the Americana Hotel, they paid little attention to the female who was singing on stage. Rick's interest was in Debbie only. And after a long time, he was happy to find that she felt the same.

"I did not think I would still be so attracted after all this time," Debbie said. They talked on and the night hours disappeared into the closing of the lounge. During the ride to Debbie's house, they reaffirmed the bond they once shared.

A FEW DAYS LATER

"I heard it through the grapevine," Donny said. "There are rumors all over the projects. I know people down here don't know shit but I got this straight from the people uptown. There is a hit out on you, Rick and they said Sam put it out."

"Okay, thanks Donny, I'll get back with you once I know what the fuck the deal is."

Rick looked in Nat's bar than drove back to 111th street, 7th Avenue.

He could not find who he searched for, yet he knew what Donny had told him was true.

Rick took the long metal box from the top shelf of the bedroom closet and laid it on the bed. He took another metal box from the floor of the closet and placed it on the floor next to the bed. He opened the long metal box and unclasped the army canvas case. He ran his hand along the stock of the M60 machine gun and he also removed the AR-15 from its holding place in the case. He began to assemble the M60.

After assembling the M60 and cleaning the AR-16, Rick opened the metal box on the floor and inspected its contents. *I knew this shit would come in handy one day.* He took out two concussion grenades and two red smoke grenades and laid them on the bed. He tapped the handles of the concussion grenades and pulled the pins. 'Now *they are ready for action*, Rick thought to himself. He tapped the AR-15 magazines together for rapid reloading action. He took the 45 caliber pistol and two magazines from under the mattress. He had had the 45 caliber magazine made to his specification, each now held 30 rounds.

Rick put on an old suit jacket and placed the grenades in the pockets. He put the AR-15 in a shopping bag along with the three magazines. He placed the 45 caliber pistol in the waistband of his pants and fastened one button on the suit jacket. He put the M60 under the bed for safe keepings until he decided just how he was going to use it.

With the AR-15 wedged between the driver's door and seat, he took the road in and out of the blocks that made up Harlem. His first course of action was a search and destroy mission to get the head of the crew and anyone else who happened to be with him.

The day light hours slowly disappeared and Rick had not found his prey. Under the cover of darkness he felt an ambush and the element of surprise were to his advantage. He sat just of the corner in the block facing the avenue. The night slowly drifted back into day and still his prey had not been spotted.

Rick had searched for several days before he learned that his target was out of town.

A FEW DAYS LATER

The rumors ran wild on the streets about Rick's partner Crime being hit and that Rick was next. The jealous and envious found pleasure in spreading the stories of Rick's demise. Rick felt the excitement of danger and it was Vietnam relief for him.

Rick laid resting on the sofa with the 45 on his chest, the ringing of the telephone brought him out of the semi sleep.

"Yeah," Rick said into the receiver.

"You're a dead man," said the voice on the other end.

"We all have to die some time. But if it's my time to go, I will be taking you with me. So, bring it. If you are as bad as you believe yourself to be, we can meet and get this over with. How about we meet in Central Park?" Rick proposed. Rick knew he could take him in Central Park using the bush of the park to cover him.

"Fuck you," was the reply. "You're a dead man!" the voice repeated before he hung up.

The phone rang almost instantly after the mystery caller hung up.

"Hello," Rick said.

"I have a collect call from a New York State correctional facility, will you accept the charges?"

"Yes operator. Hello."

"Yo Ricky, what's up my brother?" Jesse asked.

"Ain't nothing."

"I heard about your problems. Come see me," Jesse told Rick.

"I'll be there in the morning."

Jesse listened as Rick explained what had jumped off.

"What the fuck? Is he crazy?" Jesse said in disbelief. "You chill for a few days, I'm going to pull some strings. I know you want to rock his world before he can get to you. All I am saying my brother, is to be cool until I can get this matter taken care of. Sam is out of line and he needs to be set straight," Jesse stated.

TWO DAYS LATER

Satisfied with Jesse's intervention into the matter, Rick made plans to make one big move and get out of the business for good. For the type of move he wanted to make, Rick would need a partner or someone to invest. Rick had suffered some damage to his reputation with the rumors about the hit. So an investment from someone outside of the life would be best. Rick could only think of one or two people who had the kind of money he needed and just crooked enough to want to invest.

Rick dialed a number and listened as it rang.

"Universal Marking Inc.," the receptionist said.

"Yes, would you put me through to Mr. Rice's office, please."

"Whose calling?"

"Rick Talley."

"Thank you Mr. Talley. Go ahead, Mr. Talley."

"Hello Rick, my man. How are you doing?" Herb asked.

"Fine, just fine."

"What can I do for you?"

"I need an appointment to see you."

"How about the first of the week, 2 o'clock at the Round Table," Herb replied.

"That's good," Rick answered.

"See you then."

FIVE DAYS LATER

The phone rang and Rick grabbed it before it could ring again.

"Yeah Rick, its' me."

"What up, Claude? You back in the city or what?"

"No, I'm still in North Carolina. I ran into Sam down here and he wanted me to get a message to you. He said the nut you had with him is squashed and that you don't have any problems."

"Okay, thanks Claude."

"You okay?"

"Yeah, I'm cool. Look man, I'll see you when you get back in town."

THE NEXT DAY

Rick moved cautiously through the block. He had not had time to verify the message he got from his brother or Jesse, the 45 was tucked neatly in the waistband of his pants. His adrenalin still flowed because of his thoughts on how to deal with this danger if it comes.

Rick looked over his shoulder and searched the crowded street, and 47th street between 7th Avenue and the Avenue of America was a long block. At this time of day it was crowded with people, and the street was jammed with delivery trucks, cars, and cabs. *This would be a good block to make a hit*, Rick told himself. His senses were at a keen state of alert. *Why, when he should be toning them down* Rick thought to himself. Maybe because of an imagined danger or perhaps the business at hand had him up and fully alerted.

Rick took a seat in back of the Round Table that gave him an advantage. The bar restaurant was dimly lit and from where he sat he could see anyone before they saw him. Rick signaled for Herb as soon as he walked in the front door. Herb was a prominent business who had been known to lend money for a price, no questions asked. Rick had known him for a long time, some 15 years or so. Respectable, on one hand his company was the largest of its kind in the world. He was as at home with street people as he was with heads of states.

Rick ordered a vodka martini for Herb and another orange juice for himself.

"Let's get right to the point," Rick said. "I want to borrow a large sum of money for which I will pay the cost for its use."

"I don't think I can help you," Herb said. "Word is that you are not going to be with us much longer. The streets have it that your partner was killed and you are next."

"There's no truth to the rumor. My man was killed but it had nothing to do with me."

"Bullshit!" Herb said. "They want you killed and I get the news as you live it so don't try and give me that bullshit. The people that are after you are no good for business or anything else. Rick, you would be a damn fool if you let them kill you."

"What the fuck are you talking about?"

"If I were you, I would put them away and go into the federal witness protection program. By the time they get out of prison they will be old men."

"Are you crazy?" Rick asked Herb, not believing what he was hearing.

"I don't believe this shit, I ask for a meet to get a loan. I damn sure did not come here to talking about the madness coming out of your mouth."

"You know Rick, it's you who is crazy. You are acting like just another one of those street punks. I always thought you were smarter than them."

"Let me explain something to you, I would never go to the police for any reason."

"Then you're a damn fool."

"No, you're the fool! You try and walk on both sides of the streets," Rick proclaimed. "I never have trusted people like you and everything I believe myself to be confirms my beliefs about you. You square ass motherfuckers would sell your mother to save your soul. You break the law and when you can't handle the repercussions you cry like babies. Your beliefs and dedication in a cause is limited only to its success."

"Being a street hustler is not a cause," Herb defended himself.

"It's my cause, my life and I made a bond with the people who trusted me!" Rick proclaimed. "I will never betray that trust or the trust I have placed in myself to do the right thing. Yeah Herb, if that means I must go to prison or die, then I will die because this is the life I chose."

THE END
NO...
IS IT JUST THE BEGINNING?

To the many whose names were not mentioned for one reason or an-other, you and I remembered the encounter of our passing. To place each and everyone's name in print would served no purpose other than to say you are remembered. You are remembered and not forgotten.

CURRENT AND FORTHCOMING TITLES FROM
STRATEGIC MEDIA BOOKS

**DIARY OF A MOTOR CITY
HIT MAN**
The Chester Wheeler
Campbell Story

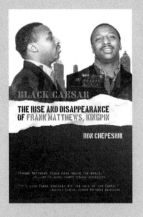

BLACK CAESAR
The Rise and Disappearance of
Frank Matthews, Kingpin

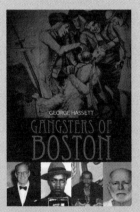

GANGSTERS OF BOSTON

JUSTICE DENIED
Bermuda's Black Militants, The
"Third Man," and The Assassinations
of A Police Chief and Governor

AVAILABLE FROM STRATEGICMEDIABOOKS.COM, AMAZON,
AND MAJOR BOOKSTORES NEAR YOU.

COMING IN 2014

AMERICAN ICON
The Legacy and Death of Marilyn Monroe

ESCOBAR VS CALI
The War on The Cartels

THE PATRIOT PRIEST:
The Story of Monsignor William A. Hemmick, the Vatican's first American Canon